We Can Take It!

We Can Take It!

BRITAIN AND THE MEMORY OF THE SECOND WORLD WAR

Mark Connelly

PEARSON
Longman

Harlow, England • London • New York • Boston • San Francisco • Toronto
Sydney • Tokyo • Singapore • Hong Kong • Seoul • Taipei • New Delhi
Cape Town • Madrid • Mexico City • Amsterdam • Munich • Paris • Milan

PEARSON EDUCATION LIMITED

Edinburgh Gate
Harlow CM20 2JE
Tel: +44 (0)1279 623623
Fax: +44 (0)1279 431059
Website: www.pearsoned.co.uk

——————————————————

First edition published in Great Britain in 2004

© Pearson Education Limited 2004

The right of Mark Connelly to be identified as author of this work has been
asserted by him in accordance with the Copyright, Designs and Patents Act 1988.

ISBN 0 582 50607 7

British Library Cataloguing in Publication Data
A CIP catalogue record for this book can be obtained from the British Library

Library of Congress Cataloging in Publication Data
A CIP catalog record for this book can be obtained from the Library of Congress

10   9   8   7   6   5   4   3   2   1

Set by 35 in 9.5/14pt Melior
Printed in China
PPLC/01

The Publishers' policy is to use paper manufactured from sustainable forests.

Contents

Acknowledgements

I'd like to thank the many people who have encouraged and assisted me in this project. My greatest thanks go to my partner Jacqui who has patiently listened to me express my thoughts on the subject material included in this book out loud in a never-ending stream. She still had enough stamina to read the manuscript from first to last and made a host of acute observations and suggestions. Second, many thanks must go to Professor David Welch, my colleague in the School of History at the University of Kent, for his comments on the manuscript and equally helpful advice. Anna Miller, Spencer Scott and the inter-library loans term in the Templeman Library at the University of Kent supported my search for, and presentation of, many different types of material that was greatly appreciated. I also owe a huge debt to the team at Pearson. Heather McCallum proved enthusiastic about the idea from the very start and has retained her enthusiasm for it throughout. In addition, she found two readers who submitted valuable reports. My thanks also go out to Melanie Carter at Pearson and Sarah Bury for editing the text with such care and attention and suggesting further improvements and refinements. Finally, as ever I must express my thanks to my parents and brother for their continuing interest and encouragement in everything I do.

Picture acknowledgements

The following are thanked for supplying and providing permission to use the images in this book:

Atlantic Syndication (Plate 2); BBC Worldwide (Plate 3); the Commissioner of the City of London Police/ the Museum of London photograph archive (Plate 5); Columbia Tristar pictures (Plate 9); Flashback (supplier of Plates 3 and 9); Hulton-Getty Images (Plate 1); the Imperial War Museum art, film and photograph archives (Plates 4, 6 and 7); Shepherd Neame Brewery (Plate 10) and D.C. Thomson Ltd (Plate 8).

Introduction

This book is about the British myth of the Second World War. It does not intend to undermine that myth because it is too deeply implanted in the hearts and minds of the British people to do that. Those who have tried to do it before, such as Clive Ponting, have singularly failed to achieve their objective.[1] Rather, this book explores the way in which the British myth of the Second World War came about and is passed on. By looking at the very substance of the myth, created, as will be argued, during the war, recreated and added to ever since, the book will seek to show how and why such an interpretation came about, is so extraordinarily resilient, and has achieved such popularity. Detailed examination of the myth proves that it is far from a fabrication, as so many of its detractors claim. On the contrary, the myth contains many elements of truth and should be viewed as a particular explanation and interpretation of events rather than as a cleverly designed falsification of reality.

There are actually many myths contributing to the one, great overarching myth of the war. This central British myth of the Second World War defies precise definition. Variants can be invoked, but the general theme is as follows. In 1939 Britain falls into war unprepared and lacking a genuine leader. In 1940 Britain gained the leader it deserved in Winston Churchill, faced humiliating defeat in France but thanks to an extraordinary rallying of the nation an Armada of small boats crossed the channel to rescue the soldiers on the beaches of Dunkirk. Britain then stood alone, without allies, surrounded by the enemy. The Battle of Britain was won by the Few in the skies over the rolling countryside of southern England. Defeat in this battle forced the Germans into an indiscriminate bombing campaign. Far from causing the collapse of Britain, the people drew together in an even tighter bond and they embarked fully on their People's War. Surviving the blitz did not bring about victory, however.

Britain went on to suffer defeats in virtually every theatre of war until Montgomery came along and won a decisive victory in the desert. After that, with new allies, it was a glorious adventure. On D-Day 'Monty' led the way back to France, and the war culminated in the suicide of Hitler and the defeat of the Third Reich. In the Pacific the Americans dropped an atomic bomb, thus ending the war completely, although it has to be said that events in the Far East have not had a prominent profile in the British myth. In 1945 Britain deserved the applause of the world because it was the only nation to have been in from first to last. It had taken the formidable blows of the enemy unaided and won through. Celebrating its victory, it created a welfare state to provide its citizens with 'cradle to grave' care in recognition that the people had fought and won their war. Since then Britain has fallen from its once influential position and it has been forced into closer contact with the nations it once fought.

However, it won back some of its former glory in 1982 when the nation used the myth of the war, which is in itself an extension of the definition of national character, to help it interpret events in the South Atlantic and liberate the Falkland Islands. Eight years later Britain firmly stood with its American ally to punish the unprovoked aggression of Saddam Hussein. Once again Britain's armed forces revealed their quality and the resolution of a people used to taking on great odds. Thus could the Second World War and British history be used as guides to action and provide parallels for contemporary events.

The myth is part of the national memory of the Second World War. It might be asked whether such a thing as a national memory exists and how it can be proved if it does. In this book memory and myth are used to describe the desire of humans to ascertain who and what they are. This is achieved partly through making a series of choices relating intimately and solely to self and partly by linking the self to a larger collective. This process is aided by the way in which humans use the past in order to assess individual and collective identities in the present. In times of individual or collective stress and upheaval these desires increase. Collective and national memories are formed in this way: groups create their own consensus on the past and its meanings and often apply these meanings to contemporary situations. This consensus is often created through tension and accommodation. The state might well wish to influence or control the way its citizens look at the past, and individuals might be gradually won round to a new position or resist it completely. Alternatively, interpretations of the past generated among small groups or communities might eventually gain national status and support. Memory in this book therefore means a collective way of looking at the past and the conclusions drawn from it. The proof that such a memory exists is found in a variety of evidence forms and, importantly, the reception given to that evidence. For example, if a particular film about a particular event is a great success with the public, then it might be assumed that the public agreed with, or was sympathetic to, its interpretation of that event. But, taking only one source and reading it in this way cannot be regarded as conclusive in itself. What this book seeks to do is prove that a collective national memory did exist by revealing the depth and breadth of the national consensus on the Second World War through the sheer homogeneity of its popular cultural artefacts. Evidence revealing a consensus of opinion on the meaning and value of the war, and the lack of any form of truly popular dissent from it, have been sought out in a wider variety of cultural forms, particularly those most accessible to the working and middle classes. These have been used as proof of the existence of a national memory and myth that contained an inbuilt value system recognised and understood by the British people (and that whether people were conscious of it or not it therefore had a political tinge to it). It is never assumed that this memory was owned and perpetuated by one particular group within society; or that it can be ascribed absolutely and without qualification to all British people, but it is argued that its broad outlines and salient points can.[2]

The overarching myth, which can be broken down into various 'sub-myths' including those of evacuation, Dunkirk, the Battle of Britain, and the blitz, all of which will be explored in this book, should never be dismissed lightly, and should never be regarded as wholesale fictions concealing a more murky reality. Myths, and the study of them, are vital for they reveal a great deal about how people relate to the past, particularly their own national past. Myths are important because they help people to make sense of their lives; they provide a popular memory of the past, which can shape expectations of the present and future. As Malcolm Smith has stated, 'A social group or a nation becomes a social group or a nation only when it has a common mythology, and a common sense of the past is a very significant element in the collective identity of any interpretive community.'[3] Jeffrey Richards, in his study of British national identity and film, has argued that for most people the imagined world of the past is far more important than historical reality (if indeed such a thing exists). He quoted George Steiner:

> Images and symbolic constructs of the past are imprinted, almost in the manner of genetic information, on our sensibility. Each new historical era mirrors itself in the picture and active mythology of its past. . . . It tests its sense of identity, of progress or new achievement against that past.[4]

Graham Dawson has analysed the way in which the Second World War has been turned into history and created a thought-provoking framework for studying myths. He attacked historians for drawing a simple division between their 'authoritative' work and the vagaries of the popular legend. He argued that historians are involved in a mythologising process themselves; they often unconsciously rework the myth even when they are seeking to attack it. This ensures that the myth is impervious to scholarly destruction and even deconstruction. Further, he claimed that the myth is not static; it has grown and developed, in fact the interaction with it by scholars guarantees its survival. Dawson then identified the various 'genres' in which writing on the Second World War can be placed: the discrete codes of the military history, the home front history, the military autobiography, the domestic biography and so on, each of which then displays its own peculiar properties. For Dawson, this use of discrete codes deprives historians of ever achieving a complete overview of the war, providing the right conditions for a mythological knowledge to flourish. Furthermore, each commentator is assuming the power to talk for others, making generalisations about the experiences of others, while privileging one source over another. This is reflected in the relative weighting we give to Montgomery's version of El Alamein, for example, which is thought to carry more 'authority' than the account of an anonymous ordinary soldier. The form of the discourse is therefore extremely important in Dawson's theory:

> Access to the major forms of public debate – broadcasting, publishing, the press, the public platform – carries the power to define, to interpret,

to offer accounts of the war, and is the precondition for entering that struggle. It is to the interface between public and private (or privatised) understandings that we can trace the object of the mythic version of World War II; produced in that moment between June 1940 and June 1941, when military danger brought political upheavals but also transformed the everyday realities of civilian life and generated a language of special significance to cope with this. Elements of the myth appear in all forms of writing, and we can describe and analyse the various constructions of the mythic which they produce. Ultimately, though, we have to find ways of relating these historical knowledges to the broader relationship of present to past, which generates popular interest in them today.[5]

This book explores the relationship of present to past urged by Dawson almost twenty years ago. Myths, then, are not to be dismissed. They are important and contain truth. It therefore seems invidious to talk of myths and truth as if they are mutually exclusive. As Malcolm Smith has noted:

Mythology has its own history, and it matters what people believe happened in the past, no matter how they learned it. Myths, in other words, are not there simply to be debunked in the name of historical accuracy; they are important historical events in their own right, and they are central to the common sense and to the history (which is part of the 'common sense') of the period in which they hold sway.[6]

The British myth of the Second World War is public and shared and has its own conventions. Public representations and memorials generalise experience and form categories in which people can organise their memories, thus creating a self-perpetuating phenomenon and experience. It is a memory which tends to marginalise moments of misery, fear and loss and value episodes of bravery, resolution and humour. But the memory is not inaccurate, it simply emphasises certain elements.

The forms in which this particular interpretation has been handed down and the media in which it was carried need to be studied. During the Second World War itself most British people got their war news from the newspapers, the newsreels and the radio, all of which were closely scrutinised by the government. But people also talked to each other as they

discussed the war news and they questioned it. This created an alternative history of the war even as it was happening, albeit one that often
complemented, rather than contradicted, the facts. Since the war, its
history has been passed down in similar ways, but perhaps the most
important medium is the visual. The Second World War is a visual war
above all else. In the popular mind the definition of a war film is one
made during or about the Second World War. These films both created
and reflected reality and so informed the development of the myths.

By contrast, the Second World War is not regarded as a genuinely literary war, certainly not in the way the Great War was and is. When people
think of war literature they think of Sassoon and Owen. Television has
replaced cinema as the medium of mass entertainment and information,
and it has allowed the Second World War to be imprinted on our minds.
This is not confined to the popular culture; museums now lay great stress
on audio-visual displays. Much of the Imperial War Museum's approach
to the war is built around providing people with access to moving images
to complement the other artefacts.[7]

Historians are therefore only one element in the shaping of the past,
there are other academic disciplines that impinge upon it, particularly
sociology and anthropology, but there are also the popular instructors,
and the most obvious and popular of these are film and television pro-
ducers who can produce irrefutable visual evidence about the war. In
addition, film and television demand neat resolutions, solid facts and
good stories. The fine shades of debate seen among academics are not
for them. The large-scale television documentaries, such as *The World
at War* or *The Nazis: A Warning from History* or *The American Civil War*,
therefore have a great power thanks to their 'realist certainty'. And fiction
films, especially ones claiming to tell true stories, *The Dam Busters*, *The
Battle of Britain* and *A Bridge Too Far* have the same effect. According to
Malcolm Smith, 'Most people learn much of their history from popular
culture, and specifically from the mass media.'[8] In Smith's persuasive
argument, popular culture determines the 'big facts' about events, leaving
historians to quibble over the 'little ones'. And the 'big facts' about the
Second World War are determined by visual sources. 'It is because they
are visual, because they rely on the claim that "seeing is believing" that
they have become very difficult to reinterpret.'[9] The big facts about the
Second World War known to every Briton are that Britain won, the

British people fought for the best reasons and showed great heroism, and that the war was won by a collective act of fortitude and self-sacrifice. The big facts do not have many nuances or ambiguities. They are the core of our belief about the war, and evidence to back up these big facts can be found in a wide variety of wartime sources and have been buttressed continually in popular culture since 1945.

At this moment we are at a crossroads regarding the 'visual memory' of the Second World War. Until very recently it was a black and white war. Black and white was regarded as the authentic experience. Indeed, as John Ramsden has shown, films such as *Dunkirk* (1958) and *The Dam Busters* (1955) were deliberately made in black and white in order to appear more like wartime films and therefore more authentic.[10] Whether the eyewitnesses to the war remember it in black and white or not, the film industry often took the decision that reality was in black and white. An interesting illustration of this issue came in October 1969 when the popular television series *Dad's Army* transferred to colour broadcasting. For Nancy Banks-Smith, then television critic of *The Sun*, it was all a little hard to take. *Dad's Army*, as a comedy about the Home Guard, seemed far more at home in black and white, it fitted the world it represented.[11]

But, over the last few years, as a generation has grown up used to seeing everything in colour the Second World War has started to be recast as a colour event. In 1997 the ITV network screened the impressive three-part documentary series, *The Second World War in Colour*, and followed it up with a second series, *Britain at War in Colour* (2000). Both series used official and amateur footage to provide a startling new angle on the war. The distance of history is suddenly eroded by these series; it is a shock to the senses after being so convinced of the appropriateness of black and white. For this is what it boils down to, expectation and not accuracy. We expect the war to be in black and white, it looks right in black and white. It is strangely different in colour. In feature films it has always been slightly different; colour became common in war films in the fifties. The Second World War is getting a colour 'make-over' for the new world. *Saving Private Ryan* (1998), *U571* (2000) and *Pearl Harbor* (2001) have all attempted to recover the 'feel' of the Second World War while using the most modern of techniques. In *Saving Private Ryan* the director Steven Spielberg deliberately over-exposed and faded his film to make it seem like the genuine colour footage. What cannot be doubted, however, is the importance of the visual medium to the memory and myth.

Many commentators on the British and the Second World War have argued that two war experiences exist: a real one, and by this they normally mean a history based on evidence of argument, dissent, division and suppression of truth, and what they define as the imagined one, created by government-controlled propaganda agencies which painted a rosy view of Britain at war and has become the basis of popular memory since 1945, thus ensuring a false, nostalgic view of the conflict. As this book will show, this division is simplistic. The real war – whatever it actually constituted – was being imagined and mythologised as it happened by its participants, both great and small, which meant it was always being recast, reframed, reinterpreted even as it continued. Perhaps surprisingly, however, the people and government between them created an interpretation of the experience as it was happening which both found acceptable. This, then, was the history they handed down. The obsessive search for the hidden truth about the British and the Second World War, conclusively proving that it wasn't all jolly cockneys and sing-alongs in shelters, is as ridiculous as saying that it was nothing but jolly cockneys and wise cracks about the Hun. Both are present and, contrary to the detractors' view, both are part of the mythologised war.

The critics of the myth of the Second World War are obsessed with what they call 'the truth' behind the experience. The way to this reality and truth is by stripping the war of its propaganda images. However, this approach appears to be based on a very simplistic understanding of propaganda. Propaganda is defined as something like, 'bad people telling good/nice people what to think by deliberately misleading them'. It takes no account of the fact that most people were not so gullible that they could not work out an absolute disaster when they saw one, that most people were more than capable of picking out of whatever information was given to them parts that were accurate and parts they rejected as nonsense. Finally, this approach completely rejects the assumption that people were only too happy to accept certain interpretations because it either made complete sense, given their understanding of their world and history, or because acceptance of it was a far better option than accepting an alternative reality. People needed to believe in something during the Second World War for it was a moment of acute crisis, and people needed to find the hope, strength and resolution to continue. The only alternative, in 1940 especially, was to negotiate with Nazi Germany, an outcome that would have had disastrous repercussions.

Geoff Hurd has rejected a simplistic definition of propaganda in his investigations of British wartime cinema. He argued that the state did not impose its ideology and agenda on cinema, and rather that cinema became a point of negotiation and transaction between 'authority' and those who were required to make sacrifices. According to Hurd, Gramscian concepts of hegemony come into play here. The ruling class negotiates with the lower classes and seeks consent for its dominance, a dominance far more than economic, being political and cultural too. This does not mean that culture is imposed from above; rather it is a process which creates a compromise equilibrium. The imposition of culture is therefore presented to the masses, who accept bits, reject others and reshape others again.[12] In the light of this, a simple conspiracy theory explaining away all myths does not appear credible.

Debunking of the myths was very popular in the Thatcher years, partly as a reaction against her abrasive concepts of nationhood, national identity and society. A division can be drawn between what might be called the 'useful revisionists' and the 'sensationalist revision-ists'. Historians such as H.L. Smith, Steven Fielding, Peter Thompson, Nick Tiratsoo, Penny Summerfield, and Ross McKibbin have examined aspects of Britain's ingrained interpretations of the war and greatly added to, and altered, our knowledge with their highly perceptive and fascinat-ing interpretations of the impact of the conflict.[13] Angus Calder was the most subtle and perceptive of the critics, skilfully analysing a crucial chapter in the popular history of Britain, the blitz. *The Myth of the Blitz* (1991) does not rely on facile divisions between reality/truth and created image. Instead, Calder attempts to explain how and why the myth came about. He shows that the myth was created by people actively accepting an interpretation of events, often inspired by the media, which then provided a model that shaped actions in time of crisis. In this sense he does not stand in the same league with other debunkers, those I label the 'sensationalist revisionists', such as Clive Ponting and Nicholas Harman. The only element of similarity is that all three identify 1940 as the year most heavily laden with mythology. Ponting's sensationalist shock-horror denunciation set out to prove that the British lurched from pillar to post in 1940. Dunkirk therefore becomes a tail of ineptitude and folly, the Battle of Britain was very nearly a disaster of equal proportions, the blitz saw morale cracking and the only way to maintain the spirit of the British people was by a diet of misinformation. This book will not try to deny the validity of such points, but will highlight the equal validity of the myth. While Ponting's *1940: Myth and Reality* caused a minor sensation when it was published in 1990, it failed to have any effect on the way the nation remembered Dunkirk, the Battle of Britain and the blitz. Nicholas Harman took a similar stance in his *Dunkirk: The Necessary Myth* (1981). He argued that it was time to forget the rubbish about a gallant British Expeditionary Force fighting its way back to the beaches and patiently waiting for deliverance. Rather it was the story of a disorderly rabble under upper-class twit officers who were interested only in saving their own skins. As research for this book began, *Their Darkest Hour* by Stuart Hylton was published. His book claims to blow the lid on the British in the Second World War by showing that people fiddled their ration books, that there was crime, that evacuation was a nasty experience and the British locked up harmless foreign nationals.[14] But this is hardly a new claim, for the great fault of the enthusiastic and committed debunkers is their poor sense of historiography and what constitutes a 'scoop'. The major part of Ponting's, Harman's and Hylton's theses could have been read in Angus Calder's *The People's War* back in 1969, not to mention Spike Milligan's very funny memoirs written in the 1970s and 1980s. Very little of it is genuinely new. Very little of it lives up to the publishers' promises of great secrets revealed for the first time between the hardcovers. And how depressing it must be for them all because the British people continue to believe in their supposed nonsense even after all the careful iconoclasm. It reveals a failure to understand the 'big facts' determined by the popular imagination and its perception of the past. It is a failure to understand the robustness of myths, the way in which they swallow criticisms and simply reshape them. As Roland Barthes noted:

Myth does not deny things, on the contrary, its function is to talk about them; simply, it purifies them, it makes them innocent, it gives them a natural and eternal justification, it gives them clarity which is not that of

an explanation but that of a statement of fact. . . . In passing from history
to nature, myth acts economically: it abolishes the complexity of human
acts, it gives them the simplicity of essences, it does away with all
dialectics, with any going back beyond what is immediately visible, it
organises a world which is . . . without depth, a world wide open and
wallowing in the evident, it establishes a blissful clarity: things appear
to mean something by themselves.[15]

This is not to say that the myth is static. Far from it. It has changed
and evolved along with Britain. Its first shift was from wartime to peacetime. In peace the history and popular memory of the Second World War
had to be readjusted. From being something solely British, the British
came to believe their achievement was something the world should
recognise and thank them for. After all, if Britain had considered peace
overtures in 1940 it might have left many nations under the shadow of a
prolonged and indefinite occupation. Throughout the 1950s, the British
felt the august glow of victory but also felt times change. As the empire
dissolved and Britain's reduced world position became obvious, the
Second World War became the nation's last glory. A decade dominated
by the Conservative party also allowed a slow erosion of the 'People's
War' idea, placing increasing emphasis on the image of Churchill, and a
desire to set the people free from interventionist controls. By the 1960s
Britain was in an economic mess. Any pretence at world power was
exposed by the decision to withdraw from east of Suez. Continued
decline in the 1970s made Britain's achievements in the Second World
War a comforting thought in a rapidly changing world. But the vision
of the Second World War still included the national epic of a people
who fought together and achieved a people's peace together. Margaret
Thatcher's Britain tended to forget the politically radical elements of the
myth, the People's War and the road to the welfare state in 1945. Instead
the nationalist element, stressing opposition to continental nations and
the glory of leadership, became far more aggressive and Churchill was
hijacked to play a part in her own cult of the leader. During the Falklands
War of 1982 the press freely compared the situation to the Second World
War and Britain's victory was perceived to have restored the great power
status Britain had so ignominiously lost since 1945. At the same time,
it was becoming obvious that Britain's increasing racial diversity was

influencing recollections and understandings of the war. The arrival of immigrants from the New Commonwealth forced the British to ask whether the war was fought by, and in the best interests of, the peoples of the whole empire. Immigrants from the empire also rightly demanded that their contribution be added to the collective history. Despite some excellent and highly accessible work on this issue, such as Christopher Somerville's *Our War: How the British Commonwealth Fought the Second World War* (1998), and an exhibition at the Imperial War Museum, the dominant narrative is still told from a white perspective.

The ugliest manifestations of the reworked memory of the Second World War have come in the form of football hooliganism. It is here that England's, rather than Britain's, decline and reaction to it are seen most sharply. English fans have sought an awful solace for the decline of their home nation by smashing European cities. Aided by the gutter press, particularly if Germany is involved in any way, the violence often appears to be a wildly misguided attempt to resurrect Britain's wartime military power. Hooligans seems to want to achieve respect by violence alone, misunderstanding the fact that Britain unleashed violence for freedom between 1939 and 1945, and that when the British army appeared in continental cities it did so as a liberator. Witlessly misreading history, England fans arrive as invaders, ironically perhaps the closest parallel is with the Nazi armies. This is something discussed in more detail in Chapter 9.

Graham Dawson and Bob West have identified a struggle to control the image of the Second World War and, through it, national identity. Their argument is that popular memory is often conservative and Conservative in its nature. They trace it beyond 1939 to the nineteenth century, arguing that the Conservative party tried to make patriotism its own from the 1870s and divorced it from any idea of dissent or class struggle. In 1940 the shock of British collapse caused a crisis in this understanding and re-opened the gates to radical patriotism, seen most clearly in George Orwell's understanding of British national identity. Then, in the 1980s, Mrs Thatcher tried to turn the meaning of Britishness and its history back to its late nineteenth-century interpretation.[16]

Many features of this general picture resonate strongly with the themes of the Conservative political discourse. . . . Churchill, the Bulldog

Breed, the soldier-heroes with their backs to the sea at Dunkirk, and the civilian-heroes who endured the Blitz – all of these are celebrated in popular representations: most commonly in terms of that phlegmatic 'national character' which blossoms when the going gets rough, and 'national unity', when 'the British people' pull together to save 'our way of life' from destruction, and to write another glorious chapter in the national annals.[17]

The effect of this, claim the authors, is to disguise the leftward lurch of British politics and society during that same period. Thus a right-wing myth of the war has competed with increasing fierceness against the People's War myth. Interestingly, for a piece wanting to dispel some of the myths and attempting to reassert the radical, People's War side of the history, it appears to fall victim to some of the myths itself. For instance, they refer to Dunkirk as the work of the people, an act improvised by ordinary citizens: 'The evacuation of the British Expeditionary Force represented spontaneous mass participation and an amazing degree moment of democratic improvisation (even if the role of the Navy was central).'[18] This flies in the face of those who have identified the evacuation as the result of the Navy's professionalism and endurance, rather than as an act of the people's will and resolution.

However, Dawson, West and Smith are certainly right to claim that the 'Road to 1945' and People's War side has been gradually sifted out or reworked to suit a conservative understanding. The accusations and recriminations resulting from the collapse of the British Expeditionary Force, the so-called 'Guilty Men' thesis, have definitely lost much of their edge. *Dad's Army* confirmed the reconfiguration of the Home Guard as a bunch of comic incompetents, rather than as a people's militia carrying with it faint whiffs of Cromwell's earlier revolutionary army. The rush to intern all aliens in 1939 has been almost completely forgotten. A xenophobic desire to 'collar the lot' does not sit easily with the image of a people phlegmatically staring fate in the eye. The Royal Navy's action against the French fleet at Oran has certainly disappeared from the memory. Forced to neutralise France's powerful warships before they fell into enemy hands, the British opened fire on their ally, killing French sailors in the process. At the time it was understood as a grim but necessary task, but now it is forgotten. While the myth is necessarily pliable, it does retain an outline cohesion, and it is that which forms part of this study.

My contention is that the British people carry a peculiar and particular history and memory of the Second World War with them. It is an image built and maintained by elements of popular, national culture: books and newspapers, broadcasting and films, museums and education. It is also an image firmly connected with a certain perspective on British history; the Second World War is placed within the context of the governing principles of the supposed national story. Prized and valued in this interpretation are the moments when Britain stood alone and took it on the chin. Interestingly, this is far more attractive to the British than the moment they began to unleash their power. To the average (if there is such a thing) Briton, words such as Dunkirk, Spitfire, Hurricane, Battle of Britain, blitz carry great meaning. They may not have any detailed interest or knowledge of Britain in the Second World War but these words touch a chord in them. But ask someone about the invasion of Italy, the invasion of Germany or the defeat of the U-boat menace and they are far less certain. Britain's memory of the war is skewed towards the early years of the conflict because this suits Britain's self-perception: resolute in a crisis and at its best when alone. 'Taking it' has been more important than 'giving it'. (Except in the case of English football hooligans who seem obsessed with reversing this aspect of national character.) A good example is the nation's deep malaise, ignorance and discomfort over the strategic air campaign. Sir Arthur 'Bomber' Harris is popularly held to be a mass murderer thanks to his direction of an indiscriminate bombing campaign. This is partly due to the fact that there was nothing sporting about his approach; he never gave the underdog a chance and always gave the impression of having the odds stacked in his favour – *very* unBritish. Given the manner in which images of the Second World War dominated the Falklands War, it is interesting to note that its greatest controversy, the sinking of the *Belgrano*, had similar overtones. Ignoring the other arguments involved, consider this explanation of the controversy. A British submarine commander makes a textbook attack, doesn't give his enemy a chance and uses the full force of his weaponry without compunction. Once again, not very British, and many are uncomfortable with it. As George Orwell noted, the British have popular poems about the retreat to Corunna and the disastrous Charge of the Light Brigade but none about Waterloo or Trafalgar.[19]

Connected with the idea of gallantly fighting against the odds is the concept of starting off on the wrong foot. The British like to think that they begin with disasters and build up to a victory. Angus Calder illustrated how deeply this had affected the nation when he cited Mike Brearley's memoirs. Brearley, as the captain of the England cricket team in 1981, saw that year's Ashes series as an example of national character: a poor start and a miraculous recovery, adding 'as a country we have specialised in doing badly at the beginning of wars and ending up victorious'.[20] In 1940, when Ian Hay told the story of the retreat to Dunkirk, he believed there was a simple historical moral behind the experience, proving there was no need for alarm:

> The British Army, by traditional usage, always seems to be compelled to start a war from small beginnings, either play for time or take desperate risks until it has built itself up into an effective striking force. The entire history of that Army is chequered with tales of early reverses or expensive resistances, redeemed in the end, as resources and experience accumulated, by the crown of victory.[21]

Britain's military history provided a reassuring map telling people where they were going. The nation had a battery of images and lessons ready to run in 1939, the war had a historical script before it started. The British people played their roles according to type and found it made sense to do it that way. Few things that happened between 1939 and 1945 were truly new to the British in the sense that their history had provided them with a guide for just such crises. As Angus Calder has pointed out, Dunkirk was the myth of an old country, not the discovery legend of a new one in the way Gallipoli is for Australia.[22]

Fitting the Second World War into the mould of national identity and history, and thus allowing it to become an understandable phenomenon, is at the heart of this book. It examines how British society has dealt with the experience of the Second World War. The media and manner in which that history has been passed on, and how it has adapted to changing circumstances, provides its dynamic.

At this point, I also feel it is important to confess that I am a part of the phenomenon I will be investigating. The Second World War that I grew up with and know is one very much shaped and defined by the elements described above. I am 32 years old and therefore never knew the war 'first hand', but I have always felt very close to it. Indeed, to say it was an obsession is not taking it too far. As a boy, my favourite toys were Airfix, Britain's soldiers and Action Man. My favourite television viewing was war films and documentaries. I have the vaguest memories of watching *The World at War* first time round; it sticks in my mind because I believed one of those burning photographs in those still powerful opening credit sequences was my granddad. It wasn't just me; my younger brother was equally interested and so were all our friends – all boys, of course. We used to pool our soldiers and Action Man figures and recreate battles. We all knew that British soldiers had fought in the desert and France. We all knew that Australian soldiers fought in slouch hats and carried machetes in swampy jungles, mud oozing into their boots. We all knew that GIs stormed Japanese machine-gun nests with flamethrowers. We all knew what a Spitfire looked like, as well as the Lee Enfield .303 rifle with sword bayonet, landing craft, a German Tiger tank, ME 109 fighters and we knew that Commandos wore little woolly fishermen's hats. We all knew about the Second World War and we all knew that British soldiers were best. There was a grudging knowledge of American involvement and a grudging acceptance of American glamour. This came in the strangest of forms; a Colt pistol for your Action Man was a highly prized article.

But how did we know? Most of our grandparents and other older relations had lived and fought through it and told us some of their memories. I had a great uncle who took part in the crossing of the Rhine, Operation Varsity, another who had been in Burma and had a Ghurka kukri knife. One of my grandfathers had been in the Royal Army Service Corps and had gathered brilliant snaps of Mountbatten taking the Japanese surrender of Singapore in 1945, along with an exciting picture of landing craft packed with slouched hatted soldiers sweeping across a broad estuary. But that was only part of the story. My father was a great organiser of Saturday afternoons out in London. We visited every museum and site of interest possible, and from this my brother and I developed a clutch of favourite places, one of which was the Imperial War Museum. This was like a wonderland; here was the adventure of the soldier's life. All the equipment, uniforms and gear we could recognise from our toy soldiers were contained in the displays and we could refine our 'anorak' knowledge: the difference between a short bayonet and a sword bayonet, the range of a 25-pound gun and what a paratrooper carried in his kit.

Our basic knowledge was then fleshed out by comics and other cheap literature. Alongside the *Beano* and the *Dandy*, I was a great fan of *Victor Comic for Boys* and *Battle*, both of which carried all sorts of fantastic Second World War adventure stories. I particularly liked the ones that were headed 'A True Story of World War Two'. Looking back on it I realise that even at the time we all knew bits were fictional, the sheer addition of the label 'True Story' to some stories proved it, however we accepted it all. This was the war, how it was fought and how it was won. Most potently, these images were underpinned by television. War films shown on television – for we were part of that shift away from cinema as the medium of mass communication – were treated with an awed respect. They were 'must see' events, particularly in an age before video recorders made it possible to view something outside its scheduled slot. All my friends knew when a war film was on and everyone would disappear to their own houses to watch it. By the time I was 14 I must have seen the whole canon of greats, black and white and colour: *The Malta Story, Reach for the Sky, The Wooden Horse, The Dam Busters, In Which We Serve, The Way to the Stars* (far too much girly stuff, not enough fighting), *The Way Ahead, The Battle of Britain, The Battle of the Bulge, The Longest Day, 633 Squadron, The Cockleshell Heroes, Where Eagles Dare, Patton*. My particular favourite was *The Guns of Navarone*. As far as I was concerned, it had everything: Commando-style raid, E-boats, death-defying climb up a treacherous cliff, girls who turn out to be spies (girls were always trouble, except when they were Virginia McKenna) and James Robertson Justice in a cameo. I remember being absolutely distraught when my parents went to see *A Bridge Too Far* and did not take me. How I envied the kids who had seen it. I had seen the poster and from that alone knew that it was a great film.

My favourite Airfix soldiers were my 1/32 scale British paratroopers and H0/00 scale Commandos. The paratroopers were in Arnhem kit and it was Arnhem that I enjoyed re-enacting most of all, using my wooden bricks as the ruins. Years later when I saw the photograph of a British paratrooper firing a mortar, his face captured between concentration and concern under the *Daily Mail*'s caption 'The Agony of Arnhem' I was moved to tears. I still am when I see it. In itself it has little value, it is just a photograph revealing only a man in uniform – a British uniform if you are aware of such things – and a weapon, but I invested it with a million times more emotional significance than that. To me it was everything that thrilled me about the British in the Second World War – incredible bravery, incredible devotion, incredible comradeship, incredible skill. And, to this day, every time I read something about Arnhem it makes me weep out of sadness for so many young lives lost, but also out of sheer admiration and, it has to be admitted, jealousy. For, ridiculous as I know it sounds given the fact that I know just how terrible, frightening, dreadful the experience must have been, I am jealous I wasn't there. I suppose I must admit to being a victim of what Graham Dawson has so brilliantly defined, the modern male with few role models other than soldiers. But I think there is something else too. I don't think it's just that I want to play with real weapons, it is because I am jealous of them for having experienced such intense emotions, for taking part in something so much bigger than themselves but to which they were each integral.

The Second World War was therefore with me constantly. I grew interested in other aspects of history in my teens, particularly the Great War, but this first enthusiasm stayed with me. I recall vividly the large-scale commemorations for D-Day in 1984, and a year later VE Day was remembered in an equally impressive way. I was an undergraduate when the fiftieth anniversaries of Dunkirk and the Battle of Britain were celebrated, and a post-graduate when VE and VJ Days were marked by a whole series of events.

This book seeks to explore this popular memory and knowledge of the war. Why do I know it in the way I do? Why was I part of a culture in which every boy I knew at both primary and secondary schools displayed these interests and obsessions to varying degrees? My own history is evidence of a culture saturated in the Second World War. I am a piece of evidence. This does not mean that I cannot detach myself and explore it. The British myth is part of me, but is something the historian in me can analyse. This phenomenon is also something on the brink of change, as is explored more fully in Chapter 9 and the Epilogue. People of my age are probably the last to be so deeply influenced by the British memory of the Second World War that has evolved since 1945. The memory is on the cusp of change and mutation thanks to a variety of reasons. Of primary significance is the ever-quickening decrease in the numbers of veterans. Most veterans of the Second World War are now at an advanced age and their ability to inspire family members with their exploits is waning. British culture has also become a good deal more diverse since the 1970s. Alterations to the broadcasting and communications laws have shattered the consensus of the Sunday afternoon television matinée and the single screen cinema. Radical changes to the racial make-up of the British population have also had an impact. As already noted, the memory of the war might still be white, but there are now far more shades and tints in it. Finally, modern visions of contemporary conflicts are placing the Second World War in a new frame. First World citizens watching television news have become used to an ironic visual interpretation of conflict: they are subjected to as many gruesome sights as a veteran of Sword Beach or the Coventry blitz, but unlike them they are utterly detached from the reality of the experience. Further, a Coventry mother worrying about her son on Sword Beach would have followed his fate by listening to the radio, reading newspapers and watching a newsreel, all of which would have been *post facto* interpretations. Now mothers may see their children on screen at the very moment they are performing their duties. Such developments are influencing the ability to create a consensus on events as they unfold and on their subsequent memory. In turn and in the light of these developments, interpretations of past conflicts are revisited and re-evaluated. As the Foreign Secretary, Jack Straw, said in regards to media coverage of the Second Gulf War:

> *But it is also worth speculating how much harder it might have been to maintain the country's morale after Dunkirk had live reports confronted the public with the brutal reality of German tactical and military superiority. Could the 'Spirit of Dunkirk', so important to national survival [in 1940], have withstood the scrutiny of 24-hour live news?*[23]

Combative news journalism has therefore made it very difficult to conceive a time in which the government and the press had joint aims and intentions. This is particularly obvious in the case of the BBC. During the Second World War it was looked at as separate from government but representing, reflecting and encouraging national aims and endeavours.

The Falklands War and the two Gulf Wars almost completely reversed this image. Both Conservative and Labour governments have accused it of working against the national interest and revelling in mischief-making. This book therefore explores a flexible memory which I suspect is on the verge of being reshaped more extensively than at any time since 1945.

Note on national identity

Individuals hold many identities to define themselves, sometimes in conjunction, sometimes singly. Thus class, religion, gender, family, status, education, region, nation are all used as labels by the individual for the individual. Nation is a particularly important identity for it is the vital link with something larger than ourselves and yet remains intimately linked to self. Nation is, in Benedict Anderson's celebrated phrase, 'the imagined community'.

The meaning of national identity, its revealing codes and history are the result of a negotiation between the nation, state and people within a broadly accepted dominant ideology. The negotiation is continual and national identity is not fixed. In 1927, Sir Ernest Baker declared nationality a cultural construct:

> Not only is national character made, it continues to be made and remade. It is not made once, for all, it always remains modifiable. A nation may alter its character in the course of its history to suit new conditions or to fit new purposes.[24]

Britain is currently undergoing such a re-negotiation and the popular history of the Second World War may well be altered with it.

Every nation has a set of values that are commonly held to define it. These are often held to be unique, but can be seen in the identity of many different countries, such as the American and French ideals of individual liberties and rights. National identities as we know them were solidified in the eighteenth century with the rise of acquisitive nation states. The British nation, as Linda Colley has shown, gained its cultural badges in the period from the Act of Union (1707) to the accession of Queen Victoria (1837).[25]

British national identity has often been synonymous with England. Many people have confused Britishness with Englishness. Foreigners can easily fall into this trap and still use the terms interchangeably. But, until recently, although there was sensitivity over the issue, England and Englishness could often be taken as shorthand for Britain. England was the political and economic powerhouse of Great Britain, giving it cultural dominance as well. With the decline of Britain as a great power, meaning a sharper decline for England, Celticism has found a new confidence, which in turn has made the British–English elision far more sensitive. The erosion of England's 'happiness' with Britain is best illustrated by football. In July 1966 England won the World Cup at Wembley accompanied by the ecstatic waving of thousands of Union Jacks. In June 1996 England played Germany at Wembley in the semi-final of the European Championship backed by thousands of crosses of St George. In this book the terms 'England' and 'Englishness' will often by used by contemporary commentators to stand for a wider Britishness. Where this is not so will be made explicit.

What were, and for many still are, the agreed badges of Britishness? What characterised and symbolised Britain from the eighteenth century and the Acts of Union? One of the greatest unifying elements was the empire. Nuances between England, Wales and Scotland were lessened by the investment in a commonly-held 'other' world. The British empire was the shining example of British qualities and superiority.

Religion also created a common bond; the British people were overwhelmingly Protestant. (Ireland is the exception to virtually every rule mentioned in this book.) When combined with island status, Protestantism fostered a sense of separation and of a unique destiny. As they overcame foreign threats to their island, the British felt they had a special relationship with God. With the growth of France as the strongest Catholic power in the eighteenth century, Britain's survival against this mighty enemy was taken as a sign of righteousness. An innate xenophobia began to express itself, foreigners were very definitely 'other'. Foreigners came to symbolise everything Britain resented. Foreigners, especially the French, were dictatorial, lacked individualism and individual liberties, lacked genuine gallantry and bravery, were conspiratorial and sly and, fatally for them, always underestimated the people of the tiny island. By 1939 little had changed, British values were clearly superior to foreign ones. Angus Calder has put the values of wartime Britain and Germany in table form. They are reworkings of earlier models:

England (Britain)	*Germany*
Freedom	*Tyranny*
Improvisation	*Calculation*
Volunteer spirit	*Drilling*
Friendliness	*Brutality*
Tolerance	*Persecutions*
Timeless landscape	*Mechanisation*
Patience	*Aggression*
Calm	*Frenzy*
A thousand years of peace	*The Thousand Year Reich dedicated to war.*[26]

It was the latest manifestation of a deep-rooted sense of separation, greatness despite size, freedom and decency. The Britain these islanders lived in developed a particular landscape. As the first industrial and urbanised nation, Britain felt the traumas of change most acutely. It created an intense reaction against the horrors of chimneys belching smoke and streets of mean houses. Symbolised by figures such as John Ruskin and William Morris, a cult of the English countryside grew up. The true glory of the nation was placed in the soil, and the soil of south-east England especially. Bucolic visions of happy peasants in charming cottages, quaffing good ale in merry inns while golden corn waved in rolling fields was the eventual result. A 'deep England' mentality affected all; to play on Simon Schama's work, memory created its own landscape of history and myth.[27]

The British, but more particularly the English, also managed to recast themselves in this landscape. One of the reasons why the English had ascended to the top of the ladder in the nineteenth century was thanks to their sheer violence. The English were very good at fighting, fighting anyone and everyone, fighting among themselves if no one else was on hand. But by the mid-nineteenth century the English gentleman had been born and is still accepted across the world as a definition of good manners, courtesy, honesty and respectability. How had this happened? The growth of a mass population led to fear of the mob and its destructive power. How was the mob to be tamed? Religion offered a partial answer. The Victorian churches strove to civilise and educate the mob. At the same time, the wind of reform swept through the British public schools system largely thanks to Thomas Arnold's work at Rugby. His insistence on creating men of character by a combination of classical studies and games set a model of gentlemanly behaviour. Victorian evangelism then threw up Muscular Christianity, a form of religion which prized chivalrous behaviour and encouraged sports of all forms. Discipline, honour and gallantry became the watchwords of the British gentleman. But these tenets were not confined to the upper classes. University settlements and public school missions to the working-class districts of British industrial towns and state education ensured the socialisation of the working classes. Of course there was rebellion against it, but crime levels dropped rapidly (also attributable to the establishment of a professional police force) and Britain, despite huge discrepancies in wealth and status, became a remarkably homogeneous and stable society.

A sense of national identity was both promoted and accepted within a process of negotiation. By the late nineteenth century, many aspects of popular culture were marked by a nationalistic, bordering on outright xenophobic, character. Music hall entertainments encouraged pride in Britain's empire and racial superiority. History lessons in state schools ensured the promotion of a particular vision of British development. The armed forces, more specifically the Royal Navy, were venerated as expressions of national power, guarding the seas, maintaining the security of the island race and the *Pax Britannica*.

All these strands came together in the Great War, when the British people revealed a high level of patriotism and a remarkable level of self-discipline and dedication. The memorials erected in the wake of the Great War symbolically enshrined the morality of the cause and Britain's race of heroes. Contrary to modern popular opinion, the 1920s and 1930s did not witness the triumph of disillusion and a total rejection of the nation's history and British values. If anything the search for consolation invested those values with even greater meaning; the deaths had to be for, and about, something. Few were allowed to doubt that the deaths were justified by the cause, and during the course of the struggle the qualities of the island race had been shown to all, friend and foe alike.[28] In 1939 the same characteristics were to be called upon. Ironically, no matter how ill-prepared it was militarily, Britain was ready for the Second World War. The tenets of history, heritage and race provided the British with the spiritual and emotional armour they needed to interpret and endure the experience.[29]

Notes

1 Clive Ponting, *1940: Myth and Reality* (London 1990).

2 Greater theoretical debate on the nature of memory and myth can be found in Martin Evans and Ken Lunn (eds), *War and Memory in the Twentieth Century* (Oxford 1997), pp. viii–xix; Graham Dawson, *Soldier Heroes: British Adventure, Empire and the Imagining of Masculinities* (London 1994), pp. 1–10; T.G. Ashplant, Graham Dawson and Michael Roper (eds), *The Politics of War Memory and Commemoration* (London 2000).

3 Malcolm Smith, *Britain and 1940* (London 2000), p. 2.

4 Jeffrey Richards, *Film and British National Identity, from Dickens to Dad's Army* (Manchester 1997), p. 364.

5 Graham Dawson, 'History-writing on World War II', in Geoff Hurd (ed.), *National Fictions: World War Two in British Film and Television* (London 1984), pp. 1–7.

6 Smith, *Britain and 1940*, p. 6.

7 Although the Imperial War Museum has sought to illustrate its Great War galleries with an equal amount of film material, it is interesting to note that the written word still has a powerful grip on the way the Great War is imagined, shown most recently in its Trench Poetry exhibition and accompanying book.

8 Smith, *Britain and 1940*, p. 3.

9 Ibid., p. 4.

10 John Ramsden, 'Refocusing "The People's War": British War Films of the 1950s', *Journal of Contemporary History* 33, 1 (1998), pp. 35–64.

11 *The Sun* 10 October 1969.

12 Geoff Hurd, 'Notes on Hegemony: The War and Cinema', in Geoff Hurd (ed.), *National Fictions: World War Two in British Film and Television* (London 1984), pp. 18–19.

13 See Harold L. Smith (ed.), *Britain and the Second World War: A Social History* (Manchester 1996); Steven Fielding, Peter Thompson and Nick Tiratsoo (eds), *England Arise! The Labour Party and Popular Politics in 1940s Britain* (Manchester 1995); Penelope Summerfield, *Reconstructing Women's Wartime Lives: Discourse and Subjectivity in Oral Histories of the Second World War* (Manchester 1998); Ross McKibbin, *Classes and Cultures in England 1918–1951* (Oxford 1998).

14 Stuart Hylton, *Their Darkest Hour: The Hidden History of the Home Front 1939–1945* (Stroud 2001).

15 Quoted in Angus Calder, *The Myth of the Blitz* (London 1991), p. 3.

16 Graham Dawson and Bob West, 'The Popular Memory of World War II and the Struggle over National Identity', in Geoff Hurd (ed.), *National Fictions: World War Two in British Film and Television* (London 1984), pp. 8–13.

17 Ibid., p. 10.

18 Ibid., p. 11.

19 George Orwell, 'The Lion and the Unicorn', in *The Penguin Essays of George Orwell* (Harmondsworth 1984; orig. 1941), pp. 131–94.

20 Mike Brearley, *Phoenix from the Ashes* (London 1983), p. 175. Also quoted in Calder, *Myth*, p. 4.

21 Ian Hay, *The Battle of Flanders, 1940* (London 1941), Foreword.

22 Calder, *Myth*, p. 7.

23 Quoted in *The Guardian* 1 April 2003.

24 Quoted in Richards, *Film and National Identity*, p. 2.

25 See Linda Colley, *Britons: Forging the Nation 1707–1837* (London 1992).

26 Calder, *Myth*, p. 196.

27 See Simon Schama, *Landscape and Memory* (London 1995).

28 See Mark Connelly, *The Great War: Memory and Ritual* (London 2001).

29 For a further exploration of these themes see: Benedict Anderson, *Imagined Communities: Reflections on the Origins and Spread of Nationalism* (London 1983); J.M. MacKenzie, *Imperialism and Popular Culture* (Manchester 1986); J.M. MacKenzie, *Propaganda and Empire* (Manchester 1984); Raphael Samuel (ed.), *Patriotism: The Making and Unmaking of British National Identity*, 3 vols (London 1989).

CHAPTER 1

. . . .

Mr Chamberlain's face: September 1939–May 1940

The first six months or so of the Second World War is not a period remembered or mythologised with any great clarity by the British people. The central myths and images of the period September 1939 to May 1940 are those of the declaration of war and lack of preparation and activity, evacuation and the role of the Royal Navy, the only element of the British armed forces actively prosecuting the war. This period is perceived as the one in which the British decided to pretend the war wasn't happening and tried to laugh it into oblivion. It is probably because of this ludicrously misplaced complacency that this early phase of the war has left an unimpressive legacy. Few images have survived in the modern memory, and those that have, such as evacuation, are often linked exclusively with the blitz of 1940–41. Given the overwhelming association of Winston Churchill with the war, many can be forgiven for their haziness over 1939; after all, Churchill was not Prime Minister during this period. Churchill's looming presence over the British memory of the war has turned Neville Chamberlain into a marginal figure, the warm-up for the main act. Yet it was during Chamberlain's period as war leader that the foundations of Britain's war memory and myth were laid. The fact that 1940 is the crucial year in the modern memory is connected intimately with the nature of the first months, for without the prerequisite of the 'phoney war' the myth of 1940 would have been robbed of its most significant aspect – that of starting off on the wrong foot – and this element is crucial to the British understanding of the war. In essence, September 1939 to May 1940 is all about starting off on the wrong foot. It was obvious at the time and its surviving fragmentary images have retained that association.

Britain is at war with Germany

The declaration of war in 1939 provided a tribute to the power of wireless. The newspaper press had been scooped by the BBC; wireless gave Chamberlain the ability to address the entire nation a quarter of an hour after the final ultimatum to Germany expired. Warned to remain close to their radios all morning, the British people heard his mournful tones bring the dreadful, but not unexpected, news. The hush that descended over the nation on that Sunday morning and the strange feelings the declaration evoked made a lasting impact on people. A middle-aged schoolmistress noted: 'At 11.15 I went up, and we sat round listening to Chamberlain speaking. I held my chin high and kept back the tears at the thought of the slaughter ahead. When "God Save the King" was played, we stood.'[1] Joan Wyndham recorded listening to the broadcast in her diary, feeling sick, and later sitting out on the steps of her house. 'The balloon barrage looked too lovely in the sun against the blue sky, like iridescent silver fish swimming in blue water.'[2] Indeed the stillness of the Sunday morning quickly became the essential image of the declaration of war. Within a few days of the outbreak of war, the General Post Office Film Unit started work on a short film recording the way in which London moved from peace to war. *The First Days* shows 3 September as an idyllic, leisurely day, with people setting out on bicycle rides, walking in Hyde Park or going to church. But then, cutting to shots of empty streets, the sound of Chamberlain's voice coming through open windows is heard. This snapshot of Britain confirmed the way memory would recall the event: a lazy day, deserted streets and wirelesses in suburban houses. Frank Capra repeated this vision in his famous wartime documentary series, *Why We Fight*. As the title suggests, the series was designed to explain the reasons to its soldiers and civilians why America had entered the war. Episode two, 'The Battle of Britain', contained a scene in which a man walking along an empty street stops to listen to the voice of Neville Chamberlain coming through the open windows of a neat, suburban house fronted by a box hedge, a quintessential symbol of British middle-class respectability.

Since the war this image has been reconstructed many times. In 1970 Granada launched its drama series *Family at War*, which proved to be a huge success gaining a regular audience of around eight million viewers.[3] The series opened with the various branches of the fictional Ashton family listening to the declaration of war on the wireless. Encapsulating the vision of *The First Days*, the shots revealed a quiet northern town, awaiting confirmation of its fate. The suburban branch of the family listened in the drawing room of a typical 1930s house, complete with bay window and sunburst decoration on the garden gate. Yorkshire Television's fine history series for schools, *How We Used to Live*, which ran throughout the 1970s and 1980s, reconstructed the moment in exactly the same way. A lower-middle-class family sit round their radio in a typically 1930s suburban home, the front garden has a sunburst gate. This Betjemanesque view of England is the prism through which we see 3 September and has been used as a visual shorthand to establish mood and time even in programmes and dramas not overtly connected with the war.

John Boorman's lavish film treatment of his semi-autobiographical story about growing up in the war, *Hope and Glory* (1987), provides the most completely realised vision of the confirmed image of the declaration of war. The film opens with Bill Rowan and his younger sister in a cinema watching the 'Saturday morning pictures'. On the screen flicker newsreel images of Chamberlain and King George VI, from the nature of the commentary it is clear that war is imminent. The scene cuts to the following morning. Bill and his sister are playing in the garden of a suburban house, the sound of lawn mowers from the other gardens is audible. A voiceover of an older man (John Hurt) announces: 'Sunday, 3rd September 1939. Everyone who was old enough and was there remembers exactly what they were doing.' Suddenly the lawn mowers stop and all is quiet while Chamberlain makes his speech. The camera pans round the concerned faces of Bill's mother and father. The room itself is a masterpiece of set design, a museum curator's vision of a 1930s' house, including Clarice Cliff-inspired crockery and leaded light sunburst windows. Boorman's camera frames the memory, confirms it as a moment when settled, middle-class worlds, such as that of Bill Rowan's Rosehill Avenue, were confident of who and what they were.

By remembering the outbreak of war in such a way, it perhaps reflects a national obsession with a world about to end, a way of life about to disappear, which, in turn, provokes a sense of nostalgia. *Family at War*'s credit sequence certainly appears to fit this interpretation: each episode opened with the shot of a beach bathed in evening sunlight, a sand castle topped by a Union Jack sat in the middle of the shot. The sand castle was then gradually washed away by the waves, accompanied by the elegiac, lyrical central section of the first movement of Vaughan Williams' Sixth Symphony. Made in the troubled 1970s, *Family at War* seems to provide a requiem for the British way of life.

Chamberlain fits into that old world, a remnant of an older age, someone who was definitely pre-war and out of place in an emergency that needed bold action. Neville Chamberlain was 70 years old when he declared war over the airwaves on the morning of Sunday 3 September 1939. He came from a family of politicians, had taken over the family power base of Birmingham and had served Conservative governments in a variety of posts before becoming Prime Minister in 1937. With his antique style of dress, Chamberlain gave the impression of being a Victorian. Always accompanied by his umbrella, he often wore a tall hat, starched wing collars and sober ties, all of which made him appear a man out of step with the age.[4] Photographs of him in 1939 reveal a thin, reedy face, framed by a narrow band of grey hair. His metallic voice had something of the tone of a headmaster dutifully expelling a boy for bad behaviour. As Angus Calder has pointed out, his physical demeanour and looks made him a cartoonist's dream.[5] Having staked so much on 'peace in our time', having thought that a man like Hitler could be reasoned with, Chamberlain has become an object of our pity, irony and sarcasm. Treated with increasing irreverence as the war effort stagnated, Chamberlain can be regarded as a symbol of Britain's rather ludicrous position in 1939: at war but not fighting, talking of a long war but making few preparations.[6]

For many, memories of Chamberlain are suffused with ridicule or humour. Spike Milligan's wonderfully eccentric and deliberately mischievous memoirs frame Chamberlain as a buffoon. In *Adolf Hitler: My Part in His Downfall*, Milligan notes that on 3 September, 'a man called

Mr Chamberlain, a man 'who did Prime Minister impersonations', looking suitably suburban, with his wife in St James's Park (Hulton-Getty Images).

Chamberlain who did Prime Minister impressions spoke on the wire-less'.[7] Milligan's wit is almost cruel, but it crystallises the accepted memory – Chamberlain as a man out of his depth, a man who impersonated Prime Ministers – with the hidden implication that, by contrast, Winston Churchill was every inch a leader, and a leader of wartime Britain too. Chamberlain is the ultimate paradox: remembered in order that he might be forgotten.

A similar thread can be found in Robert Westall's work on childhood in wartime, *Children of the Blitz*. Interviewed many years later, adults worked their childhood memories into an acerbic mode when recalling Chamberlain. A man from Tyneside, born in 1930, recalled his impressions of the Prime Minister:

> *Mr Chamberlain's broadcast was not impressive. I remembered him from the newsreels, coming out of his aeroplane after Munich, waving his little piece of paper and promising 'peace in our time'. I thought he looked like a sheep, and now he bleated like a sheep. He talked about notes being sent and replies not being received. He* regretted *that a state of war now existed between Great Britain and Germany. He sounded really hurt, like Hitler was some shiftless council tenant who had failed to pay his rent after faithfully promising to do so.*
>
> *That wasn't the way to talk to Hitler; he should be threatening to kick his teeth in. . . . I knew there'd be trouble . . .'*[8]

Memory mixed with a few, repeated images and the value of hindsight seem to be combined here to paint a picture of Chamberlain that is not so much black as grey. Noël Coward's 1942 film about life in the Royal Navy, *In Which We Serve*, included a scene in which the sailors are listening to the declaration of war. When Chamberlain announces his personal regret at the failure of negotiation, a sailor chirps up, 'it ain't exactly a bank holiday for us'. It complements the above recollection of Chamberlain; his ridiculousness was shaped and compounded by taking the war as a personal injury, almost implying that no else was sharing the experience of war.

Chamberlain has become a symbol of all that was muddleheaded, incompetent, irresponsible, complacent and, indeed, ludicrous about the first nine months of the war. With the British government taking no firm action to curb German aggression, other than to despatch the British

Expeditionary Force (BEF) to France where it dug in promptly and then did little else, the war settled down into mundane routine. This period is now known as the phoney war, but this phrase was one coined by the American press and the fact that it has entered our consciousness seems to reveal how far Britain has fallen under American cultural influences. At the time, it was known as the 'bore war'.

The 'bore war' was full of rather bizarre moments, which would have been incredible if anyone but Chamberlain had been Prime Minister. Somehow Chamberlain is the guarantee that such things could and did happen. For instance, when the BEF landed in France the British censor strongly denied it, but the French papers were carrying the story. An obsession with secrecy clearly had not been combined with a genius for news management.[9] The winter of 1939–40 brought heavy snowfalls and was the coldest for 45 years, public transport ground to a halt, and the Channel froze at Folkestone and Dungeness. But, what was blindingly obvious to everyone was made an official secret, and the press was banned from commenting on it.[10] Britain was blacked out nightly with a religious zeal, but very little thought had gone into public safety in the pitch black and accidents, particularly on the roads, rose at an alarming rate.[11]

Such a combination of factors give the bore war its air of unreality and farce, which sets it apart from the period of deep war of 1941–43 when sacrifices were obvious and life was grim. George Formby is a good example of early war; Formby is a man of the 1930s, and a man who looks out of place in 1945. His humour, his style seem to make him a symbol of a more naïve world, a world before bombing, before deaths, before Churchill. By 1938, George Formby was the top British box-office attraction, having ousted his fellow Lancastrian and equally 1930s rival, Gracie Fields. His humour was very British, particularly northern, and very working class. A mixture of innuendo and innocence, it was full of Donald McGill seaside postcard standards: overbearing landladies, courting couples, shy boys trying to woo glamorous girls and little men taking on the establishment.[12] Fields had a similar style – a simple Lancashire lassie. The lyrics of her songs romanticised the nature of everyday, working-class life combined with wistful dreams of better things. She was a phenomenon, playing to sell-out audiences, and by 1938 was the highest paid British entertainer.[13]

Like Formby, Gracie Fields worked tirelessly to entertain the troops, and both were making concert tours in France soon after the arrival of the BEF. Over 100,000 British soldiers entered a ballot to gain a ticket for her first concert in France. *British Movietone News* reported 'General Gracie holds up the war'.[14] The 5,000 winners heard her give voice to the 'emotion surging in her heart' which 'poured out in the songs the men of England love'.[15] When George Formby appeared in the spring of 1940, he was accompanied by his ukulele and sang his latest song 'Sitting on a mine in the Maginot Line'.[16] The cheeky lyrics included: 'At night myself to sleep I sing / to my old tin hat I cling / I have to use it now for everything / sitting in the Maginot Line'. Other songs of the period were equally blasé about the war. The big hit of the winter was 'We're gonna hang out the washing on the Siegfried Line', which belittled the line of fortifications Germany had built along its border with France. Such an approach to the war makes it seem like a preface to the real thing. Chamberlain, Hitler and the Nazis, and army life all become one big joke.

Even before the war, the looming emergency was provoking comedy. Will Hay's bumbling Constable Dudfoot in *Ask a Policeman* (1938) dealt with a suspected bomb according to the techniques he has learned in Air Raid Precautions (ARP) classes. Formby joined the RAF in *It's in the Air* (1938) and bungled his way through an air-raid precautions drill. Making jokes about air raids might be viewed as a sensible way of exorcising a spectre that haunted the British people, but it also hints at a lack of realism and preparation.

Of course, comedy played a part in maintaining morale throughout the war, and became even more important as the war grew grimmer. But the comedy of the bore war, as encapsulated by Formby, is of a different sort, having an innocence that is no longer accessible thanks to experience and hindsight. The comedy is almost insulting because it appears to misjudge the situation so badly. Somehow, it seems offensive to make jokes about the war when it is being downplayed so mistakenly. Humour about Hitler and the war when people realised the gravity of the situation does not have the same ability to provoke disquiet, anger or disbelief now. Today it is almost impossible to think about the lyrics of 'We're gonna hang out the washing on the Siegfried Line' without them taking on an ironic quality. We want to shout at those singing them on the newsreels of 1939, 'fools, do you honestly think it's going to be that easy?' It betrays a sense of sang-froid built not upon knowing the odds and accepting them stoically, but upon ignorance and fantasy.

Mass-Observation, a movement founded in 1936 dedicated to the sociological study of the British, investigated jokes about the war at Christmas 1939 and concluded that they were extremely popular. By August 1940 they were 'less popular', though 30 per cent of people found them amusing still. However, by the end of October 1941 fewer than 10 per cent of people were telling war jokes.[17] There is an obvious correlation between the progress and nature of the war and the level of humour found in it. Similarly, at the start of the conflict most comedians made jokes about army life, particularly the shock of joining up, and a number of comic films on this theme were made, including *All at Sea* (1939), *Laugh It Off* (1940) and *Old Mother Riley Joins Up* (1939).

Formby's *Let George Do It* is an equally fascinating example of early war film. Made in the winter of 1939–40, it was not released until August 1940 when the situation looked bleak indeed. The plot revolves around Formby's inadvertent discovery of a Nazi spy ring while performing in a British band touring Norway. Sticking to his well-established characteristics, Formby defeats the baddies by a combination of good-natured blundering and bravery, and, of course, a pretty girl and a song or two help the plot along. Undoubtedly the highlight of the film is a dream sequence in which George confronts Hitler at a Nuremburg rally. Hitler's histrionic gesturing and rants provoke Formby into action. Announcing that Hitler is his 'last territorial demand in Europe', Formby lays him out with a punch, to the obvious delight of Hitler's henchmen who joyfully take the chance to run away. The British public loved the film. Much more surprisingly so did the normally snobbish film critics. It is easy to understand why the film was a success: in August 1940 Britain was standing alone and in the shadow of threatened invasion; here was a film that made light of the situation, celebrated old-fashioned British virtues of determination and honesty and had a fantasy sequence in which Hitler got his richly deserved comeuppance. However, it also reveals a great deal about the period in which it was made, a period in which fantasy, poor judgement and bluff dominated. First, the film is set in neutral Norway, but within a month of its trade show Norway had been overrun by the Nazis, thus making comic capers in strange landscapes appear dreadfully outdated. Ealing Studios was forced to release the film with a special prologue announcing the action 'takes place in Norway, before the war spread'. Secondly, the idea that Nazi Germany was seething with internal discontent, as evoked by the deserting stormtroopers in the dream sequence, was a mirror reflection of Chamberlain's own dreams, hoping for a miraculous collapse of German morale that would end the war. In November 1939, he had written to his sister stating: 'I have a "hunch" that the war will be over before the spring. It won't be by defeat in the field but by German realization that they *can't* win and it isn't worth their while to go on getting thinner and poorer when they might have instant relief and perhaps not have to give up anything they really care about.'[18] While reading these lines one can hear in the background 'We're gonna hang out the washing on the Siegfried Line'.

A similar undercurrent of unreality runs through the Crazy Gang's grand ensemble piece, *Gasbags*. The brilliantly anarchic antics of the well-established music hall troupe are given full vent in the film. Made in early 1940, it did not reach the cinema until December, and it too revealed an equally large reality gap. At the start of the film, the gang are in RAF Balloon Command and in charge of their own barrage balloon, but high winds drag it and them away. Coming down in what they take to be France, they decide to avoid disciplinary action at home by joining the French army. But as they wander down the trenches of the Maginot Line German soldiers leap up and capture them. Realising they have in fact landed on the Siegfried Line, they are dragged up before a Nazi officer who asks them how many men are in the army. 'Ten million' says Jimmy Nervo. 'Ten million?' the Nazi officer asks incredulously, 'You haven't so many men in all your armies.' 'Ah, that doesn't include Weygand, Gort and us', he replies. (Generals Weygand and Gort were the commanders of the French and British armies respectively.) This farcical humour rests on a situation that had changed utterly by the summer of 1940, namely that there were two opposing defensive positions that might confuse crazy Britons. Even more disconcerting, although wonderfully funny, are the later scenes in a concentration camp. Knowing what happened in such places, and knowing that some knowledge of it was seeping out during the war no matter how imperfectly, has the effect of placing *Gasbags* in the world before the real war, the bore war world of fantasies and frustrations.

All of which brings the story back to Chamberlain, the presiding genius of the piece, or the one whom memory has framed as such. For a time Chamberlain and the British people walked in close harmony, both working on unrealistic assumptions. At first Chamberlain received a great deal of applause when he appeared on newsreels, but as the war stagnated and Britons realised that sanguine promises of victory needed to be backed up with sweat, his popularity began to decline. Approval of the Prime Minister was increasingly given out of a sense of patriotic solidarity rather than genuine belief in his approach to the war.[19] Then, in April 1940, Chamberlain made a speech that would have been comic had the wider situation not been so threatening. Speaking to the Central Council of the National Association of Conservative and Unionist Associations, he stated that the Germans had lost their best chance of winning the war for now the allies had caught up in terms of preparations. Hitler had 'missed the bus' he concluded. A day later, the Chief of the Imperial General Staff, General Sir Edmund Ironside, told the *Daily Express* that 'we are ready for anything they [the Germans] may start'.[20] Yet when, three days later, the Nazis invaded Denmark and Norway they caught Britain and France utterly unawares. The 'bore war' had come to an end and it would also spell the end of Chamberlain.

The Norwegian campaign also has a very low profile in the popular memory of the war, yet it was the débâcle in Norway that cost Chamberlain his job. British troops despatched to aid Norway were poorly equipped and without clear guidance as to aims and objectives. Withdrawn less than a month after they landed, the ignominious retreat of the British army led to a Commons debate that smashed confidence in Chamberlain and his ability to lead a wartime administration. On 10 May Winston Churchill became Prime Minister of a coalition government; the real war had begun.[21]

It is highly unlikely that Chamberlain will ever be rehabilitated, although historians have shown some sympathy to him and have attempted to explain how and why he took certain decisions.[22] Chamberlain is conceived as a man out of his depth and out of tune with the realities of the situation. Influential popular histories stress this image, thus ensuring that Chamberlain is viewed in a certain way. Episode two of Thames Television's *The World at War*, 'Distant War: September 1939–May 1940', is a good example. Written by Laurence Thompson and based on his highly readable and well-researched book, *1940: Year of Legend, Year of History* (1966), the episode maintains a distinctly tongue-in-cheek, bordering on sarcastic, edge. Heavy emphasis is given to newsreel footage showing newsvendors' boards with the headlines 'Never Mind Hitler, Take Your Holiday' and of children riding on elephants in London Zoo. Shots of a British army band playing in St James's Park are accompanied by the stirring tones of Schubert's *Military March*. (Unfortunately the episode missed out on the wonderful story reported in the *Daily Express* in December 1939 in which Fred Emmett, an upholsterer with a toothbrush moustache and a heavy parting in his hair, told of his dismay at being confused with Hitler. Emmett commented, 'It's a nuisance, a blooming nuisance', and he longed for the days of the Great War in which he served with the Royal Naval Air Service, 'I was all right then. I wasn't anything like the Kaiser.'[23]) The overall impression of the episode is one of muddle, irrational hopes and lethargy, with Chamberlain at the heart of it. Chamberlain is thus caught, seemingly forever, as the funny man with the umbrella who got it all so very wrong.

The Navy's here

However, the period of the bore war has left a few other fragments on the popular memory, not all of which are intimately connected with the figure of Neville Chamberlain. Images of the Royal Navy were prevalent in the first six months of the war and have rumbled down to the present day. Starved of excitement, the British press and public were whipped into a frenzy of celebration over two naval incidents in the winter of 1939–40. First came the Battle of the River Plate, fought off the coast of Argentina and Uruguay in mid-December 1939 between the German 'pocket battleship', *Graf Spee*, and three smaller British cruisers. Taking the initiative boldly, the British ships engaged the German vessel and, despite being heavily outgunned, forced her to take refuge in Montevideo, capital of neutral Uruguay. The British tried hard to rush up supporting units before the *Graf Spee* could make a dash for it, but rather than face the badly battered British force again, her master, Captain Langsdorff, took the opportunity to scuttle his ship. Then, a few months after this victory, the British destroyer, HMS *Cossack*, put a party of men aboard the *Graf Spee*'s supply ship, *Altmark*, while she lay at anchor in a fjord in neutral Norway. The British sailors released a party of British seamen due to be interned in Germany. Both incidents were used to confirm the pluck and dash of the island race and created a few weeks of terrific excitement.

News of the action in the South Atlantic was eagerly awaited in Britain; on Christmas Day 1939, *British Paramount News* proudly announced: '7,000 miles by air in a week! British Paramount News brings you dramatic pictures of battered Nazi battleship in Montevideo Harbour after overwhelming defeat.'[24] Churchill, the First Lord of the Admiralty, ordered the British ships home and arranged a triumphal march through the City of London. Just as the ships arrived, the *Altmark* incident became public. 'The Altmark Epic thrills the world', said *British Paramount News*, 'Two hundred and ninety-nine British prisoners released in spectacular fashion from Nazi hell-ship, arrive home in destroyer which saved them, and some tell their stories.'[25] Vast crowds assembled to watch the victors of the River Plate march to the Guildhall, where Churchill was guest of honour at a grand lunch. *The Times*, the *Daily Express* and the *Daily Mirror* all remarked on the size of the crowd and the atmosphere of rejoicing.[26] Winston Churchill summed up the mood when he told the assembled dignitaries, 'in a dark, cold winter it warmed the cockles of the British heart'.[27] A few weeks later, *Picture Post* issued a special souvenir issue commemorating the battle, packed with exciting photographs of the combat and grinning sailors giving the thumbs up.[28]

The Battle of the River Plate and the boarding of the *Altmark* appeared to characterise and categorise the differences between the British and the Germans. Britain revelled in the supine manner in which the Germans had reacted to the crisis. The *Daily Express* editorial on 18 December ridiculed the spirit of the Nazi navy after the *Graf Spee* had bolted for Montevideo and had then refused to meet its foes.[29] A similar line was taken by *British Movietone News*, which castigated the Germans: 'Ignominious end of the pocket battleship, sunk by Hitler, rather than face again the British naval squadron.'[30] And the *Daily Mirror* sarcastically pointed out the hypocrisy of Nazi protests at Britain's violation of Norwegian neutrality.[31] The paper also carried photographs of children giving ironic Nazi salutes to the British sailors, their faces bathed with grins. British children seemed to be proof of the stuff of the race and had had their conceptions of British power and Nazi inferiority proven. Robert Westall's Tynesider remembered it thus:

Perhaps Hitler was already beaten. The German pocket-battleship Graf
Spee *ran away from three very small British cruisers, and scuttled herself
in Montevideo harbour, though she had suffered little damage except a
shell in her bakery. The German captain said his crew could not fight
without a supply of fresh bread, and shot himself. To us kids, if the
Germans were all like the* Graf Spee, *there didn't seem a lot to beat.*[32]

The Battle of the River Plate was reassuring in the extreme.

Of course, the reason why the British had pulled it off was due to their
long history of naval mastery and the traditions of the island race. *British
Paramount News* summed it up in the headline, 'Nelson touch routs
pride of Nazi Navy'.[33] Nelson was the point of reference for all. Churchill
stated at the Guildhall: 'The warrior heroes of the past may look down, as
Nelson's monument looks down upon us now, without any feeling that
the island race has lost its daring or that the example which they set in
bygone centuries have faded.'[34] The cartoonist of the *Daily Express*
encapsulated it in a vision of Nelson coming down from his column to
buy a newspaper telling of the victory.[35] A few weeks later, celebrating
Philip Vian's cocky signal to the men on the *Altmark*, it carried a cartoon
of Drake, Collingwood, Frobisher, Nelson and 'The Navy is Here' spelt
out in flag signals with the headline 'Island race has not lost its daring'.[36]
The two incidents were therefore something to be celebrated and no
more than business as usual at one and the same time. Giving an added
emphasis to the swashbuckling atmosphere was the fact that Vian's men
had bordered the *Altmark* armed with pistols and cutlasses; it could have
been a story set in 1588, 1805 or 1940. From our perspective, it is easy to
sneer about these moments, the over celebration of minor victories in
a war that was about to become much nastier and more dangerous.
However, the successes, particularly that of the River Plate, did reveal a
difference between the Nazi naval forces and the Royal Navy: when it
came to the decisive moment the Nazis lacked nerve, whereas the British
resolve never faltered and the credit for this must be directed to Britain's
history and naval tradition. As Correlli Barnett has pointed out:

*It is hard not to think that Langsdorff's and Harwood's contrasting
fighting traditions were instinctively guided by their national maritime
heritages. Behind Harwood stood four centuries of victories in close
quarters attacks; behind Langsdorff a naval tradition barely forty years*

colourful, showing guns roaring, smoke billowing and sea boiling up into huge torrents as shells miss their target. To Britons brought up with the belief that the Royal Navy was invincible and that Britannia rules the waves, this was a jolly good confirmation of accepted wisdom. Released in the aftermath of the Suez Crisis, when Britain's inability to act without the support of the United States was proved to all, *The Battle of the River Plate* was a reassurance that all was well and provided comfort in history.

The Battle of the River Plate and the *Altmark* incident were easily woven into the fabric of British history and the annals of the Royal Navy. In turn, this set a precedent for seeing the war through a series of historical perspectives, which allowed it to become an explicable and predictable narrative. This was particularly useful for dealing with reverses, which could be explained away by historical parallels and given the reassuring conclusion that Britain always had come up smiling at the end. Years later, popular memory still sees incidents of the Second World War within this grand, patriotic narrative, meaning that the dash and glory of films such as *The Battle of the River Plate* may appear dreadfully old-fashioned to the sophisticated modern critic, but still appeal to the 'big fact'-driven history of popular culture.

Wish me luck as you wave me goodbye

Evacuation is one of the other significant memories of the bore war, although it is often blended into the memory of the blitz. Evacuation has been given a rose-tinted glow of nostalgia. It has become a cosy myth, but there can be little doubt that it was an ambiguous experience, as historians have found when questioning former evacuees. However the myth of the evacuee is still a potent symbol of the People's War, a poignant reminder of the heartache parents faced as they sent their children out of the cities rather than let them face the horror of aerial bombardment.

Everyone knows that evacuees wore shorts and caps if they were boys and short dresses if they were girls. We can all see them in our mind's eye, large luggage labels tied to their coats giving number, name, address and school, gasmasks in a little box bouncing on their hip as they march out of the school playground to the waiting buses and trains. And these children sang as they went, 'wish me luck as you wave me goodbye', which brings a tear to the eye when heard now: all that innocence and as the Admiralty allowed the production crew to join the Royal Navy on manoeuvres in the Mediterranean. Three cruisers were loaned, HMS *Sheffield* (playing HMS *Exeter*), HMS *Jamaica* (playing HMS *Ajax*) and the Indian ship Delhi (formerly HMNZS *Achilles*), which was brought back to play her former self. Thanks to some high-level negotiations, USS *Salem* was also deployed in the role of the pocket battleship *Graf Spee*.[39] Shot in Technicolor VistaVision, the effect on audiences was dramatic. When the rough cut was shown to a select audience of senior naval staff officers, Powell noted that 'the whole three rows of naval dignitaries pressed hard back in their chairs for, really, the great ships seemed about to sail out into the theatre. It was colossal. They were like children at a tea party . . .'[40] The public was equally impressed, turning it into the biggest box-office hit of 1957, although the press reaction was mixed.

The Battle of the River Plate confirmed public belief in the unflap-pability of the British and the professionalism and courage of the Royal Navy. Opening with shots of the wide expanse of the sea, a narrator's voice announces: 'This is a story of sea power'. The narration went on to say that *Blitzkrieg* tactics might have changed the face of land warfare, but at sea the problems were the same; it was a question of whether Britain could be starved into defeat. Following the *Graf Spee*'s sinking of merchant ships, the early scenes have a documentary-like quality as dates and places are captioned on screen: reconstruction elided with the historical record.

The Royal Navy is presented as the embodiment of Nelson's character, imbued with the spirit of 'engage the enemy more closely', confirmed by Anthony Quayle's forceful characterisation of Admiral Harwood: 'My intention is to attack on sight.' As the British ships go into action, Royal Marine buglers sound action stations and battle ensigns are hoisted, cre-ating an impression of glory, dash and excitement. But it is underpinned by good, old-fashioned British phlegm. The Captain of HMS *Ajax* calmly says 'Good Lord, so there is' when told that shrapnel has drilled a hole through his leg. HMS *Exeter* takes fearful punishment from the heavy shells of the enemy, but Captain Bell contemplates ramming the *Graf Spee* as a last resort. Ordered to quit the battle, Harwood signals *Exeter*, 'Can you reach Falklands?', to which Bell replies with wonderful sang-froid, 'Can reach Plymouth if ordered'. The sea battle is exciting and colourful, showing guns roaring, smoke billowing and sea boiling up into huge torrents as shells miss their target. To Britons brought up with the belief that the Royal Navy was invincible and that Britannia rules the waves, this was a jolly good confirmation of accepted wisdom. Released in the aftermath of the Suez Crisis, when Britain's inability to act without the support of the United States was proved to all, *The Battle of the River Plate* was a reassurance that all was well and provided comfort in history.

The Battle of the River Plate and the *Altmark* incident were easily woven into the fabric of British history and the annals of the Royal Navy. In turn, this set a precedent for seeing the war through a series of historical perspectives, which allowed it to become an explicable and predictable narrative. This was particularly useful for dealing with reverses, which could be explained away by historical parallels and given the reassuring conclusion that Britain always had come up smiling at the end. Years later, popular memory still sees incidents of the Second World War within this grand, patriotic narrative, meaning that the dash and glory of films such as *The Battle of the River Plate* may appear dreadfully old-fashioned to the sophisticated modern critic, but still appeal to the 'big fact'-driven history of popular culture.

Wish me luck as you wave me goodbye

Evacuation is one of the other significant memories of the bore war, although it is often blended into the memory of the blitz. Evacuation has been given a rose-tinted glow of nostalgia. It has become a cosy myth, but there can be little doubt that it was an ambiguous experience, as historians have found when questioning former evacuees. However the myth of the evacuee is still a potent symbol of the People's War, a poignant reminder of the heartache parents faced as they sent their children out of the cities rather than let them face the horror of aerial bombardment.

Everyone knows that evacuees wore shorts and caps if they were boys and short dresses if they were girls. We can all see them in our mind's eye, large luggage labels tied to their coats giving number, name, address and school, gasmasks in a little box bouncing on their hip as they march out of the school playground to the waiting buses and trains. And these children sang as they went, 'wish me luck as you wave me goodbye', which brings a tear to the eye when heard now: all that innocence and

Perhaps Hitler was already beaten. The German pocket-battleship Graf
Spee *ran away from three very small British cruisers, and scuttled herself
in Montevideo harbour, though she had suffered little damage except a
shell in her bakery. The German captain said his crew could not fight
without a supply of fresh bread, and shot himself. To us kids, if the
Germans were all like the* Graf Spee, *there didn't seem a lot to beat.*[32]

The Battle of the River Plate was reassuring in the extreme.

Of course, the reason why the British had pulled it off was due to their
long history of naval mastery and the traditions of the island race. *British
Paramount News* summed it up in the headline, 'Nelson touch routs
pride of Nazi Navy'.[33] Nelson was the point of reference for all. Churchill
stated at the Guildhall: 'The warrior heroes of the past may look down, as
Nelson's monument looks down upon us now, without any feeling that
the island race has lost its daring or that the example which they set in
bygone centuries have faded.'[34] The cartoonist of the *Daily Express*
encapsulated it in a vision of Nelson coming down from his column to
buy a newspaper telling of the victory.[35] A few weeks later, celebrating
Philip Vian's cocky signal to the men on the *Altmark*, it carried a cartoon
of Drake, Collingwood, Frobisher, Nelson and 'The Navy is Here' spelt
out in flag signals with the headline 'Island race has not lost its daring'.[36]
The two incidents were therefore something to be celebrated and no
more than business as usual at one and the same time. Giving an added
emphasis to the swashbuckling atmosphere was the fact that Vian's men
had bordered the *Altmark* armed with pistols and cutlasses; it could have
been a story set in 1588, 1805 or 1940. From our perspective, it is easy to
sneer about these moments, the over celebration of minor victories in
a war that was about to become much nastier and more dangerous.
However, the successes, particularly that of the River Plate, did reveal a
difference between the Nazi naval forces and the Royal Navy: when it
came to the decisive moment the Nazis lacked nerve, whereas the British
resolve never faltered and the credit for this must be directed to Britain's
history and naval tradition. As Correlli Barnett has pointed out:

*It is hard not to think that Langsdorff's and Harwood's contrasting
fighting traditions were instinctively guided by their national maritime
heritages. Behind Harwood stood four centuries of victories in close
quarters attacks; behind Langsdorff a naval tradition barely forty years*

old, and, with brief and rare exceptions, one of raiding and evading and ultimately of defeat.[37]

Historical parallels also ensured that the British saw the war as a continuation of the small island's ongoing national struggle against lesser-spirited, often jealous, often far bigger nations. Such parallels came easily to the British people soaked as they were in their traditions and history.

The Battle of the River Plate became etched into the popular consciousness, a process that deepened with the release of the film, *For Freedom*. In the spring of 1940, Gainsborough Studios and Gaumont British asked the Admiralty for help in the making of a film celebrating the work of the Royal Navy. Permission was gained to interview survivors and eyewitnesses of both the River Plate and *Altmark* actions. Many of these men were then used to re-enact their roles in dramatic reconstructions of the events. With the aid of these scenes, models and much newsreel footage, retired Vice-Admiral J.E.T. Harper provided expert commentary. He told the audience, 'you are watching actual men whose deeds that day wrote this splendid new page in Britain's naval history'.[38] In fact, the first part of the film is a rather plodding semi-documentary about how and why Britain fell into war, drawing contrasts between the British and Nazi way of life, only in the final thirty minutes does it become a tribute to the Navy.

However, *For Freedom* was well received when it was released in April 1940. The public seemed to appreciate the chance to see the heroes in the flesh. In effect, what the film had done was reassure the British people that the Navy was more than the equal of its enemies and set its achievements within the context of a long and proud history.

Years later, the Battle of the River Plate was to be reworked once again, this time in glorious Technicolor. Reliving wartime glories became box-office big business for the British in the 1950s. One of the grandest of these re-enactments was Powell and Pressburger's 1957 epic, *The Battle of the River Plate*. For Michael Powell it was a labour of love, having always wanted to make a film about the Navy. Luckily for Powell, his production manager, John Brabourne, was son-in-law to the publicity conscious First Sea Lord, Lord Mountbatten, which meant that Admiralty co-operation was guaranteed. Powell and Pressburger therefore had the opportunity to make a film on a large scale; no model work was required bravado trying to keep fears at bay. It is not hard to find the evidence; that is how it was reported in the newsreels, the *Daily Express* and the *Daily Mirror*: 'They packed up their troubles in their old kit bags and smiled, smiled, smiled.'[41] Evacuation is intimately linked in our memories with children. We forget that many others were moved too, including the old, crippled and infirm, expectant mothers and 20–25,000 civil servants who were decanted from offices into spas and seaside resorts.[42] Somewhere between 3,500,000 and 3,750,000 people moved to areas considered safe from bombing in the months from June to September 1939. Yet, in contrast to popular memory, of those only 827,000 were schoolchildren.[43] Indeed, it is compounded by secondary literature. Ben Wicks' otherwise excellent book on child evacuees, *No Time to Wave Goodbye* (1988), states on the jacket, 'True Stories of Britain's 3,500,000 Evacuees'.[44] The implication is that all were children.

In the joint myth and memory, these children travelled down to the countryside where they experienced a series of jolly culture shocks. Inner-city children found that milk came from cows, bacon from pigs and fruit grew on trees and did not appear miraculously on grocers' displays. The evidence can be discovered easily enough. The *Daily Express* reported 'Florence, of EC1, sees first village', and Hilde Marchant added: 'No sandbags, no air raid shelters – just the warmth and peace of an English country village. Their wit and Cockney imaginations will flourish in this gentle setting.'[45] The BBC news on 29 October 1939 included the letter of a little boy who had recently seen his first cow:

> The cow is a mamal [sic]. It has six sides, right, left, an upper and below. At the back is a tail, on which hangs a brush. With this it sends the flies away so they do not fall into the milk. The head is for the purposes of growing horns and so that the mouth can be somewhere. The horns are to butt with, and the mouth is to moo with. Under the cow hangs the milk. It is arranged for milking. When people milk, the milk comes and there is never an end to the supply. How the cow does it I have not realized but it makes more and more. The cow has a fine sense of smell: one can smell it far away. This is the reason for the fresh air in the country.
>
> The man cow is called an ox. It is not a mamal [sic]. The cow does not eat much but what it eats, it eats twice so that it gets enough. When it

is hungry it moos and when it says nothing it is because all its inside is full up with grass.[46]

We also know it as a time in which the classes came together, poor city children were billeted on yeoman farmers and the genteel middle classes. *British Movietone News* showed children at the stately home of Sir William and Lady Jowitt, and Oliver Lyttleton, later Lord Chandos, had his country home filled with evacuees. One girl wrote home to her parents, 'We have very nice food such as venison, pheasant, hare and other luxury which we cannot afford at home.'[47] Sheila Price looked back on the time she spent at Stoke Poges in the fine home of a retired colonel with great affection. She was driven to school, given piano and typing lessons, servants looked after her and she was allowed to play mini golf in the garden. In consequence, returning home was a disappointment. Equally ambiguous was Joan Porter's experience: 'I live with the results of three years of middle-class input, which helped to estrange me from my family but opened my horizons and heightened my expectations.'[48] Such evidence reveals the upper class doing their bit for the urban poor.

In contrast to the myth detailed above, reality was somewhat different. Social tensions and class antagonisms rose with the experience of evacuation. However, our common vision of evacuation has not come about due to the suppression of evidence. On the contrary, Britain went through an open spat over the issue during the winter of 1939–40, which can be found just as easily as the happy stories. Culture clashes and shocks were legion during the autumn of 1939, as Britain revealed its highly localised nature. Few country folk were used to the cosmopolitanism of Britain's inner cities, which resulted in friction over religion in particular. Liverpool Catholics, often of Irish descent, were sent to regions of strict nonconformity in Wales. Jews were often treated with great suspicion, and occasionally outright hostility. Grace Saragoussi remembers being told by her foster mother that the crucifixion was the fault of the Jews.[49] Angus Calder has noted, 'even well-behaved Jews were not acceptable to many "bridge-playing" persons in reception areas.'[50]

An even greater source of tension was the behaviour and condition of many of the evacuees. Years of living in degrading poverty and slum conditions had produced a people of the shadows. Local branches of the

Women's Institute and the Women's Voluntary Service compiled reports in which shock, disgust and pity combine:

> In practically every batch of children there were some who suffered from head lice, skin diseases and bed-wetting . . . some children [from Manchester] had never slept in beds. . . . One boy [from Salford] had never had a bath before; his ribs looked as black as if black-leaded. . . . The state of the children [from Liverpool] was such that the school had to be fumigated after reception; we have never seen so many verminous children – it appeared they were unbathed for months; the majority had scabies in their hair and septic sores all over their bodies. . . . It is hard to exaggerate the state of the [Bethnal Green] children's heads when they came; their habits were disgusting. . . . The habits of most of the [Fulham and Hammersmith] children were unspeakable and have caused great distress and expense to those who gave them billets . . . the children relieve themselves any time and anywhere.[51]

The filthy state of the children was compounded by the fact that they had been evacuated prior to the reopening of schools after the summer holiday and so had not received their usual delousing and medical inspection.

Toilet habits caused most shock and amazement to those caring for evacuees. Oliver Lyttleton wrote: 'I had little dreamt that English children could be so completely ignorant of the simplest rules of hygiene, and that they would regard the floors and carpets as suitable places upon which to relieve themselves.'[52] It was reported that one Glasgow mother, chastising her child for relieving itself in the middle of the carpet, said, 'you dirty thing, messing up the lady's carpet. Go and do it in the corner.'[53] A foster family was horrified by the sight of the children urinating against the wallpaper and that the mother left her baby in a cot soaked through with urine.[54] Many foster families aimed their ire not at the children, but at the sluttish mothers who accompanied them. A Women's Institute report declared its members 'found it hard to be sympathetic to women who could neither cook, sew, nor conform to the ordinary standards of human decency. And whose idea of enjoyment was to visit the public house or cinema.'[55] The historian, R.C.K. Ensor, complained to the *Spectator* that the countryside was now full of 'the lowest grade of slum women – slatternly, malodorous tatterdemalions'. Another historian, W.L. Burn, opined that most slum mothers saw evacuation as 'a cheap holiday of infinite duration', underlining Ensor's views.[56] A letter from a Colwyn Bay resident to *Picture Post* revealed disgust at the toilet habits of the evacuees from Liverpool and their penchant for beer. But the main focus of her attack was the dreadful behaviour of the mothers. 'The residents were happy to think that they could help by taking children, but they did not bargain for what they got. Poverty is no crime, but there is no excuse for filth. The kiddies' parents are too lazy to teach them to be clean.'[57]

This debate was certainly not a 'hush-hush' affair. Voices were heard loud and long on the subject of evacuation, and included a few bad-tempered parliamentary exchanges. Government MPs attacked the filthy habits of the evacuees and defended their rural constituents; Labour MPs denounced the slurs on the respectable working class and asked why men like the Duke of Argyll had only taken a few evacuees when he had a large house with many unused bedrooms.[58] The situation was complex, for in reality it was not a simple division between middle- and upper-class rural and suburban folk horrified by the inner-city slum class. Much debate raged on the point that in the reception areas the vast majority of foster families came from the ranks of the poor, thus placing an even greater strain on already stretched family incomes. A Women's Voluntary Service report confirmed, 'We find over and over again that it is really the poorer people who are willing to take evacuees and that the sort of bridge-playing people who live at such places as Chorley Wood are terribly difficult about it all.'[59] However, the flip side can be seen in the amazing level of work and dedication shown by the Women's Institutes and Women's Voluntary Service. These organisations were run by mainly middle-class women who had the time and energy to spare for such work.[60] Without the commitment of these women many more evacuees would have suffered from the undoubted lack of organisation and direction inherent in the official government scheme.

As the war continued the experience of evacuation began to be seen as a moment in which rich and poor were forced to look at each other and consider the kind of country they wanted to live in. In turn, this helped the cosy myth of evacuation to grow, for it could be seen ultimately as a beneficial experience and therefore something to be remembered fondly. As will be seen again and again in this book, the term 'myth' does not imply an untruth, merely a way of reading a set of events. H.G. Wells, that astute critic of the British social system, rejoiced in culture clashes providing education and improvement, and was an early and unwitting builder of the evacuation myth. 'Parasites and skin diseases, vicious habits and insanitary practices', he wrote, 'have been spread, as if in a passion of equalitarian propaganda, from the slums of such centres as Glasgow, London and Liverpool, throughout the length and breadth of the land.'[61] Richard Titmuss, the widely respected left-wing sociologist, added to the evacuation myth at the end of the war. He had little motivation to conceal nasty truths, but in his home front histories of the Second World War he confirmed a positive reading of evacuation by stressing its educational effects, forcing the two Britains to come to terms with and win the war together.[62]

This distinct vision of evacuation having been fixed, it has remained remarkably resilient. In 1969, Angus Calder reminded the British people of their public arguments on the subject in his influential work, *The People's War*, but on the whole he stuck with the idea that it had provided children with a good, if occasionally riotously unchecked, time.[63] His slightly revisionist view was felt in *The World at War* series, in which the problems of evacuation were aired. Oliver Lyttleton, by that time Lord Chandos, recalled his shock at the behaviour of evacuees. Lucy Faithfull, a children's care organiser, spoke of the poor clothing and condition of many slum children, and Bernard Kopps, the Jewish writer, told of leaving Stepney for Denham and how the billeting system made him feel like an item up for auction. But he also remembered the wonder and glory of novelties such as toothbrushes, sheets and hot water.

Another Jewish writer, Jack Rosenthal, provided an equally important interpretation of evacuation in the 1970s. *The Evacuees*, part of the BBC's highly successful 'Play for Today' series, was first televised in 1975. Semi-autobiographical, the play told the story of two Jewish brothers evacuated to a middle-class Anglican couple imbued with that slight anti-semitism once so prevalent in British society. Made to eat pork sausages and generally disoriented by the whole experience, the two evacuees represent the wartime story without its positive gilding. However, Rosenthal's popular play, with its bitter-sweet comedy, contained a nostalgic afterglow and so was not a devastating critique of the myth. If anything, it only served to reinforce it.[64]

In the 1980s, Thatcherism caused much debate on the nature of national identity, a strand of which was the examination of Britain's wartime role. Channel 4 went back to the original wartime records and in 1986 broadcast a series based on the Mass-Observation archive. The result, *A People's War*, was very much in the style of Angus Calder. The series revealed the tensions of wartime Britain and included some disturbing stories about the treatment of evacuees. Two years later came Ben Wicks' book, *No Time To Wave Goodbye* (1988). Wicks set out to collect and collate the testimonies of former evacuees. By a variety of means, including placing advertisements in newspapers, Wicks received thousands of letters from the now adult children of 1939. Aimed squarely at the popular market, Wicks' book is a wonderful read, revealing the deep impact evacuation had on those who went through it, whether as evacuee or as the foster carer. However, it is also a deeply traumatic read. Evacuees' stories of neglect and ill treatment fill page after page, the most moving being those who tell of subjugation to physical, sometimes sexual, and emotional abuse at the hands of people entrusted to look after them. Reading the book, one is left with the impression that in 1939 the vast majority of adults in British rural or suburban areas were petty-minded, wantonly cruel, hypocritical and mean-spirited. And yet, despite this generally gloomy outlook, the rosy myth of the newsreels of 1939 seeps through, as can be seen in Michael Caine's introduction. The former evacuee and celebrated actor constructed his memory according to the neat sections of a good film script:

> [Evacuation] . . . was to have a profound effect in later life on the children who were up-rooted from their homes and, with their Mickey Mouse gas-masks, despatched to live with strangers in what amounted to a 'foreign land'.
>
> I know how they felt because I was one of them, a six-year-old cockney more familiar with the smells and sounds of Billingsgate fish market than with manure and bird-song. Certainly I came in for my fair share of rough treatment from the family who first took me in, but I went on to enjoy some halcyon days over the next six years growing up on a 200-acre farm in Norfolk, which changed me from a young 'city slicker' into the country-lover I am to this day . . .[65]

It provides a perfect rendition of the myth: a city kid with no knowledge of the country, some sticky moments, but then a glorious spiritual education which transformed him into what the myths of national identity tell us every true Brit should be – a person of the soil. Wicks' own foreword provides more of the same:

> For me, evacuation from the squalor of soot-covered slums provided a view of the outside world. I saw greener pastures and was never again happy with my city environment . . .
>
> The country owes to all those who took part a debt of gratitude that can never be repaid. The face of Britain was changed for ever. The eyes of many working-class children were opened to the advantages of the few. City and country children found themselves sharing beds. The rules of the class system in Britain began to bend, heralding the introduction of changes desperately needed in a post-war Britain.
>
> An army of children, clutching tiny bags, came out of the dark and pricked a nation's conscience.
>
> The children would never be the same again. Neither would the nation.[66]

Confusingly and somewhat ironically, a book which seemingly had so much potential to damage the myth was therefore framed by the conventions of it. Wicks and Caine preface the book with the myth, establishing its contours in the mind of the reader. The evacuation myth is so powerful that it overrides the very material designed to debunk it.

Michelle Magorian has provided the most recent and influential popular reworking of the myth in her children's novel, *Goodnight Mister Tom*, which won her awards from *The Guardian* and the International Reading Association. A quick search on the internet will reveal how many schools use this as a set text, and the favourable reviews it gets from both adult and child readers. In 1998 Carlton Television adapted it on the small screen (there is also a stage musical version), starring John Thaw as the miserable old man who gradually comes to love the sad, abused, East End evacuee boy. Together they find a renewed energy and joy in life; evacuation enriches and ennobles them both. *Goodnight Mister Tom* ensures the continuation of the myth by teaching it to generations far removed from the original experience.[67]

The bore war, reflected in Mr Chamberlain's face, is remembered only in tiny fragments. It has little of the glamour of the Battle of Britain or the poignancy of the blitz. A time of confusion and ill-advised confidence in some, its few notable moments are nevertheless an important part of the myth of the Second World War. The declaration of war, evacuation and the Battle of the River Plate have each been mythologised in a particular way. Individually they are links in the 'big fact' chain of the war. These links remain impervious to the strains placed on them by the 'sensationalist revisionists', because the myths are not lies but interpretations of the truth, and so the big facts cannot be undermined.

Notes

1 Quoted in Laurence Thompson, *1940: Year of Legend, Year of History* (London 1966), p. 12.

2 Joan Wyndham, *Love Lessons: A Wartime Diary* (London 1986), p. 11.

3 *The Times* 17 February 1972.

4 *The Times* reported in January 1940 that Chamberlain had received the gift of a walking stick in the form of a rolled-up umbrella carved with a pocket-knife by an 86-year-old shepherd: a suitably bizarre fact in the almost farcical early period of the war. Quoted in Thompson, *1940*, p. 14.

5 Angus Calder, *The People's War* (London 1997; orig. 1969), p. 23.

6 A.J.P. Taylor seemed to confirm this view of Chamberlain in his highly controversial *English History 1914–1945* (Oxford 1965) in which he became symbolic of what Taylor perceived to be the muddled, contradictory and mean-spirited British foreign policy of the 1920s and 1930s.

7 Spike Milligan, *Adolf Hitler: My Part in His Downfall* (Harmondsworth 1987; orig. 1971), p. 13.

8 Robert Westall, *Children of the Blitz: Memories of Wartime Childhood* (London 1985), p. 31.

9 Ian McLaine, *Ministry of Morale: Home Front Morale and the Ministry of Information in World War II* (London 1979), pp. 36–44.

10 Thompson, *1940*, p. 13.

11 Calder, *People*, pp. 63–4.

12 For more details of Formby's film career see Jeffrey Richards, *The Age of the Dream Palace: Cinema and Society in Britain 1930–1939* (London 1984), pp. 191–206.

13 See ibid., pp. 169–90.

14 *British Movietone News* 23 November 1939.

15 *Daily Mirror* 16 November 1939.

16 *British Movietone News* 25 March 1940.

17 Figures quoted in Anthony Aldgate and Jeffrey Richards, *Britain Can Take It: The British Cinema in the Second World War* (Oxford 1986), pp. 79–80. For a discussion of Mass-Observation, see Angus Calder and Dorothy Sheridan, *Speak for Yourself: A Mass-Observation Anthology, 1937–1949* (London 1984).

18 Quoted in Calder, *People*, p. 61. For a full discussion of *Let George Do It* see Aldgate and Richards, *Britain Can Take It*, pp. 76–95. Many years later, Adolf Hitler and George Formby were mixed in a wonderfully bizarre way by Spike Milligan: a sketch in his 1970s comedy series, *Q9*, centred on Adolf Hitler, in full uniform, singing 'Chinese Laundry Blues' complete with ukulele. Formby thus continues to be a hero to many Britons precisely because he is such an unlikely example and crops up regularly in modern popular culture. In *Paul Calf's Video Diary*, Steve Coogan's notoriously ignorant character attends a New Year's Eve fancy dress party in which at least two of his friends have planned to go as George Formby.

19 See Calder, *People*, p. 61. I am also grateful to my colleague, Gill Sinclair, for providing me with access to her research on Chamberlain's personal standing in 1939–40.

20 Both quoted in Calder, *People*, p. 76.

21 For a full discussion of the fall of Chamberlain, see Thompson, *1940*, pp. 44–94 and Paul Addison, *The Road to 1945* (London 1994; orig. 1975), pp. 53–74.

22 For a good example of revisionist interpretations of Chamberlain, see John Charmley, *Churchill, the End of Glory: A Political Biography* (London 1993).

23 *Daily Express* 20 December 1939.

24 *British Paramount News* 25 December 1939.

25 Ibid., 22 February 1940.

26 *The Times, Daily Express, Daily Mirror* 24 February 1940.

27 *The Times* 24 February 1940.

28 *Picture Post* special issue March 1940.

29 *Daily Express* 18 December 1940.

30 *British Movietone News* 1 January 1940.

31 *Daily Mirror* 24 February 1940.

32 Westall, *Children of the Blitz*, p. 39.

33 *British Paramount News* 18 December 1939.

34 *The Times* 24 February 1940.

35 *Daily Express* 15 December 1940.

36 *Daily Express* 24 February 1940.

37 Correlli Barnett, *Engage the Enemy More Closely: The Royal Navy in the Second World War* (Harmondsworth 2000; orig. 1991), p. 87.

38 Quoted in S.P. MacKenzie, *British War Films 1939–1945* (London 2001), p. 65.

39 Ibid., pp. 145–6.

40 Ibid., p. 146.

41 *Daily Mirror* 1, 2 September 1939; *Daily Express* 1, 3 September 1939. For a good example from the newsreels, see *British Movietone News* 4 September 1939.

42 Calder, *People*, pp. 35–8.

43 Ibid.

44 Ben Wicks, *No Time to Wave Goodbye* (London 1988).

45 *Daily Express* 2 September 1939.

46 Quoted in Westall, *Children of the Blitz*, p. 48.

47 *British Movietone News* 14 September 1939; Calder, *People*, pp. 41, 46.

48 Wicks, *Wave Goodbye*, pp. 79, 212.

49 Ibid., p. 94.

50 Angus Calder, *The Myth of the Blitz* (London 1991), p. 62.

51 Quoted in Peter Lewis, *A People's War* (London 1986), pp. 12–13.

52 Calder, *People*, p. 41.

53 Ibid., p. 43.

54 Wicks, *Wave Goodbye*, p. 90.

55 Lewis, *People's War*, p. 14.

56 Ensor and Burn are quoted in T.L. Crosby, *The Impact of Civilian Evacuation in the Second World War* (London 1986), pp. 33–5.

57 *Picture Post* 13 September 1939.

58 See Calder, *People*, p. 42 and Wicks, *Wave Goodbye*, p. 98.

59 Calder, *Myth*, p. 62.

60 See Calder, *People*, pp. 193–5.

61 H.G. Wells, *The New World Order* (London 1940), p. 72.

62 For example, see R.M. Titmuss, *Problems of Social Policy* (London 1950).

63 Calder, *People*, p. 46.

64 See *Radio Times* 1 March 1975.

65 Wicks, *Wave Goodbye*, Introduction.

66 Ibid., p. xi.

67 Carlton Television has a website dedicated to *Goodnight Mister Tom*, see www.carltontv.co.uk/data/mistertom.

CHAPTER 2

· · · · · · · · · · · · · · · ·

A colossal military disaster: Dunkirk and the fall of France, May–June 1940

This chapter is about the myths that have arisen from the Dunkirk evacuation and the fall of France. Few people can argue with the fact that Dunkirk has become a magical word to the British. In 1940 the evacuation of the British army from the shores of Dunkirk proved to be a defining moment for the British people. It was the confirmation of exist- ing interpretations of British national character. The British people came to believe that they were facing the supreme test of their identity and traditions. This atmosphere encouraged people to look back for historical parallels and use them as guides for the present. Most believed that his- tory had proved the British to be a people blessed with unique qualities. Moreover, history had also proved that the British were destined to struggle against dreadful foes jealous of their special position in the world.

The myth of Dunkirk and the 'Dunkirk spirit' have become vital to our self-perceptions, for they underline and confirm our sense of apartness, of otherness, of self-reliance and insularity, of coolness under tremendous pressure, of surviving against the odds. These concepts of separation and of unique qualities were not invented in 1940; rather, it was their next incarnation in a long-standing national saga. A distinctive, contemporary experience was then grafted into an established national myth. This sense of being alone saw its ultimate distillation in the Battle of Britain, when the fewest of the few defeated an enemy that appeared to have uncontested superiority in every department. Surviving the Nazi onslaught ensured that its stain would be removed from the world and that the British way of life would continue. Hitler and the German people were shown that they were not going to have it all their own way. As an extremely popular television show has it, 'Who do you think you are kidding, Mr Hitler, if you think old England's done?' But the fame of Dunkirk has spread far beyond Britain. In March 2000 the *Daily Telegraph* covered South Africa's response to flood victims in Mozambique. A volunteer at a parcel collection point described the atmosphere in South Africa as 'a bit like the spirit of Dunkirk in the last war', as he recounted the offers of help and flow of donations. It seems amazing that such a term could be applied to a situation so far removed from Britain in 1940, but it is a tribute to the potency of the image.[1]

Fulfilling historical destinies

Dunkirk and the Battle of Britain continue to inspire great pride and emotion in the British people. They form two parts in the triptych of the British Second World War, the third being another event of 1940, the blitz. Powerful touchstones of national identity are encapsulated in the Dunkirk evacuation and Battle of Britain. Whatever else has happened to the nation since the Second World War, these glories cannot be blotted out. They are in the national record book; we all know it, and think foul scorn of any foreign or domestic commentator who dares to suggest otherwise. To this day we find it hard to escape the compelling attraction of the time when Britain stood alone and defiant. In November 1999, John Peel, writing in the *Radio Times* on the BBC1 documentary series poignantly titled *Finest Hour*, noted:

> Our Finest Hour is, it is generally agreed, the retreat from Dunkirk, and there may be viewers who suggest that we've had enough of the great patriotic war now. But it is clear that on some level or other we still need the war, that grimy footage of mortars pounding enemy lines, and those interviews with survivors in brightly buttoned blazers telling us the horrors they experienced all those years ago.[2]

But why did the twin events of Dunkirk and the Battle of Britain take such a hold on the national imagination? On the simple level, both moments were ones of genuine national emergency. But both crises also appealed, then and now, to a deeply-held sense of history, destiny and culture. Jeremy Paxman has summed up the three prongs of the Dunkirk legend and why it continues to attract:

> Firstly, it speaks to their sense of separateness: it was the moment when
> Britain was, finally, alone against the Nazis. . . . Secondly, it is a story
> of the success of the Few against the odds. Thirdly, it demonstrates to
> the English what they have known for centuries, that the European
> continent is a place of nothing but trouble and that their greatest security
> is behind the thousands of miles of irregular coastline around their
> island home.[3]

Standing alone, fighting weird, wonderful and incomprehensible foreigners of all sorts against great odds is something that strikes a chord in the British. Our culture is steeped in it. Tim Brooke-Taylor, in his brilliantly funny, but highly researched, investigation of national character, *Rule Britannia*, noted much the same thing:

> Pluck any name from the roll call of great British heroes and the chances
> are that he'll have made his name in some valiant, last-ditch stand
> or futile escapade, which concentrated the public imagination and
> distracted it from the general fiasco in which he was one small, heroic
> part. That's not to say that there aren't heroes that do win, but they've
> got to start as underdogs to score the full heroic tally.[4]

Pulling a gallant bunch of plucky soldiers off the beaches of Dunkirk before the might of the German army, putting a small force of jolly good chaps between invasion and the arrogance of the German air force are images which the British instinctively respond to with pride and enthusiasm. The reality of the matter is neither here nor there. That the myth was believed, and is still believed, is the important point. And, despite the huge significance of events in 1940, it was no more than the British people expected. This was a people whose culture was already steeped in images of unlikely escapades, as Brooke-Taylor implies, and so another disaster combined with a fight against the odds was merely part of the British game of life. The myth of Dunkirk was made by using the example of a particular reading of British history to inform reactions to another national crisis.

Since the nineteenth century and the rise of Britain as a great military, economic and political power, its interpretation of itself had taken on a peculiar form, or rather it modified still further an interpretation of itself which had been forming for centuries. The basic thrust of the iconography of nationality was that Britain had evolved by seeing off all sorts of threatening foreigners and had heroically withstood moments of intense peril. Combined with this was a celebration of the fact that it had been achieved by a very small island indeed. With the rise of state education in the 1870s and a mass literate working class, such concepts of nationhood spread to all. The stories of the popular heroes of empire, lionised in music halls, in books, cheap prints and on tea caddies nearly all conformed to this pattern. General Gordon is an excellent example. The realities behind Gordon's last stand in Khartoum may well be damning, but that was not the side reproduced in *Boys' Own Paper* or the sketches in the *Illustrated London News*. Rather, it was of a lone British officer taking on a seething mob of savages. Similarly, events in Zululand in 1879 were easily presentable as glorious epics. A few red-coated infantrymen alone at the remote mission station of Rorke's Drift withstood the onslaught of over 4,000 Zulu warriors. In the same year British troops fought a famous last stand against terrific odds in Afghanistan. Such events filled books like W.H. Fitchett's *Deeds that Won the Empire*, G.H. Henty's stories and the *Boys' Own Paper*.[5]

The repetition of these images created a model of behaviour and expectation in the British people which survived long into the twentieth century. Indeed, they were buttressed still further by examples of the few gambling against the odds. In 1911 Captain Scott's tiny band of fellow adventurers died in the howling wastes of Antarctica, but their deaths were presented as heroic, self-sacrificing and patriotic. Captain Oates became a hero of empire by deliberately reducing the few still more; in order to give the others a chance he staggered from the tent to die in the blizzard. Scott's last diary entry is stirring prose. In it can be detected the tiniest bat's squeaks of Churchill's rhetoric of 1940 and the language of fighter pilots' diaries, letters and memoirs:

We are weak, writing this is difficult, but for my own sake I do not regret this journey, which has shown that Englishmen can endure hardships, help one another, and meet death with as great a fortitude as ever in the past. We took risks, we knew we took them; things have come out against us, and therefore we have no cause for complaint, but bow to the will of Providence, determined to do our best to the last. . . . Had we lived, I should have had a tale to tell of the hardihood, endurance and courage of my companions which would have stirred the heart of every Englishman. These rough notes and our dead bodies must tell the tale . . .[6]

Risks, gambling, odds, not flinching from the tough options. Often sneered at now and debunked, but still believed in and encapsulated by, the term 'Dunkirk spirit'.

It might be thought that the coming of mass, industrialised warfare and killing between 1914 and 1918 sounded the passing bell on ideas of glorious deaths, and in turn destroyed the cosy image of the beleaguered people of the little island. After all, this was a war of enormous armies locked in a stalemated conflict. Where could the traditional glories be found? In fact, the familiar pool of images was fished and found to be equally applicable. When war broke out, the British had only a tiny professional army, a mere six divisions strong. In late August 1914 the British Expeditionary Force found itself facing a vastly superior German army just outside the Belgian town of Mons. This tiny force was then allegedly referred to as a 'contemptible little army' by the Kaiser. The fact that this was a mistranslation doesn't actually matter for this argument, what was reported and what people thought does. For the soldiers of the BEF it became an accolade, and they have gone down in history as the 'old contemptibles'. It hardly needs stating that the battles of the BEF were turned into modern legends almost as soon as they were fought: at Mons the British riflemen, assisted either by the ghosts of their ancestors who had fought at Agincourt or an angel, gave the over-confident Germans a bloody nose and retreated in good order.[7] On St George's Day 1917, British marines took part in a daring raid on the German-controlled port of Zeebrugge, thus the few took the struggle to the many, as had earlier happened at Gallipoli in 1915, where an Australian and New Zealand version of the few was forged in the heat of battle.[8] When the Germans achieved a great breakthrough on the Western Front in 1918, traditional ideas of remaining steady despite the circumstances dominated. Field Marshal Sir Douglas Haig, Commander-in-Chief of the British army, fell back on familiar rhetoric, telling his wilting army:

> *Many of us are now tired. To those I would say that victory will belong to the side which holds out the longest. . . . There is no course open to us but to fight it out. Every position must be held to the last man: there must be no retirement. With our backs to the wall and believing in the justice of our cause each one must fight on to the end. The safety of our Homes and the Freedom of mankind alike depend upon the conduct of each one of us at this critical moment.*[9]

One might almost say that Haig was calling for a finest hour and exhorting all to brace themselves to their duties.

In this way it can be seen that Dunkirk and the Battle of Britain had happened long before they actually occurred. The British people had a psyche and mindset that knew triumph usually came after periods of desperate peril and when others had written them off. 1940 was not so much a novelty as an apogee, the final crowning moment in a whole history of close-run things. Guiding the British people towards this conclusion were the Ministry of Information and the army. Both colluded in a campaign of suppression and misinformation in order to ensure that this one simple explanation was put upon events.[10] Fiasco became a miracle of deliverance and, it was argued, the true qualities of the British people would arise out of fiasco. This was the most sensible way to present the disaster to the British people; it appealed to their sense of history and self-identity.

In 1940 the British knew that their 'finest hour' had come. Whether all of them felt up to it is not the point, whether all of them lived up to it is also by-the-by. Far more important was the recognition that a moment of drama and destiny was at hand. That it was only to be expected given their history was also common knowledge. The British press, of every political hue, recognised it as the latest chapter in a catalogue of similar dramas. For Edward Hulton, editor and proprietor of the illustrated magazine *Picture Post*, which had a circulation of 2 million a week by 1939, the position was nothing new, Britain could take it because Britain had taken it:

This island has stoutly repelled many dread invaders. Our small trading
vessels were no match, on paper, for the 'Invincible Armada'. John
Churchill, Duke of Marlborough, amazed the world when he humbled
the experienced army and the unconquered generals of the 'Sun King'.
A nation of shopkeepers in arms brought down the 'Grand Army' of
Bonaparte. 'The Contemptible little army' lived to rout the grey hordes of
William II. Some nations are separated by a sad gulf from a heroic past;
but we are not.[11]

Dunkirk left Britain alone and in desperate trouble. Only the script
bequeathed by history could provide comfort.

On 24 August 1940, as the Battle of Britain was moving up a gear and
the struggle for aerial supremacy became even more intense, *Country Life*
presented its readers with a special edition celebrating the values of
England. For *Country Life*, the moment was comparable with the threat of
the Spanish Armada in 1588 and Napoleon's preparations for invasion in
1805. In the summer of 1940 the British were drawing upon their racial
memory:

For what is clear in the end is that the spirit of the English at that
moment [1588], or in 1805 . . . is not different from that in the present:
there is a continuity of response to danger undismayed. The words and
actions are interchangeable: one of Nelson's messages, with its natural
eloquence, would serve to express the spirit of the Royal Navy today. . . .
That is the stuff of which the English spirit is made, no less than that
dream of happiness and content which lies at the heart of every
Englishman. Is it possible that such a spirit can be conquered?[12]

Country Life was of course the journal of the landed elite and for those who
aspired to it. Historical metaphors therefore came easily to it, reflecting
the association of *Country Life* with the traditional values and meanings
of the nation.

It was a sentiment it shared with a weekly part-work, *War Illustrated*.
War Illustrated was inspired by a similar publication of the Great War. As
with its predecessor, it was edited by Sir John Hammerton and sought to
provide a highly conformist digest in words and pictures of the week's
war news. On 7 June 1940, a few days after the last evacuation ships had
left Dunkirk, it too compared the situation to 1588.[13] But this sort of

imagery was not confined to the right-leaning establishment, for the same sentiments can be seen in the centre-left publication *Picture Post*, the journal that, along with the *Daily Mirror*, became the preferred choice of the army.[14] The clarion call of history rasped out of its pages too:

> So we watch the skies – part-timers most of us, doing several four-hour shifts each week. But even those of us whose ordinary days are passed in office or factory are easily known, as much by the wind-tan on their faces as by the little blue-and-silver badge in the buttonhole. It shows, to those who look closely, a coast watcher of Queen Elizabeth's time putting a torch to an Armada beacon. We, his descendants, watch for another Armada – borne on the air. And our signals are not by beacon fires, but along the thin copper strands of countless telephone lines. Instead of Drake's fireships, our sleek, swift Spitfires – a weapon ready as Britain's weapons of other days – to seek out the enemy, to harry him, and, in the fullness of time, to destroy him![15]

When comparisons with the Armada palled, it was easy to draw upon an equally potent set of images, the Napoleonic threat. In June 1940, the *Daily Express* compared the retreating British army in France with the situation in the peninsula campaign of 1802 when a British army fell back to the Spanish port of Corunna from where it was evacuated.[16] Sir John Moore's retreat to Corunna had, in its turn, inspired one of the most popular poems in the English language, and, according to George Orwell, Corunna, like Dunkirk, 'has more appeal than a brilliant victory'.[17] A *Daily Express* correspondent trying to ascertain the mood of the country at the end of May 1940 asked a Walthamstow greengrocer for his opinion. He was told that Britain had been in tight situations in 1812 and 1918, but had come through them both. In true *Dad's Army* form, the man then told of his former army service in the Sudan and the Great War before placing a sign in his window saying: 'Are We Downhearted? No.' The *Express* had identified the 'don't like it up 'em' spirit.[18]

Contrary to popular belief, the Great War had not become anathema by 1939. The modern memory of the unmitigated futility of that conflict had not yet descended, and the resilience of 1918 was regarded as something to be emulated. Linking the men of Haig's 1918 army to a seam of events in British history, all of which revealed gallantry against the odds, *The Times* noted:

Generation after generation, to the men of Agincourt and the men who broke the Armada, to Wellington's men and Haig's men and to all who served their spirit from behind the lines, that summons has come to the people of England. They have never failed to answer the challenge, nor will they fail now.[19]

The disastrous situation in France in the late spring of 1940 was, in fact, nothing more than the old, old story, and was therefore not worth getting that alarmed about. The Minister of Information, Duff Cooper, told the public exactly that in a broadcast on 22 May:

The news is grave. There is no pretending it is not. But there is no cause for serious alarm, still less for panic. . . . Meanwhile it is the old story – sudden advances, unexpected weight of the attack, initial gains far greater speed than expected – it is the story of August 1914, of March 1918, and let us hope that it will have the same ending.[20]

That it was serious was obvious, but no one should panic was the message of Duff Cooper. He was also appealing to the British sense of history. It had all happened before, 'backs to the wall' was situation normal and the outcome was always the same: Britain won through. As Angus Calder has noted, Dunkirk was (and is) the confirmation of what British people know about their nation and its history.[21]

Having been connected with a thread of British myth, legend and history, Dunkirk quickly took on the aura of an ancient event, almost as if it was impossible to distinguish it from events centuries earlier. This sensation was reflected in *Country Life*, which commented: 'During those days travellers in the south of England encountered, on quiet railway stations among the flowery countryside, companies and battalions of bronzed, tired, but universally cheerful and disciplined lads.'[22] The term 'during those days' implies a period long since past. In fact, the last British and French troops had been taken off the beaches only a few days earlier. It also has a dream-like quality, flowers and young men, a sleepy countryside. Dunkirk was ancient fact as soon as it happened because it was easy for the public to place it within a frame of British history. J.B. Priestley felt the same. Broadcasting on 5 June, he noted: 'Now that it's all over, and we can look back on it, doesn't it seem to you to have an inevitable air about it – as if we had turned a page in the history of Britain and seen a chapter headed "Dunkirk".'[23] *War Illustrated* touched upon a similar vein. Dunkirk was the moment of supreme emergency, but that emergency was now long past: 'Never since the days of the Great Armada had the menace of the invasion of the British Isles been so acute as it was after the German westward thrust had been achieved.'[24] This was, once again, only a few days after the end of the evacuation of Dunkirk. Hammerton's point seems to be that Britain was at peril when its strength was committed to its allies, but now it was concentrated on its own island the danger was minimal. According to this thesis, Britain could glory in standing alone, for history had shown that not only was Britain often alone, but also that the British were at their best when alone.

Standing alone

It is a well-known story that when France collapsed, King George VI wrote to his mother stating, 'Personally, I feel happier now that we have no allies to be polite to and pamper.'[25] This feeling appears to have stretched to the ordinary person, for A.P. Herbert recalled a tugboat skipper yelling out on the Thames, 'Now we know where we are, no more bloody allies.'[26] This sense of relief at concentrating all efforts on the defence of the home country and standing alone reflected a genuine patriotism, founded upon centuries of belief in the apartness of Britain. A note of xenophobia certainly underpinned these comments: foreigners are not to be trusted and are not reliable. In the instance of the Second World War the foreigners happened to be Germans, but the underlying point is that those beyond this isle cannot be trusted. When Captain Alan Harper of the Royal Artillery broadcast on defensive preparations in Dover in July 1940, the text was later reproduced in *The Listener*. Harper commented on both the invidious nature of the Germans and the unity of the British people in their moment of emergency:

> *Thank God Britain is still an island, in spite of pre-war theorising by continental pundits. The obscene Goebbels and his litter in Berlin can falsify the history books, but not even Nazi propaganda can monkey with geography. . . . Our defences are formidable and methodical and behind these ever-blessed Straits. But only a few miles away is the giant army that has smashed its way through Western Europe. . . . There is no trick,*

no treachery, no murderous invention they will not use to destroy this
country, which alone stands between them and all the world's loot. . . .
Walking about in the streets reminds me of another thing this war has
done – it has wiped out any invidious distinction between soldiers and
civilians. . . . We really are all in it together . . .[27]

Winston Churchill appealed to this mixture of patriotism, insularity and
xenophobia in his speech to the Commons (he subsequently repeated this
speech on the wireless):

I have, myself, full confidence that if all do their duty, if nothing is
neglected, and if the best arrangements are made, as they are being
made, we shall prove ourselves once again able to defend our island
homes, to ride out the storm of war, and to outlive the menace of
tyranny, if necessary for years, if necessary alone [emphasis added].[28]

He implied the parallel with historical events, and made a statement of
collective will and commitment, a commitment to see it through alone. In
one sense it was no more than a statement of fact, after all what else could
Britain do short of making a compromised peace? Churchill touched
upon a strand of grim resolution. Standing alone was the *de facto* situation. And, as many knew from a soldiers' song of the Great War, it was
no good moaning about the situation, it wouldn't change it: 'We're 'ere
because we're 'ere because we're 'ere because we're 'ere.' And, as in 1914,
Britain was a remarkably disciplined nation, with a people used to
accepting difficult situations and making the best of them. It is from this
period that one of David Low's most famous cartoons dates. On 18 June
1940, the *Evening Standard* carried his sketch of an English soldier
standing on the white cliffs of Dover, his arm outstretched towards the
continent and his fist clenched. Coming from the direction of France is a
looming black cloud. The legend says, 'Very well, alone!'. Low, a New
Zealander and observer of British national character, had added his tribute and exhortation. The cartoon is the apotheosis of the bulldog spirit,
of 'backs to the wall', of taking it on the chin and it appeals to a sense of
'deep Britishness'. Robert Westall, author of several brilliantly observed
children's novels about the home front in the Second World War, and
himself a child in the war, has called it 'the greatest cartoon of the war.
I always had the feeling that David Low was actually a personal friend of

Winnie's, and possibly a member of the Government. . . . I had this picture on my bedroom wall.'[29] Westall's reflections are extremely helpful,
for they reveal that his child's mind felt there was something 'official'
about Low's work, with which he concurred. It helps us because it shows
that people were often aware of manufactured images, propaganda. But it
was not (and is not) axiomatic that images labelled propaganda were
regarded as a deliberate twisting of the truth and rejected. People accepted things they agreed with and 'knew', and in 1940 the British people
knew that the finest hour of many fine hours had arrived, sharpened still
further by the fact that 1939 had so singularly lacked fine hours.

Low summed up a common feeling of stoic resolution, but not resignation to fate, for it was not the British way; on the contrary, everything
they knew and felt impelled them to celebrate the situation. The *Daily
Express* announced, 'All right. We can take it. Now we are on our own.'[30]
A letter to the *Daily Telegraph* commented: 'To prophecy for 2,000 years
ahead is difficult – or it may be too easy. But I venture this: round about
AD 3940, when the history of these times shall have become classical, the
word "British" will be a synonym, just as "Spartan" is today. It will be
equivalent to "unconquerable".'[31] This celebration of solidarity and sep-
aration has lingered with us ever since, and is still a part of our popular
culture. The film version of the immensely popular television series *Till
Death Do Us Part*, starring Warren Mitchell as East End working-class
Tory and bigot, Alf Garnett, included a section set during the Second
World War. (The television series itself was placed in the contemporary
Britain of the late 1960s and earlier 1970s.) In one scene, Alf, the
consummate bar room commentator, tells his fellow drinkers what has
happened at Dunkirk. He denies that it was a débâcle at all, referring to it
as a 'strategical withdrawal', and adds that Churchill's plan is for the
Brits to stand together, knowing that 'your right hand will stand firm with
your left'. The point of the sketch is to show Garnett's utter ignorance of
what has actually happened, but it works on another level too, for it is a
remarkably accurate summation of the feeling of 1940. Of course the
British people knew deep down that it was a disaster, but they opted for
an explanation which allowed them to make sense of what had happened
and gave them the strength to carry on.

The British people reached into images of themselves and, with the
help of official promotion and prompting, found that the situation could

'VERY WELL, ALONE!'

'Very Well, Alone!' David Low's cartoon from the Evening Standard 18 June 1940. Years later this spirit mutated into 'Come and have a go if you think you're hard enough' (Atlantic Syndication).

be faced. Not surprisingly, the British fame for sang-froid was played upon. This allowed the real threat of the Nazi menace to be reduced and ridiculed. For *Country Life*, Hitler was a tiresome distraction and not much more: 'But whether in the country porch or in East End air-raid shelters, or in the little ships that chug their way through the Straits of Dover, the manifestations of war are being regarded much as one would a series of thunderstorms: a nuisance, even dangerous, yet not such as to upset daily routine.'[32] *War Illustrated* carried a photograph of a Kent church. On its notice board is chalked the statement: 'In future the bell will not ring except – well you know BUT the services will still go on as usual.'[33] On 13 June the government had banned the ringing of church bells – they were not to sound except to signal invasion. John Betjeman, poet and official at the Ministry of Information, pondered on this decision. His response had been to warn enthusiastic Air Raid Precautions volunteers and Local Defence Volunteers against too enthusiastic a tug on a bell rope, saying it would probably pull them up the belfry with it.[34] Both examples illustrate a refusal to take the threat seriously, a determination to shrug it off and continue with normal life.

But it was not just the British who were wallowing in their own self-image. The American press was reporting much the same thing. Britain needed American help and this required a positive image on the other side of the Atlantic. American journalists found it in the British refusal to cower and tremble. On occasion, the example of traditional phlegm could cause some doubt. Mollie Panter-Downes, writing in the *New Yorker*, could not ascertain whether the British were brave or stupid. She wondered whether it was to do with a lack of imagination. 'The individual Englishman seems to be singularly unimpressed by the fact that there is now nothing between him and the undivided attention of a war machine such as the world has never seen before.'[35]

The 'sensationalist revisionists' have sought to destroy this image of a self-confident, plucky 1940 Britain, and have marshalled much evidence to show signs of panic, small-mindedness and incompetence. But this is merely the other side of the same story; it is not *the* story of 1940. It is not the *whole* truth of the matter any more than any other history. While this side should be acknowledged, what must be said is that 1940 crystallised many aspects of British national identity and made many people realise that for their own good they should accept, celebrate and go along with them. Ian McLaine, historian of the wartime Ministry of Information, has shown that in the summer of 1940 official surveys of the mood of the people found a remarkably consistent sense of calm and reserve.[36] Occasionally this was found to be an irritant. On 24 May with the BEF in headlong retreat to Dunkirk, *The Times* asked 'Are We Really at War?' and compared the dire situation in France with the continuation of ordinary life in Britain. There was an obvious sense of frustration at the lack of urgency and seemingly misplaced energies.[37] When Charles de Gaulle arrived in London after his last-minute escape from France, he too found Britain strangely unreal. To his eyes the British stiff upper lip must have appeared offensive and obscenely removed from the realities of the situation, and he detected 'a look of tranquillity, almost indifference'.[38]

Alone, but with the Almighty

However, there was also foreboding and fear most clearly seen on Sunday 26 May, a National Day of Prayer. Churches were full, a rare occurrence, especially in a country increasingly indifferent to organised religion. Prayers were conducted for the BEF and French armies in their hour of need; it was a sign that people certainly were taking the situation seriously. But the British only began to pray when their own position started to look vulnerable. It was probably a reflection of the national chauvinism witnessed by de Gaulle. This chauvinism, when combined with a belief in a supernatural force, could lend itself to an arrogant and insouciant reading of events. In 1943, D.W. Brogan's *The English People: Impressions and Observations* was published. Brogan looked back on the summer of 1940 and implied a connection between the English and God, which made them very calm under pressure:

> A world without England would have no adequate standards of rightness; no English marks to surpass or to fail or to attain. So it has been ever since 'Britain first at heaven's command arose from out the azure main.' Whether the rest of the world was created before or after this decisive proof of divine power does not really matter. Fixed in this conviction, the Englishman can afford to rise above nearly all forms of nationalist weakness. . . . But at bottom he knows that being English is something that matters more than anything else. For that reason he was

not nearly as frightened in the summer of 1940 as he ought to have been.
It was, it is true, very difficult to see how the war was to be carried on.
German efficiency, as well as German power, was greatly admired. The
guesses at the military weakness of England, though not grim enough,
were grim. But after all what did defeat, what did surrender mean? That
Germany laid down the law to England? That sort of thing, no matter
what the experts said, simply wasn't done. And it wasn't.[39]

The English had long believed in their special relationship with the
Almighty. In 1588, His storms had dispersed the Spanish Armada
(the Armada medallion was inscribed 'the Lord God Blew and They were
Scattered'). In 1688, the 'Divine Wind' blew William of Orange to
England, allowing him to depose the Catholic James II in his Glorious
Revolution. By the nineteenth century the English had come to regard
God as a W.G. Grace-type umpire, who sat in the stands, calling the shots
of life, signalling who should go back to the pavilion. (As Clarence Day
put it: 'Aside from a few words in Hebrew, I took it completely for
granted that God had never spoken anything but the most dignified
English.'[40]) Lady Baldwin, wife of the former Prime Minister Stanley
Baldwin, equated God and country, seeing the flag of St George flying on
her local church tower she felt inspired and emboldened. She urged all
churches to keep their flags flying, showing that Britain was a bastion of
good in a sea of evil. Another woman told Mass-Observation she had had
a supernatural sensation that the Germans would never invade. While a
north London woman felt a spiritual presence saying: 'You will never
come to any harm. There is someone looking after you.'[41] Churchill told
the British that the fate of Christian civilisation hung upon their performance, but given Britain's history there was also a feeling that God
simply would not allow a German invasion.

The presence of divine intervention was seen most obviously in the
'Miracle of Dunkirk', for that was how it seemed – a miraculous delivery
largely due to miraculously calm conditions in the English Channel.
This allowed a brave, hard-pressed army to be rescued in order to fight
another day. The somewhat patchy supply of information on the British
campaigns in France and Belgium meant that the press coverage was
little more than speculation and clichés. But, despite strict censorship,
the press did consider the reasons for the British failure and retreat.

Few doubted that the army had fought heroically. The real villains were Leopold, King of the Belgians, whose decision to surrender had exposed the British flank (*British Movietone News* referred to the treacherous desertion of the Belgian King), and Chamberlain's pre-war government, which had left Britain so unprepared for war.[42]

On 31 May, Hilde Marchant, the *Daily Express*'s correspondent at Dover, reported the arrival of British soldiers evacuated from Dunkirk. She wrote, 'tired, dirty, hungry they came back – unbeatable'.[43] A similar sentiment was expressed in the *Daily Mirror*: 'And still they came back – Gort's unbreakables.'[44] In fact, the heroism of the BEF set a benchmark for the British people. According to the press they had to emulate their example. A *Daily Express* editorial remarked, 'No country has a right to ask for such heroism as our fighting men have freely given.'[45] And the *Mirror* urged, 'we shall not flag or fail. We shall not, because failure means our extinction. And because, to flag would be to prove ourselves pitiably unworthy of those brave men who lie dead along the shores of France.'[46] In response, the British people gave the BEF an extremely warm welcome. As the evacuated men landed in the ports of south-east England, particularly Dover, it was the people of Kent who greeted them first. Mass-Observation noted that volunteers turned out day and night to meet the trains in the stations, providing soldiers with drinks and refreshments, although Dover itself was described as 'flat and unemotional'. This is hardly surprising. As the nerve centre of the evacuation, Dover was a strange mixture of military camp under martial law and amazed, numb civilians, witnesses of the soldiers' first moments of safety.[47] Such was the level of jubilation, Churchill himself pointed out that 'we must be very careful not to assign to this deliverance the attributes of victory. Wars are not won by evacuations.'[48] Many men of the BEF agreed with him and were shocked by the response they received. Patrick Hadley's personal memoir of the campaign, *Third Class to Dunkirk*, published in 1944, notes that he felt ashamed of the army's 'ignominious withdrawal'. Like many soldiers he felt that the army had let the country down and might well face an angry reception back in Britain. However, he returned to a warm reception. The British people had come to an alternative conclusion. While on the train he grew confused by the sandwiches, biscuits and bars of chocolate thrust through the window at every stop. Worse still, according to Hadley, his men actually began to believe that they were heroes, thus re-writing the entire event at a stroke. Disaster and defeat were transformed into glorious victory:

> As we passed through London the little back gardens of the rows of dingy houses were gay with Union Jacks, and the words 'Well Done the B.E.F' were chalked on innumerable walls and railway wagons. In the circumstances it was hardly surprising that a large number of soldiers suddenly became aware that they were heroes and many heads were sadly turned by the enthusiasm of the welcome prepared. The rejoicing which sprang from relief at a miraculous escape was misconstrued as an expression of congratulation upon victory; and many who only a few hours before had succumbed to panic or felt the chill of fear now wrote the letters 'B.E.F' on their tin hats and shoulder straps, and accepted unquestioningly the homage paid to them by an adoring public . . .[49]

But some civilians were not impressed at all by the scenes. Mass-Observation reported an old lady who complained at the state of the troops, saying 'when I was a girl soldiers used to look smart and would never have gone out without gloves'![50] This cantankerous attitude demonstrates only the flip side of British sang-froid. For the vast majority of the public, however, the troops were heroes and that is how they have remained, despite attempts by the 'sensationalist revisionists' to expose the army as a shambles. Noël Coward's fine portrait of the Royal Navy, *In Which We Serve*, released in 1942 and the top grossing British movie of that year, included a Dunkirk sequence. HMS *Torrin*'s crew pick up survivors and take them to Dover where they disembark. As the men line up it is easy to see that their clothing is ripped and filthy, they have few weapons and look exhausted. Then a sergeant calls them to order and the strains of a military band are heard. Panning across their faces, the camera captures their latent spirit as, at the word of command, they all click to attention, chests go out, and pride is restored. They then march off in perfect time to the sounds of the band. Leading Seamen 'Shorty' Blake (John Mills) makes the only comment, 'If I wasn't so tired, I'd give 'em a cheer and no mistake.' The poignancy of the scene freezes the national myth of Dunkirk, as *The Times* noted in its review, 'that is the aftermath of Dunkirk stated theatrically, and the theatrical terms are magnificent'.[51]

Business in great waters

Even more famous than the image of the troops brought off the beaches of Dunkirk are the ships that carried them. The 'little ships' of Dunkirk are still very much part of our culture; in June 2000 the surviving ships went back to Dunkirk, as they have been doing every five years since 1965. Many hours of television were devoted to it and the newspapers covered the event. Little has changed since 1940. The Armada of ordinary launches and yachts were famous then and made a deep impression on the public imagination. As many have pointed out since, the vast majority of soldiers were actually carried away by the Royal Navy in Royal Navy vessels, but that fact has never mattered. At the time most people were impressed by the idea of ordinary people doing their bit for their boys. It was an important gesture in a conflict that was just about to become a 'People's War' in every sense.

Press coverage of the evacuation focused on the little ships and made heroines of them and heroes of their crews. Hilde Marchant, reporting for the *Daily Express*, was bewitched by the sight of 'an armada of Saucy Janes . . . this line of cheeky, arrogant little boats'. To her, as to the rescued soldiers, it was an amazing example of bravery and resource-fulness; she believed that 'this day I have seen England'.[52] While the Royal Navy was full of admiration for the behaviour of the volunteer crews, noting that many little fishing boats 'had boys of seventeen and eighteen on board, boys who have just learned to draw in their nets. They went out with their fathers and uncles, and many times dived over-board to rescue a man'.[53] A few days later, Strube the cartoonist of the *Express*, produced a cartoon of a jolly fishermen carrying a soldier out to a yacht called 'Saucy Jane'. The caption read 'All in a day's work, chum'.[54] As with so much else in 1940, it was expected to be mythological before it happened and became so as soon as it did. People were constantly told that they were living in special times, and as 1940 wore on they needed less and less reminding of it as the evidence surrounded them. In those circumstances the majority acted up to the myth they were both receivers of and participants in. Dunkirk, as noted, became ancient historical drama almost as soon as it occurred. The *Picture Post* presented it in precisely this manner as 'the Epic of Dunkirk':

The evacuation of Dunkirk has already passed into history. The world looks ahead to other operations this war will bring. But none can be more heroic or inspiring than the epic that brought to a close the first great chapter of the war. . . . Fishermen, yachtsmen, river boatmen, brought out every kind of craft. Together with pleasure steamers and row boats, they set out for Dunkirk. . . . Of acts of individual heroism, sagas will be written for centuries. The full story of Dunkirk can never be told. Out of defeat, the British and French snatched a triumph that spurs them on to meet future hardships with equal courage.[55]

It was easy to mythologise the little ships, for as with every aspect of 1940 it appealed to a world of inherited culture and iconography. Everyone knew the hulking galleons of the Spanish Armada had been fought off by much smaller ships. Everyone knew Britannia ruled the waves and that the British know 'there is *nothing* – absolutely nothing – half so much worth doing as simply messing about in boats'.[56] Ratty sculls around to his heart's content in *The Wind in the Willows* (Kenneth Grahame 1908); Jerome, George and Harris row down river with carefree ease in *Three Men in a Boat* (Jerome K. Jerome 1889) and Carruthers and Davies save the empire using only a tiny yacht in *The Riddle of the Sands* (Erskine Childers 1903). And everyone knew that the sea was Britain's ally, its moat and guardian. The British therefore had a mystical communion with the sea and ships. A British brotherhood of the sea was celebrated by *The Times*, finding a native genius in the evacuation:

The fleet engaged in snatching the hard-pressed soldiers from under the guns and bombs of the enemy was such an armada as can scarcely have been assembled for war since the Crusades. From the destroyers of the British and French navies to barges, wherries, pleasure steamers, motor-yachts and even row-boats, this motley collection of ships gave a marvellous demonstration not only of trained naval tactics, but of the daring and resources native to an island race. The bond of dangers shared and help mutually given, which has linked the British Army to their seafaring countrymen, whether of the Navy or the Merchant Service, for centuries, has been strengthened as never before.[57]

Years of Navy League propaganda, of biscuit tins decorated with Dreadnoughts, of music hall choruses of 'all the nice girls love a sailor',

combined with the very real significance of the sea to Britain's trade
and industry, meant that the image of the little ships slipped into an
all-pervasive element in British culture. A.D. Divine, writing in 1945,
recaptured the evacuation with a Shakespearian tribute to the significance of the sea:

> *Behind the British Army in May 1940, as it fell back fighting from the*
> *Dyle, lay the sea. For a thousand years that sea was the great defence of*
> *England. For a thousand years it had been the English moat. Its bays and*
> *its headlands saw the battles that held Britain inviolate from the day the*
> *house-carles broke on Senlac Hill and the Saxon power broke them. And*
> *there were years when it was more than a moat. A score of British armies*
> *in those centuries fell back upon the North Sea and the Channel, and the*
> *sea was to them a refuge; across the narrows the ships of Britain lay like*
> *a drawbridge, and by that drawbridge they crossed to safety.*[58]

The little ships of Dunkirk not only connected with the established
seafaring myths of the British, they also echoed those qualities so beloved
by the British – improvisation, amateurism and individualism. In
nineteenth-century Liberal Britain the rights and liberties of the individual had been celebrated as evidence of the enlightened glory of the
nation. This meant that the Magna Carta and 1688 played a large role in
Victorian history books, emphasising the unique political development
of Britain. When combined with a culture increasingly dominated by the
neo-classical values of the public schools, it created a Britain heavily
aware of the supposed superiority of the amateur over the professional,
and the importance of the well-rounded individual over the mindlessness of the mass. With the rise of an increasingly anglophobic Germany
after 1890, this collusion of images moved up yet another level, for the
Germans became associated with a machine mentality, lovers of strict,
unimaginative routines and rigid, impersonal modes of behaviour.
Romantic Germany was lost almost at a stroke, and the British have never
recovered it. All of these images had been deployed in the Great War. In
1940 they appeared equally appropriate.

Dunkirk, with its little ships, hastily assembled and sent out to sea,
was a perfect example of the few and the many, of sang-froid *and* native
wit and improvisation, the result of unhindered initiative. Divine saw it
in grand theatrical terms, the proof of the race:

*And when it reached the tidemark there waited for it the armada of a
fantastic improvisation. Here were no troopships long prepared; here
was no careful withdrawal. Here was only a fleet of ships' lifeboats and
motor yachts, of Dutch skoots and Flemish fishing boats, British coasters
and Channel ferries, of drifters, minesweepers, sloops, destroyers: the
strangest fleet in the history of war upon the sea; battered from the air
and from the shore, bruised, broken, and in ceaseless peril – only these
and the spirit of an awakened England.*[59]

But the most famous interpretation of Dunkirk came from J.B.
Priestley. Priestley was a well-known writer and dramatist by 1940, he
was a celebrant of the English countryside, the ordinary man's Georgian,
and a devotee of English national character. His fame increased when the
BBC began a series of 'Postscripts' to the *Nine O'clock News*. During the
Dunkirk crisis, the BBC, fearing a failure of lower-class morale, turned
to Priestley as the ideal communicator with ordinary people. His warm
Yorkshire tones contrasted strongly with the public school accents usually heard. Priestley proved to be an enormous success, gave nineteen
postscripts between June and October and received over 1,600 letters a
week from the public.[60]

For Priestley, only the British could have come up with Dunkirk,
when triumph was snatched from defeat. 'This is not the German way',
he explained, for the Germans would never make such mistakes because
they are machines without souls. He brilliantly turned Dunkirk into an
epic by emphasising the polarity between the real role of the little ships
and their employment in the evacuation. Priestley played upon the
bizarre image of seaside pleasure cruisers and the Isle of Wight ferry
deployed to pick up battered and wounded men. He saw their ordinariness, integral to the drama, and the pleasures of a British seaside holiday
– palm-readers, sand castles, ham-and-egg teas, peppermint rock – and
then contrasted it with the bombs, guns and torpedoes sent against the
ships of such familiar and homely memory. Masterfully, he created a
mechanism capable of engaging the empathy and imagination of the
ordinary listener. With great insight Priestley referred to the Isle of Wight
ferry, the *Gracie Fields*. This popular entertainer was the darling of the
north, particularly Lancashire, and so brought northern Britain into the
equation. This was a shrewd move for the evacuation had, naturally

enough, concentrated the imagination on the ports of south-eastern England. He ended on a note resonant with national character, a character marked by a fine balance between the absurd and inspired:

> *And our grand-children, when they learn how we began this War by snatching glory out of defeat, and then swept on to victory, may also learn how the little holiday steamers made an excursion to hell and came back glorious.*[61]

Improvising

Improvisation, the great weapon in the British arsenal, was also displayed in the Local Defence Volunteers. The LDV, later the Home Guard and more widely known as 'Dad's Army', is an extremely important image of Britain at war. It was an example of British defiance and self-reliance, another miracle cobbled together from nothing and held together by the spirit of national character. That was how it was seen at that time, and that is how it has come down to us, perpetuated in the evergreen television series *Dad's Army*. Initiated by a call for volunteers on 14 May 1940, the Local Defence Volunteers (renamed the Home Guard on 23 July) stood 1.5 million strong by the end of June. Its kit, uniform and ammunition shortages meant that volunteers often drilled with broomsticks or whatever potential weapons came to hand. Those in the new force had two superlative, British assets, enthusiasm and initiative. Stories of completely autonomous units lacking any sort of central guidance are exaggerated as the War Office imposed its authority from the start. But in the early days the sheer pace of events and lack of planning meant that central direction was always lagging behind. In this way myths are made. The image created by *Dad's Army* is just one reading of the reality; it so happens that it is the only one in the popular memory. To spend time labouring to replace it, as some have, is actually pointless because it does not reveal a whole new truth, merely an additional dimension to it. It does not fundamentally undermine the myth or the reality within it.

The Home Guard was also a perfect expression of the two sides of Britain in 1940. It drew many former high-ranking soldiers back into positions of command and influence and so represented the old guard.

But it was also a truly popular force, expressing the popular will and a genuine realisation of the People's War. George Orwell referred to it as 'a People's Army officered by Blimps' – a little harsh perhaps, but a neat summary.[62]

Tom Wintringham, a veteran of the Spanish Civil War, communist and regular columnist for *Picture Post*, campaigned for immediate guerrilla training and the arming of the population in order to repel invasion. His vision of the Home Guard was truly radical, it was nothing short of a new New Model Army, a Cromwellian force of political warriors raised from, for and by the people.[63] To a large extent, this is the image of the Home Guard that has been lost; it is remembered instead for its comic mixture of organised chaos and eccentric personalities. Of course, there were moments when trigger-happy men caused tragedy by shooting innocent people, but this does not detract from the validity of the other image.[64]

John Brophy, veteran of the Great War, wrote a history of the Home Guard in 1945. He identified its nature as a mixture of the radical 'Wintringham elements' and more traditional facets of national character. In fact, for a nation of gardeners which often compared its history and development with the maturing of a garden, he saw it as a perfect, organic mix:

> It symbolised and made effective the will of the British people to defend their liberties, not merely while the period of acute danger persisted, but unremittingly till the Continental despotism is overthrown. The Home Guard was a spontaneous growth of May 1940, afterwards carefully tended, trimmed, and developed, but essentially as natural and rightful a phenomenon of the British landscape as the oak or elm, the cow-byre or the suburban back-garden, the pub or the corner of the village cricket ground.[65]

Here was a genuine spirit of patriotism, a deep popular commitment to defend the nation, and one that sprang up naturally, as it would in a people so immersed in their own myths.

Brophy's book was illustrated with Eric Kennington's portraits. Kennington was a celebrated portrait painter who had been an official artist during the Great War, producing some of its most enduring images. His work in the Second World War was of an equally high quality, and his studies of the Home Guard are extremely affecting. Both the quaintly domestic nature of the Home Guard and its grim determination to defend those homes were captured by Kennington. He achieved this by painting many of his sitters in their own homes. The canvases therefore provide a provoking combination of the conventional military portrait and the mundane, the everyday. It can be deciphered as slightly absurd, but that merely confirms the very British nature of the Home Guard.

Remembering

The BBC television series *Dad's Army* is a vital medium by which people still feel connected with the values of 1940; it provides a prism through which to see the world of Britain at war, and therefore 'know' it. During the fiftieth anniversary celebrations of VE and VJ Days in 1995 sales of the videos increased markedly, almost as if people took *Dad's Army* as history. Starting in 1968, *Dad's Army* ran for nine years, totalling eighty episodes, and regularly pulled in viewing figures in excess of 21 million. It inspired many spin-offs, including games and books, two stage shows and a film version in 1971. A survey conducted in 1993 revealed that *Dad's Army* was the most popular television comedy of the past two decades. Its thirtieth anniversary year, 1998, saw it celebrated in virtually every newspaper and on television. In 1995 it was the subject of an *Omnibus* programme, highlighting its significance as a national institution.[66]

Analysing the reasons for its success is an intriguing exercise because its appeal lies in a complex web of received memory, concepts of national identity and understandings of history. However, it is very much history as it should be; *Dad's Army* touches us because it is the way we like to think of Britain in 1940. 1940 seems a golden age, a time when all were united, when Britain had a mission, when there was a great cause worthy of great sacrifices. We might all have strong opinions on current issues, such as whether the tube should be privatised or not, but it is nothing compared with our feeling that 1940 was a moment of real passion, of real issues with clear-cut options. To say that 1940 was only that is, of course, a simplification, but to try to deny that it was in any way a moment of intense emotion and clarity of vision is equally pernicious and ridiculous. To accept *Dad's Army* is merely to accept a particular presentation of the past.

Dad's Army also works because it has a much wider and deeper resonance. The characters touch a chord in British humour and national character which reaches into the deep past. Jeffrey Richards has pointed out that the characters were the latest in a line stretching through Dickens to Shakespeare. He sees the Athenian mechanicals of *A Midsummer Night's Dream*, and Micawbers and Pecksniffs in *Dad's Army*.[67] The show also played up to the British obsession with class. Captain Mainwaring, the bank manager when off-duty, is obsessed with his rank and the dignities beholden to it. Air Raid Warden Hodges, the greengrocer, is another triumph of petty officialdom, but unlike Mainwaring, he is regarded as common, a tradesman with none of the grace or style of a gentleman – Sergeant Wilson always referred to him as 'awfully rough'. The other tradesmen of the outfit, Privates Jones and Fraser, are perfectly sound, however, despite their eccentricities. Private Walker is the wide-boy spiv, a cockney with shady connections and a fag constantly dangling out of the corner of his mouth. Private Godfrey has thirty-five years behind him in Army and Navy gentlemen's outfitting, the perfect middle-class draper. The village idiot of the gang is Private Pike, a mummy's boy who is enthusiastic enough but liable to make ridiculous mistakes.[68] The characters are perfect British stereotypes and are still recognisable to this day; thus *Dad's Army* becomes a living memory of 1940.[69]

Nostalgia is an extremely important part of its charm, too. *Dad's Army* reminds us of a time when Britain was great and achieved something great, and, according to most Britons, is something for which the world still owes us. The show acts as an anaesthetic, dulling the drift of Britain into obscurity and disunity. Peter Black, reviewing the first episode in the *Daily Mail* in 1968, remarked: 'This is the summer, 1940, when the heart of England beat to a single pulse.'[70] *New Society* also identified this theme, and saw *Dad's Army* as a mythological place in which the world was comfortable and heroic. Written in the spring of 1971 against the backdrop of an ongoing postal dispute, rioting in Northern Ireland and Rolls-Royce on the verge of bankruptcy, *New Society* was forced to admit that 'it's much more comforting to remember the myth'.[71] For Tom Hutchinson writing in *The Guardian*, *Dad's Army* represented the British people's ability to turn any event into a jolly adventure, no matter what it might actually represent:

The Boa Constrictor British can swallow any number of home truths
about errors or national judgement if the criticisms are well coated with
the spittle of sentiment. A ruthless digestion then turns Chamberlain into
an endearing figure with a brolly: Dunkirk becomes a 'byronic triumph'.
And the criminal unpreparedness of 1940 emerged thirty years on as the
television series Dad's Army, *a sweetly comic celebration of the British*
amateur.[72]

The malaise that was growing in Britain in the late 1960s and early 1970s is obvious in all three of the above extracts. For the left-leaning press, the image of 1940 simply could not be accepted whole, being regarded as far too conservative and as an avoidance of the realities of that year. But Hutchinson did hit upon a subtler interpretation. He saw that the 'myth' of 1940 didn't actually mean deliberate falsification or lying, but instead it meant a recasting of events. This is actually what occurred at the time too. It just so happens that according to local circumstances it has been occurring ever since.

Yet people accept *Dad's Army* because it looks so right. It achieved its authenticity by paying a great deal of attention to period detail and, more importantly, because it coincided with what people already suspect or know about Britain in the Second World War. Norman Cohen's film version in 1971 allowed a fuller deployment of *Dad's Army*'s skill at recreating a particular interpretation of 1940. In the film, as in the television series, period authenticity was created by the use of the theme song. 'Who do you think you are kidding, Mr Hitler?' is an extremely good parody of wartime songs, having echoes of 'We're gonna hang out the washing on the Siegfried Line' and 'Bless 'em all', and was sung by Bud Flanagan, whose popularity reached new heights during the war. Snatches of other tunes and songs used throughout the film and series helped to recreate the feel of the 1940s. The Walmington-on-Sea platoon is also seen to be woefully short of arms and equipment at first, and this is, of course, played for laughs. Captain Mainwaring announces with great pride that the first consignment of uniforms has arrived, and it turns out to be LDV armbands. Thanks to the absence of rifles, Private Pike comes along with a carving knife tied to a broomstick. But, as Mainwaring tells him, 'I didn't mean you to leave the broom on the end of it, you stupid boy'. Thus the realities of the shortages of 1940 are faced, but in a comic way; no one is held responsible and no one is blamed. However, the most important way in which the film achieves its sense of authenticity is via its use of documentary material. Much newsreel footage of Nazi parades and troops is used and the newsreel material of the Dunkirk evacuation is also included. Most significantly, Mainwaring and others are seen to gather round a radio to listen to Eden's broadcast on the evening of 14 May. The film woos us in with this use of original material.

Location is extremely important in both film and series. Walmington-on-Sea is supposed to be on the south coast somewhere: it seems to be located in the Eastbourne–Hythe area (they wear Royal West Kent cap badges). With greater opportunities for location work, the film emphasises a vision of leafy, rural, wealden England. The Battle of Britain is fought in a blue sky with majestic white clouds floating past, and the white cliffs of Dover are seen on more than one occasion, again firmly linking it with other visions of 1940. The film starts with a German general looking across the channel through a pair of powerful binoculars. Improbably he sees a gentlemen's lavatory close to the edge of the cliff, from which Sergeant Wilson emerges. He seems to realise he is being watched and stares back. The scene cuts back to the German general who cannot quite believe his eyes. When he replaces his binoculars he sees the whole Walmington-on-Sea platoon ready for action and carrying a Union Jack. A shot of the cliffs at sunset provides the wonderfully comic vision of Private Godfrey watching for any signs of enemy activity through a set of opera glasses! The most potent use of landscape comes in the same scene. Mainwaring and Wilson become black silhouettes on the horizon as they walk along the cliff tops with the sun setting even lower. The scene is beautiful and a paean to a famous English landmark:

> WILSON: *It's a beautiful sunset, sir.*
>
> MAINWARING: *It's a beautiful land, Wilson. They're not going to get it you know. They're not going to get their hands on it. We shall fight to the last. We shall keep firing till we've only got one round each. And that we shall save for ourselves. By the way, how much ammunition have we got?*
>
> WILSON: *One round each, sir.*

The comic interjection stops it becoming too much of a cliché, but in doing so also adds to its poignancy. By seemingly sending-up patriotism it adds tremendously to its power and returns us to 1940 again, for it was also a time when a sense of humour was needed.

Dad's Army used humour to make its point very successfully. The differences between the British and German national character are portrayed in the juxtaposition of German invasion plans with British defensive arrangements. The Germans have an impressive HQ with a massive table map. This contrasts with the village hall and AA map book used by the Walmington-on-Sea platoon. The German general then states that three panzer divisions are ready to make the spearhead. This cuts to Mainwaring explaining that he must defend the promenade from the Novelty Rock Emporium to Stone's Amusement Arcade. The German general says divisional commanders will communicate with him via shortwave radio; Mainwaring says he will give orders by Boy Scout runners. A German sergeant tells the general that the Führer wishes to see the invasion plans; Godfrey, in full evening dress, tells Mainwaring his wife wants him to bring home a pound of sprouts. Separated by thirty years from Kennington's portraits, it has the same attributes. The insane optimism at being alone, and the desire to improvise, is resurrected and reinforced, and foreigners are absolutely other. But it was also prepared to debunk its own myth of 1940. In doing so it pulled off the cleverest of double bluffs for in doing it, as with so much else in *Dad's Army*, it actually buttressed the myth. When Wilson and Mainwaring discuss the evacuation of Dunkirk, Wilson uses a phrase Ponting would be proud of:

> MAINWARING: *Good news about Dunkirk, eh? . . . Bringing our lads back to Blighty like that was a glorious achievement. It was a great example of British improvisation getting them out of France.*
> WILSON: *Yes, it's a pity they couldn't have improvised some way of keeping them there.*
> MAINWARING: *We don't want any of that sort of talk, Wilson.*

Mainwaring is made to look the Blimpish stick-in-the-mud here and Wilson as far more canny. But once you have laughed at the joke, once you have knowingly laughed at Mainwaring's willingness to accept the best possible gloss on events, you have to admire his spirit, the never-say-die attitude, which is, after all, what we all grow up admiring as Britons. And, though Wilson may well be right, we all know full well that he is not really some sneerer from the sidelines. When, and if, it comes to it, all

'You stupid boy!' Arthur Lowe as Captain Mainwaring in Dad's Army *– a key source in our memory of the war (BBC Worldwide).*

the Walmington-on-Sea platoon are ready to die for their country and their homes.

Dad's Army reinforces the very visual nature of the memory of the Second World War. What was written in newspapers and articles and said over the radio in 1940 was visualised in *Dad's Army*. This post-war visualisation has been so effective because it has plundered the huge visual archive of the war, both in terms of still photographs and moving film. Ironically, however, there is precious little movie footage of Dunkirk. The army shipped all the newsreel photographers out of France before the evacuation got into its stride. Naturally enough this caused some resentment from the cameramen. Ronnie Noble of Universal complained in his autobiography that he was virtually flung out of France. He lamented the lack of newsreel-men because it deprived Britain of a film record of an extremely important event in its history. The only cameraman to gain any significant material was Charles Martin of Pathé, who was posted to the Navy and went over to Bray Dunes in a warship.[73] But there is a further irony. Dunkirk is so firmly fixed in the imagination entirely because of the shortage of material. It means that over the years television documentaries, films, news reports of anniversaries have relied on very few images being constantly repeated. As with the assassination of President Kennedy, if you have ever seen footage of it, you have only ever seen it from one angle in one way. There are not thousands of images, just a few vital ones that concentrate the imagination and fix it deep in the private and public mind.

The feature film *Dunkirk* (1958) had exactly that effect. It took all the extant footage and used it within a plot structure deliberately designed to create the feel of a documentary. Made by Ealing Studios, famous for its commitment to portray the national character on film, great pains were taken to ensure authenticity. Owners of small boats were tracked down and the army was approached. A radical approach to the evacuation was highly unlikely as the War Office vetted the script before providing co-operation, ensuring it was equally unlikely that the film would take a radical approach to the evacuation.[74] However, *Dunkirk*'s celebration of 1940 does not mean the absence of a critical approach. The myth has never worked by simply stonewalling.

The film emphasises its 'documentary reality' throughout, using large amounts of newsreel footage. It is spliced in almost self-consciously, not simply to fill hard-to-recreate gaps. In doing so *Dunkirk* stresses its authenticity and immediacy, which must have been far more effective on its original release when watched by people who were delving into their memories of the period. Animated maps are also used, similar to those created by Disney for Frank Capra's celebrated series of wartime documentaries *Why We Fight*. They have the effect of implying a slice of well-researched visual history. (It also hints at the *Dad's Army* credit sequence ten years in advance.) Over the scene showing the German advances across the map of Europe, Flanagan and Allen are heard singing 'We're gonna hang out the washing on the Siegfried Line'. It is clearly ironic, underlining British naïvety and lack of genuine preparation in 1940.

Often passed off as uncritical, stiff-upper-lipped adventures, *Dunkirk* is a British war film that goes out of its way to highlight the nation's problems in 1940. The 'guilty men' of the Chamberlain gang are certainly given special treatment. The lack of preparation for aerial warfare is picked out for particular emphasis. Much of the drama of the movie is concerned with the helplessness of the soldiers under aerial bombardment. When Corporal Tubby Binns (John Mills) witnesses the killing of fellow troops in a German air raid he notes ruefully, 'It wasn't the fire that killed them, they got it before that.' He replicates the spirit of the best-selling *The Guilty Men* (1940), which noted on the disaster in France that the BEF was 'doomed before they took to the field'.[75] The hard-bitten journalist, Charles Foreman (Bernard Lee), witnesses the scenes on the beaches and pronounces, 'What a mess, what a shambles we've made of this whole rotten affair.' Admiral Ramsey is seen to struggle with insouciant Admiralty staff officers who talk glibly about balancing odds rather than hand over the destroyers he so desperately needs for the evacuation. A simple repetition of a simple myth *Dunkirk* is not.

Panic is also shown. Men on the beaches fight to get into the boats and there is terror among those crowded on the moll (the main pier or jetty) during a German raid. But the army is generally absolved from blame and presented in a positive light. Lord Gort, Commander-in-Chief of the British Expeditionary Force, takes the decision to withdraw to Dunkirk as a risk, but a well-calculated and bold one. There is no hint of precipitous, muddled or incorrect thinking. 'You can't blame the army,' states Foreman, 'they had what we gave them.'

A quiet heroism is displayed, confirming the things we know about Dunkirk. Most men queue patiently waiting to board the ships, the troops on the perimeter boldly hold back the advancing Germans and a field gun team know they are sacrificial lambs, continuing to fire until overrun. On the beaches doctors and medics of the Royal Army Medical Corps calmly draw lots to decide who stays with those too badly wounded to be evacuated. In a poignant moment Lieutenant Levey's name is drawn. A Jew is therefore going to take his chances with the Nazis.

Britain is also seen to move towards greater national unity and acceptance of the reality of war. Holden (Richard Attenborough), the rather cowardly garage-owner who wants to stay safe and make a profit out of the war, is forced to confront himself by the emergency. He volunteers to take his boat to Dunkirk and bravely helps to rescue the soldiers. The Royal Navy is forced to accept civilian volunteers, thus making the struggle a People's War. Over the final sequences a voice announces, 'Dunkirk was a great defeat and a great miracle. We were alone and undivided . . . a nation had been made whole.' The myth of Dunkirk was buttressed, but it was by no means a whitewash and told a tale of a nation adjusting to war. Chosen for the Royal Command performance, the film was obviously accepted by the public, scoring the third biggest box-office success of 1958.[76]

Dunkirk as a 'witnessed event' has been boosted by its concentrated visual profile. This can be perceived even in literature. Writing many years later, Spike Milligan was fully aware of the way in which memories and images collide to create historical myths, and ascribed to himself the power to distinguish hard lines between myth and reality. And yet the first volume of his rightly celebrated war memoirs, *Adolf Hitler: My Part in His Downfall* (1971), contains a beautifully crafted scene in which the popular understanding of 1940 is recreated. It is also highly 'visual' – it could almost be directions for a film – and is worth quoting at some length:

The first eventful date in my army career was the eve of the final evacuation from Dunkirk, when I was sent out to the O[bservation] P[ost] at Galley Hill to help the cook. I had only been in the Army twenty-four hours when it happened. Each news bulletin from the BBC told an increasingly depressing story. Things were indeed very grave. For days

previously we could hear the distant sound of explosions and heavy
gunfire from across the Channel. Sitting in a crude wood O.P. heaped
with earth at two in the morning with a Ross Rifle with only five rounds
made you feel so bloody useless in relation to what was going on the
other side. Five rounds of ammo, and that was between the whole O.P.
The day of the actual Dunkirk evacuation the Channel was like a piece
of polished steel. I'd never seen a sea so calm. One would say it was
miraculous. I presume that something like this had happened to create
the 'Angel of Mons' legend. That afternoon Bombardier Andrews and I
went down for a swim. It would appear that we were the only two people
on the south coast having one. With the distant booms, the still sea, and
just two figures on the landscape, it all seemed very, very strange. We
swam in silence. Occasionally, a squadron of Spitfires or Hurricanes
headed out towards France. I remember so clearly, Bombardier Andrews
standing up in the water, putting his hands on his hips, and gazing
towards where the BEF was fighting for its life. It was the first time I'd
seen genuine concern on a British soldier's face; 'I can't see how they're
going to get 'em out,' he said. We sat in the warm water for a while. We
felt so helpless. Next day the news of the 'small armada' came through
on the afternoon news. As the immensity of the defeat became apparent,
somehow the evacuation turned into a strange victory. I don't think the
nation ever reached such a feeling of solidarity as in that week at any
other time during the war. Three weeks afterwards, a Bombardier Kean,
who had survived the evacuation, was posted to us. 'What was it like?',
I asked him.
'Like son? It was a fuck up, a highly successful fuck up.'[77]

It's all there. There is the sense of being utterly alone with no one to turn
to. Not only alone, but also unprepared for the task ahead, only an old
Canadian Ross rifle with five rounds. Then, in this moment of supreme
crisis, the ordinary is interjected – a swim on a fine, early summer day.
In such circumstances it seems absurd, but no more absurd than taking
seaside steamers to Dunkirk to take part in the evacuation. Miraculously
calm weather allows the operation to take place. The strange moment of
crisis then becomes an equally miraculous triumph. Finally, the myth
shows its resilience and strength. As in *Dad's Army*, Milligan debunks
the whole lot as 'a highly successful fuck up', but this only serves to

prove the myth still further by absorbing the alternative reality. Bombardier Kean's 'fuck up' is as real as the extraordinary heights of solidarity. Both are Dunkirk.

Dunkirk and the Dunkirk spirit have gone into our language and mental landscape. They are constant favourites of politicians and have become a form of ubiquitous shorthand. Two examples came to mind. First, *The Early Bird*, a Norman Wisdom film of 1965. Wisdom was a later incarnation of Charlie Chaplin: fighting the fight of the little man against overwhelming odds, well-meaning and never quite prepared for life's accidents and trials, but always overcoming them thanks to sheer good-humour and determination. *The Early Bird* is a typical Wisdom vehicle; he plays a milkman, the sole employee of the long-suffering Mr Grimsdale (Edward Chapman). Grimsdale's Dairies is being squeezed out by the much larger Consolidated Dairies, and one of their thuggish milkmen beats up Wisdom, telling him 'It's war, mate. Little men like you don't stand a chance.' Naturally, Norman wants to fight back but Mr Grimsdale doesn't seem to have the heart for the struggle. Then Norman plays his ace, 'You were at Dunkirk, weren't cha Mr Grimsdale? What would 'ave 'appened if we'd given up then?' This, of course, brings Mr Grimsdale to his senses and they resume the struggle, ending up victorious. The point is that this hugely successful comedian 'naturally' slipped in so many well-known elements of British national character and a reference to Dunkirk, knowing it would immediately summon up the required response in his audience.

Second, and from a quite different sphere, *Grange Hill*, the successful children's television series set in a comprehensive school. In one episode many years back, the school is under pressure to tighten up discipline at the insistence of an overly fussy local councillor. The dependable, sergeant-majorish PE teacher, 'Bullet' Baxter, tries to rally the staff room with, 'Come on, where's your Dunkirk spirit?' This elicits the sort of response from the History teacher that had *Daily Mail* readers apoplectic at loony-left schools in the 1980s, 'I don't know why everyone keeps going on about the Dunkirk spirit. Dunkirk was, in fact, a terrible defeat.' The use of Dunkirk in a drama aimed at school-aged children reflects the confidence that they would understand the image and know what it implied. This episode of *Grange Hill* also reflected the time in which it was made (*c.* 1984), but the History teacher should have known she was fighting a lost cause. Everyone in Britain knows that Dunkirk was a defeat; it is precisely because it was such a defeat that it could be turned into such a triumph. It was a History teacher showing a very poor historical knowledge of British national character and mythology.

Finally, Dunkirk stays with us in the form of the little ships themselves and their commemorative crossings to Dunkirk. The tenth anniversary of Dunkirk witnessed a large-scale commemoration of the event. Veterans returned to the beaches and were made welcome in the town. King George VI confirmed the status of the evacuation in his message to the ex-servicemen: 'As long as the English tongue is spoken it should be commemorated with thankfulness and pride.'[78] But the profile of Dunkirk was dramatically increased in 1967 by the formation of the Dunkirk Little Ships Association. It was given a publicity boost by the interest of the broadcaster, and former RAF fighter pilot, Raymond Baxter. Baxter was the unwitting owner of a Dunkirk little ship, *l'Orage*. It was only when he investigated its provenance that he uncovered its dramatic history. He became interested in gathering together as many surviving boats as possible for the twenty-fifth anniversary. In 1964, he wrote to *The Sunday Times* appealing for other little ship owners to come forward. The response was encouraging and 43 little ships sailed for Dunkirk in the 1965 commemoration. Two years later the Association was formed with the help of Commander Charles Lamb and John Knight, and they vowed to organise a large crossing every five years and smaller ones between.[79] Ever since the Association has helped keep the image of Dunkirk high in the public imagination. The crossings on the usually choppy waters of the English Channel provide dramatic photographs and television pictures. It helps reinforce the idea of a plucky, little Britain taking on awesome odds.

In 1989 a book listing all the little ships was published. Although it tries hard to provide a balanced overview, pointing out that most of the ships were requisitioned and run by the Navy, the overall impression is of the myth, stressing the role of individual volunteers coming to the aid of the soldiers. The foreword by the Duke of Edinburgh maintains the image of 1940 for generations born decades after the event:

For all who remember the dramatic evacuation of the British Army from Dunkirk in 1940, it was little short of a miracle, and the most moving

*and unexpected element of that whole astonishing event was the
intervention of what have become known as the Little Ships of Dunkirk.*

*Cockle fishermen, lifeboatmen, yachtsmen and members of the
Royal Navy put to sea in anything that would float and they braved the
mines, the 'E-Boats' and the Luftwaffe, to play their part in the rescue . . .
[it was] one of the most remarkable feats of seamanship in Britain's long
maritime history.*[80]

Echoes of the little ships at Dunkirk have transcended the decades to
us, in subtly different forms. Perhaps the last time it was seen was during
the Gulf Conflict of 1990–91. General Sir Peter de la Billière, commander
of British forces in Saudi Arabia, wanted to bolster the morale of his
troops, many of whom were homesick, especially in the run-up to
Christmas. The *Daily Star* responded, calling upon people to show their
solidarity with the soldiers by baking them cakes and sending them out
to Saudi Arabia. The response was amazing. He was swamped with gifts
and carried sackfuls on his visits to troops in the field.[81] As in 1940, it
was a moment when the many came to the aid of the few, a moment to
show solidarity with 'our boys'.

Few people have been bothered by the attempts to debunk the Dunkirk
story; it is too entrenched in the national psyche. During the sixtieth
anniversary celebrations in 2000 an editorial in the *Daily Telegraph*
summed it up. Arguments on exactly what happened are 'hardly relevant
and not worth arguing about', it noted, because although Dunkirk was a
defeat, it was 'not one without heroes'.[82] For the British, Dunkirk is about
heroism and a miracle. Others may wish to present all sorts of evidence
to the contrary, but it cannot overtake what people 'know' about the
episode because Dunkirk is taken as the entire history of the nation in
miniature.

Notes

1 *Daily Telegraph* 2 March 2000.

2 *Radio Times* 20 November 1999.

3 Jeremy Paxman, *The English: A Portrait of a People* (London 1998), pp. 32–3.

4 Tim Brooke-Taylor, *Rule Britannia: The Ways of the World and the True British Gentleman Patriot* (London 1983), p. 109.

5 For a fuller examination of these issues, see J.M. MacKenzie, *Imperialism and Popular Culture* (Manchester 1986).

6 Ann Savours (ed.), *Scott's Last Voyage Through the Antarctic Camera of Herbert Ponting* (London 1974), p. 157.

7 The myth of the Angel of Mons is an extremely interesting one. British newspapers reported sightings of supernatural intervention on the battlefield. It stemmed from a short story by Arthur Machen in which ghosts of the English bowmen of Agincourt helped fight off the Germans. In the rarified atmosphere of wartime Britain this somehow became the story of the Angel of Mons. See E.S. Turner, *Dear Old Blighty* (London 1980), pp. 54–6.

8 See Alistair Thomson, *Anzac Memories: Living with the Legend* (Oxford 1994).

9 Quoted in Gary Sheffield, *Forgotten Victory: The First World War, Myths and Realities* (London 2001), p. 192.

10 For a discussion of the presentation of the Dunkirk campaign, see Stephen Badsey's essay 'British High Command and the Reporting of the Campaign', in Brian Bond and Michael D. Taylor (eds), *The Battle of France and Flanders Sixty Years On* (Barnsley 2001), pp. 137–56.

11 *Picture Post* 8 June 1940.

12 *Country Life* 24 August 1940 (vol. LXXXVIII, no. 2275, p. 172).

13 *War Illustrated* 7 June 1940 (vol. 2, p. 610).

14 Penelope Summerfield, 'Education and Politics in the British Armed Forces in the Second World War', *International Review of Social History* 26 (1981), pp. 138–58.

15 *Picture Post* 3 August 1940.

16 *Daily Express* 1 June 1940.

17 George Orwell, 'The Lion and the Unicorn', in *The Penguin Essays of George Orwell* (Harmondsworth 1984; orig. 1941), p. 149.

18 *Daily Express* 29 May 1940.

19 *The Times* 25 May 1940.

20 Quoted in Malcolm Brown, *Spitfire Summer* (London 2000), pp. 66–7.

21 Angus Calder, *The Myth of the Blitz* (London 1991), p. 7.

22 *Country Life* 8 June 1940 (vol. LXXXVIII, no. 2265, p. 560).

23 J.B. Priestley, *Postscripts* (London 1940), p. 1.

24 *War Illustrated* 7 June 1940 (vol. 2, p. 610).

25 Quoted in Laurence Thompson, *1940: Year of Legend, Year of History* (London 1966), p. 132.

26 Quoted in Malcolm Smith, *Britain and 1940* (London 2000), p. 52.

27 Quoted in Brown, *Spitfire Summer*, p. 109.

28 Charles Eade (ed.), *War Speeches of Winston Churchill*, 3 vols (London 1951), vol. I, pp. 188–96.

29 Robert Westall, *Children of the Blitz: Memories of Wartime Childhood* (London 1985), p. 76.

30 *Daily Express* 16 August 1940.

31 Quoted in Brown, *Spitfire Summer*, p. 66.

32 *Country Life* 24 August 1940 (vol. LXXXVIII, no. 2275, p. 172).

33 *War Illustrated* 5 July 1940 (vol. 2, p. 731).

34 Ibid.

35 Quoted in Calder, *Myth*, p. 107.

36 Ian McLaine, *Ministry of Morale: Home Front Morale and the Ministry of Information in World War II* (London 1979), pp. 143–4.

37 *The Times* 24 May 1940.

38 Quoted in Angus Calder, *The People's War* (London 1997; orig. 1969), p. 111.

39 D.W. Brogan, *The English People: Impressions and Observations* (London 1943), p. 26.

40 Quoted in Brooke-Taylor, *Rule Britannia*, p. 59.

41 Quoted in Thompson, *1940*, pp. 132–3.

42 *British Movietone News* 6 June 1940.

43 *Daily Express* 31 May 1940.

44 *Daily Mirror* 3 June 1940.

45 *Daily Express* 31 May 1940.

46 *Daily Mirror* 5 June 1940.

47 Mass-Observation File Reports 1937–40: Report 167, 3 June 1940; Report 182, 10 June 1940.

48 Eade, *Speeches*, vol. I, pp. 188–96.

49 Patrick Hadley, *Third Class to Dunkirk* (London 1944), pp. 143–4.

50 Mass-Observation File Reports 1937–40: Report 167, 3 June 1940.

51 Anthony Aldgate and Jeffrey Richards, *Britain Can Take It: The British Cinema in the Second World War* (Oxford 1986), p. 203.

52 *Daily Express* 1 June 1940.

53 Ibid.

54 *Daily Express* 5 June 1940.

55 *Picture Post* 22 June 1940. *British Movietone News* also referred to it as the Epic of Dunkirk 6 June 1940.

56 Kenneth Grahame, *The Wind in the Willows* (London 1908), p. 5.

57 *The Times* 4 June 1940.

58 A.D. Divine, *Dunkirk* (London 1945), p. 9.

59 Ibid., p. 11.

60 See Calder, *Myth*, p. 197.

61 Priestley, *Postscripts*, pp. 1–4.

62 Quoted in Calder, *People*, p. 124.

63 See *Picture Post* 29 June 1940.

64 For a full history of the Home Guard, see S.P. MacKenzie, *The Home Guard* (Oxford 1995).

65 John Brophy, *Britain's Home Guard: A Character Study* (London 1945).

66 See Jeffrey Richards, *Film and British National Identity, from Dickens to Dad's Army* (Manchester 1997), pp. 351–66.

67 Ibid., pp. 355–6.

68 The fascinating point about the characters in *Dad's Army* is their very timelessness. Go back through that list and it is possible to place them all in recent, and current, popular comedy. Walker and Pike are Del Boy and Rodney from *Only Fools and Horses*, tweak Godfrey's character a bit and you have the two appalling sales assistants from *The Fast Show*, 'suits you, sir'.

69 Fascinatingly, *The Times* (1 August 1968) referred to Arthur Lowe (Mainwaring) as a fleshier version of Clement Attlee, sealing its authenticity as a genuine souvenir of 1940. Many historians have noted of Attlee that his taciturn nature, fondness for pipe-smoking and love of cricket made him a perfect example of Englishness. See Philip M. Taylor (ed.), *Britain and the Cinema in the Second World War* (Manchester 1988), p. 53.

70 *Daily Mail* 1 August 1968.

71 *New Society* 1 March 1971.

72 *The Guardian* 15 August 1970.

73 Ronnie Noble, *Shoot First! Assignments of a Newsreel Cameraman* (London 1955), pp. 27–9.

74 See MacKenzie, *Home Guard*, p. 132.

75 'Cato', *The Guilty Men* (London 1940), p. 14.

76 MacKenzie, *Home Guard*, p. 132.

77 Spike Milligan, *Adolf Hitler: My Part in His Downfall* (Harmondsworth 1987; orig. 1971), pp. 31–3.

78 *Daily Express* 5 June 1950.

79 See Christian Brann, *The Little Ships of Dunkirk* (Cirencester 1989), p. 8.

80 Ibid., Foreword.

81 Peter de la Billière, *Storm Command* (London 1992), pp. 227–8.

82 *Daily Telegraph* 3 June 2000.

CHAPTER 3

. . . .

The fewest of the few: the Battle of Britain, June–September 1940

The Battle of Britain is a potent reminder of our finest hour, it was the moment when the very few did their bit against the many. It helped perpetuate the perception that England is indeed the new Jerusalem, a green and pleasant land blessed by summer suns. The struggle in the skies of southern England seemed to provide further proof of the qualities of the island race in its continual struggle against foreign tyrants. In this moment of destiny Churchill deployed his rhetorical skills to create the blueprint of history. Moreover, the battle revealed, yet again, that the best way to fight a war is from an initially awkward position with the odds stacked against the home team. The British national myth cast it in that way, the experience did nothing to disprove it and the British have remained deaf to alternative explanations.

The Few

We all know what RAF fighter pilots of 1940 were like. For a start, they were few in number. At the height of the battle Winston Churchill told the British people that 'never in the field of human conflict had so much been owed by so many, to so few'.[1] And they thoroughly deserved their praise; fighting fiercely in the skies above southern England they kept the nightmare of invasion at bay. As the *Daily Express* remarked on

16 September 1940, 'these fine young men of ours continue to write, without halt or interruption, the most exciting story in the whole history of the world wars'.[2] Of course, those brave young men would never have stayed in the air without the dedication of ground crews, the whole administrative structure of the RAF and British workers toiling with tireless dedication in the aircraft factories. A reliance on the image of the Few may therefore be exaggerated. But there is no getting away from the fact that the British revel in the image because, in effect, the pilots were a microcosm of a microcosm. The British like to see themselves as the few and so Fighter Command became the fewest of the few.

Jeremy Paxman has seen the idea of the few as peculiarly English rather than British. He identifies Shakespeare's Henry V's Agincourt speech as its first great celebration: 'We few, we happy few, we band of brothers.'[3] The Spanish Armada certainly emphasised the same ideas, as noted in the previous chapter. In English history the Armada was portrayed as the defeat of overwhelming force by a gallant band of brothers. 1940 was simply its latest reincarnation and reinvention.

The history of the defeat of foreign enemies allowed the English to believe they had a special relationship with God; it made them the chosen people. In turn, this made the fighter pilots the cream of the British. The nation has accepted that image ever since 1940. As Britons we know that fighter pilots were young gods leading carefree lives who positively enjoyed giving the Luftwaffe a richly deserved thrashing. Since the Second World War our popular culture has reinforced this knowledge again and again, often in the most oblique ways. The popular sitcom about prison life, *Porridge*, even managed to do it. In the series, the young, good-hearted prisoner, Godber (Richard Beckinsale), is shown to be a model enthusiast, with Second World War aircraft his favourite: while building a Spitfire in one episode he remarks to a fellow inmate:

> *They saved our skins in the war, they did, them and the Hurricanes. That's what I'd like to have been, a fighter pilot. Up over the white cliffs of Dover, quick dog fight with the Luftwaffe, then back to the mess for bacon and eggs and a sing-song.*

Here are all the elements of the myth: the landscape, the carefree, 'piece of cake' characteristics of the fighter pilot and the battle for national survival. Godber refers to the image of the fighter pilot as constructed in the popular memory from popular culture itself, a sitcom.

These Few are stuck in their role as knights of the sky, gentlemen and officers. Aerial combat as a modern form of medieval jousting, requiring a chivalrous code, was not new in 1940. The Great War had seen fighter pilots eulogised as modern knights, riding their steeds high above the trenches, taking on opponents in single combat, using skill and judgement to deliver the fatal blow. In the midst of the horrors of the Western Front, with its squalor and interminable battles, the war in the air made a glamorous alternative. Aerial combat made heroes of the pilots and turned a whole generation of boys bred on Biggles stories and exciting films about the air war such as *Wings* (1927), *Hell's Angels* (1930) and *Dawn Patrol* (1938) into devotees of the chivalrous fraternity of the fighter pilot.[4] In the summer of 1940 the public looked to the skies sure of what they were to find, and they got it.

Country Life compared the pilots not only to knights, but also to other British heroes who had taken on great odds and made great sacrifices. 'Can England to its real self rest but true?', continuing with 'that self which our glorious young knights of the air are proving, in every tense hour, is as bright and true as the heart of a Sidney, a Falkland or an Oates?'[5] The *Daily Mirror* carried a photograph of the boys in duck egg blue on its front cover and centre pages under the legend, 'These Noble Knights'.[6] In September 1940, *Picture Post* reproduced some of Sir William Rothenstein's portraits of fighter pilots. The artist described one of his sitters, Sergeant Pilot V.R. Smith, as 'a medieval knight'.[7] Interestingly, Rothenstein used this term to describe a Sergeant Pilot and not an officer. Rothenstein seems to have picked his word deliberately, stressing the nobility of the other ranks in the People's War. By contrast, our image of Fighter Command is one dominated by public school boys who were undoubtedly officers and gentlemen (see Chapter 6 for the post-1945 resurgence of the officer).

But it is easy to see why the public school image should be the one handed down to us. People expected pilots to be toffs and the vast majority of images and words put before the public buttressed that. It is perhaps linked to the success of Richard Hillary's best-selling memoirs, *The Last Enemy*. Published in 1942, the book rapidly made Hillary a public figure, defining the manner, style and nature of a fighter pilot. Hillary was the son of a civil servant who spent most of his time working abroad in the colonial service. He spent his boyhood in a manner typical of the British upper middle classes – prep school, minor public school and then on to Trinity College, Oxford in 1937. While there he indulged in his passion for rowing and studied no more than was strictly necessary. He joined the University Air Squadron, and moved on to the RAF proper as a pilot officer in 1939. In August 1940, after spending time in Scotland training with the City of Edinburgh squadron, he was posted south just as the Battle of Britain was escalating. Gaining a reputation as skilful fighter pilot, Hillary found his exhilarating career cut short by the appalling burns he sustained after being shot down over the channel. It was while on convalescence that the idea of writing a book about his experiences was put to him.

The Last Enemy ensured the glamorous image of the fighter pilot as a particularly skilled practitioner of the art of war. For Hillary, aerial combat gave nobility back to war as it demanded cool calculation and a solitary pursuit against a picked enemy: 'In a fighter plane, I believe, we have found a way to return to war as it ought to be, war which is individual combat between two people, in which one either kills or is killed. It's exciting, it's individual, and it's disinterested.'[8]

When he described aerial combat and the destruction of a German fighter, he stressed its strangely detached and remote nature, but he saw in it the skills and characteristics of a swordsman:

> . . . then I had a feeling of the essential rightness of it all. He was dead and I was alive; it could so easily have been the other way round; and that would somehow have been right too. I realized in that moment just how lucky a fighter pilot is. He has none of the personalized emotions of the soldier, handed a rifle and bayonet and told to charge. . . . The fighter pilot's emotions are those of a duellist – cool, precise, impersonal. He is privileged to kill well. For if one must either kill or be killed, as now one must, it should, I feel, be done with dignity. Death should be given the setting it deserves; it should never be pettiness; and for the fighter pilot it never can be.[9]

The elevated nature of the role of the fighter pilot is exactly what the public expected. Hillary had modernised the code of chivalry and, in doing so, he reflected a theme strong in British culture since the mid-nineteenth century. The new public school ethos, which started to emerge around that time, laid a great deal of stress on the importance of good character. Shaping boys of character who were fit to govern vast tracts of the empire, lead men into battle and set an example to the lower classes was achieved by a mixture of processes, high among them the cult of games. Sport was thought to be a fine way of inculcating values of selflessness, leadership and teamwork. This was combined with Christian values and distilled into Muscular Christianity. Muscular Christianity was given expression by authors such as Thomas Hughes, of *Tom Brown's Schooldays* fame, in *The Manliness of Christ* (1880) and Charles Kingsley. Christ was portrayed as a crusader, a red-blooded manly saviour who fought chivalrously to protect the rights of the weak and the poor. In turn, Pre-Raphaelite visions of Christian knights representing all that is virtuous, and the novels of Charlotte Yonge and Walter Scott and Tennyson's Arthurian poetry created a society in which the values of medieval chivalry were highly prized. In the First World War it was easy to apply such images to fighter pilots, and little had changed by 1940.

Although Richard Hillary's description of the life and nature of the fighter pilot might still strike a chord with us, Hillary himself is not the fighter pilot with the highest profile in the public imagination. Why is that? Hillary is no longer a commonly known public hero because he is a literary hero, and the Second World War is not remembered in that way. Thanks to his literary qualities, Hillary is like a hero of the Great War, which was *the* literary conflict. Churchill, to be sure, had a command of words, but people always hear them spoken, even when they are reading them, they do not treat them as literature. It was a point made by Sir Ronald Storrs in his introduction to Eric Kennington's *Drawing the RAF* (1942): 'In this war, save for the supreme clarion of the Prime Minister's oratory, the picture has anticipated and outstripped the written word.'[10] Hillary's greatest comparator is not another fighter pilot, but Rupert Brooke. Look at Eric Kennington's portrait of Hillary and what do you see? A beautiful, blue-eyed, golden-haired god – Rupert Brooke. And, just as Brooke's beautiful face was disfigured by the insect bite that killed him, Hillary's burns seem all the more tragic given his looks.

The pilot the public knows most is Douglas Bader. Bader is a very British hero; as a leg-less fighter pilot he appeals to the British sense of the absurd and taking on the odds. He is also a visual hero: *Reach for the Sky*

(1956), starring Kenneth More, is part of the national treasure, eliding image with event, memory with act. It made the Battle of Britain an event we all witness. In fact, the Battle of Britain has a peculiarly visual reson-ance in the national memory. We all feel as if we have seen it thanks to the endless repetition, or recreation of, a set of powerful images. Angus Calder has identified the component parts of the image and its effect:

> In the nature of it, several generations in Britain remembered, or grew up with, two indelible visions of the Battle of Britain. One is from the pilot's cockpit. Film camera or prose description gives us the image of the Messerschmitt attacking, as it were, ourselves, like an immense wasp. Our paranoia is the pilot's. Our relief as the enemy hurtles blazing groundwards is his. Or, from the ground, we saw, we still see, we still imagine, the spectacle of 'our boys' duelling . . . with equally matched adversaries above our rooftops: a gallant show, perhaps leaving behind some of those vapour trails across clear blue skies which still haunt many people whose memory falsely tells them that the weather that summer was exceptionally fine.[11]

Imprinting a visual memory on the Battle of Britain obviously began during the conflict itself with the newsreels.[12] It was interpreted in other visual terms, too. Most famously by Paul Nash in his painting, *Battle of Britain*, commissioned by the War Artists Advisory Committee in 1941. Nash described it thus:

> The painting is an attempt to give the sense of an aerial battle in operation over a wide area, and thus summarise England's great aerial victory over Germany. The scene includes certain elements constant during the Battle of Britain – the river winding from the town areas across parched country, down to the sea; beyond, the shores of the continent, above, the mounting cumulus concentrating at sunset after a hot brilliant day, across the spaces of sky, trails of airplanes, smoke tracks of dead or damaged machines falling, floating clouds, parachutes, balloons. Against the approaching twilight new formations of Luftwaffe, threatening.
>
> To judge the picture by reference to facts alone will be unjust to the experiment. Facts, here, both of science and nature are used 'imaginatively' and respected only in so far as they suggest symbols for

the picture plan which itself is viewed as from the air. The moment of
battle represents the impact of the opposing forces, the squadrons of the
RAF sweeping along the cost and breaking up a formation of Luftwaffe
while it is still over the sea.[13]

It is an important picture for the way in which it makes a war memorial and historical facts out of certain elements of the Battle of Britain. An artist's mind 'stylised' the battle into a few, essential images which have been passed down into British popular culture and created the myth. The eye, and with it the impression of the battle imprinted on the mind's eye, is concentrated on vapour trails in a blue sky, a brilliant summer day, a winding river through a rural landscape, and the menacing continent. This is the national family snapshot, lovingly mounted in the photo album, a bit frayed at the edges but handed down to us, and we recognise and accept it. Exhibited at the National Gallery, Nash's painting helped support a specific understanding of the battle, particularly when reproduced in cheap postcard form.

The Few were immortalised by war artists, most notably by Eric Kennington and Sir William Rothenstein. Kennington's portraits match the skill with which he captured the spirit of the Home Guard, and portrayed the understated heroism of the pilots. Far from being a mere instrument of a propaganda machine, Kennington was no fool and knew his own mind. Passing off his work as mythological and misleading is simplistic. Kennington studied his subjects, looking for their characteristics, and he saw heroism. His portrait of the South African pilot, 'Sailor' Malan, is possibly the most famous. Malan is big and pensive, staring out of the canvas with a fixed expression; there is almost something atavistic about him, a hunter of an earlier age. A similar approach can be found in the portrait of Wing Commander Francis Beamish, who appears huge and looming, while Bader has the set look of a man used to getting his own way. There are casual heroes too, such as Squadron Leader Joseph Kyall, sitting with his flying helmet on glancing over the shoulder of the viewer. Then there are the classical ones, Flight Lieutenant Alastair Taylor, blond, slightly effeminate insofar as he seems beautiful rather than handsome, god-like, an Aerial or Mercury. Kennington painted individuals and found their characters, but placed them within a construct of heroism constant since the ancient world.[14]

Eric Kennington's Brylcreem Boy with the heart of a Knight Errant of Old: Flight Lieutenant Alastair Taylor (Imperial War Museum art, film and photograph archives).

One of the most famous posters of the war also helped to fix the image of the fighter pilot in this heroic mould. An undated poster, but presumably from the autumn of 1940, shows a group of airmen, Sergeant Pilots contrary to the myth, standing in their flying helmets looking up to the sky. The background graduates from wispy white to powder blue and has the legend '"Never was so much owed by so many to so few", The Prime Minister'. RAF blue, the blue skies of an English summer day, the emphasis on the Few and the casual young men of Fighter Command all add up to a potent definition of what Britain made of itself in 1940 – Britain conforming to the existing myth of itself, myth becoming reality and therefore unassailable.

Feature films have certainly played their part in this process. Films about fighter pilots and the Battle of Britain are actually quite small in number, although the character of the fighter pilot and 'RAF type' seem ubiquitous in the 'stiff-upper-lip' British war film. This is a tribute to the enduring strength of the image of the Battle of Britain pilot and the way in which it has created its own particular false consciousness. The all-pervasive Fighter Command pilot actually caused some resentment within the RAF during the war. As Guy Gibson, the famous Bomber Command pilot, noted:

> . . . the fighters seemed to have all the fun, walking off with the women and drinking the beer. . . . Naturally all this irked the boys of Bomber Command quite a lot. They began to take an active dislike to the flying-booted, scarf-flapping glamour boys; many a rude word was spoken between the two in practically every pub between Biggin Hill and Edinburgh.[15]

Spike Milligan told a similar story in his memoirs. As a gunner in the Royal Artillery he was jealous of the RAF pilots who stole all the girls and so tried to get a transfer. He was rejected for pilot training and didn't fancy being a rear gunner and so returned to his unit.[16]

The RAF as a sort of Wodehousian Drones' Club was captured in the biggest British box-office success of 1942, *The First of the Few*. For Jeffrey Richards, the film encapsulates national character marked by its 'sensitivity and idealism' and its 'quiet and abiding Englishness'.[17] The plot actually concentrates on the designer of the Spitfire, Reginald Mitchell (Leslie Howard), who struggled to get his work completed before he died from cancer. David Niven plays the test pilot who joins the RAF and leads his jaunty lads into battle against the Germans. Upper-class accents dominate and the RAF is seen to take a dedicated but light-hearted approach to the struggle – it is all 'a piece of cake'. Backed by William Walton's stirring music, the piece which has become a concert hall standard as the 'Spitfire Prelude and Fugue', *The First of the Few* tells you everything you always knew about the Battle of Britain, as it did to contemporary audiences.

In the 1950s a spate of films created memorials of the battle, each of them stressing the role of the officer, making it seem as if Fighter Command never had any Sergeant Pilots. *Angels One Five* (1952) treats the summer of 1940 with reverence, tracing the evolution of the young fighter pilot, 'Septic' Baird (John Gregson), into a skilful team-player under the influence of the wise 'Tiger' Small (Jack Hawkins). Baird is killed at the end, showing that pilots took great risks and were prepared to sacrifice themselves, proving themselves worthy successors to a whole host of British heroes.

A variant came in 1953 with *The Malta Story*. It tells of the resolution of the people of Malta in the face of dreadful bombing and of the RAF's attempts to defend the island. But scratch at the surface of the film and the Battle of Britain can be detected. The people of Malta, as imperial citizens, actually become British and share a finest hour with the motherland. Malta becomes another Britain, an island but even smaller, an embattled people but even fewer, an even tinier RAF force for protection against an incomparably bigger enemy. Britain and Malta share the same characteristics – stoicism, bravery, loyalty to the cause – and the RAF pilots show exactly the same qualities as those at home. Alec Guinness plays the shy young pilot, drawn into a deep emotional bond with the island, freely sacrificing himself so that it might live. Jack Hawkins plays the older head, trying to oversee the defensive organisation. Some critics found the repressed emotions of both films a bit too much to handle and teetering on cliché, but the public responded enthusiastically and they did good box-office business.[18] If myths were being peddled, a willing public was buying them.

The most important of the mythological films, *Reach for the Sky*, had a long gestation. Douglas Bader was a public hero long before the 1956 panegyric film, but he became a figure totally subsumed by his screen interpretation by Kenneth More. The Bader legend was first told in the *Daily Telegraph* in September 1940. It recounted his remarkable story of working his way back into the RAF despite the loss of both legs in an earlier flying accident. But the piece ended on a typically British note, nonchalantly announcing that after a recent minor crash Bader had bent his metal legs; however 'an artificer straightened them and half an hour later he was up in the air again'.[19]

In 1954 Paul Brickhill's biography of Douglas Bader, *Reach for the Sky*, was published. Brickhill's Bader turns out to be a crushing snob, convinced that a public school education bred a superior being, although the author does his best to save him from such charges. He notes that Bader valued those with a '"good school" background', which he felt gave men the confidence to 'lead with authority'.[20] This does not stop it being a thumping good read, exciting, full of reconstructed dialogue and very 'visual'; his words fit the images of newsreels and feature films. Quickly becoming a best-seller, and even inspiring a children's version, the film rights were snapped up. As a film, it proved to be an equally big success with the public and became the most profitable film of 1956.[21] The critics were slightly divided. For the *Daily Telegraph* it revealed the 'spirit that won the Battle of Britain', but the *Daily Herald* found the element of British understatement a little trying at times. Bader himself proved the 'piece of cake mentality' by avoiding the première altogether, preferring a Scottish golfing holiday.[22] What the *Telegraph* and the *Herald* had actually identified was the same strand in the national character and its popular construction. The spirit that won the Battle of Britain was believed to be connected intimately with the national obsession with understatement.

More's performance as Bader slightly toned down his somewhat abrasive nature, making him a more sympathetic character, but it was impossible to miss the force of his personality, self-reliance and temperament. He asks nothing of his men he would not do himself. When captured by the Germans, he reveals his British sense of humour by refusing to take them seriously, openly mocking them. At the end of the film he takes part in the first Battle of Britain Sunday fly-past, emphasising the war memorial feel of the piece. This was mirrored in the poster, in which More stands in his flying helmet looking towards the sky; it is very similar to 'the Few' poster of 1940 and so creates a link to the original mythological artefact. More recently, Bader's reputation has been subject to a great deal of debunking. Television documentaries have painted a picture of an extremely difficult and selfish person, motivated by the desire for personal glory. The metal-legged hero turns out to have feet of clay. But, as with so much else about the memory of the war, it has not recast Bader. The myth is not weakened by such charges, but in fact is made stronger because it accepts them. Few people expect saintly characteristics in someone who came back from such terrible disabilities. Only a pig-headed man could have done it, and lingering beneath the surface of both Brickhill's book and the film is exactly that characteristic.

The last movie concentrating on the Battle of Britain and RAF fighter pilots was the greatest in terms of scale, *The Battle of Britain*.[23] Released in 1969, the film strove to be a historically accurate interpretation of the battle. Spitfires and Hurricanes were bought from the Spanish and Portuguese air forces, giving the production its own mini air force. Many former fighter pilots were consulted, including Douglas Bader, Peter Townsend and the German ace, Adolf Galland. The huge scale of the film, incorporating the reconstruction of numerous aerial battles, demanded an equally impressive budget, eventually costing US$12 million. Everything was done in the name of authenticity. It was an authenticity that complemented the myth completely.

The Battle of Britain recreated Nash's painting, resurrected the characters of Kennington's portraits and even used William Walton's music. A memorial to the Battle of Britain was the result, despite its seeming intention to tell the story from both sides. The cast of characters certainly fit in neatly with earlier images. Edward Fox plays a flippant toff who, when forced to bail out, crashes through a greenhouse, dusts himself off and accepts a cigarette offered by a young boy with 'thanks awfully, old man'. Michael Caine plays a role similar to that of David Niven in *The First of the Few* – the dedicated gentleman flier, anxious to do the job properly. He even has the cliché of a faithful black Labrador (like Guy Gibson) who realises something is wrong when her master fails to return from a dogfight. Robert Shaw, with his massive, bulky presence, seems to be the incarnation of Kennington's 'Sailor' Malan. His character sees the war as a personal vendetta against the arrogant Germans who are trying to impose their will on Britain. Finally, there is Ian McShane as the Sergeant Pilot, providing the film with its working-class hero, returning the Battle of Britain to 1940 and the People's War.

The look of the battle is exactly what one would expect, in glorious colour. Aircraft wheel, dive and tumble in brilliant aerial sequences, vapour trails fill blue skies, blotched with fluffy white clouds. The England they fight over is one of rolling countryside, with parachutes fluttering down into fields where farmers with hay forks rush to the scene. London is shown occasionally, emphasising the famous u-bend of the Thames at the Isle of Dogs, but it plays second fiddle to the rural idyll. Although made twenty-four years after the war, *The Battle of Britain* has the look and style of a film made during the war, and passes on a con-struction of the war that was accepted in the summer of 1940.

Since 1969 the cinema has ignored the Battle of Britain and the fighter pilot – the shrinking of the British film industry has seen the end of the British war film – but they have appeared in numerous television dramas. The most ambitious was the 1988 adaptation of Derek Robinson's novel *Piece of Cake* (1983). Angus Calder has expertly pointed out that Robinson's decision painstakingly to debunk the myth of the Battle of Britain actually ends up supporting it. By stressing the chaos and inefficiencies of Fighter Command and its systems, the book increases admiration for the British skill of improvisation and good humour. By stressing the seemingly awesome ability of the Luftwaffe, the reader becomes more and more impressed by the *laissez-faire* manner with which the pilots treat life and death. In trying to smash the myth, albeit in a very interesting and entertaining book, one is left yelling out 'alright then, if the Luftwaffe was so much better, why the hell didn't the Germans win?' As Calder has noted, what Robinson cannot defeat is the big fact – he cannot end with a Luftwaffe victory.[24] Whatever is thrown against the myth, it will always end up floundering on the final rock inscribed 'But we still won'.

Trying to turn such an interpretation of the Battle of Britain into palat-able Sunday evening entertainment was too tough a task for the produc-tion team, and *Piece of Cake* did not inspire viewers; its approach was never likely to be palatable to the British people. Even the cast seemed to be at odds with the script, though they expressed it unwittingly. Nathaniel Parker took his role extremely seriously, feeling the weight of family history: two of his uncles were Spitfire pilots, and both were killed. He saw his role as a tribute to them, wearing one of his uncle's old flying scarves throughout the shooting. According to Parker, the cast had got inside the skins of their characters, so much so that 'it's not a cast any-more, it's a squadron, you see'. He even grew attached to 'his' Spitfire, feeling a genuine pride and affection for the machine.[25] The myth con-quers all because it feels so right and has the big facts on its side.

Some images of fighter pilots, however, have disappeared since the war, while others have grown from scratch. The lost image is that of the Yank in the RAF. During the war much publicity value was made out of Americans serving in the Royal Air Force; a special unit, Eagle Squadron, was created in 1940 to show a still neutral America what its boys were doing for decency and democracy. A clutch of movies came out of their exploits: *A Yank in the RAF* (1941), *International Squadron* (1942) and *Eagle Squadron* (1942). All three films presented the Americans as bold, but brash and rather selfish. While serving with the RAF they come to appreciate British values of sportsmanship and gentlemanly behaviour. These films were successful with the British public on their initial release, but have disappeared from the popular consciousness since.[26] This is hardly surprising, Britain's loss of status after 1945 made it reluctant to share its finest hour with anyone else, particularly with Americans, who claimed they had won the Second World War alone. *Pearl Harbor* (2001) has recently revived the Yank in the RAF, but few in Britain appreciated this and treated it with derision.

The new image, which has appeared since 1945, is of the RAF pilot as bounder and crook. It is an extension, and manipulation, of the cocky, assured, popular-with-the-girls side of pilots seen during the war. In peacetime the blue blazer, Brylcreemed hair, moustache and debonair manner veered towards oiliness and spivery. Trevor Howard played an ex-pilot who dabbles with a bunch of crooks in *They Made Me a Fugitive* (1947). In the popular 1970s sitcom *Rising Damp*, Denholm Elliott took a cameo role as a former fighter pilot who had become a conman. When Rigsby (Leonard Rossiter) discovers his chicanery he flings him out of the house with: 'Bloody Brylcreem Boys, I don't know how we managed to win the Battle of Britain. They couldn't get half you up a ladder, you were frightened of heights.' Another sitcom, *Hi-de-Hi*, set in a holiday camp during the 1950s, starred David Griffin as Squadron Leader Clive Dempster DFC, the slightly caddish ex-pilot turned entertainments manager. Nigel Havers epitomised this vision of the veteran pilot in *The Chancer*, a television series set in the late 1940s and early 1950s. Havers' character uses his suave charm to gain money, seduce women and get in and out of all sorts of scrapes. Few of these characters are despicable; they are rogues and cads rather than utter crooks. It is an interesting variant on the myth of the fighter pilot, but it has never affected the sheen of the myth of the Few.

This sporting life

The characteristic most commonly associated with the Few, because it is one they shared with their fellow countrymen, is a sporting spirit. In 1940, with the situation so threatening, transforming the struggle against the Nazis into a sporting contest was neither ridiculous nor foolhardy. It was, in fact, a very good psychological weapon in a moment of extreme crisis, giving a manageable scale to an appalling position. Moreover, the history books said it had worked in the past. *Picture Post* felt the lesson of the past; a photograph of old men playing bowls was accompanied by the caption:

> *The Game of Drake. In the garden of an Inn near Oxford the villagers finish their game of bowls. . . . What does matter is that, at a time when Europe is again despairing and England stands once more in the shadow of the invader, the English are still playing bowls.*
>
> *In the spirit of the race, whose nonchalance in the face of impending danger has exasperated and baffled its enemies since Drake broke the might of Spain with a fleet of cockle boats and a handful of civilians, burns an unquenchable flame. Playing games is not simply a preliminary to possible victory; it is symptomatic of the impossibility of England's defeat.*[27]

When a dogfight took place above Hyde Park in September, the old men playing bowls calmly carried on with their game; nothing was going to stop them because there was nothing to be alarmed about.[28]

Patience on the bowling green linked the sporting spirit with that of nonchalance and sang-froid. This sense of detachment and aloofness has had a deep effect on the way in which 1940 has been remembered and constructed. An *Evening Standard* newsvendor's bill read: 'In the Finals – Alone'.[29] These bills also kept the public abreast of the situation in the Battle of Britain, giving the impression that it was a cricket match:

'Biggest raid ever – score 78 to 26 – England still batting.'[30] *Picture Post* commented on the arrival of Australian troops, captioning photographs of them with: 'Preparation for the test match of all time: Australians in their training camp. This summer the fight is for something more than "the Ashes". There is only one decisive fixture. The Empire versus The Rest.'[31]

The single greatest example of casting the struggle as a sporting contest was Charles Gardner's famous commentary for the BBC. Sent down to Dover to cover Luftwaffe attacks on convoy shipping in July 1940, he described the scene as if it was a boxing match or a point-to-point. Although his broadcast was not transmitted until a few days later, its sense of immediacy and excitement is palpable to this day:

> . . . Ah! Here's one coming down now! There's one coming down in flames! There's . . . somebody's hit a German, and he's coming down. There's a long streak and he's coming down completely out of control – a long streak of smoke. Aah! – the man's baled out by parachute – the pilot's baled out by parachute! He's a Junkers 87 and he's going slap into the sea, and there he goes – SMASH! – a terrific column of water! – and there was a Junkers 87. There's only one man got out by parachute, so presumably there was only a crew of one in it. . . .
>
> Yes, they're being chased home, and how they're being chased home! There are three Spitfires chasing three Messerschmitts now. Oh, boy! Look at them going! And look how the Messersch . . . eh! That is really grand! And there's a Spitfire just behind the first two – he'll get them! Ah, yes! I've never seen anything so good as this! The RAF fighters have really got these boys taped![32]

A resident of Woodbridge, Suffolk, wrote to the *Daily Telegraph* expressing delight at the commentary: 'Please tell Charles Gardner to do it again. It stirred the blood of millions who heard him. War is much too serious a thing to be taken seriously – ask any fighting man.'[33] However, not all were so happy with this approach. The same issue carried a letter taking a contrary view. 'Are the dangers of deaths of brave men to be treated like a football match?', a titled lady asked. 'Mr Gardner's running commentary on an air battle filled me with a sense of shame and revulsion – that their splendour should be so belittled.'[34] There were also debates as to whether the sporting calendar should be allowed to proceed, given the gravity of the situation. But the critics missed the point, it was just because an evil force lurked on the horizon that football and cricket matches and race meetings were so well attended.[35]

That summer of 1940 was to be dominated by images of sport. Field sports, in particular hunting, had a special resonance on two counts. First, the Nazis were seen as a pest to be eradicated. Secondly, fighter pilots were seen as gentlemen hunters, pursuing their quarry across the skies. *Picture Post* carried a debate in its letters column over the social complexion of the Home Guard. One correspondent suggested that members of the gentry might regard the threat of invasion as a hunt, to the detriment of efficiency. He argued:

> The British are a sporting race with an amateur tradition, but that does not mean that it would be disgraceful for us to use professional help. The parashots [nickname for Home Guard volunteers] are being put into the hands of the squirearchy and septuagenarians in many districts. There is a danger that some of these people might be inclined to visualize a Nazi invasion as a sort of sporting afternoon, potting paratroops from the butts with a gamekeeper to load for them, and the butler bringing up the lunch-basket at noon. One admires the spirit of these gentlemen, while advocating that the 'Players' might put up a better show.

A few weeks later came the spirited response:

> . . . your correspondent, B.J. Greene, is pleased to be facetious about the service which country gentlemen are giving to the LDV. He appears to be afraid that the joy of combating paratroops might be undertaken in a sporting spirit. And why not? There is no finer spirit, and sportsmen have no scruples about destroying vermin. These men know the lie of the land, and the only alternative would be employ a gang of poachers. I, for one, would like to see some of our famous hunts suitably armed against invaders.[36]

Both quotes serve to prove the essential substance of the sporting myth. Simply by disagreeing with the sporting ethic, although unable to resist using the 'Players' metaphor himself, Greene proved the hunting metaphor was used with sincerity. British gentlemen who indulged in huntin', fishin' and shootin' were more than ready to tackle Nazi paratroopers, even if they were disguised as nuns.

Country Life applied the method and manner of the hunter to fighter pilots, confirming Fighter Command's position as the premier hunt in the country, with its Master of Foxhounds Sir Hugh Dowding. According to the article, it was this sporting temperament that set the British apart from the Teuton:

> *But the different spirit of the two corps [RAF and Luftwaffe] is the difference between fanaticism and sport; between dying for a Führer and living for victory. A sidelight on the connection between the sporting spirit and the desperate business of our warfare can be traced in the jealously guarded point of honour that forbids RAF pilots to claim victory that is not absolutely certain, even though the exigencies of fighting have now relieved them from the necessity of producing two independent witnesses. That partly explains the great increase in a day's bag after the 'pick up'. It is no irony that those terms derive from the moors, where, even in this time, the grouse are being shot, for food and stock, in much the usual way. But not every occupant of a butt is always so scrupulous in the estimate of his bag!*[37]

Here is confirmation of the aristocratic breeding thought to be responsible for victory in the Battle of Britain. Of course, Fighter Command was not like that from top to bottom. Sergeant Pilots played a massive part in winning the victory and their achievement was not overlooked – the number of Kennington portraits of NCOs reveals this – but the dominant image is not a lie, it is not baseless and was not something crudely imposed upon a credulous public. Rather, the myth served a purpose in the cause of national survival, and it was one British history and society, and, not least, its education system, had prepared the British people for.

The hunting dogs of Fighter Command were the Hurricane and the Spitfire. These two planes have become the most famous fighter aircraft of all time to the British. The Spitfire in particular exerts a magical grip on the imagination. Among the many websites dedicated to the Battle of Britain and the Spitfire, I was happy to find that a couple have recordings of a Spitfire in flight. This provided me with an extremely jolly time, playing them again and again, enthralled by the wonderful purr of its engines. Why did it have this effect on me? After all, I know very little about mechanics, have only once flown in a turbo-prop aircraft, am not a plane spotter or devoted enthusiast of aviation. And yet that sound thrilled me. The only explanation I can find is the associations I place upon it, the text and images I read into the sound. I was not clicking on to a sound, I was clicking into a scenario, an imagined past, one heavy with iconography and pregnant with meaning. The sound opened my British family photo album, and captivated me.[38] Nathaniel Parker clearly felt the same thing, remarking on the machine while filming *Piece of Cake*, 'I've never felt strongly or anything like that before, but Spitfires are different. When one flies overhead everybody, man or woman, young or old, lets out a primeval grunt: "cooaahhh".'[39]

The 'Spitfire effect' on the British people was revealed in the summer of 2000 when an Essex-based company put the aircraft back into production. Wherever possible original parts are used, but the bulk of the components have to be handmade from scratch. The cost of each Spitfire is estimated to be £1,250,000, but when the scheme was announced it was suggested that 10–15 people had already expressed an interest in purchasing one. Proof that the Battle of Britain has become a 'boy's own adventure' is provided by the sales pitch, for it was promoted as 'the ultimate toy'.[40]

But that is little different from the way they were perceived in 1940. Spitfires and Hurricanes were invested with a mysterious aura. Spitfires managed to win the lion's share of the attention thanks to the beauty of its design, even if the Hurricane was the faithful workhorse of the Battle of Britain. Sleek, graceful and fast, the Spitfire epitomised everything aerial combat was alleged to be, the sabre of the skies. E.H. Keating, an MP, complained in the summer of 1940 about the defensive attitude of mind revealed in the obsession with the fighters. He believed the public should show more interest in the offensive, in Bomber Command. Dorothy L. Sayers, the creator of Lord Peter Wimsey, refuted this attitude in the *Daily Telegraph*, touching upon the national character and its love of the underdog and 'backs to the wall' scenarios:

> *Defensive attitudes and defeatist mentality be hanged. We need not rush out, like mad psychologists to dig for hidden ambitions, when there are plenty of good, human, sentimental reasons why Hurricanes and Spitfires should have caught the public imagination.*
>
> *First, a fighter plane is, comparatively speaking, a very small machine and there is something irresistibly endearing about a very small*

thing that fights like hell . . . [and] when a ferocious giant has been
coming at one with a club, this impulse to send the hat round for Jack
the Giant-Killer is too strong to be restrained by calculations of policy.[41]

The hat doing the rounds, referred to by Sayers, was that in aid of
Spitfire Funds. The obsessive desire with which people contributed to
these funds, and the huge interest in them, reveal the core of reality
constant in the lining of the Battle of Britain myth. For all the evidence
debunkers like to bring forward of collapsing morale, of panic, of a lack
of community spirit, here is the big fact. Thousands of communities,
large and small, from across the British empire and Commonwealth
contributed to Spitfire Funds with great zest. The idea originated with
the Jamaican newspaper *The Gleaner*, which contacted Lord Beaverbrook,
at that time Minister of Aircraft Production, asking how much a bomber
cost. A week later the Air Ministry produced a figure, £20,000. The
money was immediately cabled. Beaverbrook, with his eye for publicity,
suggested through the pages of one of his newspapers, the *Daily Express*,
that each town and city in Britain should pay for a Spitfire, quoting the
sum of £5,000. Worcester and Wimbledon were the first to respond, and
were promised Spitfires named in their honour.

From there the scheme spiralled. For smaller communities, or individuals unable to pay the full amount, the Air Ministry produced a price
list of components. A guinea bought a thermometer, sixpence a rivet,
£2,000 a wing and fifteen shillings the blast tube of a machine-gun. As
Addison and Crang have pointed out in *The Burning Blue: A New History
of the Battle of Britain*, this was one of the ways in which the Battle of
Britain became truly that: Spitfire Funds drew in the whole nation. A
struggle played out over the skies of south-eastern England could appear
remote to the vast majority of the population, but the funds gave everyone a stake in the battle. Cardiff raised £20,000, Belfast £72,000, £10,000
came from Durham miners, £20,000 from Heinz factory workers, £6,400
from the tiny islands of Lewis and Harris, £50,000 from the Falkland
Islands (from a population of 3,000!), £5,000 from the Kennel Club.
Poignantly, a bereaved father sent the savings of his son, who lost his life
serving in the RAF, along with a contribution from the rest of the village
adding up to £5,000. The money rolled in at an average of £1 million a
month, and topped £13 million by April 1941. As Humphrey Jennings'

brilliant documentary film, *Heart of Britain* (1941) said, 'the Nazis will learn, once and for all, that no one with impunity troubles the heart of Britain'.[42]

Enthusiasm for the Spitfire was reflected in the popularity of a BBC special feature, *Spitfires over Britain*, broadcast on 25 June 1940 and advertised by a dramatic photograph on the front cover of the *Radio Times*. The programme covered the response of a Spitfire squadron to a German bombing attack on trawlers. Although a fictional incident, the piece aimed to be authentic, providing a record of the routines and responses of the RAF. A narrator filled in the gaps, as if he was witnessing the events, in Charles Gardner style, while the pilots were heard talking to base through their wireless sets. It was a great success, bringing home the drama of the Battle of Britain to the whole country and was a benchmark for later BBC war 'documentaries'.[43]

Et in arcadia ego

The Britain the battle was fought over was regarded as the essence of the nation. The land of the Few was defined and encapsulated by the rolling countryside of south-east England. A well-matured, well-known vision of the heart of Britain was deployed throughout the war, but most potently in the summer of 1940. This vision conceived Britain as a rural idyll, of happy country folk who toiled in fields of golden wheat. Medieval church towers dominated villages characterised by Tudor 'black and white' architecture. It was precisely because most people in Britain lived in the great industrial cities, and had been the first people in the world to adapt to mass urbanisation, that the attraction of this rural myth was so appealing.

In 1940 the rural myth was used as a visual shorthand for everything the British considered themselves to be, a reminder of what they were fighting for and the antithesis of what they were fighting against. An English village had a sense of solidity, of time-honoured codes, of rank tempered by responsibility and interdependability, of isolationism, a happy breed. Since the nineteenth century the British had been eulogising their countryside and fretting over its imminent demise. The National Trust and *Country Life* campaigned to protect rural landscapes, buildings and trades. The campaign was made all the more urgent by the deep agricultural depression of the 1920s and 1930s. During this period the countryside became more accessible thanks to road-building schemes and the slow rise in motoring. H.V. Morton's popular travel books encouraged people to search out their rural roots, and John Betjeman's Shell guides, illustrated by Paul Nash, rhapsodised over Perpendicular churches and market crosses. For those unable to afford motoring holidays, the newly discovered joys of hiking and cycling provided a link with the perceived heart of the nation. London Underground advertised the joys of the 'near countryside' in its posters, urging Londoners to go on bus trips to Epping, Chislehurst caves, Dorking and Farnham. Cockneys saw the wonders of the 'garden of England', quitting the city each summer to go 'hopping' in Kent. When the Battle of Britain broke over that garden, it was easy to perceive it as a struggle for the very heart and soul of the nation.[44]

In August 1940, H.V. Morton told readers of *Country Life* that the circumstances of the time had shrunk the nation to a village. 'It came to me that one of the most remarkable things about this war is the quiet way England has, for many of us, ceased to be a country, or even a county, and had now become a parish.' For him, this was no bad thing as there was a special and unique bond between the Englishman and the soil, which ensured the nation maintained its equilibrium. 'I think we know where this spirit of happy contentment in life comes from: it comes from the particular relation, the secret compact that the Englishman has entered into with nature.'[45]

This was not a belief confined to the Romantic right, it stretched through to the Romantic left, imbued with the spirit of William Morris and Robert Blatchford's Romantic Socialism. In a series of issues, *Picture Post* published sets of beautiful photographs emphasising the glories of the English countryside, sensing the pulse of the English people in the landscape. A radical patriotism came through its interpretation of the countryside. This was a war in which the old ways of Britain were to be defended, but at the same time the struggle was for a new and better nation. On 22 June 1940 *Picture Post* carried photos of a hay meadow in the Lakes, of a stream in Ambleside, lakes at Llyn Crafnant and the little railway bridge at Pentrevealas in Wales, remarking:

Under the sunshine of a lovely summer, the fields and woods of Britain – the fields and woods we are all fighting to protect.

This is Britain. This is the land which has withstood the tramp of the invaders for 900 years. This is the soil we are fighting for. We are not fighting to snatch what belongs to someone else. We are fighting to protect what is ours. No single Briton wants fresh territory. We are not in this war for land, for money, for 'imperialism'. We are in this war to save our homes, our freedom and – if it turns out that way – our lives. But first our homes and freedom . . . we are fighting for a chance – a chance to make a new, just and equal world . . .[46]

A few weeks later, on 6 July, the prose reached a quite remarkable purple. Photos of the villages of Kersey (Suffolk), Broadhembury (Devon), Wilmcote (Warwickshire), and a Gloucestershire village were published under the title 'The Land We Are Fighting For'. The accompanying text fulfilled Morton's vision – the whole nation appeared to have become a village. But it was no simplistic bucolic or pastoral vision, for underlying it was the urge to action and to arms, the duty of all in the People's War. It was presented as a tour of the village sights. The pub was pointed out as the place where people were free to gossip and debate as they please, without fear of reprisal. The church becomes the symbol of a Christian civilisation holding barbarity at bay, while the village school teaches children the values of decency and tolerance. Ramming home the message with great poignancy are the references to the village war memorial, on the panels of which are carved the names of those who gave their lives in the earlier struggle against Teutonic evil:

The things for which Britain is fighting now are all just up the street, all just over the way. We are fighting so that the villagers who worship shall not be persecuted for their faith. So that their children shall not have pumped into them at school the creed of domination and force. So that the men in the pub can continue to speak their minds without fearing that the man next to them is in the pay of the Gestapo. So that the villagers whose familiar names are engraved on the war memorial shall not have died for nothing.[47]

People were urged to man the barricades and prepare for invasion, they were told that the village could become a Nazi outpost if they didn't. Each Briton had to unite with his fellow countryman to ensure the safety of the nation, otherwise 'Village Britain' was doomed.

This call to co-operation, for a 'village socialism', was also seen in the Boutling Brothers short film, *Dawn Guard* (1941). Starring Bernard Miles and Percy Walsh as Home Guard volunteers standing guard on a hilltop overlooking the English countryside, the film shows the stirrings of the People's War, and how the symbols of 'deep England' could be used to impart radical messages. At one point Bernard Miles, emphasising his yokel twangs, articulates the revulsion of many against the guilty men of the 1930s who had claimed helplessness in the face of economic depression and left Britain criminally unprepared for war. He compares it to the rallying of the nation at Dunkirk, and how the communal effort had made the seemingly impossible viable:

> *Coo, look at that Dunkirk. Weren't no unemployed there. Each man had a job to do and he done it. And that's what we got to see they have in peacetime – a job. . . . There mustn't be no more chaps hanging around for work that don't come. No more slums neither. No more dirty, filthy back-streets and no more half-starved children with no room to play in. . . . We can't go back to the old ways of living, leastways not all of it. That's gone forever and the sooner we make up our minds about that the better.*[48]

A similar spirit can be detected in J.B. Priestley, the Bradford man so in love with the countryside of southern England. He revelled in the glories of the English countryside, identifying it as the true home of every Englishman. The Sunday after Dunkirk he broadcast on the wonderful spring weather. The homeliness of his subject contrasted with the scale and intensity of the experience the nation had just gone through. But he managed to fill it with historic portent, believing there had never been a spring as lovely as the one just passing into summer. By building up the timelessness of the countryside in a slow, deliberate manner he paved the way for a comparison with the awfulness of Nazi Germany, a country in love with the tinny, shrill sound of militarism. But there was also a left-leaning political message in his vision of the land. On Sunday 16 June he broadcast on his local Home Guard unit. He saw the volunteers as something from Hardy's Wessex, investing the countryside with a sense of continuity. However, he also stressed the ordinariness of the volunteers; farm-hands and labourers had come together and organised themselves, preparing to fight off the invader. This was a People's War all right, a people of a rich and sacred soil.[49]

Landscape and memory conjoined most significantly in the summer of 1940 on Dover and its white cliffs. With its castle dominating the high ground and sheer cliffs, this impressive landscape had a grip on the national imagination, and was associated with 'fortress Britain', long before 1940. Dover was the key to the nation and its first line of defence against foreign invasion. Newspaper cartoonists used it for symbolic effect throughout the Battle of Britain. Zec, the *Mirror*'s brilliant cartoonist, caught Britain's island mentality and alliance with the seas on 20 June. He drew Neptune as a British ally, sitting against the cliffs of Dover, holding his trident high as if to protect the nation, his crown bearing the tag 'HMS Crown'. 'The Old Ally still remains!' read the caption. The famous song and Alice Duer Miller's epic narrative poem, *The White Cliffs of Dover*, turned into a film in 1944 by Metro Goldwyn Mayer, connected the city and its landscape to the war most intimately.[50]

As Priestley noted, the weather of 1940 was heavenly. That's certainly the way it has been recorded in the popular memory. The seasons seemed to realise the significance of the moment and summer set out to provide it with a fitting frame. 1940 was, after all, the 'Spitfire Summer', in which the Few flew the azure skies in their duck egg blue and traced contour trails high over the hop fields and orchards of Kent where shire horses lazily clip-clopped along cobbled roads as they had for centuries and children stood on five-barred gates awestruck at the weavings of the machines overhead. In 2000 the Imperial War Museum held a special exhibition to mark the anniversary. Both it and its accompanying book were titled *Spitfire Summer*. On the opening page of Malcolm Brown's fascinating book are three definitions. The first is of 'Spitfire', the second 'summer', and the last 'Spitfire Summer', which says, 'Phrase of uncertain origin, betokening a period of historic importance in the history of Great Britain; lived through with defiance and looked back on with pride.' Peter Haining's book on the same period is also called *Spitfire Summer* (1990); and Paul Addison and Jeremy Crang hinted at an equally wonderful season in the title of their book about the Battle of Britain, *The Burning Blue* (2000). We all accept that it was a glorious summer, for it makes the drama complete. Britain struggled for its very life in the season when people feel most carefree, when people look forward to hard-earned holidays, when crops reach their peak. Hardy's influence on our national memory of the countryside is also perceptible here and, as he would have it, the contrast creates a satire of circumstances, a satire also seen in the way the long, hot summer of 1914 is remembered.

It wasn't quite like that, as Laurence Thompson has pointed out, but by the same token the evidence does not dispel the myth either.[51] May and June were warm, dry and sunny, especially June when temperatures were above average. July was unmemorable, being cool and wet, but things cheered up in August with average sunshine and temperatures. September started warm and sunny, but turned cool after the first week.[52] Not quite as we would have it, but the memory is not altogether nonsense and shapes our responses to that period. Spike Milligan encapsulates the composite and communal memory of the Spitfire Summer:

> . . . it was a wonderful 'shirts off' summer. Around us swept the countryside of Sussex. There were the August cornfields that gave off a golden halitus, each trembling ear straining up for the sun. The Land Girls looked brown and inviting and promised an even better harvest. On moonlight nights haystacks bore lovers on through their primitive course, by day there was shade aplenty, oaks, horse chestnuts, willows, all hung out wooden arms decked with the green flags of summer.[53]

1940 will forever be a song of summer.

Cometh the hour, cometh the man

The land of the Few got themselves a new tribal leader in 1940. Winston Churchill's reputation and achievements are by anyone's standards incredible, and he is a truly legendary figure. The popular vision of Churchill is as the inspirational leader of the British people in the Second World War, seeing them through both their finest hours and darkest days. He urged them on to victory thanks to the power of his stirring oratory. 1940 was the moment he came to fulfil his, and the nation's, destiny. He perceived it in those terms and acted according to those stage directions.

It cannot be doubted that Churchill's personal standing remained high throughout the war. He retained the confidence of the people, proven by numerous opinion polls, in which his popularity never dipped below 78 per cent. His personal standing was due to a number of reasons. It was partly the fact that although born with a silver spoon in his mouth, he was nevertheless an outsider. Shunned by the majority of the Conservative party in the 1930s, Churchill was not tainted by association with the Chamberlain gang of guilty men, who, it was widely believed, had got Britain into such a mess.

Churchill enjoyed himself as Prime Minister. It was, perhaps, that impression more than any other that explained his success. Relishing a fight in a tough corner, he touched upon the very essence of the nation in 1940. He gave expression to the British love of a good fight. By not accepting Hitler's peace overtures in 1940, Churchill revealed a streak of bloody-mindedness that placed him very much in tune with the nation. Robert Westall recalled Churchill's significance to his boyhood self. Far from being the spokesmen of 'mere' children, he identified the essence of Churchill's appeal. For Westall, Churchill was a gang leader, and that's exactly what he was – boss of the British gang – and he loved him for the panache with which he insulted enemy leaders, thus giving vent to the innate xenophobia of the British. Commenting on the famous photograph of Churchill posing with a tommy-gun, replete with hat and cigar, Westall enthused that he was really some sort of super-child, capable of anything. In that photograph he looks so like a child pleased with himself, and the incongruity of the hat and suit are all part of the joke on the rest of the world: 'He invariably gave the impression he was not only going to win, but was going to enjoy every minute of it. When he passed among us, people would shout, "Give the bastards one for us, Winnie," and he would lift his hat and smile obligingly.'[54] The gang leader image was reinforced by David Low's famous cartoon, 'All Behind You, Winston', in which Churchill and the new government, including such diverse characters as Attlee and Halifax, Bevin and Sinclair, all march forward with a look of steely determination on their faces, rolling up their sleeves as they go. 'The awesome thing is the rolling-up of sleeves', comments Westall, 'working men really did roll up their sleeves in 1940, very slowly and methodically, almost meditatively before starting a job or fight.'[55] Thus did Churchill appear to the British people; it was a brilliant collusion of a man who saw himself in the role of the warrior and a people happy to agree with him and play their parts too. As British backs were pushed up against the wall, Churchill was the man to inspire them. This was true for the left as well as the right, probably more so given the Chamberlainite Conservatives' suspicion of Churchill the maverick. Kingsley Martin, writing in *Picture Post*, saw him as the man of the hour who could remind the nation of its essentials: 'In Mr Churchill we have found a man of action, who sweeps all this aside and reminds us that, whatever else we are or think we are, we were born and bred British, and British we must now live or die.'[56]

Having a tremendous sense of the majesty of British history, he was in tune with a people never more aware of their past, and of who and what they were. Paul Addison has stressed that Churchill's popularity grew out of the succession of disasters which melded the people together into a fierce tribal unity. It was in this historic moment, felt most keenly by Churchill, that Britain prepared itself to stand with him in order to write the next equally significant chapter in the long history of the nation.[57]

The last reason for Churchill's popularity was the perception that he was a straight talker – ironic, perhaps, given his purple turn of phrase. People felt that Churchill didn't 'bullshit' them. Kingsley Martin commented on his speeches:

> In this war, Mr Churchill's oratory has found a new and more powerful range. As a broadcaster he alone among public men has clothed in living language the realities of this war. . . . Here at last one has got to the bed-rock, to the final and conclusive reason for Mr Churchill's hold on the nation.[58]

This militates against those who seek to undermine the myth, for it reveals a reflexive, cognisant public, suspicious of being fed utter twaddle. But, this does not make the British people ultra cynical either. Rather, it was a complex balance of accepting 'propaganda' when it made sense to them and their understanding of the world, and rejecting it when it didn't. People and state reached a knowing understanding, with Churchill accepted as the straight talker at the top.

Our image of Churchill is very much connected with his skill as an orator. Today his speeches can make people shiver with emotion and excitement, which are often used to accompany original film footage in documentaries. We imagine ourselves listening to him in 1940, inspired, as they were, to do their duty in the finest hour. However, this is where the myth is most complicated, for popular and significant as Churchill's oratory undoubtedly was, our agenda and checklist of his most important speeches is different from that of the time.

There is little doubt that Churchill's speeches were a tremendous part of Britain's war, often defining the mood of the people. John Brophy, looking back over the war in 1945, noted that Churchill's oratory was 'magnificently inflected by the sense of the historic occasion till it became far more than oratory, became, in fact, the voice of a people defiantly shaping their own destiny'.[59] Most of the Churchill speeches we regard as vital examples of his power to hold the nation enthralled were designed to be delivered in the Commons. Churchill broadcast few of these speeches; of those that were broadcast, the modern memory has often found them less inspiring. Our 'big four' of 1940 are 'Blood, toil, tears and sweat', delivered on 13 May; 'Never Surrender', 4 June; 'Their Finest Hour', 18 June and 'The Few' on 20 August. But only one of the above was actually broadcast to the public at the time, 'Their Finest Hour', which was judged to be a much less effective rendition than that delivered to the Commons.[60]

But this in no way diminishes the Churchill myth as other speeches broadcast by the BBC did receive a tremendous response. 'The War of the Unknown Warrior', broadcast on 14 July and now almost unknown, was judged to be highly effective by Home Intelligence.[61] It is easy to see why this speech registered at the time but has since been lost. Churchill addressed the moment; he encouraged the Home Guard and made a direct appeal to ordinary citizens to 'do their bit'. It lacks the stirring timelessness of 'Their Finest Hour', which we find so appealing, seeing the summer of 1940 from such a distance as we do.

Churchill's speeches often found their way into the public memory by a slightly circuitous route. 'Their Finest Hour' speech, for example, was printed under the Royal Coat of Arms as a poster and newspaper advertisement.[62] Other speeches were often printed in the newspapers. The highbrow broadsheet dailies carried them as part of their routine parliamentary coverage. Their significance is revealed by their inclusion in the popular dailies. Both the *Daily Mirror* and the *Daily Express* repro-duced the 'Finest Hour' and 'The Few' speeches in full; the *Mirror* gave over the front page to 'Their Finest Hour', while the *Express* noted, 'After Mr Churchill's speech, the mood of the people will be behind their great leader. They will challenge the enemy to come and try it on the English. For they will never yield one blade of grass of this green island.'[63] Later in the summer, the *Express* urged Parliament to allow all Churchill's speeches to be broadcast direct from the Commons. 'It is just plain foolish that such spontaneous [!] eloquence as is natural to the Prime Minister should be reserved for first-hand consumption by 615 men elected to Westminster.'[64]

The other important mechanism for imparting Churchill's words was by a newscaster reading them on the wireless. Whole speeches were often read out verbatim, then, thanks to Churchill's extraordinarily high profile and standing, people began to believe they had heard Churchill himself deliver them, as Clive Ponting and Sian Nicholas have pointed out.[65] What cannot be denied, however, is that no matter how it was disseminated, Churchill's oratory was important to the British people in their war. After the war, largely thanks to the recordings of the speeches issued on gramophone record, to Churchill's extraordinary gift for self-publicity and to the equally extraordinary cult of his personality, based on genuine wartime achievements, the memory of what Churchill was thought to have said to the British people during the conflict itself became confused and gave us a different canon of great speeches.[66] Churchill's speeches became the way in which the British like to remember 1940, and indeed the whole war; the history and nature of the experience was connected to his oratory. Although our modern memory might lay emphasis on different sections of his canon, there is no evidence to show that Churchill's speeches, taken as a whole, do not provide a genuine insight into the British people at war.

The Battle of Britain, like Dunkirk before it, served to emphasise the separation of Britain from continental Europe. It underlined Britain's perception of itself as a very special place, populated by a very special people, who were never happier than when facing a seemingly hopeless situation. Led by the inspirational Winston Churchill, the British people faced their finest hour and found a blueprint in their history – it was all part of what they expected as Britons. Since 1940 the popular memory has remained remarkably consistent, although officers and gentlemen have come to dominate the image of the RAF. Britain continues to believe in the magical Spitfire Summer. Even though it wasn't perhaps *quite* like that, it certainly was not totally dissimilar. The myths remains with us because people willed it that way at the time, they read the signs that way and made them history, and that is how it has been transmitted ever since.

Notes

1 Charles Eade (ed.), *War Speeches of Winston Churchill*, 3 vols (London 1951), vol. I, pp. 234–44.

2 *Daily Express* 16 September 1940.

3 Jeremy Paxman, *The English: A Portrait of a People* (London 1998), pp. 83–4.

4 For more details on fighter pilots in inter-war films, see Michael Paris, *From the Wright Brothers to* Top Gun: *Aviation, Nationalism and Popular Cinema* (Manchester 1995).

5 *Country Life* 24 August 1940 (vol. LXXXVIII, no. 2275).

6 *Daily Mirror* 28 June 1940.

7 *Picture Post* 28 September 1940.

8 Richard Hillary, *The Last Enemy* (London 1997; orig. 1942), p. 15.

9 Ibid., p. 97.

10 Eric Kennington, *Drawing the RAF* (London 1942), p. 33.

11 Angus Calder, 'The Battle of Britain and Pilots' Memoirs', in Paul Addison and Jeremy Crang (eds), *The Burning Blue: A New History of the Battle of Britain* (London 2000), pp. 193–4.

12 Some good examples are *British Movietone News* 15 July 1940, 5 August 1940, 22 August 1940; *British Gaumont News* 16 September 1940; *Pathé Gazette* 7 October 1940.

13 Quoted in Paul Nash, *Paul Nash: Paintings and Watercolours* (London 1975), p. 95.

14 See Kennington, *Drawing the RAF*.

15 Quoted in Robert Murphy, *British Cinema and the Second World War* (London 2000), pp. 216–17.

16 Spike Milligan *Adolf Hitler: My Part in His Downfall* (Harmondsworth 1987; orig. 1971), p. 55.

17 Anthony Aldgate and Jeffrey Richards, *Britain Can Take It: The British Cinema in the Second World War* (Oxford 1986), p. 53.

18 See S.P. MacKenzie, *British War Films 1939–1945* (London 2001), pp. 150–1.

19 *Daily Telegraph* 16 September 1940.

20 Paul Brickhill, *Reach for the Sky* (London 2000; orig. 1954), p. 186.

21 MacKenzie, *British War Films*, p. 153.

22 See *Daily Telegraph* 7 July 1956; *Daily Herald* 6 July 1956; *Daily Express* 6 July 1956.

23 Although Czech director Jan Sverak's powerful 2001 movie about Czech pilots in the RAF, *Dark Blue World*, had a plot line revolving around the Battle of Britain, due to its very limited distribution this interesting film has failed to make any impact on the British public.

24 Angus Calder, *The Myth of the Blitz* (London 1991), p. 163.

25 *TV Times* 1 October 1988.

26 For a discussion of these films, see H. Mark Glancy, *When Hollywood Loved Britain: The Hollywood 'British' Film 1939–1945* (Manchester 1999), pp. 117–28.

27 *Picture Post* 6 July 1940.

28 Angus Calder, *The People's War* (London 1997; orig. 1969), p. 151.

29 Quoted in Tim Brooke-Taylor, *Rule Britannia: The Ways of the World and the True British Gentleman Patriot* (London 1983), p. 110.

30 Calder, *People*, p. 150.

31 *Picture Post* 6 July 1940.

32 Quoted in Malcolm Brown, *Spitfire Summer* (London 2000), pp. 92–3.

33 Ibid., p. 93.

34 Ibid.

35 Ibid., pp. 67–8.

36 Ibid., p. 73.

37 *Country Life* 24 August 1940 (vol. LXXXVIII, no. 2275).

38 A good example is the website www.spitfires.flyer.co.uk. Accessed 10 July 2001.

39 *TV Times* 1 October 1988.

40 *Daily Telegraph* 23 July 2000.

41 Quoted in Brown, *Spitfire Summer*, pp. 112–13.

42 For the Spitfire Funds, see Brown, *Spitfire Summer*, pp. 110–13; Calder, *People*, pp. 149–50; Peter Haining, *Spitfire Summer: The People's Eye View of the Battle of Britain* (London 1990), pp. 38–9; and Paul Addison and Jeremy Crang (eds), *The Burning Blue: A New History of the Battle of Britain* (London 2000), pp. 248–9.

43 See Brown, *Spitfire Summer*, pp. 107–8, and Sian Nicholas, *The Echo of War: Home Front Propaganda and the Wartime BBC, 1939–45* (Manchester 1996), pp. 190–227.

44 For an extended discussion of these ideas in 1940, see Calder, *Myth*, pp. 180–208.

45 *Country Life* 24 August 1940 (vol. LXXXVIII, no. 2275).

46 *Picture Post* 22 June 1940.

47 Ibid., 6 July 1940.

48 Quoted in Malcolm Smith, *Britain and 1940* (London 2000), p. 50.

49 See J.B. Priestley, *Postscripts* (London 1940), pp. 5–8, 9–13, 54–9.

50 See Rory Semple's forthcoming PhD thesis, 'Dover's Bunker Mentality: Dover, its People and its Tunnels in the two World Wars' (University of Kent).

51 Laurence Thompson, *1940: Year of Legend, Year of History* (London 1966), p. 139.

52 Ibid.

53 Milligan, *Hitler*, p. 33.

54 Robert Westall, *Children of the Blitz: Memories of Wartime Childhood* (London 1985), p. 77. The Germans used this photograph to prove Churchill's gangster habits in the magazine, *The Sniper*. I am indebted to Professor David Welch for this reference.

55 Ibid., p. 79.

56 *Picture Post* 1 June 1940.

57 Paul Addison, *Churchill on the Home Front* (London 1992), pp. 326–34.

58 *Picture Post* 1 June 1940.

59 John Brophy, *Britain's Home Guard: A Character Study* (London 1945), p. 15.

60 Calder, *People*, p. 79.

61 PRO INF1/264 Home Intelligence Daily Report, 15 July 1940.

62 See for example, *Daily Express* 21 June 1940.

63 *Daily Express* 19 June 1940.

64 Ibid., 23 August 1940.

65 See Clive Ponting, *1940: Myth and Reality* (London 1990), pp. 157–60; Nicholas, *Echo of War*, p. 57.

66 See John Ramsden's excellent article on the post-war Churchill cult, 'Churchill: "The Greatest Living Englishman"', *Contemporary British History* 12, 3 (Autumn 1998), pp. 1–40.

. . . .

CHAPTER 4

London Pride has been handed down to us: the blitz, September 1940–May 1941

The blitz, the name given to the German bombing campaign against Britain, is linked with Dunkirk and the Battle of Britain to form the third panel in the triptych of 1940. And, along with these other two events, is an experience the 'sensationalist revisionists' are keen to debunk.

Blitz comes from the German *Blitzkrieg*, meaning lightning war, and implied an all-arms campaign of short, shocking intensity. It was thus a misnomer when applied to the prolonged bombing of British cities, but the name stuck and it will never be changed. Although there is some debate over exactly where and when the blitz began and ended, it is generally agreed that it commenced with the bombing of London on 7 September 1940. For the next 76 nights (excluding 2 November when the weather deterred the Luftwaffe) London was raided. In October and November, the Nazis extended their attack to other British cities, most notably Coventry on 14 November. The bombing continued until mid-May 1941, but then petered out as Hitler's attention was taken up by the final preparations for the invasion of the USSR.

Along with its 1940 stable-mates, the myth of the blitz is vital to British national identity. According to this memory, it provided, and continues to provide, proof of the distinct qualities of the island race. It is remembered as the moment when the Few of Churchill's island stood shoulder to shoulder, regardless of class or creed, and withstood the 'full terror, might and fury of the enemy'.[1] Instead of buckling, the people laughed and joked their way through it, full of wonderful British sang-froid. King and Queen came to know their people and their people them, as all did their bit without murmur. The myths of the blitz are defined by a set of visual images that define London and the provincial cities under bombing. These visual images then impart messages of defiance, solidarity and togetherness, and improvisation in the face of a powerful enemy. By surviving this experience, Britain bought the freedom of the world. Like most events of 1940, the blitz is something the British people can look on with pride, and the endurance and fortitude of the nation in the face of it is something the world should thank us for now and forever more. In this way is the blitz remembered and conceived.

Malcolm Smith points out that the blitz and 1940 have been interpreted in two ways, creating two competing political mythologies, one of the left and one of the right. For Smith, the left-wing myth emphasises the collapse of the bad, old guard (as symbolised by Chamberlain), the rise of Attlee and his fine team of colleagues, the triumph of the British people in the face of adversity and a distinct move towards 1945 and the welfare state. The right-wing interpretation stresses the deep patriotism of the British people, the greatness of the island race and its standing in world affairs, and Winston Churchill's stature as leader. According to Smith, in the 1960s the left-wing version came under increasing attack from new left criticisms of the compromises made by the Labour party in wartime and the immediate post-war years, while the new right would come to criticise the Conservative party for not recognising that the country was being hijacked by the left during the long years of war. The triumph of Thatcherism in the 1980s ensured that a right-wing interpretation would become dominant, playing up the elements of patriotism and greatness while playing down the elements of state intervention and the first shoots of the welfare state.[2]

The 'sensationalist revisionists' of the myth of the blitz have made many attempts to tear it down. They have revelled in the fact that crime rose during the blitz, and have gleefully reproduced reports on low morale. They have highlighted that Britain's survival was hardly a unique occurrence to be celebrated as such, pointing out the example of German and Japanese endurance in the face of determined bombing. Clive Ponting certainly took this view in *1940: Myth and Reality*. But, as Malcolm Smith has pointed out, Ponting's argument is limited in its usefulness:

> *The myth was made not* primarily *to mislead the British, as Ponting implies, but to help them to survive not just another political mess but the greatest threat in their national history. That myth was necessary to help them to make sense of the disaster, and to fight on. The alternative was to come to terms with the Nazis: in the circumstances, whatever was needed, it was not Ponting's notion of reality.*[3]

As Smith would argue, the big fact remains: Britain did not crumble during the blitz, it survived and remained the sole nation in arms against the Nazi empire.

The blitz continues to play a large role in our national memory. It remains impervious to debunking and is continually reinforced. According to the historian Lucy Noakes, the blitz is becoming *the* central event in the public memory of the war.[4] She suggests this is because the blitz is an easily understood, dramatic story that does not require much expert knowledge of military, diplomatic or political history. The exciting elements often appeal to children and, as the blitz was something that affected the Home Front, it is an experience with which women can empathise. The Imperial War Museum's Blitz Experience is identified by Noakes as an important medium through which people gain knowledge of the campaign. Museums, and especially one as prestigious as the Imperial War Museum, are powerful shapers of perceptions; they confer authority on interpretations of the past. People visit museums in order to gain knowledge and in the belief that the collections of artefacts and explanations are legitimate and learned. Therefore when something like the blitz 'become[s] the subject of numerous or particularly important museum exhibitions and displays, aspects of the past can change their meaning. They cease to be just a part of *history* and instead have the potential to become part of our shared, national, *heritage.*'[5]

Welcomed by the warm tones of a cockney Air Raid Precautions warden, the Blitz Experience allows visitors to sit in a replica of an East

End air-raid shelter. Once in the shelter, the warden introduces the visitor to the other occupants and their voices are heard. Bombs fall around the shelter, including one near miss which makes the visitors rock on their benches. A museum guide then leads visitors out into a street which has been wrecked by bombing, while the voices of the shelterers and emergency services personnel annotate the scene. Finally, the ARP voice bids the visitors farewell and tells them not to forget. Although the Blitz Experience allows the visitor to hear the screams of an hysterical woman and states that the East End certainly was not ready to face the aerial onslaught, the overall atmosphere is that of the myth: the voices in the shelter sing 'Roll Out the Barrel', cockney humour brightens the more sobering moments and the final words of the ARP man exhorting the visitor not to forget those who endured the blitz are poignant reminders of bravery and stoicism. Significantly, a script emphasising the horrors of the blitz was rejected in favour of this more 'upbeat' version.[6] The Blitz Experience is dramatic and moving, and while it contains no untruths, it is sanitised. It is also tremendously popular, with long queues forming outside the exhibit, and it is a must for all schools visiting the museum. Knowledge of the blitz is therefore perpetuated and interpreted according to the broad parameters of its myth. Yet people do not get a sense of their heritage through museums alone, and so the many other ways in which the blitz has been perpetuated also need to be examined.

Visualising the London blitz

The blitz is very definitely a visual memory. Pictures of the blitz have retained their haunting qualities. We can imagine the look of the blitz because so many photographs were taken of it, because films were made about it during the war, and post-war films and television have repeated and reconstructed these images. Moreover, the blitz feels like a film. It has a great script: a small gang of fiercely independent people refuse to cave in to the bad guys. The bad guys decide to punish this wilful defiance in an appalling show of might. Despite the hardships, the small gang becomes even more tightly bound, laughs in the face of terror, takes everything the forces of evil can dish out and sends them packing. A simple story, but full of drama, full of powerful images and, for the British, scripted a long time before 1940. Once again, 1940 (including Dunkirk and the Battle of Britain) was the remake of the national epic.

In the *Daily Mail*'s wonderfully anglo-centric opinion, the blitz provided the crucial image of the war. On 29 December 1940, its front page carried a shot by staff photographer, H.A. Mason, of St Paul's cathedral standing proud while wreathed in smoke and flame. The headline proclaimed 'War's Greatest Picture'. Mason described taking the photograph to the *Mail*'s readers: 'Glares of many fires and sweeping clouds of smoke kept hiding the shape. Then a wind sprang up. Suddenly, the shining cross, dome and towers stood out like a symbol in the inferno. The scene was unbelievable. In that moment or two I released my shutter.'[7]

As Malcolm Smith has highlighted, fire fitted the established Judaeo-Christian mythology. Fire is apocalyptic and redemptive. The British people also knew that London had already faced one great fire, and its Wren churches were the symbol of resurrection after that event. In 1666 a phoenix had arisen from the ashes, and so it would again in 1940. Londoners and Britons had their historical script and they stuck to it.[8]

Such images as Mason's were joined, even during the war, by documentary film interpretations. The titles of the best are still well known: *London Can Take It!* (1940), *Christmas Under Fire* (1940) and *Fires Were Started* (1943). Wartime feature films also imagined and reconstructed the blitz, as in *Mrs Miniver* (1942), *In Which We Serve* (1942) and *Demi-Paradise* (1943). A way of framing, recalling and memorialising the blitz had been established. Since the war, documentaries, television dramas and films have drawn heavily on this original material, often treating reconstructed scenes as real footage. Like Dunkirk, great reliance has been placed upon relatively few images. A uniform image of the blitz has therefore come down to us. Whether we realise it or not, if we have seen a documentary on the blitz, then we have seen images from *London Can Take It!*, *Christmas Under Fire* and *Fires Were Started*. All three were government-backed propaganda films and all three were made by the same man, Humphrey Jennings. An artistic, message-laden vision of the blitz is our inheritance, but it does not necessarily follow that it is a mistaken one, a cover-up or a fabrication.

What becomes obvious from the visual record and the way it has been used since the war is that London is *the* city of the blitz. St Paul's cathedral shrouded in smoke dominates the memory just as it once dominated the London skyline. It was the crucial image of the Crown Film Unit's *London Can Take It!* Primarily made to influence opinion in the neutral United States, the film had a commentary written and spoken by the London-based American journalist, Quentin Reynolds, and was a great success on both sides of the Atlantic. Opening with a low-angle shot of St Paul's, the dome of the cathedral is confirmed as a symbol of both the capital and the nation. Backed by the majestic tones of Vaughan Williams' *London Symphony*, the film balances the stoic attitude of Londoners against the enormous task of fighting a mighty enemy. 'I can assure you that there is no panic, no fear, no despair in London town; there is nothing but determination, confidence and high courage among the people of Churchill's Island.' Quentin Reynolds' deadpan, matter-of-fact style combined with his alleged aloofness ('I am a neutral reporter') gave the documentary a sombre authority. It is an authority buttressed by a knowledge of Britain's affinity for and with its past. 'It is hard to see five centuries of labour destroyed in five seconds.' But 'a bomb has its limitations', Reynolds concludes, 'it can only destroy buildings and kill people. It cannot kill the unconquerable spirit and courage of the people of London. London can take it!' This final statement is delivered over an image of Marochetti's statue of Richard the Lionheart, the sword held high bent by bombing, and framed by the smashed windows of Westminster Hall in the background. Thus the film ends with a vision of the medieval past and one that symbolises the unity of monarchy and people in the form of Richard and the Houses of Parliament and the continuity of British history.

Retitled *Britain Can Take It!* for its domestic release, the film was greeted with enthusiasm. When it was shown in a Scottish mining village, the Ministry of Information projectionist recorded, '*Britain Can Take It!* was by far the most successful film. The reasons, I think, were because of the neutral reporter, the emphasis on the common people and the fact that it showed what the war was like.' A Mass-Observation report noted that it was 'the most frequently commented upon film, and received nothing but praise'.[9] If the actual situation was so very different from that portrayed on screen, then the film would surely have been rejected as patronising and insulting.

History brooded over Londoners during the blitz, but at one and the same time the blitz was becoming part of History. By this I mean the epic story of the nation. Past and present were fused. The heavy hand of History was most potently felt in the haunting spectacle of burnt-out Wren churches. In the winter of 1940–41, Wren's churches took on a double meaning: they became symbols of the glory of seventeenth-century London and of the heroic resistance to the modern barbarous enemy. Therefore the churches were, and are, a reminder of what Churchill called 'our long history', emphasising the weight of the past on British shoulders, and an epic moment in our recent history. Muirhead Bone's *St Bride's to St Paul's*, a sketch taken from the roof of a building just behind St Bride's, is an excellent example of this phenomenon. The sketch shows the intense damage inflicted on the few blocks between the church and the cathedral. Fire-bombs have gutted St Bride's south aisle and transept, and firemen's ladders still lie in the adjacent lane. Combined with the leafless trees and the snowy pavements (despite the recent fire), it creates a sobering picture of death and destruction. However, it is also a vision of majesty and redemption, for the tower of St Bride's remains intact and soaring, as does the noble dome of St Paul's cathedral, which still dominates the skyline. In 1944 London Underground commissioned a series of posters from Walter Spradberry, one of which showed the dome and eastern apse of St Paul's towering over the rubble. Underneath the image ran the legend '". . . the principal Ornament of our royal City, to the Honour of our Government, and of this our realm" from the "Letters Patent under the Great Seal of England the 12th day November 1675"'. Commenting on his work, Spradberry noted that it was to convey 'the sense that havoc itself was passing and with new days come new hopes'.[10] The poster implies that the great phoenix of the Great Fires (1666 and 1940) has spread its wings. London Has Taken It! London Has Arisen.

'Destiny has given England the torch of liberty to hold', said Quentin Reynolds in *Christmas Under Fire*, 'she has not let it slip.' Presiding over the blitz was also a profound sense of History having thrown up yet another leading role for the nation in the grand drama of world affairs. London felt this onus with particular force. It was a force that inspired and framed the actions of ordinary people. On 21 September 1940, the Lord Mayor of London made a radio address to the United States. It was a message of Churchillian rhetoric: 'Today London stands as the very bulwark of civilization and freedom. These streets of my city will be defended to the last. London City has sometimes been attacked, but never sacked. London has steeled herself for resistance and victory.'[11]

Noël Coward produced an equally poignant tribute to the spirit of London and its history, which resonates to this day, in his song 'London Pride'. Often simplistically referred to as a dilettante playboy, Coward was also a profound patriot with an instinctive knowledge of the spirit of ordinary Britons. Inspired by Londoners' resolution and endurance, Coward's song brilliantly sentimentalises and celebrates both the everyday details and the grand panoply of the city's history. His song referred to the spirit of the past infusing the present. It celebrated the stoic endurance of rich West Enders, frequenters of the Ritz, and the ordinary Londoners sipping pints in the 'Anchor and Crown'. For Coward the city, smudged by the smoke of both chimneys and bombs, was a symbol of indomitable pride and the never-ending glory of everyday people inspired to heights of quiet heroism by their history and nature.

The heroism of ordinary Londoners during the blitz cannot be denied, in particular those who enlisted in the fire services. In 1938 the expansion of the Air Raid Precautions and Civil Defence services led to the creation of the Auxiliary Fire Service. Drawn from ranks of civilian volunteers, the men and women of these services, often fighting prejudice from pre-war unionised specialists, carried out untold acts of bravery and endurance while holding down other jobs or occupations. Reynolds told the audience of *London Can Take It!* that every night of the blitz a 'people's army of volunteers' swung into action. This was far from a trick of high rhetoric. *War Illustrated* noted, 'Today, when every other citizen of London is close to being a hero, the fire fighters stand out. There are no words to describe their fearlessness.'[12]

The work carried out by these men and women has provided some of the most potent images of the blitz. Police Constables Arthur Cross and Fred Tibbs chronicled the blitz in photographs for the City of London Police. One of their finest is of the Salvation Army headquarters at 23 Queen Victoria Street crashing downwards. A diagonal line of window frames and bricks falls like a stage curtain, while the diagonal of a fire engine's ladder points in the opposite direction, creating an image that the memory holds tight. The surrealism of a building perfect in form, but not solid and stiff, descending downwards allows us to stand in the middle of a moment of time – the viewer is on the cusp of when before became after. Like the entire British memory of the Second World War, the photograph is a historical record but one that is still unfolding – the rubble and dust of the bombing have not settled in both the original photograph or British society. Leonard Rosoman, a fireman artist, captured a similar moment in his painting *Falling Wall*. Based on a genuine incident, it is a first-hand account of the horror and courage of the blitz. Suffused in an ochre-orange-red, the painting shows a wall falling on to firemen, tiny black silhouettes about to be buried alive. Rosoman painted the vision. His colleague, William Sansom, a journalist, recorded it in a short story, *The Wall*. As with Rosoman's painting and the photograph of Queen Victoria Street, the greatest impression made is that of time freezing:

> *Three of the storeys, thirty blazing windows and their huge frame of black brick, a hundred solid tons of hard, deep Victorian wall, pivoted over us and hung flatly over the alley. Whether the descending wall actually paused in its fall I can never know. Probably it never did. Probably it only seemed to hang there. Probably my eyes only digested its action at an early period of momentum, so that I saw it 'off true' but before it had gathered speed.*[13]

Memories and images frozen in fire are fundamental to the blitz, forming the manner in which it has been remembered and continues to be viewed. When combined with the heroism of the fire services, the image is completed. Soon after the blitz ended, the Ministry of Information took these elements and made a chronicle of one bombing raid that has become a legend, Humphrey Jennings' *Fires Were Started*.

The film tells the story of the ordinary men and women of one East London fire sub-station. The majority of them are working-class volunteers, who are joined at the start of the film by Barrett, a middle-class writer. Genuine fire service volunteers filled all the roles, with William Sansom taking the role of Barrett. Jennings stressed the easy-going comradeship of the men, a comradeship put to the test when the never-seen enemy bomb a local warehouse. In fighting the fire, one of the team, Jacko, is killed. Jacko's last look at the camera is one of grim heroism; he holds hose and guide rope in a vice-like grip, his face a mask of resolution and duty. To a people used to reproductions of eighteenth-century naval portraits, Lady Elizabeth Butler's canvases and the stoic looks on

23 Queen Victoria Street, May 1941. It is still crashing down on us over sixty years later (the Commissioner of the City of London Police/the Museum of London photograph archive).

the faces of Scott and his men in their last photograph at the South Pole, Jacko's face and attitude was no surprise, but his class and accent might have been: a shopkeeper became Britannia's shield.

Fires Were Started was begun in late 1941 but not released until 1943; it is therefore a document and chronicle of the blitz made after the event. The effect of the film was to freeze its image for posterity by creating a memorial to it while the war was still raging. It was a memorial constructed from a set of interpretative codes established during the blitz itself; a formula for the presentation of the blitz was encapsulated in *Fires Were Started* and has become the standard. Significantly, although the press greeted it with almost universal enthusiasm, the British public were only mildly interested in it. Jennings was just a little too artistic, a little too reflective for his own good.[14] Since the war, *Fires Were Started* has been used as a source of contemporary material, thus helping to blur the difference between the 'genuine' record and Jennings' highly controlled and stylised near-contemporary interpretation. Although an interpretation, *Fires Were Started* is not a fabrication; Jennings carried out months of painstaking research, he knew his material and was astounded by the heroism and devotion to duty he found in the Auxiliary Fire Service.[15] Jennings provided a visual poem of the blitz, a poem founded in the realities of the situation.

The second London image to encapsulate the blitz is that of people sleeping on the platforms of London Underground stations. We can all see those powerful photographs in our national memory. They symbolise a people unafraid and unruffled by the venom of the enemy and make us proud to be British.

During the 1930s, British governments had considered civil defence and came to a dreary conclusion. The British working class was thought to be particularly susceptible to panic and disillusion in the face of an aerial onslaught. Plans were laid to counteract mass civil disobedience and for the rapid disposal of the thousands of bodies which air raids would leave in their wake. When it came to shelters, the government considered it best to protect people in small groups. Communal shelters, it was argued, would create conditions for an agitator's field day. It would also encourage a 'deep shelter' mentality, leading people to become H.G. Wells' morlocks, tunnel dwellers who would never break the surface and resume their jobs in vital war industries.[16]

Such an approach to civil defence made the government reluctant to accept the use of the Underground as a shelter. At the same time, it was surprised that so many people wanted to take shelter in the tube, as was admitted in the semi-official publication, *War Illustrated*.[17] Londoners simply took matters into their own hands and occupied them. There was no panic, no argument. People bought platform tickets and took shelter. Unsure of what action to take, the government had to concede to this *de facto* occupation. When Labour MP, Herbert Morrison, was drafted into the post of Minister of Home Security he formally accepted the situation. But Ponting quotes from the diary of Jock Colville, Churchill's Private Secretary, claiming that Churchill wanted to ban others from using the Underground, but was happy to use a disused tube station himself.[18] However, Calder argues that Churchill was in favour of the use of the Underground, but had initially followed the opinions of civil servants and other ministers. When it became obvious that people were using the tube, Churchill sent a huffy minute, 'Pray let me have more information about this, and what has happened to supersede the former arguments.'[19] People felt safe in the tube, therefore it was good for morale. A Mass-Observation report recorded, 'Many undergrounders come to believe in the place, its ambience, as protection almost sacrosanct in qualities.'[20]

At first conditions in the tube were primitive. There were not enough toilets, little was done to improve ventilation and mosquitoes thrived in the hot, humid conditions. *Picture Post* published letters of complaint.[21] Improvements were pioneered by councils of shelterers, which petitioned the Ministry of Health. Eventually better facilities were introduced, including first-aid posts, improved sanitation and bedding.[22] This was an example of people power; as *War Illustrated* announced, 'Democracy Finds Itself in London's Tube Shelters'.[23]

But Underground stations were not entirely bomb-proof and there were some disasters, such as at Balham in October 1940 when 600 people became casualties. In March 1943, a panic broke out at Bethnal Green tube after a nearby explosion. The mass of people rushing to the station caused some to slip on the steps and in the resulting crush 197 men, women and children were killed. The official report into this dreadful accident was suppressed at the time as being bad for morale. However, in 1993 a memorial commemorating the incident was unveiled at the station, and thus the story became 'official' and part of the national memory.

Official, purpose-built public shelters became part of the government's thinking only at a very late stage, and many were incomplete when war broke out. Flat-roofed and brick-built, public shelters stood at many street corners or on bits of spare land. The construction of shelters was hampered by a lack of cement and many were built without any at all. Damp, shoddily built with insufficient conveniences, public shelters gained an evil reputation. Many people refused to use them, fearing for their safety – hence Londoners' occupation of the Underground. Mass-Observation recorded numerous complaints, 'A breath of wind would knock them down'; 'The flat roof makes them such a lovely target'; '£93 they cost and they're no damn use at all'; 'A bomb fell near one and blew the five of them and the shelter four yards along the road'.[24] A letter to the editor of *Picture Post* demanded more shelter-building from the government and condemned the supposed lack of cement as a poor excuse when cement factories in Durham had been closed down for lack of work.[25]

As with the case of the Underground, the people took matters into their own hands. South Londoners colonised the Chislehurst caves in Kent; families set up homes there and special trains allowed men to join their loved ones after a day's work. The caves gained their own barber shop, church services and entertainments. Similarly, the residents of Haggerston, Hackney, took over their local church hall. The vicar and mayor helped to make the place more homely, and despite its complete lack of ability to withstand bombs, it was a place where people felt safe. Far less salubrious were the railway arches of the London–Tilbury–Southend Railway in Stepney. Vast steel and cast iron girders gave these arches a feeling of solidity and security and people flocked to them. Fashionable West End society went east in search of the exotic tales told about the arches, full as they were with the cosmopolitan mix of the East End – Jews, Lascars, Chinese, West Indians, Irish Catholics and Indians. Even these places were improved by the people themselves; 'Mickey's Shelter', also in Stepney, was a large cellar that sometimes attracted ten thousand people. Eventually a shelter committee was formed and, playing on the publicity sparked by the shelter's infamous reputation, was able to establish a canteen donated and fitted by Marks and Spencer.[26] Far from supine collapses of morale when sheltering in large groups, it not only bolstered morale, but the British people revealed that they could also make up for undoubted government error and lack of provision.

The pre-war government's preferred choice of shelter, the Anderson, a corrugated iron hut named after its designer Dr David Anderson (and not the Minister for Home Security, Sir John Anderson, as often stated), was capable of holding up to six people and was strong enough to withstand anything short of a direct hit. Being a surface shelter and one designed for domestic use, the government saw it as the best antidote to 'deep shelter' mentality. Unfortunately, the majority of British people did not have gardens in which to erect these shelters. Those who did, found they were damp and prone to flooding unless carefully caulked. When Morrison took over Anderson's post, he oversaw the introduction of a second type of domestic shelter, this time designed for indoor use – a solid rectangular steel frame, which often doubled-up as a table.[27]

With the possible exception of the Morrison shelter, all the forms of air-raid protection mentioned have etched their way on to the national memory. During the blitz, a large library of photographs was collected. As noted, we have all seen people lying on the platforms of the Underground, but equally we have all seen photographs from other public shelters and people curled up in their Andersons. *London Can Take It!* and *Christmas Under Fire*, both made during the blitz, captured on film people queuing for, and resting in, the shelters. Since the war, this image of Britons taking it has been often repeated. *The Battle of Britain* (1969) included scenes shot on the platform of the disused Aldwych tube station; this was a fascinating decision, revealing the holy aura surrounding the blitz, for who would have noticed the difference had the scene been shot in a studio? Somehow the blitz was too important for that. The film, serving as a memorial, had to be accurate in every detail.[28] A tableau similar to that seen in *The Battle of Britain* can be found in 'The Battle of Britain Hall' at the RAF Museum, Hendon. It serves to reinforce the message that Londoners endured and came out victorious. In John Boorman's *Hope and Glory* (1987), the bombing scenes see the family take shelter in the Anderson, as befits the suburban aspect of the film. Of course, *Dad's Army* had its Anderson shelter scenes; in one episode Captain Mainwaring is continually bothered by the enormous bulk of his wife sagging through the springs of the upper bunk. Viewers of Channel 4's popular *The 1940s House* series, and visitors to the tie-in Imperial War

Museum exhibition, were also shown the interior of an Anderson shelter and, more unusually, a Morrison. The environment of the blitz is thus before us; we know what it looked like.

In fact, it is far easier to be exposed to the shelter than it is the bombed landscapes, despite the fact that the British people lived with bomb-sites for years afterwards. So dominant is the vision of the shelters that the statistics for their use can be a shock. It was estimated that the largest number to seek shelter in the Underground was on the night of 27 September 1940 when 177,000 people entered. Although this represented the equivalent of the population of Southampton, it was less than 5 per cent of those left in London. A survey conducted in November revealed that only 4 per cent of Londoners regularly sheltered in the tube. Nine per cent went to a surface public shelter, and 27 per cent used domestic (mostly Anderson) shelters. This left over half of the remaining population either at work, on some form of ARP duty or taking what shelter they could within their own homes.[29] But in the myth nearly everyone takes shelter because that is what the easily available evidence shows.

The spirit of those taking shelter from the Nazi bombers is intimately entwined with these visions. The morale of those who faced bombing has interested the debunkers of the myth of the blitz. Both Clive Ponting and Stuart Hylton have taken great pains to show that during the blitz morale came close to cracking on many occasions and have scorned the notion of the chirpy cockney smiling in the rubble. Evidence of poor morale, near hysteria and the contrary expression of shock, catatonia, can certainly be found. Mass-Observation surveyors noted hysteria in an East London shelter. After Nazi bombers overwhelmed the small cities of Coventry and Plymouth, it was equally clear that morale had been very badly dented. People were said to be in a daze, had lost faith in their leaders and had succumbed to a feeling of helplessness. Much of this evidence was collected by the government and did not become public, although rumours could not be stopped. In such an atmosphere, it was inevitable that these rumours would proliferate. After Liverpool received a heavy blitz, it was widely accepted as common knowledge that martial law had been imposed. Where this idea originated is unclear but many believed it.[30]

Suppression of evidence is key to the Ponting thesis. He suggests that the myth of the blitz and 1940 was made by withholding material and lying: 'This book goes behind the scenes to examine many of the facts and episodes that were kept carefully concealed at the time', he notes in the introduction.[31] However, these facts are not the whole story. While it cannot be doubted that some material was withheld, it also needs to be noted that the myth is based on a core of truth. It is far too big and strong to crumble under such accusations because there is equal evidence to show that people *did know* about the dark side of the blitz and still maintained their morale and spirit of defiance. H.R. Pratt Boorman, owner and editor of the *Kent Messenger*, provides a good example. In 1942, a year in which some shocking defeats dented morale until victory came at Alamein in October, his book, *Hell's Corner: Kent Becomes the Battlefield of Britain* was published. Instead of painting the perfect propaganda picture in a black year, Pratt Boorman's story tells of heroism and trauma. Recounting the day bombs fell on the small town of Lenham, he told of an old lady of 80 found sitting in her house with 'her gas mask on, a saucepan on her head, sobbing for all she was worth'.[32] Another anecdote concerned a trip to London in which tea at the Charing Cross Corner House was interrupted by a raid. The orchestra played tunes to encourage community singing 'but it was half-hearted'.[33] Not quite the 'roll out the barrel spirit' in that story. Most shockingly, he also referred to the looting of bombed houses, 'amazing though it seems, there are some people mean enough to steal from those whose houses have been bombed. If discovered they can be punished by death.'[34] Crime, particularly larceny, did go up in the war.[35] Clearly, people knew about it, spoke about it, complained about it. Information and knowledge of the issue was not entirely suppressed then, nor has it ever been. *Britain at War in Colour* (2000), a Carlton television documentary made for the popular market, which might be considered susceptible to repeating clichés, also made the fact of looting clear by quoting the diary of a woman whose blitzed house had been struck by thieves.[36]

In fact, popular histories of the blitz have rarely drawn a veil over this flip side. The most influential television history of the war, *The World at War*, included the testimony of an East Londoner who witnessed Churchill receiving a fierce rebuke from women salvaging belongings from their bombed houses. At Christmas 1981, I received the *Hamlyn Children's History of Britain*. It was a book I loved for its dramatic account of the nation's history, but the darker side of the home front in the Second World War was not omitted:

> *The spirit of neighbourly co-operation, heroic defiance and self-
> discipline was not so universal as the government pretended, of course.
> Crime did not stop during the wartime 'blackout'. . . . More work was lost
> through strikes in 1943–44 than in some peacetime years. All the same,
> the British had good reason to feel proud of themselves.*[37]

I seriously doubt whether the *Hamlyn Children's History of Britain* can
be labelled a dangerously subversive or revisionist piece of children's
literature. Rather, it simply repeated what was already well known; and,
if a children's book was carrying such an interpretation years before the
works of Ponting and Hylton were published, the supposed novelty of
their work seems overstated.

Secondly, the final line of the above quotation is significant. Even
once the darker side of the home front has been taken into consideration,
the final analysis is that '*the British had good reason to feel proud of
themselves*'. This is the element Ponting and Hylton refuse to deal with
so steadfastly. For where there is undoubted evidence of 'bad behaviour',
there is at least an equal amount of evidence revealing heroism, self-
sacrifice, humour, resolution and stoicism. 'An historian cannot damage
the myth without appearing petulantly wilful', wrote Angus Calder,
'because the myth soaked deeply into the very first-hand evidence which
he must come to at last if he wishes to destroy it.'[38] I will come to the
'soaking-in' process later; first the positive evidence needs to be studied.

Evidence of positive morale, which defines the broad contours of
the myth, is not hard to come by. Towards the end of October 1940, a
young observer with Mass-Observation noted: 'Considering what they
[Londoners] have been through, they appeared to be remarkably cheerful
and friendly, and the worse the conditions the more laughter there
seemed to be.'[39] Cheerful cockneys became the stock-in-trade cliché
of the press. *War Illustrated* seemed to find them on every corner of the
capital. On 20 September it carried the headline 'London Feels the Full
Blast of Nazi Fury / Mark of the Nazis on Humble East End Homes / But
"We Can Stick It" Say the Cockneys.' On 11 October it stated, 'This is
the War of the Unknown Warriors / Courage and Cockney Humour Go
Well Together', on another page 'Londoners Lose Homes But Not Their
Hearts', a week later 'London Carries On in the People's War / They Go to
Deep Shelters with High Hearts'.[40] Of course, changing the caption of a

photograph can alter its meaning or interpretation entirely, but *War Illustrated* revealed other forms of evidence showing humour combined with defiance and resilience. On 8 November it printed a collage of photographs of signs hanging in shops and businesses. 'Business As Unusual! / Inspect our Bargains in Blasted Goods / No Reasonable Offer Refused'; 'Reynell and Son / We have withstood every war since 1812 / We shall withstand'; 'Accommodation / H&C in all bedrooms – air raid shelter / Facing Sea and Enemy'; 'We have no [window] panes Dear Mother now'. It concluded with the photograph of an upside down mannequin, legs pointing in the air propping up a sign saying 'BLAST'.[41]

Flippant shop signs burrowed their way into the imagination in other ways. In *London Can Take It!*, Reynolds announced, 'London shops are open as usual. . . . In fact, some of them are more open than usual' over footage of a shop's smashed windows. Thirty years later, when Thames Television made *The World at War*, an East Londoner remembered and recalled this type of humour: 'It was not an uncommon sight to see "No windows but plenty of spirit" or "Sorry we've got no front door, don't trouble to knock come straight-in" and you'd see these funny little notices put up outside the door.'[42] Of course, it could not have been like that throughout the war, the myth does not claim it was, but by the same token, it was there and it could not have been only the supine vision painted by Ponting and Hylton.

The provincial blitz

London set the standard for the rest of the country during the blitz. The way the London blitz was reported and interpreted ensured that other British cities had to react with equal fortitude, resolution and courage. Here myth and reality co-existed, they fused and informed each other to the point where it becomes impossible and fruitless to attempt to distinguish between them, as the debunkers seek to do with such vigour. The highly controlled presentation of London meant a behavioural norm had been established by the autumn of 1940 that demanded emulation by others. In turn, this ensured London's status as *the* city of the blitz, *the* model of survival, and encouraged Londoners to remain cheerful so as not to let the mantle slip. If there is such a thing as the myth of the blitz, then it was not a fabrication devised afterwards. Even less was it a fabrication devised by those in power and forced on the majority. Rather, a blurring occurred: the genuine actions of ordinary people were reported and lionised which created a genuinely popular heroic image few wanted to fall short of. The spirit of the blitz has thus become the heritage and folk memory of the British people and remains impervious to assault because the so-called myth is 'soaked into the very first-hand evidence itself'.[43]

As the Luftwaffe spread its attentions across Britain, a sense of competition with London was often inspired in the provincial cities. *War Illustrated* heaped praise on those endeavouring to 'Take It' in the way London had:

> *Lest Londoners should imagine that theirs is the only city where*
> *dwell such heroes, let us not forget that the same experiences, the*
> *same heroism, and the same glorious victory have been endured,*
> *demonstrated and won by the firemen and people of Coventry,*
> *Manchester, Bristol, Southampton, Sheffield, and half a dozen other*
> *great provincial cities. Truly 'you can't lick the people' when they are*
> *fighting for their own homes.*[44]

When the small, but vital, port city of Plymouth was hit in a particularly devastating set of raids, *War Illustrated* once again found heroism in the provinces. Under the headline 'Of Course, the British People "Can Take It"', it noted:

> *Plymouth was given a severe battering by Nazi bombers on the nights of*
> *20 and 21 March 1941, as part of Hitler's campaign to put our principal*
> *ports out of action. But the spirit of Plymouth's people was undaunted,*
> *finding expression in a Union Jack fluttering above the ruins and the*
> *oft-repeated wish: 'Let the RAF give the Germans what the Germans have*
> *given us.'*[45]

A perverse pride was found in the trauma, as was revealed in the headlines of the local press: 'PLYMOUTH ASSUMES THE MANTLE OF COVENTRY', 'CITY DEVASTATION WORSE THAN COVENTRY – SAYS US ENVOY', and '"ASSUMED MANTLE OF COVENTRY": LONDON OPINIONS'.[46]

Mass-Observation reporters found that people in Southampton were convinced they had faced raids far worse than those on Coventry and were annoyed that the national press had not picked up on this fact.[47] London clearly stood by itself, on an entirely different level of 'Taking It', but there was fierce competition to be second, and Coventry was obviously the city to beat.

Perhaps the corner of the country most proud of its reaction to the Nazi threat was Kent. It was the county closest to the enemy after the fall of France and felt keenly its position as the 'frontline county'. Kent skies were full of aircraft during the Battle of Britain and its inhabitants felt the first rumblings of the blitz long before the campaign against London started. Close to London, yet isolated on the long toe which sticks out into the Channel and North Sea, the people of Kent developed a brand of intense local patriotism during the preliminaries to the blitz proper.

H.R. Pratt Boorman's *Hell's Corner: Kent Becomes the Battlefield of Britain* (1942) told the story of 'Old Nick', a former Regimental Sergeant Major in the Royal West Kents, who put up a 'Business As Usual' sign over his bomb-damaged window and entrance to the shop he had owned for over 30 years. Visiting an anti-aircraft battery at the height of the Battle of Britain, Pratt Boorman wondered how the men could stand the strain of constant bombing and action stations:

> If you ask them they just shrug their shoulders and say, 'Well, it's my job.'
>
> But that is not the real answer. The real answer is that they represent the spirit of the people of Kent – the determination not to give in, no matter what the cost; absolute refusal to be driven away from their homes and from their jobs.
>
> It's that spirit that will win in the end.[48]

Dover became the key symbol of Kent's resistance and, by extension, British determination. In the wake of the fall of France, Dover became the front line and heavy bombing began in July 1940. Already carrying the weight of its symbolic history as the key to Britain, Dover was quickly laden with another historic parallel. In the Great War, the British had placed enormous emotional significance on the defence of the small Belgian city of Ypres. Ypres, the outpost of the Channel Ports, as it was known, burned its way into British hearts. Many of the marks, sites and features of the landscape became well known to the British, one of which was the notorious Hellfire Corner on the Menin Road. A few weeks after the opening of the German campaign in 1940, Dover was christened Hellfire Corner. An onus was therefore laid on the people of Dover to emulate the heroism and stoicism of the British and Imperial armies defending the Ypres salient between 1914 and 1918. Harry Watt celebrated the resistance of the city in his film, *Dover: Front Line City*. Made in 1940, it stressed the calm attitude of the inhabitants and their determination not to be shifted from their homes. It was an important message in the light of Nazi claims of widespread panic and flight. Pratt Boorman recalled a similar feeling of resolution: 'Reluctantly I left Dover. Like every other Britisher I left full of admiration for the spirit of defiance amongst its people. . . . Dover makes you proud to be British.'[49]

The provincial blitz revealed just as many local government shortcomings as that on London. Small cities were often overwhelmed by the disaster and morale undoubtedly fell; occasionally those in responsibility failed to do their duty effectively and with fortitude. Unlike the blitz on London, the Luftwaffe rarely visited the smaller cities on a continual basis, night after night. This had a far deeper effect on morale than facing the enemy constantly; just as a city thought it had escaped, the bombers might return, jarring and denting fragile nerves. A cockney survivor of the blitz said 'you can get used to it. You can get used to anything.'[50] But 'getting used to' was a symptom of routine, and the provincial cities were often denied this appalling luxury. Despite these problems British cities remained firm. Initial shock and horror were overcome and they took it.[51]

Of course, at the time the failures of local government and collapses in morale were not covered in the press. This does not mean that people were ignorant of such matters, merely that in the final analysis they too preferred the heroic picture and did their best to conform to it – the alternatives held little attraction. Seeing the blitz as an heroic moment added additional chapters to already proud local histories, or created a heritage in new communities. As Malcolm Smith has pointed out, after the war local histories of the blitz proliferated, often published by and compiled from the archives of local newspapers. Very few, if any, criticised civic government or the lack of preparation, but all told of the heroism and endurance of the inhabitants. Such records were clearly accepted by many, as the sales reveal: Plymouth's history, *It Came to Our Door*, by H.P. Twyford, was published in 1946, went through three reprints and was reissued in 1949 and 1975. January 2002 saw the *Kent Messenger* print the fifth edition of its book, *Kent at War*, by Bob Ogley. Written by a local historian, the author acknowledges his debt to Pratt Boorman's original works and the archive of the newspaper. The county motto provides the title for the Foreword, *Invicta* (unconquered), and sets the tone for the book. Lavishly illustrated with the newspaper's wonderful collection of photographs, the book is a proud record of Kent's part in the war. Comedy and pathos intersperse the text and help to underline the proud memory. Of particular significance is the section covering the Baedeker Raid on Canterbury in June 1942. (Hitler had promised to raze Britain's historic monuments to the ground using the famous Baedeker tourist guides to provide the list of targets.) In attacking Canterbury, the Nazis struck at a vital symbol of England, its heritage and self-perception. But by surviving the attack, the inhabitants and the remnants of the city fabric combined to become symbols of the unconquerable nature of the island race and its centuries of history. The history was said to endure in the spirit of the living; it was proclaimed at the time and again in 2002 in *Kent at War*: 'As the great clean-up continued, scores and scores of Union Jacks were draped from the windows of damaged buildings. Historic Canterbury had died that night, but the message from its inhabitants was crystal clear.'[52] Stating that such responses reveal nothing more than a Pavlovian response to government-inspired propaganda initiatives are of no importance. The big fact remains, the city survived and its inhabitants took it.

The people who bought the initial wave of books were survivors; they knew the facts, yet they bought histories that the debunkers would regard as fatally flawed. 'They were surely buying a pattern', Smith has noted, 'a local historical map against which they could orientate their personal and family experience, and thus make sense of their own experience as part of a larger story.'[53] Making sense of the story is the function the received interpretation of the blitz performs for the British people.

Standing together

'All pulling together' is the final element in the blitz myth. According to the standard interpretation, the blitz, like evacuation, forced the British people together as the Nazi bombers knew no distinction of class, wealth or status. As with evacuation, the real situation was a bit more ambiguous than this rather simplistic understanding. Nevertheless, the boldest features in the popular memory are not fragments of the imagination.

During the blitz much was made of the indiscriminate nature of the raids, affecting the smart and fashionable districts alongside those of the working class. *London Can Take It!* showed a gaping hole in one of Nash's Regent's Park crescents. When Buckingham Palace was hit, the King and Queen were photographed amid the damage, stressing the common fate of the British people.[54]

While this chapter was being written, news came through of the Queen Mother's death. Fascinatingly, the newspaper coverage has made much of the role of the King and Queen during the blitz. However, rather than stressing the *primus inter pares* role presented during the blitz, the memory seems to have been refocused. Much of the material has implied that the King and Queen played vital leadership roles, setting an example to their people. Proof of Malcolm Smith's thesis of a new-right hijack of the memory of 1940 might be found in this evidence, that is the people's role in their own defence and destiny was downplayed in order to stress an old-fashioned division of leaders and led.[55]

Class divisions certainly made themselves felt during the blitz. For example, the Dorchester Hotel converted its Turkish baths into an exclusive air-raid shelter:

> . . . a neat row of cots, spaced about two feet apart, each one covered
> with a lovely fluffy eiderdown. Its silks billowed and shone in the dim
> light in pale pinks and blues. Behind each cot hung the negligee, the
> dressing gown. . . . The pillows on which the heads lay were large and
> full and white. . . . There was a little sign pinned to one of the
> Turkish-bath curtains. It said 'Reserved for Lord Halifax.'[56]

The Savoy Hotel converted its underground banqueting hall into a dormitory-restaurant, which became the subject of a demonstration on 15 September 1940, when a gang of East Enders broke in during the air-raid alert. Real class tension of a bitter and intractable nature was missing, however, for the all clear soon sounded and the crowd withdrew quietly and with good grace, and, it is rumoured, after making a collection for the head porter![57]

Although Nazi bombing was indiscriminate, it was generally aimed at the industrial zones of British towns and cities; it was therefore inevitable that the poor would suffer more than the rich. It was equally inevitable that the working class and poor would grumble and complain at any instance of wealth and privilege buying preferential treatment. However, the disciplined, well-established British working class remained remarkably wedded to a routine of work and simple domesticity. The blitz was a people's experience, and victory was assured by their attitude. Although this attitude was reassuring to the government, the resilience of working-class morale was never taken for granted. McLaine has noted the Ministry of Information's sensitivity on this subject and the related issue of class antagonism. Constant attention was paid to these concerns, particularly during the blitz. Yet Home Intelligence found very little hard evidence of damaging class antagonism in this period.[58] Old-fashioned Conservative fears about the moral fibre of the working class can be detected in these obsessions, and reveals how such ideas survived the establishment of a coalition government.

More supportive of the pulling-together vision was the social composition of the Air Raid Precautions' and civil defence services. Here it is possible to see all ranks combining to defeat the enemy, albeit in a very British manner. ARP wardens, as local volunteers, reflected the area they served. Sometimes it was difficult to recruit in working-class areas largely because far fewer people had enough spare time to volunteer for extra duties. However, a 1939 Mass-Observation survey in a west London borough found that about two-thirds of the ARP volunteers were working class.[59] Complementing the work of the ARP was that of the Women's Voluntary Service (WVS), an overwhelmingly middle-class institution. Thus class distinctions might exist, but it did not mean that any one class took on the bulk of the work, and it could not be said that entire classes were shirking their duties and responsibilities.

Class distinctions have always been admitted in the British vision of the blitz, but it has been neatly emasculated of fractious overtones by expressing it through comedy. *Dad's Army*, for example, was based on class: Mr Mainwaring's middle-class aspirations condemned him to constant sparring with Mr Hodges and his own clerk, Mr Wilson. The white-collared Mainwaring always referred to Mr Hodges, the lower-middle-class greengrocer and ARP warden, as a tradesman. While Mr Wilson, his professional inferior, was actually a social superior having attended a minor public school and possessing a drop or two of aristocratic blood. It created that most British of all scenarios, class confusion resulting in social ambiguity. In the war, Tommy Handley's fabulously successful radio comedy, *ITMA* [*It's That Man Again*] (see next chapter), contained the wonderfully working-class charlady, Mrs Mopp. In one episode, Mrs Mopp described her fire-watching duties which she shared with a man she considered to be her social superior, 'ever so polite he was too, sir. Always said "pardon" before he took his boots off.' (Night fire-watching duties also became the subject of numerous saucy jokes, as it was rumoured that male–female teams alone on the roofs of buildings could indulge in all sorts of 'goings-on'.)

The blitz made heroes out of ordinary British people; it cast them on to the centre-stage of history. Because so much was asked of them, their aspirations and needs could no longer be ignored or dealt with in a piece-meal manner. In the midst of the destruction the British people had to be offered reconstruction, they had to be told that their world would not only be replaced, but would be replaced with something better. Queen Elizabeth herself felt as much. Writing to her mother-in-law, Queen Mary, in October 1940, she noted: 'The destruction is so awful, and the people so *wonderful* – they *deserve* a better world.'[60] A People's Peace, no matter how far off that seemed, had to be accepted, although no one was quite sure what form it would take in the winter of 1940–41. This understanding of the blitz has been under pressure since the late 1970s. Instead of celebrating the role of the people in the creation of a new world, the emphasis had been laid on the role of the people and their leaders in withstanding foreigners, stressing the 'standing alone' factor. Clearly this was the case, but in foregrounding one factor, it marginalises a complementary one that was once so important to the memory of the blitz.

During the blitz shortcomings in authority and government, both national and local, were certainly highlighted. Contingency planning had often been unbalanced or mismanaged, and many local governments failed to do anything at all. Once disaster struck, some authorities revealed little reactive power or initiative. Equally, some people behaved very badly indeed or collapsed under the strain, conducting themselves with little of the famed blitz spirit. Balancing these elements, however, are the innumerable tales of heroism. Most people acted heroically in the minor key by simply carrying on as normal in utterly abnormal situations

– they went to work and got on with their everyday lives, which was vital
to the overall war effort. Others acted heroically in the major key, fighting
fires, rescuing people from ruins, treating and caring for the wounded
and distressed or serving tea to thirsty firemen and rescue squads when
fires were still burning hot and unexploded bombs remained in the
vicinity.

The blitz survives as a vivid cultural memory, literally burnt into our
minds by the staggering number of visual records it created. Landscapes
that are turned into surreal variants of their former condition make
easily remembered images, as do ordinary domestic scenes played out
on Underground platforms or in tiny corrugated iron huts. In that crazy
landscape the British people carried on and took it alone, and
bequeathed a remarkable cultural, social and political legacy to succeed-
ing generations.

Notes

1 Charles Eade (ed.), *War Speeches of Winston Churchill*, 3 vols (London
   1951), vol. I, pp. 188–96.

2 Malcolm Smith, *Britain and 1940* (London 2000), p. 93.

3 Ibid., p. 29; also see Clive Ponting, *1940: Myth and Reality* (London 1990),
   p. 171.

4 Lucy Noakes, 'Making Histories: Experiencing the Blitz in London's
   Museums in the 1990s', in Martin Evans and Ken Lunn (eds), *War and
   Memory in the Twentieth Century* (Oxford 1997), pp. 89–104.

5 Ibid., p. 89.

6 Ibid., p. 99.

7 *Daily Mail* 29 December 1940.

8 See Smith, *Britain and 1940*, pp. 81–3.

9 Quoted in James Chapman, *The British at War: Cinema, State and
   Propaganda, 1939–1945* (London 1998), p. 99.

10 Oliver Green, *Underground Art: London Transport Posters 1908 to the
    Present* (London 1990), p. 98.

11 *War Illustrated* 4 October 1940.

12 *War Illustrated* 18 October 1940 (vol. 2).

13 William Sansom, 'The Wall', in Dan Davin (ed.), *The Oxford Book of Short Stories from the Second World War* (Oxford 1984), pp. 20–3.

14 See Anthony Aldgate and Jeffrey Richards, *Britain Can Take It: The British Cinema in the Second World War* (Oxford 1986), pp. 218–45.

15 Brian Winston, *Fires Were Started* (London 1999), pp. 19–46.

16 See Angus Calder, *The People's War* (London 1997; orig. 1969), p. 179.

17 *War Illustrated* 22 November 1940 (vol. 2).

18 Ponting, *Myth and Reality*, p. 166.

19 Quoted in Calder, *People*, p. 184.

20 Tom Harrisson, *Living Through the Blitz* (Harmondsworth 1990; orig. 1976), p. 113.

21 *Picture Post* 5 October 1940.

22 See Calder, *People*, p. 185.

23 *War Illustrated* 22 November 1940 (vol. 2).

24 Quoted in Peter Lewis, *A People's War* (London 1986), p. 50.

25 *Picture Post* 5 October 1940.

26 See Calder, *People*, pp. 182–3.

27 See Harrisson, *Blitz*, pp. 37–8.

28 See Leonard Mosley, *The Battle of Britain: The Making of a Film* (London 1969), p. 37.

29 Harrisson, *Blitz*, p. 111.

30 Ibid., pp. 62–3, 134–5, 210–13, 240–1.

31 Ponting, *Myth and Reality*, p. 2.

32 H.R. Pratt Boorman, *Hell's Corner: Kent Becomes the Battlefield of Britain* (Maidstone 1942), p. 10.

33 Ibid., p. 19.

34 Ibid., p. 90.

35 Ponting, *Myth and Reality*, p. 142; Calder, *People*, p. 337.

36 *Britain at War in Colour*, Part One: 'Darkest Hour'.

37 Neil Grant, *Hamlyn Children's History of Britain* (London 1981), p. 284.

38 Angus Calder, *The Myth of the Blitz* (London 1991), p. 143.

39 Ibid.

40 *War Illustrated* 20 September, 11 October, 18 October 1940 (vol. 2).

41 Ibid., 8 November 1940.

42 *The World at War*, Episode Four: 'Standing Alone, June 1940–May 1941'.

43 Calder, *Myth*, p. 143.

44 *War Illustrated* 17 January 1941 (vol. 3).

45 Ibid., 10 April 1941.

46 Quoted in Harrisson, *Blitz*, p. 221.

47 Ibid., p. 149.

48 Pratt Boorman, *Hell's Corner*, pp. 36–7, 97.

49 Ibid., pp. 116–17.

50 *The World at War*, Episode Four.

51 See Harrisson, *Blitz*, pp. 132–276 for a discussion of the effect of the blitz on British provincial cities. It is clear that despite the problems with morale, people 'bounced back' as they had in London.

52 Bob Ogley *Kent at War* (Westerham 2002), p. 124.

53 Smith, *Britain and 1940*, pp. 85–6.

54 See Lewis, *People's War*, pp. 69–70.

55 For examples, see *Daily Telegraph* 1 April 2002; and *Sunday Express* 31 March 2002.

56 Ingersoll, quoted in Calder, *People*, p. 186.

57 Calder, *People*, p. 167.

58 See Ian McLaine, *Ministry of Morale: Home Front Morale and the Ministry of Information in World War II* (London 1979), pp. 92–8.

59 Ibid., p. 197.

60 Ibid., p. 524.

CHAPTER 5

Over-sexed, over-paid and over here: the home front, 1941–45, Yanks, women and Auntie Beeb

For the British people the Second World War was a total war. It demanded the mobilisation of every resource, every citizen, every ounce of energy and treasure. During the course of the war the British broke taboos, debated the future of their country with great vigour, accepted hardships and privations. Unsurprisingly, the effect of such intense effort has left an indelible mark on modern British culture and the pool of public knowledge of the home front is wide, even if it isn't very deep. Most people know something about rationing, particularly the lack of nylon stockings, causing women to stain their legs. They will recognise the character of the spiv and the slogan 'Dig for Victory', that women found American servicemen wonderfully glamorous and many became GI brides. This chapter will therefore concentrate on those images that have a high profile in the popular memory of the home front: rationing, the role of the BBC, sex, and the position of women. Such images and concepts are given an academic slant by the increasing significance of the home front in National Curriculum History studies and university courses. Our knowledge is curiously balanced between two poles: the 'sacred' – the British people heroically playing their part in the titanic struggle for survival – and the 'profane' – the British people engaged in all sorts of behaviour, some of which was, perhaps, improper. So does this provide the chance to divide the real experience of war from that devised by government and mellowed by memory and nostalgia? The answer has to be not really, for, as noted so often, the division between the contemporary reality of war and the remembered version is not a particularly valid or valuable one because no such clear lines have ever existed. Instead, this chapter will be slightly different from the others. It will also examine those elements of the British war story that are long since forgotten but that were once considered to be of absolute and vital importance. There is now very little popular knowledge of Britain's wartime affinity with the USSR or the political divisions that were so fiercely felt and expressed. This chapter will reveal that the memory of the home front is a complex one, shot through with areas of contrast, light and shade.

Rationing

The British people suffered many intrusions into their lives during the Second World War. They were in constant danger of falling victim to enemy action and their lives were transformed by a government which suddenly developed an appetite for regulation, intervention and instruction. If not conscripted into the armed forces, a person could be compelled into some other form of national service which might entail enforced relocation to a different area of the country altogether. In the name of the war effort the government regulated the supply and nature of not only luxuries but every other necessity too. State power meant that the war was inescapable, even during leisure time.

A little buff-coloured book with detachable, perforated-edged coupons and the name and address of the owner on the front is the most potent symbol of the war on the home front. Combining the elements of state power and the individual, even now the ration book is crucial to our understanding of the Second World War, being one of the most ubiquitous souvenirs of the conflict, pressing itself into the national memory. Ration books were first issued in January 1940. Initially, rationing was applied to very few products and allocations were generous. However, during the summer of 1940 regulations became more stringent, more and more items were covered by rationing restrictions and allocations decreased. 1942 saw a sudden tightening, largely thanks to the parlous state of the Battle of the Atlantic, as prodigious shipping losses forced increased parsimony.[1]

Rationing worked on a points system with each item covered by the scheme given a points allocation. People could purchase these items provided they had the requisite number of valid coupons; coupons allocated to one product could not be used to buy another, nor could they be hoarded over a long period and used in one great spree. But the system could not ensure a steady supply of all foods. Certain items disappeared for the duration of the war, most famously oranges and bananas. There are myriad stories of wartime children utterly bemused by their first sight of such luxuries and, as the anecdotes have it, most decided to eat the lot, skin and all. More basic, but vital foodstuffs, such as eggs and milk, could be equally hard to get hold of. The introduction of substitutes did not alleviate the situation, as most people hated the powdered versions. Another contender for most detested substitute was the increasingly dark bread. The British were a race of white bread eaters in 1941 and were highly suspicious of the National Wheatmeal Loaf of 85 per cent extraction, which was introduced to save shipping space by cutting down on grain imports. In 1943 a Mass-Observation survey found approval of the bread measured a mere 14 per cent.[2]

Whatever the ills of the system, most people welcomed it and even wanted it extended. Lord Woolton, the tireless Minister of Food, was determined to ensure 'fair shares for all' in accordance with the mood of the country. The Wartime Social Survey of 1942 recorded that only one person in seven was dissatisfied with rationing and nine out of ten housewives approved of it.[3] At the same time this was a defensive reaction: rationing stopped other people getting exactly what they wanted if they had the time, money and leisure to procure it. It can be labelled a typically British solution: it brought everyone down to a certain level and so maximised the misery not the equality. Thus, despite the outward level of support for rationing, no one was actually that happy with it. The other great problem with the 'fair shares for all' mentality was that it took no account of differing needs. In arriving at the figure that the average man needed 3,000 calories a day, the government had made no concession to those working in heavy industry. A coal miner or metal smelter might need somewhere in the region of

4,500 calories a day. Fair averages did not make sense. As Angus Calder has pointed out, 'the general pattern was that dockers, miners, shipyard workers and iron and steel workers were less well nourished, absolutely, not just in relation to their much more arduous work, than clerks or workers in light industry'.[4]

Contrary to the popular perception, not everything was on ration and nor was it impossible to 'eat out'. (A surprising number of my students ascribed the work's-canteen menu blackboard seen in Humphrey Jennings' *Listen to Britain* as pure propaganda, citing the impossibility of eating a meal untouched by the rationing system.) Restaurants and cafés continued to operate throughout the war, although menus were greatly affected. Government-run British Restaurants offered good, solid food at a reasonable price and enjoyed a boom as a result, as people saw them as a way of saving valuable ration coupons. However, the by no means unfounded rumour that the rich could buy what they wanted where they wanted was a cause of deep and clear resentment.

A rising tide of agitation against those thought to be avoiding the strictures of the rationing system forced the government to act. Woolton imposed draconian punishments for sharp practice by shopkeepers and anyone attempting to profit from the black market. By 1944 over 900 inspectors were employed, ensuring compliance with the regulations, a definite outward sign of the government's commitment to maintaining the credibility of, and confidence in, the rationing system.[5]

This darker side of rationing does not have a high profile in our memory, but it is there nevertheless in the form of the spiv. The character of the spiv is still recognised, but now he is recalled only as a comic character rather than a parasitic felon making money from the deprivations of honest citizens. During the war, both the comic and the criminal images were commonly ascribed to the spiv. The comedian Sid Field was loved for his imitation of the spiv, complete with the clichéd trademarks of a camelhair overcoat, wide-lapelled suit, wide tie, trilby hat and pencil-line moustache. By contrast, the 1945 film *Waterloo Road* presented the spiv in a very poor light. A young soldier (John Mills) goes absent without leave in order to win back his wife (Joy Shelton) who has been dallying with a spiv (Stewart Grainger). Grainger portrays his character as a feckless, self-obsessed person utterly unmoved by the plight of his country or fellow citizens. Of course, decency, in the form of Mills, a symbol of the nation in arms, triumphs. But here was an open admission that not all were rallying to the cause.

After 1945 the spiv lost this disquieting image and became fixed in the alternative comic pose. George Cole provided the perfect caricature in Launder and Gilliat's cinematic adaptations of Ronald Searle's St Trinian stories. Introduced in *The Belles of St Trinian's* (1954) as 'Flash Harry', Cole slid round with a conspiratorial demeanour, trilby turned down low over his face and vast overcoat tightly buttoned to the neck. He takes bets for the girls, markets their illegally distilled gin and generally connives in their shady practices. When told to look less conspicuous by the equally crooked headmistress, he replies with great assurance 'Me lady? I'm the invisible man' and stalks off accompanied by a barrel-organ tune, that most working-class of sounds. (Years later George Cole was to reprise this role in a slightly different guise as Arthur Daley, the incorrigible wheeler-dealer of *Minder*.) Wartime spivs were recalled with affection in *Dad's Army* in the form of James Beck's excellent interpretation of Private Joe Walker. Always on the fiddle, a cockney (naturally!), Walker has the stereotypical Ronald Coleman moustache and takes deep drags on his cigarette which was, of course, always held in the far corner of the mouth. By making Walker a crook with a heart – despite all his criminal ways he still does his bit by joining the Home Guard – the spiv was turned into an integral part of the positive image of the People's War. The British have retained their affection for such characters as can be seen in the enormous success of *Only Fools and Horses*, a sitcom based on the attempts of two South London brothers to become millionaires by selling 'Trevor Francis tracksuits from a mush in Shepherd's Bush' and who possess the same basic characteristics of the charming spiv.

Auntie Beeb

Surviving the food shortages and frustrations of rationing in wartime Britain was made slightly easier thanks to the constant stream of advice from the Ministry of Food. Woolton appeared regularly on the radio and in short films, as he explained the policies of the Ministry in a clear and concise manner and provided tips on how best to use rationed and unrationed food. Every weekday morning at 8.15 the BBC broadcast the *Kitchen Front* to the nation. Dr Charles Hill was the great star of

Kitchen Front; his reassuring, warm tone explored the body and its secrets in a truly British way – there was an obsession with the stomach and bowels. 'The Radio Doctor' was such a success that his programme lasted for ten years and he later joined the board of the BBC and became Chairman. Here was a society far from denying the reality of its position; on the contrary, it turned the situation into a national rallying point, proving once again that the Brits were at their best when their backs were against the (kitchen) wall.[6]

This type of regular broadcast made the BBC the crucial instrument of national information, entertainment and unity. In 1939 nearly 9 million radio licences were sold in Britain. Unlike the American 'free for all', the British government had been determined to control and regulate broadcasting and had given the British Broadcasting Company a monopoly in 1922. In 1926 the BBC became a corporation and had its monopoly guaranteed by public charter. Despite the issuing of licences through the Paymaster General's Office, the BBC was not a government organisation. Indeed, earlier in that year, and before the changes to its structure, Churchill had been much vexed by his inability to use the organisation as an instrument of government propaganda during the General Strike. Under its austere director general, John Reith, the BBC developed a rather stuffy reputation, favouring high-minded entertainment, and gained the nickname 'Auntie Beeb', reflecting its somewhat priggish ways.[7]

War brought great change to the BBC. The government was extremely interested in its potential to reach listeners across the planet and so the scale of its operations expanded enormously. Indeed, it revealed its power on the very first day of war as it proved to be the crucial instrument in disseminating the news of its outbreak. Given additional funding by the state, while still remaining independent, the BBC increased its foreign language services from 8 to 47. The BBC's wartime ubiquity, and the image of people listening to their wireless sets throughout the conflict, has made it a significant part of the British popular memory.

The war also forced a change in domestic listening habits. With people working longer hours in more complex shift patterns, the ability to read a whole newspaper from cover to cover diminished, thus making the radio the crucial source of news and information. Air raids and the blackout often interrupted other leisure pursuits and so the domestic wireless set became the focus of home entertainment.

Newsreaders became stars as the war introduced a slightly more personal approach to their craft. From the summer of 1940 newsreaders had to announce their names, thus allowing listeners to put names and voices together. Thus John Snagge, Alvar Lidell, Wilfred Pickles, Frank Phillips, Bruce Belfrage and Fredrick Allen became, in Calder's words, 'better known than cabinet ministers'.[8]

In drab wartime Britain most people longed for jollity and so radio comedy became extremely popular, none more so than *ITMA* [*It's That Man Again*], which gained vast listening figures. Tommy Handley played both linkman and feed to a variety of characters played by his small team of associates. Handley presided in a number of guises, including the Minister of Aggravation, His Washout the Mayor of Foaming at the Mouth and Squire of Much Fiddling. *ITMA*'s secret lay in its ability to turn the stresses and tedium of the war into comedy. Government rules and bureaucracy were parodied in the Minister for Aggravation and his Office of Twerps, and spy-mania was ridiculed in the inefficient agent Funf. In 1942, a year in which defeat after defeat depressed the British and caused the *Daily Mirror* to lead a campaign against the influence of superannuated Colonel Blimps, *ITMA* introduced Colonel Chinstrap, a bibulous old chap with the catchphrase 'I don't mind if I do'. Once again, there was no denial of Britain's problems. Rather, there was an open acceptance of the situation but this was turned into comedy and thus made bearable.

After Handley himself, the presiding genius was Mrs Mopp, the charlady, with the wonderful catchphrase 'Can I do you now, sir?' The British repression of sex and its consequent delight in innuendo, as also seen in Donald McGill's seaside postcards and so eloquently explored by George Orwell, was given full vent in this character.[9] Although most *ITMA* recordings sound very dated now, such humour continues to play a part in the national culture. *The Fast Show*'s Arthur Atkinson, with his 'Where's my washboard?' catchphrase, and sidekick Chester Draws are affectionate caricatures of Britain's music hall and radio comedians.

After comedy the most popular BBC programmes were music-based ones. The (still) iconic figure of Vera Lynn, 'the forces' sweetheart', was given her legendary status by the radio. The BBC Music Department had always been wary of popular, sentimental songs, no doubt feeling the influence of Reith, but became particularly obsessed during the war.

Constantly fearing that nostalgic, syrupy songs about home might undermine the morale of servicemen, they sought to drive them from the airwaves. Somewhat ironically, at exactly the same moment, one of the BBC's great successes was *Sincerely Yours – Vera Lynn*, a programme in which Lynn sang sentimental ballads non-stop for homesick servicemen who wanted to dream of their sweethearts. Despite its high listening figures and the obvious loyalty of servicemen, senior officials, including the Deputy Director-General, were deeply opposed to Lynn's programme. Fears were even expressed on the *Brains Trust*, when 'Is Vera Lynn's programme harmful to morale?' was asked. After consulting with Army Welfare psychiatrists, the BBC decided to launch a counter programme in June 1942 which relied on stirring marches rather than slushy crooning. The *Daily Telegraph* was certainly happy, announcing 'Back to Merry England songs', but the public clearly wasn't and *Melody Maker* urged people to send complaints to their MPs. The BBC was forced to compromise and sentimental songs crept back into programmes. Sian Nicholas has noted:

> As producers soon recognised, just as in the First World War, loosely
> defined nostalgia for home provided a far more potent and popular
> morale-booster both home and overseas than thumping jingoism. If
> Gracie Fields and 'There'll Always be an England' was the Second World
> War equivalent of 'Tipperary', Vera Lynn and 'We'll Meet Again' was the
> direct successor to 'Keep the Home Fires Burning'.[10]

Another great success was *Workers' Playtime*, an adaptation of the forces' programme *Garrison Theatre*, which was broadcast live from a war factory. It came about with the active support of Ernest Bevin, the Minister of Labour, and was broadcast every Saturday lunchtime from 31 May 1941 and became thrice weekly from 28 October. The show consisted of entertainment broadcast live, usually from a canteen, and by its second anniversary had been performed in front of 270,000 workers in factories, rest centres, hospitals and hostels and had a regular audience of 7 million.[11]

A similar programme, *Music While You Work*, set out to unify the forces, ordinary civilians and factory workers. According to Sian Nicholas, '*Music While You Work* was one of the most remarkable innovations in British broadcasting, a programme that deliberately set out to be aesthetically and intellectually commonplace, providing repetitive light background music, a propaganda programme without propaganda.'[12] But, unlike *Sincerely Yours – Vera Lynn*, this programme was upbeat and popular for it. Most people wanted music to provide a rhythm and background to their work and so pieces with a good beat and plenty of punch were required. Eric Coates provided the programme with its own signature tune, 'Calling All Workers', in September 1940. Though some factory owners thought that it hindered production, the government, workers and many other bosses thought it helped greatly and by 1943 almost 7,000 factories with 4 million workers were tuning in. By 1945 the programme reached over 9,000 factories and 30–40,000 small plants.[13]

Reacting to its various audiences with some skill, the BBC broadcast a host of programmes aimed at specific sections of the forces. So popular did the Forces Programme become that it regularly attracted six listeners out of ten.[14] *Ack Ack – Beer Beer* found talented service personnel in Balloon Command and Anti-Aircraft batteries, Doris Hare, accompanied by Debroy Somers and his orchestra, presented *Shipmates Ahoy*, a programme for merchant sailors which was broadcast live from a London theatre, and the big radio comedies often had special service editions.

One of the war's greatest radio successes, *Brains Trust*, grew out of the demand for all types of information from servicemen. Donald McCullough, a former advertising man, was the 'Question Master', and the three regulars were the zoologist Julian Huxley, the philosopher Cyril Joad (brilliantly parodied by one of Richmal Crompton's wartime *Just William* stories as Professor Know-all) and a retired naval officer, Commander A.B. Campbell. The programme quickly established a large audience – at its peak 10–12 million listeners a week – and the panel was deluged with queries sent in by the public.[15] A vast array of topics was discussed, including many debates on religion, morality, science and, most radically, their implications for British society. In the middle of a deep, dark period of the war the interest shown in *Brains Trust* reflected the increasing radicalisation of the British people as they began to ponder the deeper implications of the war. As Sian Nicholas has noted, this was an example of the BBC reacting to public debate rather than setting the agenda.[16] Significantly, it came on to the airwaves at exactly the moment the government was on the ropes over Britain's dismal performance in virtually every theatre of war, when the new, radical political party Common Wealth was making its biggest impact and in the immediate run-up to the Beveridge Report.

Beveridge Report and political antagonism

The Beveridge Report came out at a crucial moment, just after Britain's first great victory, El Alamein, and just before the Red Army's success at Stalingrad. After years of hanging on the British people were given a glimpse of the end of the war and thoughts turned towards ensuring a more equitable post-war world. The atmosphere of 1942 was therefore receptive to new ideas and Beveridge promised something new and revolutionary – whatever historians might have thought about it since.

Few government reports have ever sold large numbers, but the 650,000 copies purchased in the months after the report was published gives some indication of the enthusiasm with which it was received. Sir William Beveridge, a quiet, calm, Liberal civil servant, had unleashed a document of immense power. Anthropomorphising humankind's problems, Beveridge identified five great giants that could be defeated only by state action: Idleness, Want, Squalor, Disease and Ignorance. In adopting this metaphorical language, Beveridge engineered a very English social revolution for he had tapped into the deep consciousness of the English language, employing the imagery of Bunyon and *The Pilgrim's Progress*. Promising social security from 'the cradle to the grave', Beveridge gave the British people a domestic focus for victory. Victory was not simply a matter of defeating external foes, it was also a matter of defeating internal ones. Only a full welfare state was acceptable to a British people who had risked everything, strained every sinew and endured the full fury of the enemy. Two weeks after the publication of the Report, Gallup conducted a poll asking people whether they had heard of it. Of those questioned, 95 per cent affirmed that they had some knowledge of the Report and 90 per cent wanted it enacted in full.[17] However, Churchill was not at all interested in welfare schemes. His mind was on grand strategy and he wanted to shelve all such talk until victory. The Conservative party began to divide as some followed Churchill's example, while others wanted to face up to the demands of the British people and begin planning a Tory peace. Labour gave its support to the Report but was deeply vexed by

Conservative opposition to embark on any sort of planning for its imple-
mentation. This approach caused much irritation in the Labour ranks,
leading to an outright revolt of backbenchers who wanted a more dramatic and immediate commitment. Passions had been aroused by the
Beveridge Report that reflected the fragility of the wartime political truce.
Although Churchill was the absolute opposite of Chamberlain in terms
of character and attitude to the war, the Chamberlainite Conservative
tenets of caution and extreme gradualism in regards to domestic and
financial policy still dominated the party. It was an atmosphere Churchill
was loath to change, having an equal distaste for anything that smacked
of socialism. On the other side was the Labour party, urging a distinct
departure in welfare policy. The two philosophies agreed to disagree
during the war but keeping the disagreements off the main public agenda
became increasingly difficult. Attlee just held on to party discipline,
using the rallying cry of the war effort, but others outside the party were
not prepared to keep quiet. People's Warriors were coming forward to
champion the Beveridge Report and cause unease in the government
ranks.

Common Wealth, founded in July 1942 when the war situation looked
black indeed, was the party to do this. Led by Sir Richard Acland, a former Liberal MP converted to socialism, Common Wealth had arisen from
the Forward March movement he had formed with J.B. Priestley. Never
numbering more than 15,000 members, about one-fifth of them in the services, Common Wealth soon proved a formidable force at by-elections,
even if it did lack the clout to compete nationally. Driven by Acland's
zeal, it had an energetic earnestness as it fought all forms of corrupt practice, urged the efficient prosecution of the war and called for immediate
social and welfare reform rather than postpone such schemes until
victory was assured. Of great appeal to young professionals, it made its
biggest impact in suburban areas but failed to penetrate Scotland or
Wales where the Labour party held firm.

In the light of the wartime electoral pact, whereby the coalition parties
did not contest the party of the former incumbent at by-elections,
Common Wealth was often the only alternative available to the local electorate. Revealing the radicalisation of the British people, Common
Wealth achieved its most remarkable successes against the Conservative
party.

Its first by-election victory came in April 1943 at the rural constituency of Eddisbury in Cheshire. Calling for an immediate second front and 'Beveridge in full now', the Common Wealth candidate, a young Battle of Britain pilot, toppled the Conservatives. Other successes followed, most notably in West Derbyshire, home to the Dukes of Devonshire at Chatsworth. The constituency had been dominated almost exclusively by the Cavendish family, and the Duke's son was adopted as Conservative candidate when the seat became vacant in January 1943. But, with Common Wealth assistance, Charlie White, an independent socialist, managed to take victory. Deference to the lord of the manor was clearly crumbling.[18]

Here are chapters from our Second World War history that are often missing from our modern national memory. Fierce argument and dissent are not easily incorporated into the dominant imagined form of national uniformity in the face of the enemy. But it is crucial to the People's War story in other ways. For here is the assertion of the working class on the page of history, here is the road to 1945 writ large in which the British people, by their own efforts, ensured change for the better. And, instead of concentrating on aspects of dissent, the story that has emerged is one of self-congratulation at the peaceful revolution thanks to the deeper, almost Blakean, radical patriotism of the workers. 'Home Fires, Britain 1940–1944', episode fifteen of *The World at War*, written by Angus Calder, contains two interviews which eulogise the image of British society, but particularly the working class, as heroically labouring for a combined victory against fascism abroad and social ills at home. J.B. Priestley noted: 'The British people were absolutely at their best in the Second World War. They were never as good before, certainly not in my life time, and, I'm sorry to say, that they've never been quite as good since.'[19] Similar sentiments were expressed by Michael Foot:

> There was a great community spirit during the war. It is the nearest thing that I've ever seen in my lifetime to the operation of a kind of socialist state, that is a democratic socialist state, of citizens believing that they could influence by their actions speedily what was going to be done and that the whole world could be changed by the way they operated. They saw that the world was changed by their actions in the war and they

thought that could be translated into political action as well. It was
extremely exciting.[20]

Far from remembering the internal arguments in the British family, we
now nostalgically ache for such a society, a society in which Britons were
at their best, a society in which citizens could influence events, a society
in which Britons knew what to do and how to go about it. This vision of
a united society driven by high idealism is the last surviving remnant of
the old Labour party's vision of the People's War.

British workers and our gallant Socialist ally

A reflection of the increased radicalism of the British people in the middle
of the war was the intense feeling of admiration for the Soviet people.
This story of our wartime history is missing completely from our modern
imagination. With the advent of the Cold War and Britain's adherence to
a supposed special relationship with the USA, the wartime appreciation
of the USSR was quickly squeezed out of the national war story and has
never been reinstated.

When the Nazi invasion of the Soviet Union began on 22 June 1941,
the British empire found it had the most unexpected of fellow combatants. The vast majority of Britons regarded Communism and the Soviet
Union with deep distrust. It was a distrust deepened by the Nazi–Soviet
Non-Aggression Pact of August 1939, the Red Army's role in the parti-
tioning of Poland just a few weeks later and then its invasion of Finland.
In Britain, the invasion of Finland had evoked much sympathy for the
bold, valiant Finns in their struggle against overwhelming odds. It was a
scenario Britons were familiar with and, as a sporting nation, they were
keen to see the underdog win. Victory for the Soviet Union in this short
but vicious war was secured only after some humiliating reverses and
after receiving expert advice from their new German friends. This suspicion of the Russians evaporated over night in June 1941; from being the
only active enemy of Nazi Germany, the British suddenly gained a huge
ally. Even the most consistent anti-Soviet critic, Winston Churchill, re-
ajusted his position. On the first night of the invasion he addressed the
British people on the radio and painted a picture of charming Russian
villages raped by the brutish invaders. Sir John Colville, his secretary,

recalled Churchill's justification of his volte-face: 'I have only one pur-
pose, the destruction of Hitler, and my life is much simplified thereby. If
Hitler invaded Hell, I would make at least a favourable reference to the
Devil in the House of Commons.'[21]

As the Nazi invasion gathered momentum and forced the Russian
people to take desperate measures to defend their nation, British admiration for the Soviets soared. Mickey Lewis, a lathe-operator in a gun
workshop, recalled the fellow feeling for the Soviet people:

> This was a war in which working-class people knew what was going on.
> We had working groups and we used to meet to discuss politics. The
> feeling in the country was very pro-Soviet because of the heroic way they
> were fighting. People here felt tremendous admiration for the terrific
> heroism in the Leningrad siege. Everyone felt the same. There was
> absolutely no anti-Soviet feeling.[22]

Margaret Cohen, a teacher working in Coventry, began campaigning
for a public declaration of greetings and solidarity to send from the
women of Coventry to the women of Stalingrad. The first call gained
7,000 signatures, which rose to 30,000 by the time the siege of Stalingrad
was over.[23]

British workers gave the 'Tanks for Russia' week their full support
when it was launched on 22 September 1941; it was also noted that production always rose and labour relations were more harmonious when
the plight of the Soviet Union was invoked.[24] The Ministry of Information
was initially fearful of this pro-Soviet feeling, but slowly realised that
praise for the Soviet war effort was good for home front morale too.[25] On
22 February 1943, in the aftermath of the Nazi defeat at Stalingrad,
British cities celebrated a Red Army Day with pageants, music and
passionate speeches. A similar day of celebration in November 1942
had been equally popular, and a year later the BBC's special feature on
the siege of Leningrad and the Soviet counter-offensive gained 9 million
listeners.[26] Also in 1943 Anthony Asquith's quaint celebration of Anglo-
Soviet friendship, *Demi-Paradise*, came to cinema screens. Laurence
Olivier starred as a Russian engineer, Ivan Kutznetsoff, who comes to
Britain to discuss plans for a new form of ship propeller. At first he finds
it hard to adjust to English customs but eventually comes to respect
and like the people, just as they take to him. By turning Anglo-Soviet

relations into a gentle comedy of manners, the film avoided making any point about the profound differences in political cultures.

Humphrey Jennings interpreted the Anglo-Soviet friendship in an equally subtle manner in his 1945 film, *A Diary for Timothy*. A sober, moving documentary following the first nine months of baby Timothy's life, Jennings' camera recorded a 'Salute to the Gallant Red Army' with a children's choir providing the musical background. So bizarre is the juxtaposition of the heroic Red Army soldier with British schoolchildren singing folk songs that it is possible to detect a flash of humour in Jennings' otherwise sombre film. Other images hit deeper: shots of British women queuing for coal in freezing weather are accompanied by the sound of the BBC announcing great Russian advances on the Polish front and the Russian national anthem. Workers' armies enduring for a people's victory is the message, but the homely faces of the women strip the scene of its political radicalism. Instead there is simple admiration for their stoicism.

The loud and long announcement of sympathy for Russian soldiers and workers should not be misunderstood as British sympathy for Communism. Angus Calder has shown that the Communist Party of Great Britain was unable to capitalise on this affection for Russia. Instead, it was the mainstream Labour party that was best able to present itself as the ally of all workers and which eliminated much of the subversive potential of this affection for the Soviet Union.[27] Alexander Werth, the Moscow correspondent of *The Sunday Times*, was employed by the BBC to provide a fortnightly round-up of the war on the Russian front and from the Russian perspective. *Russian Commentary* soon gained an audience of 4 million. Keen to stress that Stalin was no longer interested in worldwide revolution, merely the defence of his own country, and that the Russian people were just like the British, working to stop an aggressive power desecrating their land and culture, Werth helped depoliticise Soviet Communism and create the 'Uncle Joe' image.[28]

As noted, it is hard now to detect any element of this fervour for Russia. Only occasionally does it surface in the popular culture. Fans of Spike Milligan will find it in his comic war memoirs. In *Rommel? Gunner Who?* (1974) he tells of route-marches accompanied by a song with the tune of 'Vive la Compagnie':

SOLO: The might of the nation is wielded by one
OMNES: Vive la Joe Stalin!
SOLO: He isn't half knockin' the shit from the Hun!
OMNES: Vive la Joe Stalin . . . etc.[29]

It is a reminder of the wartime feeling that Russia was doing all the fighting while Britain made encouraging noises from the sidelines. In the summer of 1941 George Orwell wrote: 'The favourite quip now is that we are giving Russia all aid short of war.'[30] Thirty years later Spike Milligan gave Orwell's comments bizarre validity with yet another of his wonderful, crazy anecdotes about life in the Royal Artillery. This one, concerning the capture of a pig running amuck through the streets of Bexhill, ends on the lines: 'Somewhere on the steppes of Russia squadrons of Red tanks were advancing on all fronts. But England too was in there somewhere.'[31] Whatever tiny fragments of the Russian alliance we are left with now are comic ones.

Another element of the home front missing from our image of the war, and in many ways connected to the discussion of empathy with Russia above, is that of industrial unrest. After the terrible depression of the 1930s and its devastating effect on Britain's heavy industries, the war proved a boon. Full employment was guaranteed thanks to total war. Indeed, such were the demands of modern war that Britain found itself facing an acute labour shortage, particularly in the coalfields. With full employment came renewed trade union confidence. Workers' rights and conditions could be argued with vigour without fear of the sack and a prolonged period on the dole. Though Ernest Bevin endeavoured to minimise strikes and industrial unrest by imposing arbitration mechanisms on industry, even his impeccable trade union credentials could not stop tension from boiling over in certain sectors. In 1943 1,800,000 working days were lost in 1,785 strikes and 1944 saw the loss of 3,700,000 days.[32] Coal miners took their chance to press for redress of longstanding grievances. Working in appalling conditions for the most vital of war resources, coal miners were outraged that mine owners continued to stack up vast personal profits while their sacrifices were granted scant reward. As demand for coal rose and the labour available fell, the government took the drastic measure of diverting one conscript in every ten to the mines. The Bevin Boys, as they became known, valiantly though they tried, were hardly the answer to the structural problems of British mining made so graphically obvious by the war.[33] Despite all its problems, British industry rose to the challenge of war and achieved incredible successes. In the vital struggle for finished war materials Britain outstripped its allegedly better organised Nazi foe with some ease. Tanks, aircraft – particularly bombers – guns, radios, radar sets poured off British production lines. In contrast, Germany did not move into total war production until 1942.[34]

Paeans to the British worker can be found. The visual poet laureate of Britain's wartime effort was Humphrey Jennings. His works provide the backbone of our shared visions of the home front. If you have seen a documentary about wartime Britain it is highly likely that you have seen clips from his powerful tributes to the ordinary people, *Heart of Britain* (1941) and *Listen to Britain* (1942). The historical evidence that has pressed itself on to the national conscience is therefore something created by and for the state. Accepting such an image does not mean gullibly swallowing a government-sponsored lie. Rather, it is the accept-ance of one particular vision of wartime Britain. To be sure, there are other, radically different, stories to tell and alternative interpretations, but it does not follow axiomatically that the dominant imagined war is a total fabrication.

Jennings' two short films made for the Ministry of Information cele-brate the diversity of British life. Undeniably, Britain is shown as a land of classes but that is part of its very diversity and the class structure is in no way divisive. Britain is a land of deep harmony. Working-class culture is embraced and dignified – the choral tradition of Britain's northern industrial cities, exemplified in shots of the Huddersfield Choral Society exalting in the 'Hallelujah Chorus', dominates *Heart of Britain*. For Jennings, the badges of working-class identity did not mean a cheap or lowly culture: in *Listen to Britain* ordinary servicemen and women, deliberately identified by the focus on the rank insignia on their uni-forms, are seen studying artworks at a National Gallery exhibition of war artists. *Listen to Britain* also shows us wartime heroes still significant today. Flanagan and Allen singing 'Underneath the Arches' in a factory canteen encapsulates our vision of the community spirit we identify as one of wartime Britain's greatest assets. Bud Flanagan has stayed with us as the voice behind *Dad's Army*'s theme song, 'Who Do You Think You

Are Kidding, Mr Hitler?', that most perfect pastiche of 1940s popular taste. Jennings captured what we now expect of wartime Britain: Bruce Belfrage's announcement of victory at El Alamein is cheered by factory girls sitting at their benches; a female lathe-operator singing along to 'Yes, My Darling Daughter' played on the factory loudspeaker system: here are the people winning their war. It is a vision of unity, happiness despite the conditions, decency, dignity and harmony we envy so deeply. Of course, many would say this nostalgic longing for a world that never really existed is extremely dangerous, not to mention pernicious, as it turns legend into fact. Yet just because Jennings' view cannot be regarded as true of all the people all of the time it does not stop it from being true of some of the people some of the time.

Women

An integral part of Jennings' tribute is a salute to the labour of British women. The role of women in the People's War is one that has come back into the public consciousness after largely disappearing in the 1950s and 1960s. With the growth of women's history and gender studies in the 1970s and 1980s, the need to recognise and study the role of women in the Second World War was asserted. However, it was never a mission to recover a story suppressed since its inception, rather it was the recovery of something openly debated and discussed during the war years.

The Second World War was the first in which British women had taken part as enfranchised citizens, and the twentieth century's crucial test of citizenship has been service to the state in time of war. Facing a significant shortage of labour, Britain went further than any combatant nation by gradually conscripting and enlisting nearly all women. Women were enlisted through various acts: the National Service Act 1941, the Registration of Employment Order of the same year and the Employment of Women Order 1942. It created a situation whereby all women aged between 18 and 40 could be conscripted by the government. In turn, this had a significant effect on the type of women in employment; by 1943 47 per cent of the female industrial force was married, and one-third had children.[35] Absenteeism was high, which can only partly be explained by domestic duties and problems. There was the constant issue of prejudicial and intolerant attitudes from the male workforce, poor pay and lack of facilities. It became increasingly difficult to persuade women to serve their country by working in factories, most wanted non-industrial jobs. The problem was exacerbated by the Ministry of Labour's insensitive approach to female demands and needs, often believing that women wanted to take simple options, even going as far as implying that many would rather be prostitutes for the sheer profit margins than patriotically support the nation.[36]

Wanting to produce a positive image of women in war, the Ministry of Information enthusiastically supported the successful film production duo Frank Launder and Sidney Gilliat in their plans to make a film celebrating women in the factories. *Millions Like Us*, released in 1943, emphasised the importance of female labour to the war effort. Horrified by the thought of factory work, the young, naïve heroine, Celia (Patricia Roc), is told by another woman: 'There's nothing to be afraid of in a factory. Mr Bevin needs another million women, and I don't think we should disappoint him at a time like this. The men at the front need tanks, guns and planes. You can help your country just as much in an overall as you can in a uniform these days.' Celia gradually gains confidence and begins to like her job making aircraft components. She finds that living in a government hostel is not so bad and makes friends with a variety of women from different backgrounds. But the film skil- fully avoids the trap of patronising its audience by being too upbeat; the downside is also explored. The foreman tells them, 'Now you'd better understand there's not much glamour in a machine shop', and Celia's life is touched by tragedy as she marries a young air-gunner who is soon killed in action. Here was the gritty reality of war: a reality that was not denied by the government because it was impossible to avoid the fact of casualties, but the way this experience was interpreted could be shaped in particular ways. Thus Celia's tragedy can only be palliated by the victory of the just.

Another powerful image of women's war work was that produced by the artist Dame Laura Knight. In 1943 she was commissioned by the War Artists Advisory Committee to paint the heroine of the factories. Ruby Loftus was the first woman to be employed on the highly skilled work of screwing the breech ring of the Bofors gun. Considered to be the prerogative of a man with a nine-year apprenticeship behind him at the Royal Ordnance Factory, Loftus had gained the skill by the age of 21 after two years' training. Knight painted Loftus at her lathe and produced a masterpiece of heroic realism, which (unwittingly?) reflected the pro-Soviet celebration and idealisation of the working class. Hair tied up in a turban, clad in a blue overall, Loftus bends over her lathe with a look of concentration and experience. In the background other women are involved in similar tasks. Produced in postcard form, this very English Stakhanovite was distributed to factories across Britain.[37]

Since the war the role of women in factories has become less prominent. Though most dramas set during the war hint at it, they often don't do much more than that. The reason for this omission from the dominant modern memory is probably because women retreated from the workplace with rapidity in 1945, thus leaving very little evidence of their important contribution to victory. Historians have debated the long-term significance of this movement into the male sphere of employment for many years. Arthur Marwick, an exponent of the idea that war is an engine for social change, believes war work brought women out of their homes and into a wider world which may have been temporary for some but established a significant precedent, with the result that the post-war world could never return to its 1939 standards.[38] A more subtle argument has been advanced by Penny Summerfield. She has shown that the Second World War forced the complementary forces of patriarchy and capitalism, prevalent in the powers of the state, to face up to the problem of labour supply which demanded female workers. She contends that in trying to achieve a solution suitable to both capitalism and patriarchy, the state often severely constrained the role of women and did little to alter the unequal position of women within British society.[39]

Seemingly more glamorous were the women's uniformed services. By 1945 over half a million women were serving in the Auxiliary Territorial Service (ATS), the Women's Royal Navy Service (WRNS), the Women's Auxiliary Air Force (WAAF), the Air Transport Auxiliary (ATA) and the First Aid Nursing Yeomanry (FANY).[40] Although women were mainly employed on ancillary tasks such as clerking and cooking, some were trained as mechanics, while others ferried aircraft from factories to their new bases or were deployed on anti-aircraft batteries in mixed-sex crews. Running alongside the military services was the uniformed Women's Land Army, which included a timber unit.

Dame Laura Knight's Ruby Loftus Screwing a Breech Ring: the vital contribution of women to the war effort (Imperial War Museum art, film and photograph archives).

A life of exciting adventure seemed to be the promise of the women's uniformed services. This idea was given a huge boost by Abram Games' sensual recruiting poster. Dominated by the profile of a cool blonde, Games' poster was soon withdrawn at the insistence of MPs who felt it encouraged false expectations (and might also attract the wrong sort of woman). In 1943 the ATS was the focus of a feature film, *The Gentle Sex*. Much derided by modern commentators for its male view of woman-hood, the film was very popular at the time, particularly among women.[41] Like *Millions Like Us*, it attempted to promote life in the services but not by showing it in too one-sided a manner. But as with factory work, it was Laura Knight who produced the most potent images of women in uni-form. In 1940 she painted a number of women decorated for their actions: *Corporal Robbins with Assistant Section Leaders E. Henderson MN and Sergeant D. Turner* and an individual portrait of *Corporal Daphne Pearson GC*. Pearson had dragged a pilot from a burning bomber packed with bombs and shielded him from the blast of the explosion with her body. For her actions she was awarded the Empire Gallantry Medal, which was later transmuted to the George Cross. In Knight's portrait, Pearson sits looking at the sky, the peaceful Malvern countryside in the background. Her face is one of dedication and quiet heroism, a tribute to gallantry. But the finest of Knight's wartime works is *A Balloon Site, Coventry*. Commissioned in 1943 to recruit 'the right sort of woman for Balloon Command', the painting shows women pulling on the guy-ropes of a slowly rising balloon while the chimneys of Coventry are smoking in the background.[42] It captures the intense physical strain of the work – at first women were not considered strong enough for this task, but when this stance was dropped in 1941 it was still found that a crew of 16 women was required to replace a male crew of 10.[43] At the same time, it also reveals the significance of balloon barrages, for the operational factories of Coventry are the fruits of the labour. Knight's biographer, Caroline Fox, states that she succeeded 'in making this appear both a heroic and glamorous occupation'.[44]

The physically demanding nature of life in the services often out-shone the exciting image. Terese Roberts, a gunner on an anti-aircraft site, recalled washing in ice-capped fire buckets and Elaine Burton bemoaned the lack of proper lavatories.[45] Joan Wyndham's fascinating diaries reveal her shock at the impersonal nature of her WAAF medical

and the instruction not to attend if menstruating.[46] Land girls often faced
an even harder regime, working on backbreaking tasks from dawn till
dusk and occasionally facing the hostility of their surrogate communities.[47] But the majority of women who served remember their time in
uniform with pride. Mickie Hutton Storie, a former member of a search-
light team, who joined up despite her parents' disapproval, noted:

> I cannot stress enough how well these girls behaved in action, even
> though sometimes German bombers would dive down the beams with
> machine guns blazing away, trying to put the light out. They still went
> on duty, even when the telegrams arrived that their husbands had been
> killed or injured at Arnhem. It was a marvellous feeling of just working
> together. It was utterly marvellous.[48]

As with factory work, post-war interpretations of female service
life are hardly numerous. Lucy Noakes has suggested that the need to
maintain the image of women as home makers and mothers was – and
continues to be – the dominant stumbling block:

> There is little or no room in this popular memory of Britain at war for
> women in uniform, although many women served as members of the
> ATS, the WRNS and the WRAF [sic]. Instead, women represent the
> nation's values, the family at home that the men are fighting to defend.
> Active images of women in wartime are mediated through the need for
> women to retain a relative degree of passivity in the public narrative
> of war.[49]

Proof of this rule can be found in its two most significant exceptions.
In the 1950s two popular films provided an alternative history by showing a reality hidden in wartime. *Odette* (1950) and *Carve Her Name With
Pride* (1958) revealed what the wartime state could not – that women,
mothers, wives and home front workers for victory were actually being
sent on highly dangerous missions behind enemy lines. Starring the
well-known British actress, Anna Neagle, and directed by her husband,
Herbert Wilcox, *Odette* told the story of Odette Sansom, a young
Frenchwoman married to an Englishman. This mother of three was
recruited by the Special Operations Executive in 1941 and sent to France.
Meeting her contact, Peter Churchill (played by Trevor Howard in the
film), she worked as a courier in the area around Cannes. When their

circuit was penetrated by the Nazis, they fled but both were soon captured. With great skill she managed to convince the Nazis that they were
married and that Peter was the nephew of Winston Churchill. This story
saved both from execution and when the allies approached her prison,
the commandant drove her to the American forces and presented her as
the niece of Churchill, no doubt hoping it would save him from an awful
retribution.

Neagle played Odette as a woman of great passion who puts service
to the cause of freedom above that of motherhood. Her loyalty to her
comrades is that commonly attributed to men in wartime and so she
combines the emotions of a woman with the temperament of a man. A similar theme runs through *Carve Her Name With Pride*. Virginia McKenna
played Violette Szabo, an Anglo-French woman who had married a
French Foreign Legion officer killed at El Alamein. Szabo, like Odette
Sansom, was a mother who took the agonising decision to leave her home
in order to defend the homes of millions. Captured by the Germans just
prior to D-Day, Szabo was executed at Ravensbruck concentration camp
along with two other female Special Operations Executive agents, Denise
Bloch and Lilian Rolfe. McKenna's Szabo is a neat, homely woman;
Robert Murphy has remarked that she retains her virginal appearance and
attitude even after the birth of her daughter.[50] But it is exactly this trait
which gives the film its emotional power; she is so sweet a person caught
up in such a dreadful situation confronting enemies who retain not the
slightest vestige of human decency. Murphy believes the success of these
two films reveals a reaction against the conformist society of the 1950s
and provided proof that woman did indeed do great things in the cause of
allied victory.[51] Both films have now taken on an almost clichéd quality
precisely because they are the only examples of their genre and have
been repeated so often.

In the late 1980s the ITV network revived the female spy story for television in the drama series *Wish Me Luck*. The darker, more old-fashioned
view of women as Mata Haris, sexually sophisticated manipulators of
men, has been recently resurrected in the film version of *Enigma* (2001),
Robert Harris' best-selling novel (1995). Based on the code-breaking
centre at Bletchley Park, the story entwines two male visions of women.
Hester Wallace, played by Kate Winslet, is dependable, honest and therefore almost inevitably lacks sexual poise. Claire Romilly, played by

WE CAN TAKE IT!

Saffron Burrows, is a sensual siren who calls the brilliant code-breaker Tom Jericho (Dougray Scott) to his doom. Sebastian Faulks provided a further variant on this type of story in his novel *Charlotte Gray* (1998), and its subsequent adaptation for cinema (2001).

The only other film version of women's life in uniform to make any sort of impact on the public is *Land Girls* (1998). *Land Girls* has a remarkably old-fashioned feel to it, almost as if it is a government-approved wartime feature. Following three women from very different backgrounds, played by Anna Friel, Catherine McCormack and Rachel Weisz, the film shows their gradual acceptance of country life and codes. At the same time, the grumpy farmer eventually comes to appreciate and respect them as they show increasing skill and judgement in their work. As with the British popular perception of the war, the film does not attempt to disguise difficulties or tensions but presents them as obstacles overcome by the spirit of a united people. Once again, facts are not denied but are reworked to be included in a story underpinned by a particular moral. Tales of unmitigated misery from land girls there must be, but does that necessarily mean that Joan Shakesheff's pride at 'doing something worthwhile' is a false memory shaped by a nostalgic desire for a Britain that never existed in reality?[52]

Evidence of a more mundane reality is certainly not hard to find. Men on the home front rarely readjusted their role to help accommodate women who had taken on war work. Most women continued to play domestic roles, caring for children and running the household. In wartime this often meant queuing for hours, mending clothes long after they would normally have been discarded and trying to ensure childcare during work hours. Even women without a job would have found their traditional role a lot harder to perform in the difficult circumstances imposed by war.

Living with the war

This effect of war on everyday routines has been passed on to us. *Family at War* certainly highlighted the stresses and strains the conflict placed on women. Jean Ashton is worn down by the burden of war, worrying constantly about the safety of her grown-up children, and the ongoing struggle to maintain any semblance of ordinary family life drives her into an early grave. Derided as a piece of nostalgia by some critics, as has been noted, *Family at War* was sober and realistic as well as celebratory. Those who, like myself, were at secondary school in the 1980s were also shown the realities of wartime home life, albeit in a much less harrowing way, in *How We Used to Live*. Most recently, Channel 4 scored a great popular success with its series *The 1940s House*, which was accompanied by a special exhibition at the Imperial War Museum and a handsome coffee table book (2000). The series found a family willing to take on the role of time-travellers and placed them in a typical 1930s house restored to its 1940 condition. Nothing of their modern life was allowed to remain as the series sought to show the reality of the 1940s. Here was *How We Used to Live* for adults. A particular feature of the programme was the way in which the trials and tribulations of wartime life forced the family to become a tighter unit, and this might explain its success. In our increasingly atomised world, where relationships seem far more ephemeral and fragile, this tribute to community and interdependence struck a chord.

Time travel and the comparison between our world and that of wartime Britain also lay at the heart of one of the BBC's greatest successes of recent years. Laurence Mark's and Maurice Gran's *Goodnight Sweetheart* consistently achieved high viewing figures, ran for six years (1993–99) and even has its own fan-run websites. The star of the show is Gary Sparrow (Nicholas Lyndhurst), a television repairman. Lost in the East End, Gary asks a policeman for directions. Told to go down an alley and then ask again at the Royal Oak pub, Gary walks into the 1940s. Gary's life then becomes a balancing act between his wife in modern London and a romance with the publican's daughter in the 1940s. Obsessed with the spirit of the 1940s, the show made great efforts to recapture the feel of the time and the characters of George Formby, Noël Coward and even Clement Attlee made appearances. In fact, what the series captured was the spirit of *Dad's Army* – that of affectionate tribute – and so buttressed our generally positive image of British society in the Second World War. Given the success of the comedy, it is hard to argue against the idea that Britain has a continuing obsession with the conflict.

Songs and throwaway references to films and stars of the war were an integral part of the 'authenticity' of both *Dad's Army* and *Goodnight Sweetheart*. The popular tastes of the 1940s tell much indeed about its spirit and whether our memory has become a mere parody of the situation. Cinema was the great pastime, and became even more popular in wartime, particularly for women. After working long hours, often missing the company of men, the cinema was a place of comfort and escape.[53] Feminist historians such as Sue Harper and Antonia Lant have studied the representation of women on the screen and the extent to which women's tastes were catered for. Harper has stated that women in wartime cinema were used 'to signify forbidden wilfulness (*The Wicked Lady*, 1945), ratified monogamy (*In Which We Serve*, 1942), innocent sensuality (*Lady Hamilton*, 1941), doomed feminism (*Thunder Rock*, 1942), proletarian doggedness (*Millions Like Us*, 1943) or aging support (*The Prime Minister*, 1941).'[54] However, as she also points out, it was men, with the input of very few women, who made most of these films. Despite this, she believes that some films can be regarded as 'belonging' to women:

> Although during the war women were largely excluded from the film-making process by a combination of industrial structure, official policy and cultural conditioning, the male progenitors of such films as The Wicked Lady or Lady Hamilton should be regarded as female 'substitutes', even though they were doubtless motivated partially by cupidity and acquisitiveness.[55]

The demands of war industry, pulling in more and more female labour, created a vast army of women factory workers who were often burdened by dull jobs and long hours. These women longed for colour, excitement and glamour in their precious leisure hours and one studio in particular, Gainsborough, gave it to them. Most critics loathed Gainsborough melodramas with their bodice ripping, slashed-shirt romping. Slammed for their shoddy history and unashamed excesses, Gainsborough's films were, however, just what hundreds of thousands of British women wanted.

The Wicked Lady (1945), Gainsborough's most successful film, starred Margaret Lockwood and James Mason as a pair of outlaw-lovers. Set in a heavily stylised seventeenth century, *The Wicked Lady* shows the past to be a place of romance, intrigue, dashing men and sensual pleasure. Margaret Lockwood is attracted to robbery after becoming bored of her dull husband and life in the countryside. Revelling in the excitement of highway robbery, she ends up paying for her bad ways by dying alone and in agony. By contrast, the good girl whom she has wronged (Patricia Roc) gains the love of a decent and honourable man who will make her very happy. But the moral lesson of *The Wicked Lady* is actually far more ambiguous. Lockwood's character may get her comeuppance but her life is so much more glamorous, sexy and rewarding than Roc's that the benefits of virtue appear stultifying. Sue Harper has shown how young women, and adolescent girls in particular, idolised Lockwood's image and aspired to copy it. She quotes a Birmingham survey in which 67 per cent of schoolgirls admitted imitating Lockwood, 'thus endorsing Ted Black's instinct that she had "something with which every girl in the suburbs could identify herself"'.[56]

As well as films that hinted at sexual intrigue, women liked romances. Some of the most financially successful films of the war years were the Hollywood-made British melodramas such as *Waterloo Bridge* (1940), *Mrs Miniver* (1942), *Random Harvest* (1942) and *The White Cliffs of Dover* (1944). All four films were produced by Sidney Franklin for MGM and each of them 'centres on the pain and anxiety caused by wartime separation or loss, and each offers a strong, maternal and caring woman as a source of safety and serenity amid the heartaches of war'.[57]

It is a rural, idyllic, hierarchical village England which is celebrated and perpetuated in these MGM films. Ironically, the harmony of this strictly class-based England, which was so popular at the British box office, was facing intense pressure due to the realities of war. *Random Harvest* is typical of this mini genre: men and women find love and contentment, often across class barriers, and, despite the odd fractious moment, British society retains its cohesion due to deeply entrenched values of respect, humility, duty and service. A box-office smash in Britain, *Random Harvest* was the most successful film of 1942 revealing a public eager to soak up tear-jerking heartstring-pullers.

Mrs Miniver, the biggest financial success of them all, introduced the middle class, often missing from the Hollywood British film in favour of the aristocracy–working-class binary relationship. The middle-class Minivers are actually a lot closer to an American understanding of what an ordinary family should be; the British middle class was probably not quite as 'ostentatious' as MGM perceived them. However, coinciding entirely with British middle-class opinion is the emphasis on the Minivers as representative of the nation and its core values. Mrs Miniver is the ideal matriarch, caring for her little children during the horrors of an air raid, worrying about her hot-headed son, Vin, an RAF pilot, and gradually pacifying the rather cantankerous Lady Belton, who worries that her granddaughter is lowering herself by falling for Vin Miniver. Belham, the Kentish village where the Minivers live, is the ideal feudal unit, dominated by church and manor house. At the same time, it is the ideal unit of co-operation, interdependence and sheer fortitude and bravery. Mr Miniver sails off to Dunkirk in his little boat while his wife tackles a Nazi airman in the kitchen. At the end of the film, the villagers gather in the blitzed church for Sunday service. Death has come to the village thanks to the Nazis. Vin has lost his wife and Lady Belton her granddaughter. By sitting with Lady Belton, Vin joins her in stoic accept-ance of loss and reveals war crossing class boundaries and creating unity. The film ends on a stirring note of vigour as the clergyman urges them all to greater heights of endeavour and self-sacrifice:

> *Why, in all conscience, should these be the ones to suffer? I shall tell you why! Because this is not only a war of soldiers in uniform. It is a war of the people – of all the people – and it must be fought not only on the battlefield but in the cities and villages, in the factories and on the farms, in the home and in the heart of every man, woman and child who loves freedom. . . . This is a People's War! It is our war! We are the fighters!*

Mrs Miniver was an extraordinary box-office success in both the USA and Britain and topped the British box-office charts in 1942. The British people clearly wanted melodrama in their drab, hard-pressed wartime lives. This was melodrama of a particular nature as it combined elements of the wartime reality with fantasy and so provided 'realistic escapism'. But the acceptance of a hierarchical, class-based Britain on the silver screen by no means meant that the British people were content to accept it in their everyday lives; 1942, as has been noted, was a year of tremend-ous upheaval.

The British public taste in films was therefore a little ambiguous. 'Decent' romance was enjoyed, but they also accepted hints at more saucy goings-on. To what extent was this a reflection of wartime realities and how has it been understood in the modern image of personal life in the war? John Costello's work has shown how the conditions of war created a situation in which attitudes towards sex altered.[58] Male and female lives were uprooted and transplanted to new environments or routines and in doing so forced a re-evaluation of morals. For many, out of sight meant out of mind and infidelity lost its power to shame and reign in desires. Contradictory forces were unleashed by the war: those of heightened emotion due to fear, feelings of instability and the unpredictability of events. It provoked a 'do as you please for tomorrow you may die' attitude. At the same time, the war had its own monotonous, all-pervasiveness that provoked a desire for emotional release and excitement.

Sex, Poles and Yanks

Inevitably sexual morals became a matter of concern to many and those of servicewomen were thought to be the most lax. A Mass-Observer surveyor overheard the outraged opinion of a man in a Chester pub: 'Those ATS girls are a disgrace. They come into this pub at night and line up against that wall. Soldiers give them drinks and then when they're blind drunk they carry them out into the street. And we're paying public money for them too.'[59] So widespread did such rumours become that a committee was convened to investigate the sexual conduct of servicewomen. The issue was intimately connected with concerns over the drop in legitimate births, and the concomitant rise in illegitimacy and the growing use of contraceptives. Between 1940 and 1945 there were 255,000 births, out of which around 102,000 were illegitimate, representing a huge increase on the pre-war illegitimacy rate.[60] But it was the increase in venereal disease that caused most morbid interest and debate. Obsessed with efficiency, the army was convinced that VD would undermine its abilities as a fighting force. It was a continuation of a debate given much time during the Great War, but unlike the Great War responses, the government broke all taboos about the subject and began a full campaign of public education. In the autumn of 1942 the Ministry of Health began to publicise the problem of sexually transmitted diseases and placed a series of advertisements in the press giving information and advice. Lurid posters were produced warning men and women against careless attitudes towards sexual hygiene *and* moral probity.[61] Men appear to have lost their shame about this subject quite quickly and sought medical attention earlier, thus bringing down male VD rates noticeably. However, women probably still felt shame at contracting the disease and female VD rates remained high.[62]

Angus Calder referred to mid-war Britain as the India-rubber island as it contorted itself to meet the demands of total war. By 1944 the rubber island had made room for 1,421,000 allied, dominion and colonial troops. The arrival of such vast numbers from an equally wide variety of countries and backgrounds increased the opportunities for both platonic and physical relationships. Such relationships often caused deep resentment in British men, but over the years they have become an important part of the myth of the home front.

Early in the war Polish pilots were often identified as the charming lotharios sweeping British women off their feet. Spike Milligan's memoirs capture the weak joke they had become by 1943. After suffering the disappointment of receiving no mail, a fellow gunner tells him to cheer up, 'You can read my letter, my wife's pissed off with a Polish pilot.' A month later Sergeant Dale announces ''Ere! My missus has run off with a bleedin' Polish airman!' 'That's funny,' announces another gunner, 'so 'as mine. They must be short of planes.'[63] Ironic proof of the attraction to Poles is found in the recollections of a lecturer who tried to interest the ATS in the long-term prospects for Poland but failed miserably. 'On the next occasion an enterprising officer at a similar unit had the talk billed under the heading "Would you marry a Pole?" As some of the girls had, the discussion which ensued was lively in the extreme.'[64]

But it was the Americans who became the most exotic prize, and they were much envied by their British comrades for their superior pay and better quality uniforms. Often considered to be enjoying the life of riley by British servicemen while they fought the real war, it wasn't long before the Yanks gained the epithet most Britons still recognise: 'over-sexed, over-paid and over here'. The arrival of large numbers of GIs created a stir in communities across Britain. They brought huge pieces of hardware with them – lorries, tanks, self-propelled guns – and in vast quantities too. On a more domestic level, they also brought items severely rationed in Britain. Americans had sweets, cigarettes, butter and a host of other commodities in profusion. When combined with uniforms that made them look like officers and accents heard only at the cinema, it was hardly surprising that many women caught in drab wartime Britain started relationships with American soldiers. At the end of the war around **80,000** GI brides left Britain for the USA.[65] Strenuous efforts were made during the war to maintain the image of Americans as decent allies who had no intention of 'stealing' British women. What went unnoticed then, and is lost in the popular memory today, obsessed as it is with the idea of dashing GIs, is that many were sober, shy, lonely young men who led quiet lives while encamped in Britain. Pamela Winfield, who first met Americans as a 17 year-old at a Wimbledon town hall dance, recalled that 'in fact we found out that the majority were small-town boys, straight out of high school, and church-going. The vision that they were all wild and woolly was not fair.'[66]

The film *Daily Mail* readers voted as their favourite of the war, *The Way to the Stars* (1945), was a story of Anglo-American co-operation tinted with a hint of romance. An excellently crafted film with a touching Terence Rattigan script, *The Way to the Stars* tells the story of an RAF airfield taken over by the US Air Force. The remaining RAF personnel gradually come to terms with the boisterous Americans and both mix in the bar of the local hotel. Johnny Hollis (Douglass Montgomery), an American pilot, strikes up a friendship with the hotel owner, Toddy (Rosamund John). Missing his wife and children, Johnny finds Toddy an understanding friend. She is a widowed mother, having lost her husband, an RAF pilot, in a raid over Germany. Drawn closer together, the two teeter on the verge of a romance but decency and mutual respect prevail and the moment passes. At the end of the film, Johnny reveals the new union of the great English-speaking family by sacrificing himself. Returning from a mission in a crippled bomber still carrying part of its load, he refuses to save his own life by bailing out and allowing the bomber to crash somewhere near the village, possibly endangering the villagers. Instead, he attempts to land the bomber at the airfield, knowing and accepting the vast risk involved. Johnny dies that others might live. Moviegoers were extremely moved by it, and C.A. Lejeune, critic for the *Observer*, believed it had identified the sinews holding together the Anglo-American friendship and alliance:

> [It is] the only film I have ever seen that succeeds in explaining the
> Englishman to the American, and the American to the Englishman with
> good humour, good sense and clarity. It does this in the frankest possible
> way, by admitting that any difference that exists between British and

> *American manners must necessarily present itself to the American as*
> *an inferiority on the part of the British, and to the Englishman as an*
> *inferiority on the part of the American; but that there are things deeper*
> *than manners, which both nations admit to be superior, and which they*
> *have in common.*[67]

The reality behind this vision of shared moral and political objectives
was that Britain was utterly bankrupt, heavily in debt to the United States
and in no way an equal partner.[68]

During the war, therefore, officially approved views of American servicemen were positive ones. 'Americans in British wartime features are
"over here",' as Sue Harper has noted, 'but they are neither overpaid nor
oversexed.'[69] Since the war the popular memory has tended to focus on the
idea of the GI as a glamorous leading man. Two films released in 1979,
Hanover Street and *Yanks*, were a curious mixture of wartime genre conventions consciously resurrected, but this time the women who fall for
Americans have sex with them too. *Hanover Street* stars Harrison Ford
as an American pilot and Lesley-Anne Down as Margaret Sellinger, an
English woman with a husband serving in the forces. Unlike *The Way to
the Stars*, however, this relationship becomes physical. *Yanks* became
the more famous of the two largely due to the performance, and looks, of
Richard Gere. Playing an army cook, he falls for Jean (Lisa Eichhorn), an
English woman living near the camp. Emotional upheaval comes in the
form of Jean's long-standing engagement to a British soldier. But Jean and
Matt are portrayed as having deeper physical desires than her British
fiancé and so their relationship becomes the natural one. With the former
boyfriend out of the way, the lovers do not find immediate contentment
as British prejudices towards American servicemen are highlighted.
However the two survive their troubles, held together by the strength of
their love.

Partly inspired by the success of *Yanks*, the ITV network launched
a television drama series centring on the lives of American airmen based
in a small English village. *We'll Meet Again* came to the screens in 1982
– somewhat ironically, full-page advertisements promoting the drama
appeared in British newspapers on the day they announced an imminent
invasion of the Falklands.[70] Romance was at the heart of the drama,
as British women fell for American airmen. Few of the romances ran

smoothly as the village men are shown to be a mostly suspicious and unfriendly bunch keen to keep Yankee paws off British girls. The women who fall for the Americans are from a wide range of backgrounds, and include the lady of the manor (Susannah York). Although married to an officer serving in North Africa, she cannot resist the gallant CO, at least ensuring an affair with someone of similar rank. *We'll Meet Again* hit all the buttons of popular memory – fun-loving Americans giving away rationed goods with generous abandon, miserable British men sullenly brooding over the presence of the bloody Yanks and, of course, the strains of Vera Lynn.

A slight variant on the handsome American can be found in *Hope and Glory* (1987). Here a French Canadian replaces the GI. Dawn Rowan (Sami Davies), hardly more than a schoolgirl when she meets him, rapidly falls in lust and then love, ending the film with a war baby. British culture has obviously accepted the idea of wartime relationships, including infidelity. Significantly, however, it is an acceptance of female love and transgression. There are few images of British soldiers having affairs, of sailors with wives in every port or foremen using their position to flatter female workers. It is possible to find soldiers having sex with prostitutes in Spike Milligan's war memoirs, but the whole thing is suffused in comedy with the atmosphere of a smutty seaside postcard.

Attitudes towards sex did change during the war; without some shift our popular images would not have taken shape. Anyone reading Joan Wyndham's two published wartime diaries will see how she progresses from rather naïve convent girl to sexually experienced WAAF, discovering the joys of masturbation and experimenting with bondage along the way.[71] Sue Harper implies a degree of liberation, mentioning the increased use of cosmetics, particularly as a reaction to dull, Utility brand clothing.[72] However, it was liberation of a limited sort. For Lucy Noakes, the stream of advice on how to look good in uniform, how to get the best out of cosmetics and maintain good looks is something that reinforced traditional gender roles.[73] It is also very clear that the blame for spreading venereal disease was placed on women, with men's behaviour hardly ever mentioned. So-called 'good time girls' were thought to be even more responsible for the increased numbers of those suffering from sexually transmitted diseases than prostitutes, and girls of up to 23 years of age could be sent to borstal for sexual laxity.[74]

Women were under constant exhortation to remain chaste and wait for their husband or fiancé to return from the war. Women's magazines warned against infidelity; Constance Holt, the wartime editor of *Woman's Own*, recalled its clear and uncompromising advice:

> '*You can't do this to your husband, or even your fiancé, while he is away fighting for his country. You must break it up or wait until after the war and resolve it. You must not see this man'. We'd go as far as that – that was the advice we gave them.*[75]

As Lucy Noakes has argued, such attitudes revealed the buttressing of traditional gender roles rather than their realignment or redefinition. Two, opposed forces were therefore at work, one liberating and new, the other traditional. In the Second World War the state encouraged women to take on men's roles, but at the same time reassured men in uniform that their women were ready to play doting wives and mothers as soon as they returned. Balancing these two female roles and ensuring that women were ready to do both was a tricky proposition. Graham Dawson has developed a complimentary position with regards to male behaviour, stating that the image of the soldier hero provides men with a constant model of masculinity, shaping their perceptions and actions, which remains impervious to – and a defence against – changes in the economy and its concomitant re-ordering of working lives and roles.[76] Thus, men and women were expected to fulfil their traditional gender roles in the Second World War. 'Women and men, while fulfilling their roles as useful wartime citizens, were expected to do so within existing con-structions of femininity and masculinity.'[77] Performing men's jobs did not necessarily emancipate women because their essential relationship with, and relative position to, men did not change.

A good measure of how far values were *perceived* to have changed came in July 1945 when the Archbishop of Canterbury used a sermon to urge a rejection of 'wartime morality'. It was warmly welcomed and sup-ported by other ecclesiastics.[78] Far from facing a wave of protest from people happy in the land of lotus-eating, the majority of British people probably agreed with this stance. A return to normality was wanted by all, but that was hardly possible. Britain was financially and econom-ically ruined in 1945, rationing would have to continue and become even more stringent, demobilisation would take a long time, the fruits of

victory would not be tasted for many years. However, most women were
prepared to give normality a try, starting with their exodus from the
workplace. The vast majority of women re-embraced their roles as wives
and mothers with remarkably little fuss. And who can blame them?
Overworked, underpaid, forced to labour in often appalling conditions,
many women wanted the security and relief of their former roles. The
home – and all its myriad demands – still looked better than the workplace, especially if the main breadwinner was coming home and eager to
reassert his position after so many years of disorientation.

Nothing represents this desire for a return to normality better than
that most English of films, *Brief Encounter* (1945, the same year as *The
Wicked Lady*). Now seen as a quintessential reflection of British culture,
it was far from an unqualified success on first release with many finding
the film either too painful in its treatment of adultery or lacking credibility in its retreat from it.[79] *Brief Encounter* is the story of a middle-class
woman (Celia Johnson) who escapes from her humdrum life as wife and
mother to find romance with a charming doctor (Trevor Howard), but
overcome by a sense of guilt and remorse she puts duty first and breaks
off her affair regardless of the pain it causes. From its ambiguous initial
release to the equally ambiguous reactions to it today, *Brief Encounter* is
a symbol of our mixed memory of wartime sexual and romantic life.
In turn, this seems to be a reflection of our own debates about personal
relationships, giving authority to Noakes' assertion that the memory of
the war alters and changes along with society itself, and where it remains
static it does so for similarly contemporary reasons.[80]

We seem to be equally happy accepting both pure romance *and* sexual
adventure as the qualities of wartime private lives. In 1993 the Imperial
War Museum staged one of its most successful exhibitions, 'Forces
Sweethearts', designed to reveal personal feelings and emotions from the
First World War to the Gulf War, though the main emphasis was on
the Second World War. The exhibition was also aimed at 'feminising'
the museum, and it certainly worked. 'Coachloads of old ladies made
unprecedented visits to Lambeth', as Margaretta Jolly has noted, 'and tak-
ings rocketed at a time when all museums were struggling to keep themselves viable.'[81] Although the exhibition did cover some saucy aspects,
such as soldiers' pin-ups, its main thrust was romance, and heterosexual
romance at that. Gay relationships, abortion, sexually transmitted diseases,

heartache and death did not play a role. In some ways the exhibition was almost a modern version of the idealised private lives promoted by the state and self-appointed moral guardians during the war. However, it was clearly a vision most people found acceptable and it turned Joanna Lumley's accompanying book into a best-seller (1993).

But at the same time as celebrating the stoic acceptance of painful separations and romantic reunions, we accept and acknowledge the affairs and illegitimate babies. Our popular culture is full of such examples. That most excellent of radio comedies, *Round the Horne*, in its routine send-ups of British wartime attitudes, contained a sketch about a returning officer asking his wife for news of the children. He proceeds to list a stream of very Anglo-Saxon names, but the penultimate is Abdullah, and he adds 'You know I've worried a lot about young Abdullah'. Sexual infidelity was something to be joked at by the 1960s. Similarly, Channel 4's 1992 adaptation of Mary Wesley's *The Camomile Lawn* (1984) was treated like a nudge-nudge joke there was so much illicit sex, but few seemed to believe it had besmirched our glorious wartime reputation. For all the jokes about it, *The Camomile Lawn* was actually a powerful piece of television, showing shifts in attitudes towards sex and relationships. *Family at War* treated infidelity seriously, showing its effects on the Ashton family. Once again, it becomes obvious that the warts-and-all truth about Britain in the Second World War, believed to be suppressed in the common memory by so many revisionist commentators, is far from valid. However, very dark facts like abortion and sexually transmitted diseases are still far from discussed or acknowledged. The grubby underside of the Second World War can be found in popular culture such as the BBC television productions of *Imitation Game* and *Licking Hitler* but they are hardly icons like *Reach for the Sky* or *The Dam Busters*.

Our acceptance of both the 'good' and the 'bad' in wartime private lives fits our contemporary understandings of relationships. We argue whether the merits of greater sexual freedom are healthier than older values of the sanctity of marriage and the family. It is in the context of this debate that we can best place modern reactions to *Brief Encounter*. There are a number of different positions and groups to be identified. The first represents those who see it as the embodiment of a value system completely lacking in today's Britain, much to its detriment. The second accepts the great emotional pull of the film, has some nostalgic longing for the world it supports, but is capable of gentle mockery. An excellent example of this was found in the *Victoria Wood Christmas Special 2001*. She provided a superb parody, turning it into a lesbian affair. But the parody worked due to her obvious affection for the original; it was the homage of someone who knew the nuances, language and nature of 1940s British film culture. A third group finds the film moving but symbolic of all that was wrong with Britain in 1945. It is viewed as a tragedy of unfulfilled desire, of damning adherence to a muddleheaded system which valued duty above personal happiness. Thus, the common perception of wartime relationships and attitudes is far from a narrow or simple one. It is an area of contradiction and debate, but in no way endangers the overall image of unity and endeavour.

The popular memory of the home front therefore contains many elements translated directly, if rather loosely at times, from the war. The great mythologised elements are still very much part of our memory. GIs, rationing, spivs and the concept of a unified people fighting a People's War. But, this does not mean a simple memory; it is one that acknowledges transgression and shadows. Missing from it are some significant parts of our Second World War history. The deep respect and fellow feeling for the Russian people and the Red Army, the fierceness with which political issues were fought and the levels of industrial unrest are hardly understood today. Britain's imagined war is a curious phenomenon. It reflects a desire to see it as the finest hour without ever becoming a complete whitewash. It is not a monolithic story and explanation of the war because the war itself did not have a simple, single story or explanation at the time. The real war and the mythical war will therefore always be intertwined.

Notes

1 For general details of the rationing scheme see Angus Calder, *The People's War* (London 1997; orig. 1969), pp 276–80 and Peter Lewis, *A People's War* (London 1986), pp. 154–76.

2 Lewis, *People's War*, pp. 154–5.

3 Calder, *People*, p. 405.

4 Ibid.

5 Ibid., p. 407.

6 Ibid., p. 383.

7 For a full history of the BBC, see Asa Briggs, *History of Broadcasting in the United Kingdom*, 3 vols (Oxford 1974).

8 Calder, *People*, p. 359.

9 See George Orwell, 'The Art of Donald McGill', in *Penguin Essays of George Orwell* (Harmondsworth 1984; orig. 1942), pp. 19–46.

10 Sian Nicholas, *The Echo of War: Home Front Propaganda and the Wartime BBC, 1939–45* (Manchester 1996), p. 239.

11 Ibid., p. 133.

12 Ibid.

13 Ibid., pp. 135–7.

14 Calder, *People*, p. 362.

15 Ibid.

16 Nicholas, *Echo of War*, p. 249.

17 Lewis, *People's War*, p. 228.

18 For details of wartime politics, see Paul Addison, *The Road to 1945* (London 1994; orig. 1975).

19 *The World at War*, Episode Fifteen: 'Home Fires, Britain 1940–1944'.

20 Ibid.

21 Quoted in Calder, *People*, p. 260.

22 Quoted in Lewis, *People's War*, p. 200.

23 Ibid.

24 Calder, *People*, p. 262.

25 Nicholas, *Echo of War*, p. 170.

26 Calder, *People*, pp. 347–9; Nicholas, *Echo of War*, p. 169.

27 Calder, *People*, pp. 348–9.

28 Nicholas, *Echo of War*, p. 168; Ian McLaine, *Ministry of Morale: Home Front Morale and the Ministry of Information in World War II* (London 1979), p. 198.

29 Spike Milligan, *Rommel? Gunner Who?* (Harmondsworth 1974), p. 23.

30 Quoted in Calder, *People*, p. 262.

31 Spike Milligan, *Adolf Hitler: My Part in His Downfall* (Harmondsworth 1987; orig. 1971), p. 53.

32 Calder, *People*, p. 395.

33 Ibid., pp. 431–42.

34 John Keegan, *The Second World War* (London 1989), pp. 170–8.

35 Sue Harper, 'The Representation of Women in British Feature Films, 1939–1945', in Philip M. Taylor (ed.), *Britain and the Cinema in the Second World War* (Manchester 1988), pp. 168–202.

36 Ibid.

37 Caroline Fox, *Dame Laura Knight* (Oxford 1988), p. 102.

38 See, for example, Arthur Marwick, *British Society since 1945* (London 1982), pp. 67–71.

39 Penelope Summerfield, *Women Workers in the Second World War* (London 1984). See also Penny Summerfield, *Reconstructing Women's Wartime Lives: Discourse and Subjectivity in Oral Histories of the Second World War* (Manchester 1998).

40 Figures quoted in Robert Murphy, *British Cinema and the Second World War* (London 2000), p. 153.

41 For example, see Antonia Lant, *Blackout: Reinventing Women for Wartime British Cinema* (Princeton, NJ 1991), pp. 89–99.

42 Quoted in Fox, *Dame Laura Knight*, p. 102.

43 See Lewis, *People's War*, pp. 138–9.

44 Fox, *Dame Laura Knight*, p. 102.

45 Quoted in Lewis, *People's War*, pp. 136–7.

46 Joan Wyndham, *Love Lessons: A Wartime Diary* (London 1986), pp. 180–2.

47 See Calder, *People*, pp. 428–30.

48 Quoted in Lewis, *People's War*, p. 138.

49 Lucy Noakes, *War and the British* (London 1998), p. 120.

50 Murphy, *British Cinema*, p. 118.

51 Ibid.

52 Quoted in Lewis, *People's War*, p. 144.

53 For the role of cinema in wartime, see James Chapman, *The British at War: Cinema, State and Propaganda, 1939–1945* (London 1998); Anthony Aldgate and Jeffrey Richards, *Britain Can Take It: The British Cinema in the Second World War* (Oxford 1986).

54 Harper, 'Representation of Women', p. 170.

55 Ibid., p. 198.

56 Ibid., p. 194. See also Sue Harper, *Picturing the Past: The Rise and Fall of the British Costume Film* (London 1994).

57 H. Mark Glancy, *When Hollywood Loved Britain: The Hollywood 'British' Film 1939–1945* (Manchester 1999), p. 90.

58 See John Costello, *Love, Sex and War: Changing Values 1939–1945* (London 1985).

59 Quoted in Lewis, *People's War*, p. 134.

60 Calder, *People*, p. 312.

61 See Lant, *Blackout*, pp. 75–9; and Harold L. Smith (ed.), *Britain and the Second World War: A Social History* (Manchester 1996), pp. 32–6.

62 Lant, *Blackout*, p. 313.

63 Milligan, *Rommel?*, pp. 56, 123.

64 Quoted in Noakes, *War and the British*, p. 66.

65 Calder, *People*, p. 312.

66 Quoted in Lewis, *People's War*, pp. 207–8.

67 Quoted in Aldgate and Richards, *Britain Can Take It*, pp. 286–7.

68 As A.J.P. Taylor put it, the war created an 'economic Dunkirk' for Britain. See his *English History 1914–1945* (Oxford 1965), p. 599. For a provocative interpretation of British reliance on the USA and the economic consequences of the war, see Correlli Barnett, *The Audit of War: The Illusion and Reality of Britain as a Great Nation* (London 1986).

69 Harper, 'Representation of Women', p. 183.

70 See *Daily Mail* 2 April 1982.

71 See Joan Wyndham, *Love Lessons* and *Love is Blue: A Wartime Diary* (London 1986).

72 Harper, 'Representation of Women', p. 177.

73 Noakes, *War and the British*, pp. 64–74.

74 Harper, 'Representation of Women', p. 179.

75 Quoted in Lewis, *People's War*, p. 152.

76 Graham Dawson, *Soldier Heroes: British Adventure, Empire and the Imagining of Masculinities* (London 1994), pp. 282–92.

77 Noakes, *War and the British*, p. 51.

78 Harper, 'Representation of Women', p. 177.

79 Richard Dyer, *Brief Encounter* (London 1993), pp. 4–7.

80 Ibid., pp. 12–13.

81 Margaretta Jolly, 'Love Letters versus Letters Carved in Stone: Gender, Memory and the "Forces Sweethearts" Exhibition', in Martin Evans and Ken Lunn (eds), *War and Memory in the Twentieth Century* (Oxford 1997), pp. 105–24.

CHAPTER 6

Bless 'em all: the British army, 1941–45

The British remember the war fought by the armed services with pride. The nation celebrates the victory of a people's army that overcame many setbacks and defeats to beat off its powerful enemies. The memory contains many elements lionised during the war and thus builds on the original interpretation of events. This chapter will therefore concentrate on images of the British soldier, and battles and campaigns that retain a profile in the popular memory. At the same time, the British have also forgotten and lost many aspects of the war fought by the armed services that were considered important at the time. As with most other aspects of the national collective memory of the war, sections have been reshaped, re-emphasised or re-ordered, while still shadowing that known, accepted and celebrated during the conflict itself.

The essentials of the British Second World War we know today were put together between 1939 and 1960. Our contemporary conception of the war is the result of a strange fusion of images produced in wartime and reactions to a glut of post-war remembrances. The most potent mediator of the British version of the war was the cinema, in particular the on-screen reworking of the Second World War that occurred during the 1950s. Although ticket sales reached an all-time high in 1945, cinema-going continued to be the essential social habit of British people in the 1950s. During that decade British cinema relived the Second World War in a string of box-office successes. These films were consumed by both those who had experienced the actual events and the young baby-boomers born after 1945, and this confirmed and framed a particularly British reading of the Second World War. The cinema did not exist in isolation but was buttressed by a seemingly endless supply of novels, reminiscences and autobiographies, cartoon books and serious histories all peddling an equally anglocentric interpretation of the war. Given the amazing success of these cultural products, it is equally astonishing that they have received so little serious critical attention. British academics and cultural commentators have proven Orwell right time and time again:

> The really important fact about so many of the English intelligentsia [is] their severance from the common culture of the country. In intention at any rate, the English intelligentsia are Europeanized. . . . In the general patriotism of the country they form a sort of island of dissident thought. England is perhaps the only great country whose intellectuals are ashamed of their own nationality. In left-wing circles it is always felt that there is something slightly disgraceful in being an Englishman and that it is a duty to snigger at every English institution, from horse racing to suet puddings.[1]

The popular cultural artefacts of the Second World War are just such an English institution that has been sniggered at, and which have resulted in the neglect of significant indicators of public taste. As John Ramsden has pointed out, despite the fact that the British film industry produced a vast number of war films in the 1950s, the organisation charged with the promotion of British cinema, the British Film Institute, rarely shows them at its National Film Theatre and not one of these films is due for examination in its *Film Classic* series of books.[2] Derided for their stiff-upper-lip values, for their relegation of women, for their cardboard portrayals of the working class and foreigners, the British 1950s war film is now regarded as the most appalling reflection of our hidebound, intolerant, old-fashioned national character. The fact that they were wildly popular is ignored. What Michael Paris has called the 'pleasure culture of war' dominated the 1950s and ensured that a new generation of young Britons would see the experiences of their parents in a particular manner.[3] As Peter Hennessy, whose excellent study of British post-war life, *Never Again*, and child of the 1950s, has commented 'we spent the fifties in cinemas absorbing an endless diet of war films in which Richard Todd and Kenneth More convinced us that there is a singular mixture of insouciance, bravery and flair that we [British] could bring to the conduct of international affairs'.[4] Britain's finest hours were relived and placed in a history of many other fine moments by such films as *They Were Not Divided* (1950), *Angels One Five* (1952), *The Battle of the River Plate* (1957) and *Sea of Sand* (1958). On a simpler level, the 1950s explosion of war films was probably due to the commercially excellent combination of best-selling literature waiting to be snapped up for film treatment on subjects which formed such an important part of life for so long. The top two best-grossing British movies in each year between 1955 and 1960 were war films, and in 1951 the top British box-office stars were those found most often in uniform: John Mills, Jack Hawkins, Trevor Howard, Richard Todd, Dirk Bogarde, Jack Warner and Leo Genn. By 1955 Kenneth More had joined the list.[5]

Stereotyped as boys' own heroics for their glorification of war in which disillusion is outlawed, in fact British 1950s war films rarely contained elements of gung-ho machismo, concentrating instead on underplayed heroism, for which they are, of course, equally pilloried. Elements of the People's War were undoubtedly lost in the 1950s; the stereotyping of other ranks and the writing-out of women and civilians is clearly seen in these British war films, whereas they were a major part of the wartime effort and imagery. But the films rarely contain outright lies. Authentic from a particular angle might be the best description of British war films in the 1950s, and it was an authenticity validated by popular approval which has gone into national mythology and memory. The shared ground between the wartime knowledge and image and these films is therefore of great significance in determining the extent to which there was a cultural shift in emphasis between 1939 and 1945 and the post-war world. It is also important to note that the influence of these films did not die with the decade. They gained a whole new audience through television. 'Having once established their transition to television, these films acquired a permanent life after death, and arguably shaped the central view of the Second World War for the next two generations in their approximately annual re-screenings.'[6]

Visualising the army

In 1939 the public's image of the army was mixed. The Navy was the guardian of the home *and* far-flung empire, while the RAF was seen as the instrument most likely to defeat the enemy by delivering destruction to his very heart. By contrast, the army was associated with the Western Front and the drudge of trench warfare. Dogged, determined and thoroughly British though its spirit might have been, many wondered whether it was simply an old boys' club officered by men similar to David Low's famous cartoon character, Colonel Blimp, a ridin', huntin', fishin' and shootin' soldier of the old school. Affection for the army undoubtedly went up when it came reeling back from Dunkirk; 'our brave boys' struck a chord in every heart. But from Dunkirk to El Alamein it was hardly a glorious procession. Aside from the odd victory, the army seemed to lurch from disaster to disaster. In the Western Desert, where there were successes, the army always seemed capable of snatching defeat from the jaws of victory. For example, General O'Connor's brilliant advance was checked in a situation engineered by the British themselves. Just as O'Connor was about to administer the knockout blow, Churchill and Wavell (O'Connor's commander) denuded him of troops and equipment for the ill-advised Greek adventure. British soldiers arrived in a situation they could do little to improve and found that while their backs were turned Rommel had arrived in the desert. It made the Ministry of Information's rather plodding, and at times curiously inaccurate, film, *Wavell's 30,000* (1942), designed to inform the public of a British success, totally redundant by the time it was released and it was soon withdrawn. The army needed an image makeover. It had recognised the value of good publicity for many years and had created the post of Director of Public Relations back in the 1930s, but it took some time for effective wartime propaganda to be produced. In 1940 the Army Film Unit was established, later to become the Army Film and Photographic Unit.[7] Consisting of army-trained photographers and men from the film industry, the AFPU became an efficient organisation capable of high-quality work.

Some of the most poignant and long-lasting images of the war came from the AFPU. An excellent example is the photograph of an officer, pistol on lanyard held outstretched, leading his men with their bayoneted rifles across a sand dune as a huge shower of dust and sand erupts behind them. Here is the British army at its most resolute and professional, a professionalism admired all the more for having been conjured up from amateur conscripts.[8] Another shows British troops on Queen Sector, Sword Beach on D-Day. British troops laden with kit seem to be in the aftermath of battle: some are helping wounded comrades, while others are checking their gear. In the foreground are the head and shoulders of a soldier moving out of shot; standing beside him in profile is a man surveying the scene. It is the embodiment of battle and the British spirit – here are men who have come through a terrible experience and are making their first attempts to comprehend it. We see what they suffered for us. 'The entire imprint of what it was all about is registered in that one photograph', wrote Ian Grant, a cine man who was with the photographer, Sergeant Jimmy Mapham, 'it became the first to be wired to the world and clearly hammered home the message – this is D-Day.'[9] AFPU newsreel has provided another D-Day image of intense power which has also been seen over and over. It shows the doors of an assault boat swinging open with the beach in sight. The backs of heavily laden soldiers are captured in the final moments before they clamber down and go into battle. The wedding-ringed hand of an unseen soldier taps the back of the leading man in good luck and support. This tiny gesture of comradeship and feeling at a moment of global significance is amazing. It transforms faceless soldiers into 'our boys' preparing to do something of immense risk on our behalf. (Although they are, ironically, Canadian soldiers, there is still the intimacy of the Commonwealth link and the fact that the men are wearing exactly the same kit as British troops.) It is history on the verge of being made and the viewer – whether in 1944 or now – asks what happened next? Did both of them survive or was it their last action before death?[10] These images have been reproduced in countless documentaries and books, and have become snapshots of experience, pinnacles of an iceberg concealing a great weight of subconscious meaning. They are symbols of British resilience and heroism and represent qualities modern Britons would like to believe they maintain.

Such images freeze moments of high drama and poignancy and have the power to provoke deep emotions. The phlegmatic British can cope with this only by allowing correctives that puncture the bubble and reintroduce the prosaic. Edward Ardizzone captured this during the war.

His sketches and watercolours of British and Commonwealth soldiers show neither the heroism nor pity of war. Instead, they encapsulate the mundane and accepting nature of the soldiers. In one sketch, men drink tea while looking at freshly dug graves. There is no prophecy in the piece and its title is direct and utilitarian, *Tea Break*. Rodrigo Moynihan's work is of a similar nature, recording the soldiers of the British army in all moods, none of them self-consciously heroic or important. Similarly, H.M. Carr's portrait of Sergeant B. Montague of the King's Royal Rifle Corps in his desert kit is a remarkable piece of work. Montague is the hero who has seen it all. Relaxing with a cigarette in his hand, he stares at the viewer not with pride but simple acceptance of his lot. He is the spirit of the British army. He is heroic precisely because of his unheroic nature. Thus British military success in the Second World War is often downplayed and often teeters into comedy. Spike Milligan's memoirs illustrate this point perfectly. He maintains a humorous contempt for his fellow conscripts and himself as soldiers, especially when compared with the efficient, professional Germans. An annotated sketch comparing German and British soldiers reveals the Germans to have a brain zone, an anti-semitic zone, legs for marching in any direction and a small area dedicated to sex. By contrast, rather than a brain zone the British have an area dedicated to thinking about tea. The region from the neck down to the waist is concerned only with food, beer and chips. From the waist to the ankles is the sex region and the feet are charged to football.[11] A lazy afternoon in Algeria finds him reflecting on the thoughts of the men: '. . . what were they thinking? Pint at the Pub? Watching Millwall at the Den? A walk with the Girl on Sunday? See? The lazy sods, that's all they ever think of! Booze, sex and football.'[12] James Sims' recollections made a very similar point: 'Getting the English soldier worked up enough to defend democracy was an uphill task, as the average soldier appeared to have only three basic interests: football, beer and crumpet.'[13] It has become accepted as an article of faith that the Germans always 'looked the part' compared with the British, which was also a reflection of a greater professionalism. Ivan Moffat, a British scriptwriter with an American official film unit, recalled seeing the vast numbers of German prisoners captured by the British and Americans in the spring of 1945. For Moffat, the Germans retained an air of superiority; they were the real army even in defeat, they 'were probably more professional and a better trained army

H.M. Carr's portrait of Sergeant B. Montague, 'A Desert Rat': the embodiment of British stoicism (Imperial War Museum art, film and photograph archives).

than we were'.[14] He also remembered the smell of leather, a material used far more widely by the Germans than the allies. Spike Milligan told of a despatch rider who approached and asked some questions. On his departure a comrade expressed his suspicions. The questioning had led him to suspect that the man was a spy. The response was instant and withering: 'Don't be bloody daft Shap, he was too scruffy to be a Kraut.'[15] As a relative of mine told me years ago: 'Son, compared with the Germans we always looked like sacks of shit tied up in the middle.' Few veterans have ever disagreed with this idea. This is not to say that the assertion is true, rather it is the British sardonic reaction whenever they are praised too much or the emotional atmosphere becomes too heightened.

Largely because of this humour the army survived the handicaps of under-funding, muddled thinking and a series of defeats, and by 1945 this conscript force, lined with a smattering of pre-war professionals, was victorious. It was a remarkable achievement and is something the veterans can look back on with pride. In 1944 Carol Reed paid tribute to it in his film, *The Way Ahead*. Following a group of conscripts from a wide variety of backgrounds, Reed's film was made at the request of the army, anxious as it was to reassure new recruits that it would care for them and make them proud to serve their country. Mixing comedy and drama effectively, *The Way Ahead* celebrates the ordinariness of the British soldier and in doing so reflected nothing more than the truth. A good deal of authenticity was injected into the film by refusing to give the new recruits any great sense of idealism or political motivation. They make few comments about the glory of fighting for democracy or freedom and it is freely shown that they were dragged from their homes and jobs. As David French has pointed out: 'Few of the conscripts enlisted after 1939 had much relish for soldiering or fighting, and few were motivated by a highly developed ideological commitment to the political cause of eradicating Nazism.'[16] *The Way Ahead* cannot, therefore, be accused of taking a highly simplistic and overly rosy view of the average British citizen-soldier. But the film also shows this very same unwilling bunch graduate into a disciplined and intelligent force capable of dealing with the enemy. The final scene is a miniature masterpiece: the platoon is due to attack under cover of a smoke screen and the soldiers grimly fix bayonets in preparation as the camera pans down their ranks. Once given the order to move they set off with steely determination on their faces as

William Alwyn's score rises in the background. The men disappear into the fog and the caption 'The Beginning' appears on screen. Many in the audience must have been reminded of Winston Churchill's comment on the victory of El Alamein by this device: 'Now this is not the end. It is not even the beginning of the end. But it is, perhaps, the end of the beginning.'[17] But it also ties in with the title; here is the British army marching towards victory and beyond to the New Jerusalem of the welfare state and homes fit for heroes. Victory was indeed merely 'The Beginning'. Thus the British army is seen as a reflection of its society and is celebrated for being nothing more than a collection of salesmen, rent collectors, farm hands and caretakers. Many years later Carl Davis did exactly the same thing in music when he was commissioned to provide the score for *The World at War*. Carefully avoiding bombastic overstatement in all his music for the series, Davis' original score was for a small orchestra and deliberately 'unheroic', deploying a 'musical language consciously derived from Bartok and Shostakovich'.[18] 'Blood, Sweat and Tears' was the piece he wrote to accompany scenes of British soldiers. He captured something of the swagger of the Eighth Army in the desert and the exuberance of D-Day, but ensured an everyday ordinariness by using the piano and clarinet rather than more heroic instruments. Watching scenes of Churchill tanks rumble along Belgian lanes in pursuit of a fleeing enemy seems a peculiarly mundane event when framed like this, but in a curious way is made all the more poignant because of the disjuncture. Davis' piece is moving in the extreme and a perfect memorial to a phlegmatic people's army. It reminds contemporary Britons of when their nation was morally and physically great.

Desert rats

The theatres of war in which the army fought are ranked in the public memory. The one that dominated until fairly recently was the desert campaign, thanks to a number of factors. During the war itself the significance of the Western Desert campaign had a high profile. As John Keegan has noted: 'At the time it bulked very large in British eyes, being the only focus of engagement between a British army and the enemy anywhere. . . . Tactically . . . it was a very small war indeed . . . though its strategic implications were considerable.'[19] Initially, the Western Desert was important to the British because it provided a buffer for the Suez Canal. Italy's entry into the war and the subsequent disruption to Mediterranean shipping then diminished the importance of this link to Britain's eastern empire. But the Western Desert did not decrease in significance, as it became the forward defensive position of the vital Persian oil fields. It was also the only place where the British could risk a campaign against the enemy. With the British army too small and inexperienced to risk a hurried invasion of continental Europe, only the peripheral theatres remained as locations in which they could show the Axis powers that they were capable of fighting and wearing down their forces. Anthony Eden admitted as much in *The World at War*:

> We decided that the only place we could fight the enemy was the desert, North Africa. There was nowhere else. We couldn't hope to make a landing in France in any foreseeable future and therefore couldn't injure the Germans that way. So the two possibilities were [strategic] bombing and fighting in the Middle East, and that is why from the very early days we began to push, agitate, ask for more armour in the Middle East.[20]

But why did the desert war retain its romance and interest long after 1945? Part of the answer must lie in the fact that it was perceived to be a clean war, involving soldiers who respected each other in a ding-dong struggle that appealed to the sporting side of the British people. Above all, the desert campaign seemed to follow the British love of unequal struggles, last-man stands and successes despite the odds. Thus Tobruk saw the British and Commonwealth troops cast as defenders of their small port-fortress against a well-equipped and superior enemy; and at El Alamein Britain displayed its usual trait of pulling off a last-minute victory that turned the tide of the war. Moreover, it was a victory fought and won by Britain and its Commonwealth (with the aid of units from the occupied countries) and thus kept the British end up before the Americans and Soviets dominated the agenda. Even the German com-mander, Rommel, gained admiration for showing British qualities: he was equally capable of achieving success despite the odds. But, perhaps the desert war also draws out a deep-rooted British cultural romance. Since the nineteenth century the British have displayed a love of such wildernesses, encapsulated by the popularity of Doughty's *Travels in*

Arabia Deserta (1888) and T.E. Lawrence's *Seven Pillars of Wisdom* (1935), and seen since the Second World War in films such as *Lawrence of Arabia* (1962) and *The English Patient* (1996).

At the time, the desert war was given a good deal of coverage by the British press. After seeing their early successes wiped out by Rommel, the British exchanged the emotions of victory for those of crisis. The press fell back on the usual mixture of stressing resilience under pressure and ingenuity in the face of danger, and coverage was therefore similar to the presentation of Dunkirk. The key symbol of this became the port of Tobruk. Besieged by Rommel, its garrison refused to collapse and was held stubbornly by Australian and British troops. After nearly seven months the siege was lifted thanks to a British offensive and the defenders were relieved. In June 1942 it was surrounded once again, only this time the port was not prepared and after a short siege the defenders were forced to surrender. Like the surrender of Singapore earlier in the year, the fall of Tobruk was a shock. A symbol of hope and resolution had been destroyed. Having been defended so stubbornly for so long in 1941, its collapse was all the more surprising and troubling to a British people unaware of the full complexity of the situation. Churchill was devastated, and hearing the news in Washington also left him feeling belittled in the eyes of his ally. A good indication of the significance of the defeat can be detected in the rich use of language – very similar to that used to describe Ypres, a site sacred to the British of the Great War. The *Daily Express* referred to Tobruk as 'ground that had been hallowed by the blood, valour and success of our fighting men', and so felt its loss keenly as 'a disaster for the defenders of Egypt and a great blow to the hopes of this nation'.[21] But, as with the earlier loss of Singapore, it was hoped that light could come from the darkness: 'Tobruk can be a symbol. Its loss can fire in every one of us a new spirit, an immense revival in our national strength.'[22] In a sense, recovery from the loss of Tobruk was easier than that of Singapore because it still left the British with a job to do – defend Egypt – and was not an end in itself, as Singapore had been in February 1942 (which probably explains why Singapore has disappeared from the common memory). Thus every effort was now going to be put into another backs-to-the-wall situation and the British still had a chance of revealing their best qualities.

The crisis came just a week later in the First Battle of Alamein. Now almost totally forgotten except by military historians, this vital battle

brought Rommel to a standstill and allowed the British and Commonwealth forces time to recover. The spirit of Dunkirk was resurrected
by the *Daily Express*, which poured praise on the long-suffering British
soldier: 'Give your praise to that stout fighting man who carries so
splendidly, who bears so worthily, the traditions of a warrior race.'[23]
According to this interpretation, sticky situations were the contractual
lot of Tommy Atkins.

Just a few months later the British got what they had long dreamt
of, an outright victory at the Second Battle of El Alamein. The headline
in the *Daily Mirror* proclaimed, 'Rommel Routed / Huns Fleeing in
Disorder', and added, 'Rommel's desert army, blitzed as no German army
has ever been blitzed before, is in full retreat with the Eighth Army in
close pursuit of his 'disordered' columns'.[24] From this point on the
Montgomery legend started to take shape. The *Daily Mirror* printed his
picture on the front page under the title, 'He dished it out' and beneath
the text emphasised the novel sense of complete victory:

> For the first time in this war a German Army has been really blitzed. The
> famous Afrika Korps could not stand up to the ceaseless pounding that
> General Montgomery and the Eighth Army have dished out. Twelve days
> of this terrific fight have broken Rommel's crack troops. They are in full
> retreat falling back in disorder.[25]

The editorial was gleeful, and it is hard not to be aware of the palpable
sense of novelty in the sensation of victory:

> The latest news of the great battle in Egypt is magnificent. Rommel and
> his Afrika Korps are fleeing in disorder. That, surely, is the best news we
> have had since the war began. Whatever difficulties we have yet to face
> we have cause for great rejoicing today. For rejoicing and heartfelt
> thanks.[26]

When the BBC announced the victory the drama was intense. Normal
programming was interrupted as listeners were told to standby for 'a
special Cairo communiqué, which has come in since the *Nine O'clock
News*'. Bruce Belfrage then came on air and, his voice quivering with
excitement, stated: 'Here's some excellent news, which has come during the
past hour in the form of a communiqué from G[eneral] H[ead] Q[uarters]
in Cairo. It says the Axis forces in the Western Desert after twelve days

and nights of ceaseless attacks by our land and air forces are now in full retreat. Their disordered columns are being relentlessly attacked by our land forces and the allied air forces by day and night.'[27]

Victory had come the way of the British people and none too soon. Churchill ordered that the church bells be sounded for the first time since 1940, only this time it was to salute the Eighth Army rather than to warn of an invader. At a Mansion House luncheon he then added his own tribute to the soldiers and used one of his most romantic images: 'Now . . . we have a new experience. We have victory – a remarkable and definite victory. The bright gleam has caught the helmets of our soldiers, and warmed and cheered all our hearts.'[28] Behind Churchill's 'bright gleam' was the weight of history, for his mind was doubtless conjuring up a parallel with the gleam of sunlight on crusaders' armour and the glint of finely worked swords and shields. The modern British infantryman was striding in the footsteps of Richard the Lionheart and Henry V.

The newsreels made much of Alamein too. The unity of the Commonwealth was celebrated in its moment of long-awaited revenge against the formerly formidable enemy. *Pathé Gazette* took particular pleasure in pointing out the role of the 51st Highland Division, a unit that had been sacrificed in the Dunkirk evacuations leaving a feeling of bitterness and resentment in the Highlands. In this version the domestic controversy was turned outwards, for it became a story of revenge over the Germans:

> Let us give praise to these men in battledress. Men of the Home County
> Regiments, the Australians, New Zealanders and South Africans, the
> Indians and our other Allies from overseas. But with what glory does
> the 51st Highland Division fill the picture. A reconstituted division
> which has today avenged the loss of the previous 51st which passed
> into eclipse at St Valerie at the end of the Battle of France. What a
> glorious rebirth.[29]

The success of the Eighth Army's fame was hammered home by the release of *Desert Victory* in March 1943. Produced by the Army Film and Photographic Unit, *Desert Victory* was a masterpiece of the documentary movement. Excellent photography taking full advantage of the dramatic desert landscape, a robust, clear commentary, a good score and careful editing combined to leave the viewer with a deep impression of the skill, dedication and endurance of the British and Commonwealth forces.

For this is the overriding image of the film. For once looking every bit like soldiers in their usually ludicrous baggy shorts, the ordinary troops are infused with an intense dignity and stature. Charging German positions, ducking to avoid explosions, sweating in unswept minefields, the soldiers take on heroic size, reminiscent of Charles Sargeant Jagger's memorial sculptures. Tributes are paid to the allies – the Americans for supplying some of the hardware, the Free French and Poles – but striding the centre stage are the men of the British empire. The finale shows the Tripoli victory parade as bagpipes skirl, men march in perfect formation and high on the ramparts flutters the newly raised Union Jack. These are the men of the People's Army in the People's War, men who knew why and what they were doing thanks, in part, to an enlightened command struc-ture typified by Monty: 'General Montgomery realising that a citizen army fights best when it knows exactly what's going on, saw to it that the plan of battle was known to everybody, from general to private soldier; and it came down from one rank to another, until the chain was complete', as the commentary states. These highly motivated men of the Eighth Army become a reincarnation of Cromwell's New Model Army and Monty 'a man who lives as sternly as a Cromwell – and who is as much a part of his modern ironsides'. Even now, so many years after Alamein, *Desert Victory* is a stirring film and it is thrilling and comforting to accept its message of British greatness and extreme magnanimity. In 1943 it was a sensation. In a Mass-Observation survey it emerged as the third most popular film of the year, and the general public echoed the critics' acclaim.[30]

Accompanying the release of the film was a glossy Ministry of Information booklet, *The Battle of Egypt* (1943; the initial title of *Desert Victory*).[31] Deliberately designed to replicate the layout, size and nature of *Picture Post*, the publication is a high-quality, illustrated history of the Alamein campaign. The propaganda effect of the text is all the more effective for its extremely low-key approach. Devoid of high rhetoric, the booklet's style is one of solid, no-nonsense prose explaining clearly and effectively the course of the battle. The rather dour text is then more than balanced by the brilliance of the photographs, many of which appear to be stills from *Desert Victory*. At much the same time another Ministry of Information booklet, *The Eighth Army*, was published. Over 100 pages long and well illustrated, it told the history of the unit from September 1941 to January 1943.[32] Using the same prose style as *The Battle of Egypt*, *The Eighth Army* is a good read and leaves the reader in no doubt as to its professionalism and efficiency. The military historian John Keegan has referred to these works as 'a model of what sensible propaganda can achieve'.[33] In words and pictures Winston Churchill's bright gleam was indelibly imprinted on to the helmets of the desert army. The 1939 image of the army had been finally eclipsed.

Alamein became a British legend, and though military historians have debated its significance since 1945, it remains a high point in the war for the British. In 1977 the military historian Correlli Barnett gave a talk on Radio 4 in which he noted the outlines of the legend. Calling his talk 'Myth versus History', Barnett commenced with a quote from the German philosopher Otfried Müller, who defined myth as 'a narrative which combines the real with the ideal'. Within this structure the British public had simplified the story of the campaign to a few, easy points: before Alamein all was confusion and disaster in the army but Monty came along and saved the day. This position was given credence by Churchill in his much quoted statement: 'It may almost be said that before Alamein we never had a victory. After Alamein we never had a defeat.' But, as Barnett pointed out, he was often misquoted by the omission of the word 'almost'. By dropping this simple word the subtlety of Churchill's point was lost completely and a myth made. Churchill had undoubtedly made much of the battle, needing an all-British victory at that dark moment in the war, and the nation's impending subordination to the USA demanded it. For Barnett, Alamein was a battle fought more for reasons of morale and politics than military strategy and he urged popular history to adopt a revisionist attitude. He stated: 'The war is thirty years behind us now. Do we still need myths? Is it not time that popular history, like historian's history, came to terms with the facts?'[34] Of course this assumption rests on the belief that historians are collectors and guardians of absolute fact and interpretation is standard and unchanging. History and myth adapt according to society and its culture.

A riposte to Barnett's position might well be 'so what?' If Alamein was a victory demanded more for political and morale reasons, does that necessarily disqualify it from being labelled a great moment in itself? And to what extent was the battle militarily worthless if it fired the British with a sense of confidence and restored pride? Admittedly, the Western Desert was a sideshow, but Alamein was one of a clutch of markers revealing the turning tide of the war.

The desert war has certainly rumbled on in the popular imagination. In the 1950s it was as a favourite location for war films. The daring adventures of the Long Range Desert Group were saluted in Guy Green's *Sea of Sand* (1958). John Gregson, Richard Attenborough and Michael Craig starred in this drama which celebrated the teamwork of the war and showed men with different attitudes settling down to fight together. It was a box-office hit in 1958, as was another desert drama, *Ice Cold in Alex* (1958). Unlike many other 1950s war films, this one contained a central female interest which gave it a fascinating twist. A mixed group of army personnel, including Sylvia Sims as a very sexy nurse, and led by John Mills, attempt to get back to British lines after the fall of Tobruk. Mills plays a nervy, twitchy character held together by alcohol and the thought of it, a far cry from his stereotypical dependable type roles. Eventually, after an epic trail across the desert, they make it to Alexandria and order ice-cold beers in a bar. When Carlsberg Lager decided to resurrect this scene for an advert a few years ago it boosted public knowledge of the film and revealed once again how the war, real and imagined, still influences our popular culture and is regarded as a persuasive image.

Other aspects of the legend survive and have grown stronger largely due to the recollections of veterans. One of the most important is that of the 'purity' of the war in the desert and therefore its cleanness and gallantry. Fought between small armies, the British and Commonwealth on one side and the Germans and Italians on the other, and far from any other campaign of war, the desert became a private contest of skill and mutual respect. The German General Johann Cramer told *The Times'* correspondent that 'the war in North Africa was a gentleman's war'.[35] Another German veteran confirmed this in an anecdote told in *The World at War*, which revealed the chivalry of the campaign: 'Sportsmanship showed on both sides. Football games were not interrupted by artillery fire during certain periods.' Laurence Olivier's narration asserted: 'The peculiar conditions of the desert bred a comradeship that was unique in the whole war. For many, the desert war was a private war, the last to retain any pretence of chivalry.'[36] Is this friendship a myth? Are the qualities of this campaign mere tricks of memory and the imagination? It seems not. As I write, the sixtieth anniversary of Alamein is rapidly approaching and there has been a sudden rush of new books and reprints. One of the new works is called *Alamein: War Without Hate*. The introduction stresses the unique quality of the war in the desert and the remarkable friendship between the veterans of both sides shown at a 1999 reunion in the Rommel Barracks, Germany.[37]

The landscape of the desert certainly denuded war of its disquieting twentieth-century elements. There were no towns or villages to provide refuges and obstacles for defenders, which would in turn demand that an attacker flatten them. There was no civilian population as such which removed all fear of causing death and destruction to non-combatants. The terrain itself was vast and empty, giving battle and manoeuvre a seemingly textbook quality. Barnett wrote in his highly successful history of the campaign, *The Desert Generals*, that 'The desert war of 1940–43 is unique in history. . . . The desert campaign was . . . war in its purest form.'[38] 'This land was made for war,' as Olivier put it in *The World at War*, 'here is no nubile, girlish land, no great, virginal countryside for war to violate.'[39] Such conditions allowed it to be remembered with fondness as a clean war, regardless of the actual nature of the fighting. But, significantly, this strips it of ideological and xenophobic overtones, a rare quality in the British popular memory of the war. It is the antithesis of the memory of the blitz, for that is one in which the Germans are the undoubted bad guys, using an underhand form of war in an attempt to impose an alien way of life on the British. Denuded of German atrocities on civilians, British qualms about strategic bombing and the other nasty baggage of total war, the desert war has offered the British a glimpse of war as romantic adventure and daring-do between two finely matched sides. War as sport once again.

Another element of the desert myth is that of good Germans. This came about thanks to the needs of post-1945 *realpolitik*, and in turn increased the sensation that the desert war was a very special one. The descent of the Cold War, the advent of the two Germanys and uncertainty over the Soviet Union's intentions suddenly made it necessary to rehabilitate the West Germans as a decent, freedom-loving people who could be trusted. An integral part of this was the promotion of German ex-servicemen as men who had fought for their country with skill and passion but not necessarily motivated by Nazi ideology. The Afrika Korps and Rommel were the perfect vehicles for this vision.

During the war many British soldiers had come to admire Rommel and even the British press admitted his skill and courage. Explaining away defeat after defeat as the work of a military genius was actually a much more convenient way of avoiding a too detailed scrutiny of British military practice. Montgomery's predecessor, General Auchinleck, felt that this admiration was bad for his men's morale and ordered his subordinate commanders to downplay references to Rommel lest he be taken as an unbeatable, omniscient god.[40] However, there can be little doubt that the British army and people retained an interest in Rommel throughout the war and after. In 1950, at the start of the 'war renaissance', Desmond Young, a veteran of the desert war, published his biography of Rommel. Auchinleck's preface revealed why this member of the hated enemy was so revered in Britain. Admitting that Germany has produced many great generals, Auchinleck said Rommel displayed something extra. He 'stood out amongst them because he had overcome the innate rigidity of the German military mind and was a master of improvisation'.[41] Unbound by slavish adherence to the rules, Rommel was almost a Brit; and like the British he could pull something out of the bag when things looked bleak indeed. Rommel became one of Britain's own. Auchinleck then touched on another reason for Rommel's continued high profile in the post-war years, praising his 'stout hearted adversary . . . [which] may help to show a new generation of Germans that it is not their soldierly qualities which we dislike but only the repeated misuse of them by their rulers'.[42] Thus Auchinleck spoke the language of the Cold War and the two Germanys. Wanting West Germans to become loyal allies in the quest to contain Communism, they had to be given some role models. Rommel was the ideal 'good German', someone Germans could look up to as a man of honour and dignity, respected by his former enemies and untainted by the death camps. A more controversial biographer, David Irving, known for his provocative histories of Nazi Germany, also picked up on his romantic image, which, he argued, contrasted so deeply with that of his political masters. 'He was said to have revived a long-forgotten style of chivalrous warfare. In a war brutalized by the Nazi extermination camp and the Allied strategic bomber, Rommel's soldiers were ordered to fight clean. Prisoners were taken and treated well. Private property was respected.'[43]

In 1951 *Desert Fox* was released, a biopic of Rommel based on Young's phenomenally successful biography (it went through eight editions in the year of publication alone). James Mason played the general as an honourable man, deeply concerned by the actions of the Nazi party, who then endangers himself and his family for the greater good of Germany by taking part in the anti-Hitler 'July Plot'. A big success at the box office, it spawned another film, *Desert Rats* (1953), in which Mason reprised his role as Rommel, but this time concentrating on the siege of Tobruk.

Rommel is also part of a double act, for he is intimately connected with the Montgomery legend. Montgomery was Britain's most successful soldier of the Second World War, leading the British army to victory after victory. At least that is the way the public sees him, or should that be *saw* him? Academic opinion about Montgomery has always been divided, but since his death the public has been drawn in as popular histories have questioned and probed. 2001 saw the publication of *The Full Monty: Montgomery of Alamein 1887–1942* by Nigel Hamilton, his official biographer. Far from proving that dead generals are the stuff of arcane debate in tiny circles, the reaction in the press was lively and impassioned.[44]

Often taken as a typical Briton, Montgomery was in fact far from it. The brashness, the self-confidence, the desire for the limelight were all very unBritish. Nigel Hamilton detected in these aspects of his character the influence of his early years in Tasmania, noting elements of 'an Australian bravado and no-nonsense approach to life'.[45] It might then be thought that this maverick, eccentric soldier would show an equally cavalier and flamboyant approach to battle. Far from it, however, for the other side of Montgomery's character was one of attention to detail and devotion to method and planning. Thus Montgomery is the most ironic of British heroes, he lacks the essential credentials: he is not associated with improvised last-man stands, fights against overwhelming odds or snatching improbable victories from the jaws of defeat.

But he did have a very British pigheadedness, eccentricity and sense of insularity. The eccentricity was part of a carefully controlled and promoted self-image. This was seen most clearly in his clothes and headgear. Never one to wear the regulation uniform, Monty made sure both his troops and the public knew him by his highly individual wardrobe. Tatty jumpers, parachutists' smocks, baggy shorts and equally baggy khaki trousers were topped by singular hats: a beret sporting the general staff crest with the tank corps badge, and a slouch hat covered in regimental badges. Montgomery revealed his character at a war factory in the spring of 1944. Sent to boost worker morale, he praised the nation for its innate superiority over the Germans, then roused the audience to a climax by telling them that his job was 'fighting the Germans or anybody else too who wants a fight' before revelling in the storm of applause.[46] The smile on his face as he delivers this line is as curiously manic as the storms of laughter and enthusiasm that greet it. It seems to say, 'bring 'em all on. We know we have many enemies and we just don't care.'

His crowning glory was to accept the unconditional surrender of all enemy forces in northern Germany in May 1945. Montgomery acted like Will Hay's famous officious schoolmaster, as he treated high-ranking German officers like naughty boys who had been dragged into his office for a stern telling off. It revealed fully both Monty's eccentricity and his Britishness.[47]

After the war Montgomery used his position to mould the developing shape of its history and had no problem with false modesty. In books and a BBC television series he did nothing to downplay the idea of his own genius. The British are, of course, very suspicious of self-congratulation and slowly a revisionist reaction set in. Much of it was completely justified as it evened out many of his distortions and overstated assertions. But in typically British fashion it went much, much further than that. The Montgomery myth was not merely toned down, it was demolished; every aspect of his life, both personal and professional, has been exposed to damning criticism. Montgomery's attitudes, particularly towards family life and women, are paraded as appalling, disgusting, even depraved. Such criticism is akin to that bestowed on so many 'great dead white men' for it lacks the most fundamental of historical skills – context. In many respects Montgomery's attitudes were simply those of his time and class, exaggerated very likely, put over with far more candour almost certainly, but not entirely abnormal. Modern Britons might not like them, but they were fairly common currency in the old Britain with its essentially nineteenth-century value system.

Operation Overlord

In the spring of 1944 the British press promoted the forthcoming invasion as the next round in the ongoing Montgomery–Rommel bout. *British Movietone News*'s special D-Day edition showed shots of Montgomery 'about to strike once more his old enemy, Rommel, whom he has hitherto always defeated'.[48] Alongside the desert war, Dunkirk and the Battle of Britain, D-Day is probably the most important campaign in the public popular memory of the Second World War. At the time the overwhelming feeling was one of entering the final act of a great drama and of having come through a test of national character. Shots of British soldiers landing in the *Movietone News* D-Day special were accompanied by the same sentiment, only in a more utilitarian manner, 'They tell their own story, I think. The story of how four years after Dunkirk; four years after Hitler thought it was all over bar the shouting, Britain came back.'[49] D-Day was presented as the direct result and reward for surviving an epic examination, and no newspaper did it with more panache than the workers' and soldiers' favourite read, the *Daily Mirror*:

> *On a memorable occasion, and at a time when there seemed little left to us except hope and that sublime obstinacy which is the British character expressed in terms of adversity, the Prime Minister, with inspiring pessimism, promised us blood, tears and sweat. It is blood, tears and sweat that we face again today, but in a very different mood. Then the skies were grey. Now they are ablaze with the light of triumphs achieved, and victory to come. On behalf of those who have gone forth in courage and cheerful fortitude to fight this epic battle we, at home, offer our prayers and pledge ourselves to support them in mind, in spirit, in material, to the utmost of our capacity. The curtain rises on the closing scene of the greatest human conflict the world has ever known. . . . As our hearts swell with pride and awe; as we contemplate the perils and glories of the battle; as we offer up our humble supplication; we can, with reason, select a sacred invocation for the battle cry, and say, with Montgomery: 'Let God arise and let His enemies be scattered.'*[50]

The inspiration was probably King George VI's D-Day radio address, in which he urged his subjects to remember 'this time four years ago [when] our nation and Empire stood alone against an overwhelming and implacable enemy, with our backs to the wall'. Then the British, 'tested as never before in our history, in God's providence . . . survived the test: the spirit of the people, resolute, dedicated, burned like a bright flame . . . which nothing can quench.'[51] In 1588 the Lord God had blown and

England's enemies were scattered, in 1688 the Divine Wind brought forth a Glorious Revolution, in 1940 in God's (and Rupert Brooke's) English Heaven the RAF brought low the invader and in 1944 His enemies were scattered through the endeavour of British soldiers. Here was the nation's history and destiny, easily understood by all and accepted entirely.

1940 thus went into the 'deep history' of the old nation and became its reminder in the 1944 present of endurance and valour. None could deny that the present was a moment for boldness and sacrifice, and in finding 1940 an example to draw on, the historic significance of that year was once again affirmed: none would ever be able to deny the story of 1940 lightly.

D-Day was reworked in the public imagination in the epic film *The Longest Day* (1962), an adaptation of Cornelius Ryan's best-selling book of the same title (1960). A galaxy of stars was deployed in a carefully plotted film that viewed D-Day from the American, British, French and German points of view (but omitted the important Canadian contribution). Great action sequences, lavish sets and attention to detail combined in a film that must have seemed like a celluloid war memorial to the original audiences in 1962. Darryl F. Zanuck's film concentrates on the American role, but the British contribution was not forgotten and it certainly played upon British national stereotypes. Kenneth More, cast as a beach-master complete with pipe clamped between his teeth and a gruff bulldog named Winston, injected his part with typical British sang-froid. Oblivious to the dangers, he directs traffic off the beach and towards the front. When a bren carrier breaks down in front of him, he states that his grandmother's remedy for all mechanical problems was to hit the offending machine with a big stick. Raising his walking stick, he gives the carrier a thump that duly brings it back to life. Thus myth, anecdote and history were mixed in *The Longest Day*.

In 1984 and 1994, the fortieth and fiftieth anniversaries of D-Day were marked with large-scale commemorations. Veterans paraded in Britain and Normandy, taking their friends and relations with them. The media left the British in no doubt as to the value of the invasion and the glory of the sacrifice made. During the fiftieth anniversary celebrations the *News of the World* gave away a special commemorative issue (as did most other newspapers) and praised the veterans as 'the best of Britain'. *The Times* presented its commemorative issue as a memorial to the men who fought

– 'It is a tribute to their valour, deeds and sacrifices' – while the editorial in the main newspaper commented on the importance of keeping the memory alive: 'These rituals of remembrance also stretched out a hand to those born long after Operation Overlord, for whom D-Day is history rather than memory.'[52] Inspired by this surge of interest Steven Spielberg made a war memorial in film with his box-office success, *Saving Private Ryan* (1998). Although it settles down to become a fairly predictable post-1945 war movie, the first twenty minutes set on Omaha beach are stunning, awful, exciting and horrifying, giving an impression of combat that many have praised for its realism and lasting impact. This story of D-Day is told from a solely American perspective and ignores the contribution of Britain and Canada. However, the film had a deep impact in Britain, reminding people of the sacrifices a previous generation had made in order to liberate Europe and bring peace to the world.

A bridge too far

In marked contrast to this concentration on D-Day is the relative lack of knowledge of subsequent events. This is partly due to the nature of the contemporary coverage. Reportage of the period from D-Day to the surrender of Germany was mostly uninspiring, and reads that way today. Undoubtedly, the taking of major cities and the smashing of German armies were given full coverage and the papers were splashed with dramatic headlines, but the overwhelming sensation is of grind, a slow, inexorable grind to victory. Operation Market Garden in September 1944 provides the great exception, as it has all the credentials of a great British moment. Journalists and other commentators rose to the drama of the occasion with consummate skill largely because Arnhem gave them the chance to use the rhetoric and imagery their education and experience had prepared them for. Market Garden was bound to become myth, opening as it did during the Battle of Britain thanksgiving commemorations. Newspapers made much of Sunday sermons disrupted by the roar of the aerial Armada as it made for Holland and Belgium.[53] It then became an epic of the happy few, a gallant band of Britishers facing an enemy superior in size and equipment but not in skill, determination or humour. Richard McMillan, a reporter with the *Daily Mail*, witnessed the return of those who managed to reach British lines after eight days of incessant fighting defending a tiny, but ultimately untenable, enclave:

> *Struggling through a hurricane barrage of fire from 88mm guns, tank cannon, and machine-guns, the last survivors of the noble band of British Airborne troops who held the Arnhem bridgehead for nine days were ferried over to our lines during Monday night.*
>
> *I saw the tragic but heroic cavalcade of bloody, mudstained, exhausted, hungry, and bearded men flood up from the river bank after going through 230 hours of hell.*
>
> *Many were stretcher cases. Many were wrapped in blankets. Some hobbled with sticks. All were so completely exhausted that they could hardly keep their eyes open. They were beaten in body, but not in spirit. 'Let us get back again; give us a few tanks and we will finish the job,' they said.*[54]

While Alan Wood, the *Daily Express* journalist who had landed with the assault troops, wrote: 'This is the end. The most tragic and glorious battle of the war is over, and the survivors of this British airborne force can sleep soundly for the first time in eight days and nights.'[55]

Thus Arnhem was not a defeat, it was a grave celebration, another Dunkirk, another Gallipoli, as the airborne forces evacuated themselves from the wrong side of the Rhine with fortitude, endurance and skill. The *Daily Mail*'s editorial rolled out the rich tapestry of British history as the men were compared with the thin red line of the Crimea, the charge of the light brigade (apt in more ways than one), Rorke's Drift, Lucknow, Ladysmith and Sir Richard Grenville. The vital and potent element in this imagery was the connection with desperate causes, forlorn hopes and gallant last stands. Denying that the operation was ill conceived and thus avoiding some of the more controversial points of comparison with these historical events, high rhetoric was deployed to cover up yet another British military disaster, magnificent and strangely noble as it was.[56]

Defeat was made acceptable by turning it into another epic of the island race. After so many victories Arnhem stood out all the more poignantly, and in doing so reinvigorated the British sense of insular solidarity. Humphrey Jennings caught it beautifully in *A Diary for Timothy* (1945). Baby Timothy's family sit round listening to a BBC report on the grim situation at Arnhem. The looks of deep concern on their faces are extremely moving. Each one is clearly thinking intently of the men trapped in their ever-decreasing enclave. But such deep emotions are also a reflection of a family spirit. It is a sombre celebration of a fiercely felt sense of interdependence.

A year later the cameras arrived in Arnhem to shoot the film *Theirs is the Glory* (1946). Made as a tribute to the men who fought at Arnhem, it starred them too, many of the original participants taking part in the recreation. Directed by Brian Desmond-Hurst, *Theirs is the Glory* is a peculiar film as it walks a tightrope between straight, rather prosaic, reconstruction and deeply moving elegy. This was achieved in two ways. First, Desmond-Hurst employed Stanley Maxted and Alan Wood to repeat their original despatches and in so doing they became the Greek chorus of the tragedy. Secondly, by the addition of a prologue and epilogue: at the start of the film the camera shows men in a Nissen hut preparing for action, but at the end the camera returns and pans over the empty beds of the now dead, wounded and missing while Leo Genn's voiceover recalls their names and that 'they were just ordinary men'. Reactions to the film were overwhelmingly positive. Leonard Mosley wrote a moving review for the *Daily Express*: 'It takes you by the throat and shakes you. It shows you what men can do, what heights simple people can reach, in the ultimate moments of death and pain and horror.'[57] The opinion of the *Manchester Guardian* emphasised the epic nature of the story and caught the British love of romantic failure:

> *The story of Arnhem has, of course, one transcendent quality – the quality not of Salamis but of Thermopylae. Arnhem was a failure. The poetry of war, we are told, is in the pity of it; but it is in war's failures that the pity and the poetry are greater and more noble.*[58]

However, the *Monthly Film Bulletin* made the shrewd point that the film was actually invested with emotion by its viewers rather than by its creator: 'The poetry comes less from cinematic virtues than from emotion recalled.'[59] Arnhem was obviously a word capable of causing deep emotion and had a clearly understood, and commonly accepted, narrative underpinning and defining it.

Arnhem appeared on screen again in 1977 in Richard Attenborough's hugely expensive production, *A Bridge Too Far*. Treated in a lukewarm manner by both critics and public alike, the film certainly suffers from trying to do too much. In attempting to tell the whole story of Market Garden, Attenborough was over-ambitious, which is probably why the compact and easily understood drama of Arnhem is the most successful section of the film. Attenborough skilfully caught the transformation from initial high hopes gradually to surrender and retreat. The final scene of wounded British paratroopers waiting to be taken prisoner while singing 'Abide With Me' is deeply moving and leaves a feeling of admiration for such brave men. Designed as an anti-war film, highlighting the arrogance and conceit of those in high command who played games with men's lives, *A Bridge Too Far* failed because Attenborough couldn't quite get the right balance, especially over Arnhem. The sheer intensity of his portrayal of the action leaves the viewer in a state of ambiguity: should they admire or should they regret? This is the problem of Arnhem. It may have been a dreadful failure and waste of lives, but to call it so unambiguously is interpreted as a slur on the intense courage and resourcefulness of those who fought there.

The high points in the British memory of military operations in the Second World War have a broad similarity to other elements of the popular recall. Standing out most prominently are aspects connected with unequal struggles, resilience, eccentricity and humour. It is a memory largely connected with the initial interpretation of events, then given added definition by the 1950s war film and book genre and hasn't altered greatly since. It may well be a myth, building on myths current during the war, but it is a myth accepted as history. The initial function of the myth was to give the British strength during the trial of total war. Since 1945 it has become history because it offers an easily understandable interpretation of events. Some would argue that the myth is dangerous and distorting, while others judge it acceptable within the 'big fact' structure, for the myth incorporates reality and can never be labelled completely inaccurate.

Notes

1 George Orwell, 'The Lion and the Unicorn', in *The Penguin Essays of George Orwell* (Harmondsworth 1984; orig. 1941), pp. 161–2.

2 John Ramsden, 'Refocusing "The People's War": British War Films of the 1950s', *Journal of Contemporary History* 33, 1 (1998), p. 35.

3 Michael Paris, *Warrior Nation: Images of War in British Popular Culture 1850–2000* (London 2000).

4 Peter Hennessy, 'History in the Making', *Director*, September 1992, p. 27.

5 Ramsden, 'Refocusing "The People's War"', p. 42.

6 Ibid., pp. 36–7.

7 For more details, see James Chapman, *The British at War: Cinema, State and Propaganda, 1939–1945* (London 1998) and S.P. MacKenzie, *British War Films 1939–1945* (London 2001).

8 This photograph was taken by Sergeant Chetwyn of the AFPU (IWM 18909). Fascinatingly, as with the material mentioned in note 10, these soldiers are not actually British, but Australians, and the photograph was taken during a training exercise prior to the battle. I am grateful to Alan Wakefield of the Imperial War Museum for his assistance with this matter.

9 Quoted in Jane Carmichael, 'Army Photographers in North-West Europe', *Imperial War Museum Review* 7 (no date), pp. 15–22.

10 These remarkable images were taken by an automatic camera fixed to the stern of a landing craft. I am grateful to Roger Smither of the Imperial War Museum for his help with this matter.

11 Spike Milligan, *Rommel? Gunner Who?* (Harmondsworth 1974), p. 129.

12 Ibid., p. 66.

13 Quoted in David French, *Raising Churchill's Army: The British and the War against Nazi Germany 1919–1945* (Oxford 2000), p. 133.

14 Quoted in BBC broadcast *D-Day to Berlin*, 8 May 1985.

15 Milligan, *Rommel?*, pp. 88–9.

16 French, *Churchill's Army*, p. 122.

17 Charles Eade (ed.), *War Speeches of Winston Churchill*, 3 vols (London 1951), vol. II, pp. 341–5.

18 Jerome Kuehl, cassette liner notes, *The World at War*, Decca KDVC 6 820 013-4.

19 John Keegan, *The Second World War* (London 1989), p. 272.

20 Quoted in *The World at War*, Episode Four: 'Standing Alone, June 1940–May 1941'.

21 *Daily Express* 22 June 1942.

22 Ibid.

23 Ibid.

24 *Daily Mirror* 5 November 1942.

25 Ibid.

26 Ibid.

27 Quoted on *BBC 1922–72*, fiftieth anniversary discs BBC50.

28 Eade (ed.), *Speeches*, vol. II, p. 342.

29 *Pathé Gazette* 12 November 1942.

30 MacKenzie, *British War Films*, p. 110.

31 *The Battle of Egypt* (London 1943). Print runs and sales figures for these booklets are difficult to ascertain. However, some indication of their popularity can be given from the example of the booklet *The Battle of Britain, August–October 1940: An Air Ministry Record of the Great Days from 8th August–31st October 1940* (London 1941). In its first (unillustrated) edition it sold two million copies and the second (illustrated edition) sold 900,000 copies in ten days. I am indebted to my colleague, Gill Sinclair, for providing this information.

32 *The Eighth Army, September 1941 to January 1943* (London 1943).

33 John Keegan, *Six Armies in Normandy* (London 1982), p. 5.

34 Correlli Barnett, BBC radio talk 'Myth Versus Reality', broadcast 6 December 1977.

35 Desmond Young, *Rommel* (London 1950), p. 148.

36 *The World at War*, Episode Eight: 'The Desert: North Africa 1940–1943'.

37 John Bierman and Colin Smith, *Alamein: War Without Hate* (London 2002), pp. 1–8.

38 Correlli Barnett, *The Desert Generals* (London 1960), p. 21.

39 *The World at War*, Episode Eight.

40 Young, *Rommel*, pp. 23–5.

41 Ibid., p. 9.

42 Ibid., p. 11.

43 David Irving, *The Trail of the Fox: The Life of Field Marshal Erwin Rommel* (London 1977), p. 4.

44 See, for example, *The Sunday Times* 25 February 2001, 12 October 2001; *The Times* 4 March 2001, 19, 21, 27 September 2001; *The Times Literary Supplement* 19 September 2001.

45 Nigel Hamilton, *Monty: The Man Behind the Legend* (Wheathampstead 1987), p. 7.

46 *Pathé Gazette* 6 April 1944.

47 See *British Movietone News* 10 May 1945; and also see *Daily Mirror* 5 May 1945 for comment on his attitude towards the Germans.

48 *British Movietone News* 8 June 1944.

49 Ibid.

50 *Daily Mirror* 7 June 1944.

51 Ibid.

52 *News of the World* 5 June 1994; *The Times* 6, 7 June 1994.

53 *Daily Herald* 18 September 1944.

54 *Daily Mail* 28 September 1944.

55 Ibid. His column was syndicated to the *Daily Mail.*

56 Ibid.

57 *Daily Express* 12 September 1946.

58 *Manchester Guardian* 14 September 1946.

59 *Monthly Film Bulletin* October 1946.

CHAPTER 7

Take that, Fritz!:
Commandos, prisoners of
war and the boys' own war

As this book shows, the modern British memory of the Second World War is made up in the main of elements sketched during the war itself. Most unusually, however, one part of this memory has been added since 1945. Knowledge of life in enemy captivity, and of those who attempted to escape it, is something that we are far more familiar with than those who lived through the war years. The exploits of prisoners of war are a bonus memory gifted by victory.

Along with special forces, prisoners of war are the most influential vehicles for passing on the British popular history of the Second World War. These two groups are presented as the embodiment of national characteristics and the spirit that got Britain through the dark days. Since the war they have become standard symbols of the conflict and have played a large role in literature, films and television aimed at, or attractive to, young adults. The version of the war contained in these interpretations has, in turn, become the target of much satire and humour. Like fighter pilots, special forces and prisoners of war have become mythological figures of the conflict, but despite the attacks of satirists, these figures have remained impervious to debunking.

Commandos and prisoners of war

The success of the German army in the early years of the war and Britain's inability to strike back at the continent with an invasion, led Churchill to demand an elite force capable of 'setting Europe ablaze'.[1] The result was the Commandos. Many serving soldiers volunteered for this new unit, lured by the thought of action and adventure. In 1941 the Commandos launched their set-piece debut raids against Norwegian targets. The first was the destruction of various installations in the Lofoten islands and the second an attack on Vaagso island. Both were regarded as potential propaganda coups and film crews were despatched. The successes of the subsequent newsreels far outstripped the military value of the actions. *Pathé Gazette* treated the Vaagso raid to a special edition, mixing exciting shots of the action with an equally rousing commentary:

> *Attack!! From the bowels of waiting ships clamber the Commandos. . . .*
> *Two landings will be made on the snow-clad islands of Maaloy and*
> *Vaagso. By now the German garrison is aware of danger. Up go their*
> *Verey Lights, probing the darkness to see the dim outline of our invading*
> *force. Then, with a firepower of nearly 50 shells a minute, every gun on*
> *our warships opens up in a furious broadside. All hell is let loose as the*
> *coastal batteries are smashed into pulp.*[2]

To the British public the Commandos were like Bomber Command, they left the nation's calling card across Europe.

On the night of 28 March 1942 the Commandos took part in an even more daring raid. The target was the huge battleship dock in the French west coast port of St Nazaire, as destruction of the dock would seriously disrupt Germany's ability to deploy its major warships in the Atlantic. Breaking into the heavily defended dockyard required fast motorboats and a rapid deployment. An old destroyer was then smashed into the gates of the dry dock. The story had all the elements of an exciting epic. It was presented as the ultimate adventure in the press, topping the assaults on Lofoten and Vaagso. Here was the proof of Britain's natural dash, initiative and élan. In addition, here was the core material for later popular novelists such as Alastair Maclean. It was certainly the essence of the boy's literature and comics I read in the 1970s and 1980s.

The most daring Commando operation of the whole war turned out to be the most disastrous, although the lessons learnt from the débâcle helped ensure the success of D-Day two years later. Planned as a large-scale raid, the assault on Dieppe in August 1942 saw the loss of almost half the attacking force, with the bulk of the casualties from the ranks of the Canadian contingent. Sheer bravery and fortitude had not been enough to overcome poor planning and strong defences as the Germans responded with professional efficiency. Back in Britain the press crowed another daring triumph. 'Big Hun Losses in 9-HR Dieppe Battle' claimed the headline of the *Daily Mirror*, and added 'the news of this offensive stroke will hearten our expectant people at home'.[3] The day after the raid Spike Milligan recalled sitting in a pub with his arm in a sling after suffering an accident in training. Mistaken for a hero of Dieppe, he was treated to drinks all night long.[4] And yet today only serious students of the conflict know anything about Dieppe. Commando stories are known only as a collective generality.

Presented as a success, the Dieppe raid certainly did not dampen the public's enthusiasm for Commando stories. Commandos were the embodiment of the national genius, cheeky in the face of overwhelming odds and resolute and resourceful when under pressure. The publication of the Ministry of Information's booklet on the Commandos, *Combined Operations 1940–1942*, in the spring of 1943 was used as a chance to stress that these most modern of warriors were in fact the continuation of an English tradition. The exploits of Elizabethan sea dogs provided the heritage and pedigree, as Drake, Essex and Howard all knew 'how a combination of sea and land forces could inflict hurt on an enemy'.[5] The *Daily Telegraph* recommended the book to its readers, stressing the details of the St Nazaire raid plus 'many other thrilling Commando episodes, some entirely new to the public'.[6] While it was indeed a good read, the booklet was not a simple glorification of the Commandos; the high losses of the Dieppe raid were mentioned but, by stressing the raid's deep impression on the Germans, the casualties were cleverly turned into a necessary and worthy sacrifice.

However, it was not all boys' own adventure stuff. During the war the army put forward a more sober view of combined operations that balanced the exciting stories with great force. Wishing to emphasise the vital importance of secrecy and security among all ranks, the army approached Ealing Studios to make a training film. A full-scale feature film was the eventual result, *Next of Kin* (1942). The film told the story of a raid that nearly goes disastrously wrong thanks to unwitting security leaks at many levels. Success is achieved eventually but only after the British have suffered many casualties. When Churchill saw it he was extremely concerned by its dark tone and believed it would traumatise cinema viewers. As a result, *Next of Kin* – the title comes from the phrase much heard in wartime Britain, 'the next of kin have been informed' – was released only once 80 feet of the most graphic material had been cut and the genuine raid on St Nazaire had taken place. Revealing a toughness of fibre, an ability to face the realities of the situation and a stoic desire to learn lessons, the British people reacted to the film with great enthusiasm. Within two months of release it had been seen by approximately 3 million people and made the Ministry of Informa- tion £95,308 in profit. Far from being unable to face the truth and com- forting themselves with propaganda tales of constant success, the response to this film shows a gritty realism in the British people. Some must have gone along as a duty, knowing they were in for a harrowing time for the film still has plenty of scenes of British soldiers lying dead or injured, slaughtered even before they could leap from their assault boats. A London woman with two sons in the army was absolutely con- vinced the film was genuine footage and went into a state of extreme shock.[7]

This jarring portrayal did not survive after 1945, for in the post-war years the glamorous image asserted itself as the only interpretation of the Commando. *The Green Beret*, an adventure story about the Commandos, went through fifteen paperback editions between its first edition in 1949 and 1956.[8] In the 1950s and 1960s cinema lionised the special operation in such films as *The Cockleshell Heroes* (1955) and *The Guns of Navarone* (1961). *The Cockleshell Heroes* recreated a Royal Marine raid on Bordeaux harbour and was given a good deal of help by the forces, including marines as extras, and the provision of canoe and drill courses. Prince Philip, along with a host of senior officers, attended the royal pre- mière, giving the film an additional seal of approval. When the Prince suggested some inaccuracies, the film company decided to incorporate his advice and shoot additional scenes, all of which helped sell the film as a truly authentic account.[9]

Unlike *The Cockleshell Heroes*, *The Guns of Navarone* was not based on a real event but a best-selling Alastair Maclean novel (it had twenty-one paperback printings in the ten years from its first edition in 1957).[10] Sporting an all-star cast which included Gregory Peck, Anthony Quinn, Anthony Quayle and David Niven, this lavish adaptation has become a fixture in the popular culture thanks to repeated television outings. In 1997 it was adapted for Radio 2 with Toby Stephens cast in Peck's Major Mallory role and given a new lease of life via the BBC's Radio Collection series of tapes. It is the ultimate boys' own adventure and confirms every schoolboy's knowledge of the Commandos – they have specially-adapted kit, can cause explosions like no one else, scale cliffs, take out vastly superior numbers of Germans and escape from the trickiest of tricky situations.

In the spring of 2002 Channel 4 screened a documentary series called simply *Commando*, in which the wartime history of the unit was explored. Each episode gave the impression that the production team was genuinely surprised to find that these men lived up to the clichés about them. The veterans interviewed seemed either extremely eccentric or extremely ordinary. This truly extraordinary bunch of men were treated in a curious way by the documentarists, part tongue-in-cheek, part respectful and part poignant. The tongue-in-cheek aspects never seemed too disrespectful, however, as they matched their characters so perfectly – an original member and enthusiast for the unit, Major Peter Churchill, is referred to by all who remembered him as a madman who took his sword and bagpiper on operations, while new recruits had to find their own billets and were allowed to take their landlords' and landladies' pets along on route-marches. The overall impression was that everything about the Commandos was bizarre and therefore very British. Such details proved the foil and cover for the highly emotional moments in which tearful veterans recounted losing close friends and comrades. Perhaps unwittingly, the documentarists had continued a traditionally British way of looking at the war – balancing constantly the horror with a self-deprecating humour. This obsession with a rare breed of British soldiers is still seen in our culture only now it is SAS troopers and the special forces generally that have come to dominate. Andy McNab and *Bravo Two Zero* (1993) is the next step on from St Nazaire and Commando books.

It might also be argued that the public interest in modern captivity stories, such as the experiences of Terry Waite, John McCarthy and the coalition pilots and western civilians held by Saddam Hussein during the Gulf War, are connected to the ongoing fascination with prisoner-of-war escape adventures. After the Great War tales of escape from German captivity had been very popular. Indeed, Major Pat Reid, the man who wrote the greatest of the Second World War escape stories, his autobiographical *The Colditz Story* (1952), admitted that he had been an avid reader of those tales in his youth.[11] During the war itself escape stories were rarely printed in newspapers or given much coverage. Tales of individual intrepidity on this small, but intense, scale were swallowed by bigger events. The forces were also keen to keep those successful escapees out of the limelight for security and safety reasons: no one wanted the Germans to find out how the trick had been pulled off. After the Second World War the public revealed a taste for prisoner-of-war stories, particularly if they involved escapes and were based on real adventures. Thus books like Eric Williams' *The Wooden Horse* (1949), *The Colditz Story* and Paul Brickhill's *The Great Escape* (1951) became huge best-sellers: *The Colditz Story* went through seventeen editions in ten years.[12] Unsurprisingly, these books were snapped up by film companies and translated into a different medium.

The presiding spirit of the books, and the subsequent films, was that of the public school novel. The reader immersed in any of these escape stories could be forgiven for confusing them with *Tom Brown's Schooldays*, *Stalky and Co*, *Loom of Youth* or the Billy Bunter stories. Thus German guards become prefects to be avoided or outwitted, camp commandants seem decidedly headmaster-like and escaping is a jape akin to raiding the tuck shop. It is similar to the vein of British humour in which Channel 4's *Commando* series treated its subjects. Other ranks are not thick on the ground in these war stories, and like public school novels the main characters are gentlemen; officers alone indulge in grand escape plans and sit on escape committees discussing various ventures. When these stories were projected on the big screen in the 1950s, giving them an even larger audience, a retreat from the People's War image can be detected. The industrious, dedicated and skilful privates of wartime propaganda are relegated to bit-part players in escape stories – if they appear at all. This was partly a reflection of the truth. Under the rules of the Geneva Convention officers were exempted from labour and thus had the time and leisure to conceive escape plans. Other ranks were in no such position and were deployed to keep wartime Germany ticking over. For the average prisoner-of-war private, the evening was a time to collapse exhausted not indulge in clandestine recces and shuftis round the camp. Inspite of this, prisoner-of-war/escape movies attracted audiences by their celebration of shared British values. The British sense of humour often came into play, for the Germans, no matter how threatening and awful, are always shown to be twits, much as they were in wartime comedy. The plots also have a strong streak of competition in them, revelling in games and sport. In effect, the escape becomes a sports contest and the British love a good contest. *The Wooden Horse* is dominated by the eponymous vaulting horse, while in *The Colditz Story* a French athlete escapes from the castle by leaping over the fence. Finally, the prisoners are always forced to improvise, forging identity papers, clothes, guns and other bits of equipment. Given the British obsession with improvisation, chucking things together at the last minute and generally making do, which was always cited as a reason for success at Dunkirk and in the blitz, it is little wonder these novels and films were successful.

The British public clearly did not reject this return to supposedly upper-class values, despite the fact that the war was one of the people, had led to a crushing Labour election victory and resulted in the creation of the welfare state. The films *The Wooden Horse* and *The Colditz Story* were smash hits in 1950 and 1954 respectively. But for us perhaps the quintessential escape story is *The Great Escape*. John Sturges' 1963 version of Brickhill's novel parachuted in some American stars to keep MGM's domestic audience happy and balanced them against British stiff upper lips captured by Richard Attenborough, Nigel Stock and Donald Pleasence. Gordon Jackson, personifying 'plucky' Scotland, represented British regional interest. A big money spinner at the time, it has become embedded in British culture thanks to numerous Christmas and bank-holiday television screenings and its catchy Elmer Bernstein tune. Everyone has heard of *The Great Escape*, to the point where it has become cliché. The theme to *The Great Escape* is now chanted on football terraces and can be used as a mobile phone ring-tone. In his autobiography, Stephen Fry compared his arrest to an incident from the film, and it has given comics and satirists a veritable field day. *Round the Horne*'s version was

'Escape from Stalag Limpwrist', a mercilessly camp parody in which Kenneth Williams announces that he was taken in the rear in the Ruhr and had to bail out. A fellow prisoner catches sight of his DSO ribbon and states: 'It's not often you see that. . . . Well not in someone's hair.' The late 1980s/early 1990s BBC Radio comedy, *Lenin of the Rovers*, starred Donald Hewlett in a virtual reprise of his role as the colonel in *It Ain't Half Hot Mum*. Regaling the men with his Second World War exploits, he tells them of his escape from the notorious Stalag Teasmaid where authentic German documents had been forged using only a potato. A version of the Second World War therefore lives with us still, in a form very different from the official histories but in touch, no matter how thinly, with the spirit of the time.

Boys' own war

Both Commando and escape stories provide the exciting legends of the Second World War and both are the staples of the conflict told to children, and young boys in particular. Throughout the conflict boys were offered a pleasure culture of war, glorifying the role of the British and Commonwealth forces. Veteran boys' fiction writers like W.E. Johns and Percy Westerman reshaped their Great War adventures into pieces suitable for a new generation.[13] Wartime paper rationing and a rationalisation of the market saw the number of boys' papers reduced and the quality of their print and illustrations diminish, but the stories themselves continued to capture imaginations. Many tales centred on the secret adventures of undercover agents, such as the *Rover*'s serial about a British spy working in a Nazi school for saboteurs. Unsurprisingly, Commando stories proved popular; in 1942 the *Hotspur* carried a serial about the 'Black Flash Commandos' and W.E. Johns produced a new character, Captain Lorrimer King, the hero of *King of the Commandos* (1943). Loosely based on the real Commando leader Lord Lovat, King is a natural leader of men as he is from a family with long-standing military connections and an aristocrat to boot. However, once on a mission he stresses that all are comrades and the objective is the only thing that matters. On an operation in France, King (or Gimlet as he is known thanks to his gimlet-eyed stare) and his men discover a British boy who has been waging his own private war against the Nazis since 1940. This theme of boys helping soldiers in their missions is one that recurred again and again in post-war boys' fiction and was clearly designed to make boys empathise with the characteristics of 'warrior masculinity'.

Johns was also behind the most important children's fictional female role model of the war. In 1941 he produced *Worrals of the WAAF*. Far from being an anaemic character, in keeping with older stereotypes of women, Worrals is studious, has a good sense of humour, is a fine pilot in the Air Transport Auxiliary and she always confounds men who don't think she is up to the job. Johns even wrote a scene in which she kills a German, thus breaking a taboo. In *Worrals of the WAAF*, she finds herself confronted by a German fighter while delivering a Spitfire; with ruthless determination Worrals shoots down her opponent. Dorothy Carter developed a similar female pilot character, Marise Duncan. In *Comrades of the Air* (1942), Duncan pilots a Red Air Force bomber. When the bomber crashes she and her comrades are forced to fight their way back to Russian lines, but only after they witness the brutal manner in which the Germans treat the local population. Boys did not therefore maintain a monopoly on combat fiction in the Second World War.

Curiously, while children told a Mass-Observation survey that they hated the war, the popularity of war literature shows that children were prepared to fantasise about it.[14] War games and toys also proved popular despite this ambivalence and in 1939 toy manufacturers were caught out by the sudden desire for war toys. By 1940 the industry was responding as lead soldiers and board games with war themes came on to the market. War toys went in and out of fashion according to the actual situation, thus at Christmas 1939 and in early 1940 model forts and a board game based on the Maginot Line were popular. But, as Quentin Reynolds pointed out in *Christmas Under Fire*, by December 1940 these were collecting dust on top shelves and aeroplanes were the most sought after toys. A year later British industry moved into total war production and the manufacture of toys ground to a halt. This placed more stress on homemade war toys and self-devised war games. Many commentators noted these forms of play and activity and often remarked on their complexity.[15]

In the immediate aftermath of the war there was a desperate, and understandable, desire to forget the experience and move on. However, as post-war austerity gradually gave way to a consumer society and a nation suddenly eager to relive its finest hour according to a relatively simple set of images, the conditions for a flourishing war toy industry were created, and perpetuated what Michael Paris has called 'the pleasure culture of war'. The children who took part in this 1950s war revival were often those born towards the end of the conflict or in the 1945–48 baby boom. This 'youth bulge' created a market the economy was keen to exploit and the excitement of war was a highly sellable product. For these children and youths the war produced by the toy, entertainment and publishing industries, when combined with what their parents told them, created history during a period in which the nation's great power status had slipped away. The Second World War as a simple struggle of good against evil, native wit, invention and humour against dour, plodding, unimaginative enemies was set. When children set it into the context of their school history lessons, it provided yet another example of strange foreigners determined to undermine the plucky island nation.

In the 1950s the Second World War started reappearing in comics. The *Lion* offered a serial on the 'Lone Commandos' followed by the 'Naval Castaways'. Printed in full colour and brimming with action-packed stories, the *Eagle* soon became the essential boys' comic of the period. Though its main character, Dan Dare, was a 'pilot of the future' who fought the evil alien Treens, the *Eagle* did not ignore the war and provided articles on arms of the services and biographies of important and famous participants. From the 1950s boys' comics were moving away from their nineteenth-century position of 'intellectual enlightenment' towards one promoting 'emotional intensity'.[16] Television was also forcing the stories to become more visually dynamic and dramatic. These trends were seen most clearly in D.C. Thomson's highly successful titles such as *Hotspur*, *Wizard* and *Rover*, all of which regularly featured exciting war stories.

Running alongside the weekly comics were the booklets, pioneered by the Amalgamated Press in 1958 with *The War Picture Library*. These offered a single, full-length, comic-strip story. D.C. Thomson soon muscled into the market with the *Commando* series, which started publication in 1961 and is still running.

Children and teenagers collected *War Picture Library* and *Commando* titles avidly, as well as reading the weekly comics *Victor*, *Battle* and *Warlord*, and each Christmas accompanying annuals were released. It is possible to identify continuing motifs and themes in these comics and annuals. First, many of the heroes are either other boys in their mid-teens who are caught up in the war accidentally or Non-Commissioned Officers (NCOs). Boys could easily identify with other boys and, as Dawson has suggested, the NCO has a particular resonance for boys. As brave, resourceful figures subject to the orders of higher authority, the NCO was the perfect 'fantasy-similar' for a well-behaved schoolboy. Secondly, the comics often blurred fact and fiction. *Victor* carried a weekly 'true story' from the First or Second World Wars, normally detailing the events lead-ing to the award of a Victoria Cross or other decoration. The inside covers of the annuals also carried true stories, reducing events to one dramatic cartoon sketch with a caption box providing details. For example, the 1980 *Victor* annual showed Hurricanes and Heinkels over London in a Battle of Britain scene, while the inside back cover portrayed British bombers over Cologne. Between these scenes the annual contained fictional stories about an RAF fighter pilot, a Royal Navy torpedo boat mission, an Eighth Army raid on the Afrika Korps involving troops on camels, RAF bombers over Italy, 'Pasty' White in a daring spying mission and Joe Bones 'the human fly' and scruffiest soldier in the British army climbing a sheer cliff to sabotage German coastal guns. Story and history merged in these annuals.

The third element typical to the comics, annuals and booklets is the high reliance on Commando or 'behind-the-lines' type action. In the true story sections, the St Nazaire, Dieppe and Bruneval raids were continual favourites, while combined operations adventures featuring motor launches, torpedo boats, kayaks and paratroop assaults dominate the fictional stories. High drama and excitement were guaranteed in such stories and provided boys with the plots for many of their war games and fantasies. The fourth element is the relegation of women. Women do not appear in many of these stories other than as mothers, sweethearts and wives confined to the domestic sphere and in need of masculine protection. Graham Dawson has noted that romantic plots in adventure stories bored him as a boy. He suggests a deliberate reading-out of women from the plot, a denial of the heroes' desire for love and the maintenance of a 'distinctively gendered reading of the narrative as an unalloyed adventure'.[17]

The final common element is the portrayal of the enemy and the manner in which the recourse to violence is justified. All enemy soldiers

A boys' own war: Commando *book front cover from 1969 (D.C. Thomson Ltd).*

were portrayed in highly simplistic terms. The Japanese were cruel, inscrutable fanatics who screamed 'Banzai' in every attack. The Germans were all blond and well built, often shown to be good soldiers, but always overcome by the sheer dash and imagination of the British. They spoke in the cod-German so beloved by those who satirise this version of the war: 'Himmel!', 'Donner und Blitzen!', 'For you Tommy ze vore is over'. By contrast, the grand allies were often ignored; there were few Americans or Russians in these publications, a great exception being 'Johnny Red' in *Battle*, an RAF pilot who flew with the Red Air Force. By contrast, Commonwealth troops, particularly the Australians – soldiers famed for their resilience and humour, qualities likely to be valued by boys – were often included. The rationale behind the violence towards the enemy is never explained except in the most obvious immediate way. The enemy is cruel, bullying and foreign and therefore deserves punishment. Few, if any, comic book heroes make any sort of statement about freedom, tolerance or democracy as motivations for fighting.

This was the very British war the children of the 1960s and 1970s grew up with. Everyone knew that the enemy was a very dodgy type and so the motivations and justifications for fighting did not have to be articulated in a sophisticated manner. But it was also a remarkably clean and sanitised war. Despite the violence men died quickly and honourably, wounds required bandages, a helping hand from a mate and a swig from the canteen. Those maimed, disabled, blinded or mentally disturbed by combat did not exist. It was also a clean war in another sense: there were no concentration camps, atrocities or internecine complications. The British war was a struggle of good against bad in which it was clear that the British were the forces of good, held all the aces up their sleeves and would win. This was the war I not only read about but played too.

Airfix has been teaching British boys, adolescents and quite a few adults too about the hardware of the Second World War since 1949. Although the first kit was actually a Ferguson tractor, it did not take the company long to branch out into planes, tanks and warships. The company itself was run by two ex-servicemen. Ralph Ehrmann, the chairman, had been a bomb-aimer with the RAF and John Gray, the managing director, an armourer in the army. Both men were determined to make their kits as accurate as possible and encouraged close links with the services and later the Ministry of Defence to help ensure authenticity.

Cheap to produce, using modern plastic-moulding techniques, and equally cheap to purchase, Airfix kits soon became an essential pastime for British boys. In 1953 the company produced its first Second World War model, appropriately enough it was the Spitfire. The box told purchasers that 'This aircraft fought in all theatres during the last war and together with the Hurricane formed the backbone of RAF Fighter Command' and it was an immediate success.[18] Since then the Spitfire has been reissued in revised kit form many times and retains a high profile in the model range. A model shop owner has affirmed that 'my best selling kit is the Airfix Series 1 Spitfire. I sell more of those than almost anything else. If you want turnover that's the way to go.'[19] Despite the vast leaps forward in aviation and its shadowing by model manufacturers, five of Airfix's six best-sellers remain models of Second World War aviation: the Spitfire Mk 1, the Hurricane Mk 1, the Lancaster and Mosquito bombers and the Messerschmitt 109. Of the twenty most valuable original Airfix kits on the collectors' market seven are Second World War related.

Alongside the model kits, Airfix produced plastic soldiers and battle scenarios. Thus through the 1970s it was possible to collect figures representing Second World War British paratroopers, Commandos, support infantry, Eighth Army, Australian infantry, American marines, Japanese infantry, German infantry and Afrika Korps. It was also possible to purchase El Alamein, Stalingrad, D-Day and Guadalcanal 'battle sets', and a model pontoon bridge complete with tanks.

Almost as stimulating as the models themselves were the packaging and box illustrations. Airfix prided itself on box art and, significantly, employed an artist who had formerly worked for the *Eagle* and *Swift* comics. Roy Cross produced the box art from the mid-1950s until the early 1980s and in doing so buttressed the images boys had witnessed on the big and small screens and imagined while reading books. Cross provided a visual history of Second World War combat which was heroic and exciting. One enthusiast, who built Airfix models throughout his 1960s childhood, said of Cross' work: 'It was most daunting in its precision and realism. Can I make a model that good? That is real war on those boxes, real bullets.'[20] The new 1970 Spitfire kit (possibly a response to the interest generated by the 1969 epic *The Battle of Britain*) showed two Spitfires flying above wispy clouds with ME109s streaking earthward in spirals of smoke, while far below is the verdant English countryside.

Warship kits invariably showed plumes of smoke and fire belching out of guns while boiling torrents of water spout skywards from near misses. Occasionally the artwork rewrote history. The 1968 Fairey Battle kit showed these aircraft attacking bridges that are crumpling in flames. The illustration appears to be making reference to the Battle squadrons' assault on the Meuse crossings in May 1940, an operation that was actually an unmitigated disaster for the crews of these obsolete aircraft.

Airfix shrewdly realised that its products could be tied-in with other examples of the Second World War in popular culture. In 1974, to coincide with the BBC *Colditz* series, a Colditz glider kit was launched complete with a twelve-page illustrated booklet about it written and signed by Major Pat Reid. (A board game also inspired by the series was released at much the same time.) Together with Action Man, Airfix provided many boys with the tools to re-enact the Second World War in play with plots taken from films, books, comics and relatives' recollections.

The ubiquity of prisoner-of-war and Commando stories in British film and popular fiction turned their dialogue into cliché, and this language was used by boys in play. These well-known turns of phrase then became the basis for satire and humour. Matching the sardonic humour of the combatants themselves, the British as a whole have always retained a slightly irreverent attitude towards the performance of the armed services in the war. But it is a humour not so much based on the reality of the actual experiences as the manner in which they have been presented since 1945: the interpretation has often become the focus of the humour. There are two different strands of humour. The first is generally positive and is often driven as much by the way the war has been presented and represented as by the experience itself. The second strand is a lot darker and the satire far less affectionate, and its profile is a lot lower in the popular culture and memory.

It was during the 1960s that the Second World War was opened up to satirical humour and comment. This was due to a number of factors converging. The war was re-imagined in the 1950s, a process that had retained elements of the original experience while reshaping or re-emphasising others. By the early 1960s a generation had reached maturity whose only knowledge of the war was through this reworking rather than one gained by direct experience. Significantly, this generation had grown up in more affluent and favourable circumstances than any other in twentieth-century British history, giving it a greater degree of self-confidence and assertiveness. At the same time, Britain's rapidly declining global position encouraged a reappraisal of the war, Britain's role in it and its consequences.

This combination of circumstances made the approach subtly different from the trail-blazing radio comedy, *The Goons*. Spike Milligan, Peter Sellers, Harry Secombe and Michael Bentine were all ex-servicemen who had gained an insider's knowledge of the forces and war. Their send-ups allowed them to create marvellous caricatures of the services, while life in the services was still firmly grounded in images common to the popular culture and held in affection. Barely a week went by without *The Goons* including some form of reference to service life or including a military character, invariably 'old school' and Blimpish. The 'Operation Christmas Duff' episode provides a good example. It included jokes about the NAAFI (services' canteens) being an enemy fifth column, upper-class twit officers, HMS *Ajax* depth-charging for raisins and RAF bombers dropping Christmas puddings.[21]

The crazy humour of *The Goons* then gave way to younger performers who added satire to the inheritance they had received from these pioneers. The satire boom of the 1960s was led by younger men like Alan Bennett, David Frost and Peter Cook, all of whom were prepared to treat British institutions irreverently but not without affection and understanding. British radio comedy was also moving into a new era as fresh writers, such as Barry Took and Marty Feldman, emerged with shows like *Round the Horne*. The 1960s therefore witnessed a comprehensive reassessment of the Second World War according to the comic muse.

But, as befitted a generation that had grown up at the cinema, the war was mainly recast as a parody of the great (and not so great) films. Feldman and Took revelled in satires of wartime films, particularly the clipped, stoic dialogue of Coward's *In Which We Serve* and *Brief Encounter* (or *Brief Ecstasy* as they re-titled it). Kenneth Horne always introduced these parodies with a perfectly framed announcement, for example: 'We in England have a great tradition in film-making, particularly during the war when we made those never-to-be-forgotten epics of "Keep It Up", "Stick It Out", "Take It On the Chin", "I Knew You'd All Volunteer", "Good Heavens, an Orange", "Jack, Darling, What's Happening to Us?" school of film. Here's an excerpt from one such naval

drama. . . .' It included dialogue reminiscent of so many hospital scenes
in which devoted women visit their wounded men:

> BETTY MARSDEN [playing the great actress Dame Celia Molestrangler]:
> What's it like, Charles?
> HUGH PADDICK [as 'ageing juvenile, Binky Huckerback']: At the front?
> BETTY MARSDEN: At the front.
> HUGH PADDICK: Not too bad. It's not too bad at the back either, but she's
> done the sides beautifully.[22]

Alan Bennett, Peter Cook, Dudley Moore and Jonathan Miller provided an equally acute observation in *Beyond the Fringe*. The sketch
'Aftermyth of War' included a section based on Humphrey Jennings'
work and *A Diary for Timothy* in particular, the British love of disaster,
the war as a great sporting contest, and a brilliant pastiche of the self-
sacrificing officer dialogue found in so many films. The result was a skit
on stiff-upper-lipped devotion to duty combining *The Way to the Stars*
with *Angels One Five*, epitomised in this exchange between Cook and
Miller:

> PETER: Perkins! Sorry to drag you away from the fun, old boy. War's not
> going very well, you know.
> JON: Oh my God!
> PETER: We are two down and the ball's in the enemy court. War is a
> psychological thing, Perkins, rather like a game of football. You know
> how in a game of football ten men often play better than eleven . . . ?
> JON: Yes, sir.
> PETER: Perkins, we are asking you to be that one man. I want you to lay
> down your life, Perkins. We need a futile gesture at this stage. It will raise
> the whole tone of the war. Get up in a crate, Perkins, pop over to Bremen,
> take a shufti, don't come back. Goodbye, Perkins. God, I wish I was going
> too.
> JON: Goodbye, sir – or is it – au revoir?
> PETER: No, Perkins.[23]

The whole sketch is utterly dependent on the ability of the audience to
read the signs. Without a common knowledge of the images it means
nothing, particularly the Jennings section and its word-for-word inclusion of the lines: 'The music you are listening to, Timothy, is German

music. We are fighting the Germans. That is something you are going to have to work out later on.'[24] The audience may not have identified Forster's commentary for *A Diary for Timothy* exactly, but would definitely recognise the general style and derivation.

Far from diminishing over the years, British comedians have continued to be fascinated by the war, and more particularly perhaps by the post-1945 war film. *The Fast Show*, a popular 1990s comedy, produced its own pastiche entitled 'The Valiant Years (1956)'. Opening with a British platoon under fire from a German pillbox, the officer turns to his men and asks for a volunteer to attack the position. The officer's stare descends on one soldier who announces 'Well, I'm not going'. Inverting the genre completely, the entire platoon then decides to surrender. Harry Enfield took a similar angle with a satire on the later 1960s war films, starring actors who were past their first flush of youth by that time, in his spoof documentary of the great actor, Sir Norbert Smith. 'The Dogs of War' was thus placed in the action-adventure mould defined by such films as *Where Eagles Dare* and *Wild Geese* and was acted by an excellent spoof cast, including Norbert Smith, Dick Booze, Richard Smashed and Oliver Guinness, who were all clearly modelled on actors in the Richard Burton, Oliver Reid and Richard Harris moulds.

The caricature of Germans has also provided fertile ground for British comics. As well as playing a host of Indian Army-type colonels, Dick Emery often adopted the monocle and jackboots of the German officer. *'Allo 'Allo*, a popular situation comedy series of the 1980s, included similar pastiches of aristocratic German officers, plus twisted Gestapo agents and melodramatic French resistance fighters. Jeremy Lloyd and David Croft's comedy was a parody on the earlier BBC occupation dramas, *Secret Army* and the *Fourth Arm*. However, *'Allo 'Allo* walked an extremely thin line between a satirical reworking of a genre and old-fashioned British xenophobia in which all foreigners are inherently comic and inferior.

Despite this disquieting element, the comedy has generally been affectionate and self-deprecating. But, this does not mean the acceptance of a new history of the type urged by the 'sensationalist revisionists' in which British myths are shown to be pernicious, government-inspired cover-ups of a far nastier reality. Far from it in fact, for this comedy is a celebration of Britain's eccentricity and insularity. Self-deprecatory comedy is also a symbol of self-confidence. Only a nation that knows what it is and where it is going can afford to be ironic. It might be said that as Britain loses this sense of direction it is becoming increasingly difficult to be self-deprecating. This trend is particularly marked in England, the nation most deeply scarred by Britain's decline, and its subsequent effect on English national identity: the football hooligan at an England match is most definitely not ironic or self-deprecating.

Others have urged Britain to come to terms with the Second World War and its effect on British society and culture by advocating darker, less affectionate comedy. As with the material already discussed, this phenomenon was also a part of the 1960s with a 1950s precedent. A quartet of films took an ironic look at the conflict starting in 1961 with *The Long and the Short and the Tall*, followed in 1967 by *How I Won the War* and was completed a year later with *The Long Day's Dying* and *Play Dirty*. All four questioned the relationship between officers and men, conscripts and professionals and individual's motives for fighting. The plots included British soldiers accidentally gunned down by their own side, and a platoon sent behind German lines to mark out a cricket pitch. The precedent had been set in 1956 by the Boulting Brothers' film, *Private's Progress*. Starring Ian Carmichael as the young private who is gradually deprived of his innocence thanks to army life, the film portrayed the wartime army as an institution motivated entirely by self-interest in which everyone was 'on the fiddle'. Many critics disliked the cynicism, but in the year of the Suez Crisis and the consequent questioning of Britain's global role, it was a notable exception to the established interpretation of the war. However, it is highly doubtful whether many of these films would be recognised now. In contrast to *Play Dirty* or *How I Won the War*, *The Dam Busters* and *The Great Escape* are still very much with us.

The myths and legends of gallant prisoners of war making jokes at the expense of the German guards, of Commandos armed to the teeth fighting like devils and then smiling cheekily for the camera are an essential part of our understanding of the Second World War. Undoubtedly, these images are highly stylised and deny the horror of killing and the boring drudgery of captivity. While the British may still hold such figures in affection and admire some of their qualities, the stereotyped image survives only in close association with the comic send-up. British humour has kept simplistic interpretations in check. Stiff upper lips and boys' own adventurers have been constantly cut down to size since the 1960s, at least by comedy. It allows for the survival of a myth without letting the myth become too fantastic.

Notes

1 A phrase Churchill used to Hugh Dalton, head of the Political Warfare Executive, which is often quoted. See Martin Gilbert, *The Second World War* (London 1989), p. 106.

2 *Pathé Gazette* 5 January 1942.

3 *Daily Mirror* 20 August 1942.

4 Spike Milligan *Adolf Hitler: My Part in His Downfall* (Harmondsworth 1987; orig. 1971), p. 114.

5 *Combined Operations, 1940–1942* (London 1943), p. 9.

6 *Daily Telegraph* 18 May 1943.

7 See Anthony Aldgate and Jeffrey Richards, *Britain Can Take it: The British Cinema in the Second World War* (Oxford 1986), pp. 96–114.

8 John Ramsden, 'Refocusing "The People's War": British War Films of the 1950s', *Journal of Contemporary History* 33, 1 (1998), p. 39.

9 Ibid., p. 52.

10 Ibid.

11 Pat Reid, *The Colditz Story* (London 1952), Prologue.

12 Ramsden, 'Refocusing "The People's War"', p. 39.

13 See Michael Paris, *Warrior Nation: Images of War in British Popular Culture 1850–2000* (London 2000), pp. 186–221.

14 Ibid., p. 221.

15 Ibid., pp. 219–21.

16 Ibid., p. 231.

17 Graham Dawson, *Soldier Heroes: British Adventure, Empire and the Imaginings of Masculinities* (London 1994), p. 253.

18 Arthur Ward, *Airfix: Celebrating Fifty Years of the World's Greatest Plastic Kits* (London 1999), p. 28.

19 Ibid., p. 94.

20 Ibid., p. 98.

21 Spike Milligan (ed.), *The Lost Goon Shows* (London 1987), pp. 10–35.

22 *Round the Horne*, BBC Enterprises 1988, ZBBC 1010.

23 Roger Wilmut (ed.), *The Complete Beyond the Fringe* (London 1987), pp. 72–8.

24 Ibid., p. 77.

CHAPTER 8

· · · · · · · · · · · · · · · ·

It ain't half hot mum:
the forgotten campaigns

Just as the British have revised and reshaped many aspects of the Second World War to suit themselves, they have also forgotten much about it, as was revealed in Chapter 5 on the home front. In terms of Britain's military effort, the elements least known in the public consciousness are usually those that fail to fit the nation's self-perception and these elements have spawned few myths. It is also significant that most of these missing campaigns failed to achieve much recognition at the time and thus their absence reflects a continuing trend rather than a new departure. This has certainly helped to create a slanted popular history and has ensured that many veterans of these campaigns retain a residual resentment at their omission from the accepted role of honour.

Colonel Bogey: the Far East and Italy

Of all the campaigns involving British and Commonwealth forces in the Second World War, the campaign in the Far East is unique for its utter lack of distinction in the British popular memory. Virtually unknown and ignored at the time, it is largely unknown, and ignored, now and very few cultural artefacts of the epic struggle in Burma have come down to us. The reasons for this distain for the war in the Far East are complex. On the one hand, the Burma campaign should have been, and should be, celebrated. After all, it seems to fit the British self-perception of time and history perfectly – a poor start was guaranteed by miscalculation and incompetence, only for victory to be achieved despite the odds. The Fourteenth Army, which took on the Japanese forces in Burma, came back from the dead, reinvigorated by a new commander, General Sir William Slim, a true hero of a People's War having worked his way up to high command from a relatively humble Midlands background. It was a campaign in which a romantic adventure took place behind enemy lines as Orde Wingate and his Chindits harassed supply lines and communication centres. Heroic resistance was put up against fanatical Japanese onslaughts at Kohima and Imphal, saving India from invasion. By the end of the war the Japanese forces in Burma had been comprehensively beaten, suffering 'the biggest disaster in the history of the Japanese Imperial Army'.[1]

Yet for all that only serious students of the Second World War have heard of Kohima or Imphal or the immense feat of crossing the wide, fast flowing River Irrawaddy. The reasons for this national amnesia probably lie partly in what came immediately before and partly in what came immediately after the campaign.

Churchill, like many others in the British government and armed forces, was convinced that Singapore was an impregnable fortress. Dominated by an impressive and modern naval base, Singapore was the key to Britain's defences in the Far East. In order to forestall Japanese aggression, Churchill decided to despatch a naval deterrent to Singapore in the autumn of 1941. Wanting the Japanese to consider the implications of this move, he let it be known publicly that HMS *Prince of Wales*, the newest battleship in the Royal Navy, along with an older battleship, HMS *Repulse*, were being sent east.[2] Large crowds turned out in Cape Town to welcome the *Prince of Wales* when she arrived in November 1941, and locals took the crew away for receptions, parties and sightseeing tours. It was an extraordinary act of hospitality and a reflection of the awe in which battleships were still held.[3] The next stop was Ceylon and then it was on to the great naval base at Singapore. As at Cape Town, the locals turned out in numbers to witness the arrival of the beautiful ships. *The Singapore Free Press* echoed the feeling that battleships were the supreme weapon of war and therefore the best guard against attack:

> It is big news not only for Singapore and Malaya but for the whole of the
> democratic countries bordering on the Pacific; it is bad news for Japan

which may begin to see the shattering of her hopes for an unopposed naval advance to the south.[4]

Even more confident of the 'battleship effect' was Major Fielding Eliot, a military correspondent, whose syndicated column appeared in a variety of newspapers, including the London *Daily Telegraph* and the *Malaya Tribune*. According to Eliot, the new arrivals would keep the Japanese navy from venturing into the South China Sea. 'In fact, the arrival of some British battleships at Singapore would render the Japanese naval problem in the Pacific quite hopeless.'[5] Turning to Japanese naval aviation he made a fatal blunder, claiming it was the weakest branch of the imperial navy and would never be able to cope with the attrition of war. He was clearly ignorant of Japan's 1941 output of 5,088 military aircraft.[6]

Within a few days of reaching Singapore these two ships set out to attack Japanese invasion shipping heading for Malaya. Far from providing Churchill's 'decisive deterrent', both ships were sunk by Japanese torpedo bombers, thus wiping out Britain's main defensive strategy at a stroke. Initially the British public took this defeat well, but it did not last. Home Intelligence noted a change, recording, 'there is increased criticism of the naval authorities concerning the loss of the *Prince of Wales* and *Repulse*'.[7]

The British were still debating the reasons for this defeat when it was announced that Malaya had fallen and the Japanese were besieging Singapore. The supposedly invulnerable fortress island proved shockingly easy to invade and subjugate and the garrison surrendered on 15 February 1942. The capitulation of Singapore forced Britain to accept its greatest military disaster since 1 July 1916, the infamous First Day of the Somme, and its biggest capitulation since Yorktown in 1781. When the fall of Singapore was announced by Churchill the enormity of the defeat could not be hidden which, perhaps for the first time, revealed a hint of desperation in the leader and his nation, a feeling reinforced by Churchill's decision to play the Dunkirk card: 'Here is the moment to display that calm and poise combined with grim determination which not so long ago brought us out of the very jaws of death.'[8] The newspaper coverage emphasised the heroic defence of Singapore but whereas other epics of the Second World War have, at the very least, a core of truth to them into which positive readings could be planted, the appalling reality of Singapore was, and has, remained resistant to such silver linings. The *Daily Telegraph*'s editorial agreed with Churchill's appeal to the nation: 'This is one of the moments when the British nation can show its quality and its genius', but coming just a few days after the Nazi capital ships *Scharnhorst*, *Gneisenau* and *Prinz Eugen* made a run for Germany through the English Channel in what was labelled 'the Channel Dash' without serious interference from either the RAF or the Navy, such exhortations seemed thin.[9]

The victorious Japanese forces revelled in their success, forcing the British to witness a humiliating formal surrender ceremony in which the commander of the Commonwealth forces, Lieutenant-General Arthur Percival, marched through the ranks of his men forlornly carrying the Union Jack. Captured by Japanese newsreel cameras, this scene can still make Britons squirm. Unsurprisingly, the British were angry and disillusioned by this national disaster, but it was not the end of the problem for the Japanese then turned their attention to Burma and maintained the momentum. In an act of self-protection the British seemed to blot the eastern theatre out of their minds as if it was too painful to consider. By the time the tide turned in Burma it was too late to refocus attention as the campaign in north-west Europe dominated the agenda. Even victory in Burma was not enough to drag the struggle into the limelight; defeat of the Germans had left the British feeling that the main task was already complete. After the war the victory itself soon looked worthless as Burma took its independence and refused to become a part of the Commonwealth. Many of the troops involved in the liberation of Burma had been from the Commonwealth and empire, particularly India. But in 1947 Indian independence appeared to give the British even less reason to celebrate this great imperial effort. Burma was an ironic victory. It is a shame it is unknown to the nation for if ever the new, multiracial Britain wanted to find an aspect of the Second World War in which all could share, and feel equal pride, it is in the Burma and Far Eastern campaigns. Alongside Britons from the home islands fought Indians, Burmese, Africans, Australians, Malaysians, Chinese and the aboriginal islanders of the region.

An attempt was made to show the British people what the self-styled 'Forgotten Army' had achieved. In October 1945, two months after Japan surrendered, *Burma Victory* was released. Made in the same series that started with *Desert Victory* (1943) and included *Tunisian Victory* (1943) and *True Glory* (1945), its post-hostilities appearance meant that it 'fulfilled the role of historical record' rather than a direct propaganda function.[10] Though rightly praised by the critics for its dramatic but clear narrative recounting the long and arduous campaign, it failed to achieve the impact of *Desert Victory*. It was a film too late.

The images the British do retain of the struggle against the Japanese do not, on the whole, pertain to the fighting itself but to the fate of British and Commonwealth prisoners of war, and there are relatively few of them. Of greatest significance is David Lean's 1958 masterpiece, *The Bridge on the River Kwai*. Adapted from Pierre Boulle's 1954 novel, it provides a brilliant examination of human wills and characteristics and is thus not quite the traditional 1950s British war film. However, its deep and lasting impact cannot be denied. Recently I paid my first visit to the River Kwai, joining a coach trip from Bangkok. Our Thai tour guide's first question was to ask who had seen the film. Around 40 people from a range of countries were on the bus – I identified Indians, New Zealanders, Australians, Dutch, Germans, French and Greeks – and all appeared to know the film regardless of age, which also meant that all were capable of humming the theme tune of 'Colonel Bogey'. The guide's commentary then unwittingly reinforced the idea that the film was an authentic interpretation of the bridge's construction, and it was very clear from the reactions of my fellow tourists that they took the film as an accurate reproduction of history. *The Bridge on the River Kwai* has therefore had an international impact, reshaping an aspect of the Second World War and keeping it alive in the modern, popular memory.

Not quite so well known as *The Bridge on the River Kwai*, but a significant influence on British attitudes towards the war in the Far East, was the 1956 film version of Nevil Shute's best-selling novel, *A Town Like Alice* (1950). Concentrating on the fate of women in Japanese captivity, the film avoids painting all Japanese as fanatical monsters but certainly does not attempt to redeem them either. A powerful and poignant drama, particularly as Jean's (Virginia McKenna) romance with an Australian soldier Joe Harmon (Peter Finch) blossoms, *A Town Like Alice* celebrated British decency and integrity. Ivan Butler's opinion that the film 'showed national *sang-froid* reduced almost to freezing point, no single member of the party of civilians caught in the hands of the Japanese cracking by so

A rare familiar moment in a forgotten war: Alec Guinness as Colonel Nicholson in The Bridge on the River Kwai *(1958) (Columbia TriStar).*

much as a millimetre' appears to pay it a backhanded compliment.[11] Emotion is there; it is merely presented in a very British way. The end scene in which Jean has reached Alice Springs and is reunited with Joe Harmon is deeply moving entirely because it is so restrained.

In the 1980s women prisoners of the Japanese were brought back to public attention in the highly successful BBC television drama, *Tenko*. The lives of a wide range of women were followed, from the wives of high-ranking British officers through the lower-middle-class wives of colonial civil servants and merchants to Australian army nurses, Eurasians and Dutch women captured in Java. Rescuing women from oblivion, the series revealed their endurance and bravery in the face of often cruel Japanese treatment. However, lest the drama degenerate into mere cliché, the complication of a relationship between a prisoner and a Japanese guard, which results in the birth of a child, was explored, stripping the story of a simple them-and-us divide. Running for three series from 1981 to 1984, *Tenko* gained an audience of 14 million per week and is remembered with a good deal of affection. An active website run by its fans bears testimony to its continuing high reputation.

Another television series remembered with warmth provides the only other major image of the war in the Far East still in our culture. *It Ain't Half Hot Mum* ran on the BBC for eight series between 1974 and 1981. Written by Jimmy Perry and David Croft (the writers of *Dad's Army*), *It Ain't Half Hot Mum* followed the fortunes of an Entertainments National Service Association (ENSA) unit situated somewhere in the jungle. Bearing a similarity to Peter Nicholls' play *Privates on Parade* (1982), the comedy was generated by the mixture of largely unsoldierly types who made up the unit. Melvyn Hayes played a camp female impersonator, Don Estelle the extremely short singer in his ludicrously baggy shorts and large pith helmet and John Clegg was the well-spoken pianist, always referred to as 'Mr Lah-di-Dah Bombardier Graham' by the Sergeant Major. Presiding over them were two stereotypical stiff-upper-lipped officers played by Donald Hewlett and Michael Knowles, while Windsor Davies turned in excellent performances as the permanently outraged Sergeant Major. Disgusted by their lack of martial prowess, his waxed moustache would quiver on his red face as he yelled out insults. Towards the end of its run it was derided for its too simplistic depiction of the Indian punkah wallahs, one of whom was played by a blacked-up British actor

(Michael Bates), himself a former Indian Army soldier. But the main joke behind the series was the sheer ridiculousness of the British. Thus *Bridge on the River Kwai, A Town Like Alice, Tenko* and *It Ain't Half Hot Mum* have created a fragmentary vision of the war in the Far East, a vision far removed from the real Road to Mandalay.

Hazy and fragmented memories are not confined solely to those campaigns fought outside Europe. There is general ignorance concerning the war in Italy, for example. Given the British penchant for Italy, its glorious scenery and beautiful cities one might have thought that its invasion would loom large in the popular imagination, but this is simply not the case. Even the bold amphibious moves against Salerno and Anzio are forgotten. The process of forgetting began even while the operations were still under way. Looking at the press coverage of the campaign it is easy to detect a growing sensation of boredom and frustration as the allies struggled to gain every inch of ground. Triumphs were acclaimed, but were accompanied by a sense of intense trial and tribulation, as was illustrated by the *Daily Mail*'s reaction to the fall of Monte Cassino after months of siege: 'The capture of Cassino is a first-class victory. It could only have been accomplished by stubborn and determined fighters who refuse to be defeated by weeks and months of frustration and disappointment.'[12] It was in stark contrast to the desert war; at least when things were going badly for Britain in the Western Desert there was the perverse thrill of excitement and adventure as vast chunks of territory exchanged hands rapidly and often more than once.

Far from launching a lightning campaign in Italy, the allies found themselves slogging away at tenacious German resistance. The hopes and expectations aroused by the collapse of the Italian armies and the surrender of the Italian state were quickly dashed by the speed with which the Germans recovered. The geography of Italy helped the Germans; hilly with numerous rivers, the landscape gave them the advantage of natural barriers, which made it hard for the allies to use their material superiority to most effect. After a while the Italian campaign descended into a stalemate not too far removed from the attrition battles of the Western Front in the Great War. Perhaps this is the reason for its low profile in our modern memory. At the same time, it became increasingly obvious that Italy was a sideshow, especially once Montgomery departed for Britain – the real event was going to be in France. After the war Churchill's caustic comments on the Anzio landings served as an epitaph on the entire campaign, from which it still hasn't escaped: 'We hoped to land a wild cat that would tear the bowels out of the Boche. Instead we have stranded a vast whale with its tail flopping about in the water.'[13]

There are some equally surprising omissions from the public memory concerning the 'real war' in France and Germany after D-Day. The final few months of the war are still largely unknown to the British, despite the fact that British and Canadian troops fought with great skill and determination in the invasion of Germany, bagging vast numbers of prisoners and taking such famous and important towns as Cologne, Hamburg and Bremen in the process. The operations included an elaborate and brilliantly executed Rhine crossing, which included the largest aerial assault in history, Operation Varsity. Launched on 23 March 1945, over 3,000 aircraft and 1,300 gliders carried British airborne units to the far bank of the Rhine. Germany's most formidable western natural barrier had been breached and it allowed the British and Canadian armies to advance side by side with the Americans who had crossed further south. German resistance was stubborn throughout the last months – they were now fighting for their homeland – and each victory was won only after a tough contest. Here the qualities of the British infantryman can, and should, be praised lavishly and remembered with pride and thanks. But who has heard of Operation Varsity apart from its few remaining veterans or serious students of the conflict? Why do the British not hold such occasions high in our popular memory? Could it be because the nation has no affection for victories won with the application of large-scale, cold, calculated professionalism? Could it be that they just aren't romantic enough? It is strange that the British do not like winning like this; they are less interested in this mechanical deployment of overwhelming force in a thorough and absolute manner. Give them another Arnhem or Dunkirk, or a great victory only after 'a damn close run thing', like El Alamein, and they are happy.[14]

Reaping the whirlwind: Bomber Command

Another missing chapter in the public history of the Second World War is that concerning the British strategic air offensive against Germany. During and after the war the most glamorous service was the RAF.

Modern, seemingly untroubled by the unwarranted influence of super-annuated old colonels, the RAF was both the cutting edge of science and technology while also fulfilling humankind's oldest, most romantic dream, that of flight. But in the post-war years the positive image came to rest more and more on Fighter Command rather than on the service as a whole. The explanation for this development is found in the British people's increasing unease at the wartime role of Bomber Command. In an act of collective amnesia the British decided to forget that they had dedicated more energy to the prosecution of a bomber war than any other combatant nation. Gradually overtaken by the haunting photographs of Dresden and dozens of other German cities, the shadow of the atomic bomb and official ambivalence to the veterans of the Command and its most vociferous Commander-in-Chief, Sir Arthur 'Bomber' Harris, the British turned their backs on the bomber boys.

It was very different in the middle of the war itself. With the army unable to invade the continent at that stage, the Navy engaged in a largely defensive battle, Bomber Command was the only instrument capable of offensive action against Germany. Rationed, besieged, facing disaster at almost every turn, the British people demanded a German bloody nose and supported the bomber as the only weapon likely to deliver it. Night after night the bombers flew to cities in Germany and occupied Europe, and over Germany at least they launched an indiscriminate area bombing campaign. Coverage of this campaign was ambiguous to say the least. On the one hand the British media celebrated the righteous retribution brought to all Germans, but on the other it stressed the legitimate assault on industrial targets only.[15]

In 1941 the Crown Film Unit made one of its most celebrated documentaries, *Target for Tonight*, chronicling the story of one aircraft on a raid. Made by the famous documentarist Harry Watt, *Target for Tonight* was a model of the genre. Watt used no actors, relying on serving Bomber Command personnel including the then Commander-in-Chief Sir Richard Peirse and the dialogue was written after Watt and his team had spent months studying the force. When the film was released, both public and critics enthused over the realism of the piece: here was the vital war winning force in action. But the bombing mission itself was staged using studio models and the film claimed a degree of accuracy Bomber Command knew to be well beyond its capability.[16]

Having established a reputation as the cutting-edge of British offensive action, Bomber Command maintained a high profile in the press until the end of the war. But, as a backlash occurred, Bomber Command was denied its place in the 1950s war films fest except for one glorious and stunningly successful celebration, *The Dam Busters* (1955). The reasons why this raid has been allowed to remain in the memory while every other aspect of Bomber Command's role has been excluded or treated with scorn are simple. Every element of the dams' raid can be found on the Great British checklist of what constitutes an epic: it was a huge gamble, it was the brainchild of a brilliant and eccentric mind and it was carried out by a tiny band of brothers. In addition, it was also a precision raid on a well-defended industrial target and therefore has none of the moral ambiguity of the Hamburg firestorm raids (although, in fact, the raid did cause considerable loss of non-combatant lives).

Known by everyone, the story of *The Dam Busters* hardly needs recounting. A jolly good bunch of British and Commonwealth chaps get together to execute a daring and technically challenging raid. History and image have elided in the case of the dams' raid, creating a popular version of a complex event. Richard Todd has become Guy Gibson, leader of 617 squadron. Partly thanks to its stirring march by Eric Coates, *The Dam Busters* has become a unique part of modern British culture. The music is hummed at football matches and causes an almost instantaneous outspreading of the arms in imitation of the Lancaster bomber. And, like the theme for *The Great Escape*, it too can be downloaded as a mobile phone ring-tone. It has been parodied in adverts too which has undoubtedly helped prolong its life. The most noteworthy parody is that produced for Carling Black Label Lager, which not only used the film's imagery but also buttressed our latent sense of germanophobia, albeit in a comic way. The camera pans over a Mediterranean holiday resort showing Germans marching round the pool intent on claiming the best sun loungers. A young British holidaymaker witnesses this from his hotel balcony and bowls his Union Jack towel over the rail. As *The Dam Busters* theme rises in the background, the towel skips across the water like the bouncing bomb before unfolding itself on a lounger. Deployed to suit the anti-culture of modern Britain, a seemingly standard 1950s British war film has therefore become a contemporary cultural icon too.

But, in terms of presenting Britain's bomber war on film, *The Dam Busters* is almost a lone example. Films such as *Appointment in London* (1953), a sensitive exploration of the stresses Bomber Command crews were subjected to, starring Dirk Bogarde, was largely ignored at the time and is almost unknown now. Len Deighton redressed the balance a little with his brilliant and sympathetic novel, *Bomber* (1970), which provided an insight into the workings of Bomber Command and was given a powerful large-scale dramatisation on BBC Radio 4 in 1993. But it has proven extremely difficult to rehabilitate the image of Bomber Command. When the Bomber Command Association commissioned a statue of the unremembered Harris for St Clement Danes, the RAF Church, it caused controversy. Split and divided as over few other aspects of Britain's Second World War role, some Britons supported the scheme while others saw it as an appalling calumny, giving tacit approval to a war criminal.[17]

With British military operations in support of NATO or United Nations resolutions now often led by air strikes claiming to hit targets with precision, leaving no 'collateral damage', the implications of the strategic air campaign of the Second World War remain a live issue which make it even harder to integrate it into the nation's positive popular war history.

'When Britain First at Heaven's Command': the Royal Navy

The role of the Royal Navy in the Second World War is another casualty but for slightly different reasons. The vital Battle of the Atlantic struggles to capture the imagination, lacking glamour and excitement. This indifference does a vast disservice to the thousands of merchant seamen and sailors who toiled against the twin dangers of the sea and a determined enemy. The Battle of the Atlantic and its vital role in keeping open the nation's arteries was brought home to the British people in the 1950s through a novel and a film. In complete contrast to the essential but routine duties of convoy protection were the clashes between surface vessels. For the general public the use of big guns against enemy ships is naval warfare and therefore has the ability to grab attention and interest. However, for the Royal Navy great fleet actions were very few and far between in the Second World War. The conflict never came close to a second Trafalgar; there wasn't even a second Jutland, the disappointing major fleet engagement of the Great War. When warships did clash, the press made much of them and they lingered in post-war memories.

Early in the war the Royal Navy proved its worth to the nation by its actions against the *Graf Spee* and in the Norwegian campaign, as discussed in Chapter 1. These incidents were followed by a string of operations that made very good copy: an attack on the Italian navy in Taranto harbour, a further humbling of the Italian fleet at Cape Matapan and a gallant, desperate fight to assist in the defence of Crete. Set against these positive views of the naval war were numerous disquieting losses. In October 1939 a German submarine penetrated Scapa Flow's inadequate defences and sunk the battleship *Royal Oak* while she lay at anchor. News of this disaster was suppressed for months. The loss of the famous battleship HMS *Barham* in November 1941 was announced after a two-month delay and the dramatic newsreel footage of her sinking was not released until the end of the war.[18] But it was impossible to avoid mentioning losses and defeats altogether.

One of the greatest shocks came in May 1941 when HMS *Hood*, the pride of the fleet, was sunk by the *Bismarck*. Fortunately for the British, a few days later revenge was extracted as the *Bismarck* was herself sunk after a long and arduous hunt. The editorial of the *News Chronicle* carried the sense of retribution at the sinking of the *Bismarck*. 'When the *Hood* blew up, the Navy set its teeth and went all out for vengeance. Now the account is paid.' The editorial went on to explain that Hitler's strategic loss was far greater than Britain's. Having fewer capital ships to risk, the loss of the *Bismarck* was a huge blow to German designs on Britain's naval supremacy.[19] Therefore, they suggested, the loss of the *Hood* was not too great a disaster.

HMS *Ark Royal* had an aura similar to that of the *Hood*, graceful, dependable and dignified. Reported sunk on so many occasions and yet always turning up to play a vital role in operation after operation, the *Ark Royal* was held in tremendous affection by the British people, reflected so obviously in the newspaper reports of her sinking in 1941. Paul Holt noted in the *Daily Express*, 'that this fine ship of war acquired, spontaneously and gradually, a spiritual tradition'. '*Ark Royal* went down "like a gentleman"' said the *Daily Express* headline, and its reporter – who happened to be on the ship when she was hit – found proof of the famed discipline and professionalism of the Royal Navy as the men left the ship in an orderly and unhurried manner.[20] Unlike many other disasters and reverses in the war, the loss of the *Ark Royal* provoked a strangely reflective reaction. There was the usual helping of stoicism – how the British can take hard knocks on the chin – but also the admission of 'a few shy tears' at her fate.[21] The Ministry of Information dedicated an entire illustrated pamphlet to the *Ark Royal* and attempted to articulate the spiritual bond with the ship felt by both her crew and the British people:

> *The gallant company had been close to death many times and they had reached the peaks of life. Together they had created that indestructible fellowship which had become the spirit of the* Ark.
> *This is not fanciful, nor is it a little thing. That spirit was real, if imponderable, and more enduring than the ship herself. And those of the* Ark *will take it with them in other ships and other aircraft, out to sea and into the sky.*[22]

When the *Hood* was sunk there was undoubtedly a deep sense of shock, but that had been repaid within days by the destruction of the *Bismarck*. *Ark Royal*, by contrast, had been in so many scrapes and had defied the enemy by wilfully continuing to sail long after the many declarations of her loss by fascist propagandists that her eventual demise seems to have hit the British people like the death of a close friend. The mourning of her loss seemed to epitomise the unique and intimate connection of the island race with its Navy. Used as we are today to air travel and a much smaller Royal Navy and British merchant fleet, we find this mystical connection hard to understand.

The sinking of the *Ark Royal* was announced a week after the naval drama *Ships with Wings* was released at the cinema. *Ships with Wings* (1941) is a movie many film critics and academics love to hate. Stereotype Italians and Germans gesticulate and goosestep through it without a shred of subtlety. The British heroes are all jolly good public schoolboy types who carry out their duty like faithful gun dogs, and the women are all adorable homemakers who wait patiently for their men to return, anxiety shown only by the tiniest furrow on their spotless foreheads. Opprobrium has been heaped on this film, condemning it for its acceptance of a rigidly class-based society and its lack of realism. And yet the public loved it, ignoring the critics' contempt and bemusing those who have sought to celebrate the 'quality' end of British film production; the film struck a chord with the people. It is a strange quirk of the People's War that such a vision of an ordered, class-based society was accepted with such enthusiasm. But accepted it was, much to the disgust of those who have sought evidence of deep pools of resentment in British society, of active social oppression or of an unsatisfied avant-garde taste in the British working class.[23]

A similar veneration for a well-ordered, respectable and hierarchical society was found in the greatest naval film of the war and one of Britain's greatest ever films, *In Which We Serve* (1942). It came about only after a long struggle with the naval authorities, for despite the success of naval films, the Admiralty remained largely aloof to the need for film propaganda. At first this position was sustainable due to the huge respect the public had for the Royal Navy. But a reaction set in as more details of disaster became public, and when, in February 1942, the Germans successfully completed their 'Channel Dash' the Navy came in for some harsh criticism. It was in this climate that the Admiralty suddenly became interested in a feature film.

The presiding genius behind the project was Noël Coward, a man who had gained a great respect for the Royal Navy as a result of his friendship with Lord Louis Mountbatten. Many within the Navy thought that Coward was not fit to play a role in a film about the senior service, due to his 'infamous' reputation, and it took some high-level wrangling to get the production underway. But Coward's project proved to be a masterpiece. A brilliant cast, including John Mills, Bernard Miles, Coward himself, Celia Johnson, Kay Walsh and Joyce Carey, gave excellent performances and brought to life the famed family feeling of the Royal Navy. *In Which We Serve* stressed that in this family all have their place and station and its harmony and efficiency is utterly dependent on all realising and accepting this system. By linking the sailors' home lives to their role in war, Coward made the film accessible and meaningful to a wide audience, drawing in all mothers and wives of servicemen. He was also determined not to patronise his audience and so fought a battle with the censor to show the loss of British ships. Here was propaganda at its best, not trying to deny reality but working it into the moral of the piece. Starting with the sinking of HMS *Torrin*, the film is built round a succession of flashbacks that show the men at home and at work, each of which stresses the interdependence of all ranks and orders. Beautifully observed, the film provides a poignant snapshot of mid-war Britain and an excellent tribute to the Royal Navy. Public reaction to the film was unanimously enthusiastic; it was the most successful British film of 1943 at the box office, and second only to Hollywood's *Random Harvest*, and in 1945 was remembered as one of the best films of the war.[24] *In Which We Serve* still has the power to move and is a reminder of Britain's former naval greatness and supremacy and the unique qualities the island race attributed to itself. At the end of the film, Leslie Howard speaks the final words over shots of naval ratings parading:

> *Here ends the story of a ship, but there will always be other ships, for*
> *we are an island race. Through all our centuries the sea has ruled our*
> *destiny. There will always be other ships and men to sail them. It is these*
> *men, in peace or war, to whom we owe so much. Above all victories,*
> *beyond all loss, in spite of changing values in a changing world, they*
> *give us, their countrymen, eternal and indomitable pride. God bless our*
> *ships and all who sail in them.*

Perhaps this is why it has proved enduringly popular, a comfort to Britons who these days rule the waves only occasionally.

The golden age of British war films in the 1950s and early 1960s saw the release of many successful naval films, each maintaining the positive wartime image, such as *Above Us the Waves* (1955), *The Battle of the River Plate* (1957) and *Sink the Bismarck* (1960). But the film that sticks out in terms of enduring appeal and quality is *The Cruel Sea* (1953). Far from sticking to the standard formula of the British post-1945 war film, *The Cruel Sea* is marked by its dour realism and lack of glamour, and thus departs significantly from the stereotypes and clichés critics of the British myth find so misleading. While never doubting the validity of the cause, or the endurance and bravery of the men, *The Cruel Sea* reveals the toll war takes on the individual and its sheer grinding drudgery. Based on Nicholas Monsarrat's best-selling novel of the same name, published in 1951, Ealing's fine film concentrates on the unglamorous Battle of the Atlantic in an unglamorous convoy escort ship. Jack Hawkins produced one of his finest performances for the film as the dour Captain Ericson, who fights his conscience and his failing nerve to retain his grip on command. There are no dashes in pursuit of enemy battleships or sudden landings of troops on enemy coasts. Instead, this close adaptation of Monsarrat's novel shows the stress of keeping convoys in good order, gut-wrenching U-boat attacks in the middle of the night and the helplessness of torpedoed ships. In doing so, both the novel and film version confirmed the British in their 'backs-against-the-wall' position. The struggle against the U-boats appears so unequal, the odds so stacked in favour of the aggressor that victory was a miracle. It was not until the 1980s and the excellent German television drama *Das Boot* that the British saw the Battle of the Atlantic from the other side.

Second in the top-grossing films of 1953, *The Cruel Sea* has retained its reputation as a minor classic. The book was part of the old O-Level English syllabus and has recently been added to the GCSE syllabus.[25] This is an interesting decision as the novel, like the film, stresses a male world in which women play little role other than as spectators. Angus Calder has deemed it a novel 'sexist virtually by intention' and has commented on the fact that 'British civilians in general are treated with contempt and ridicule'.[26] But that does not make *The Cruel Sea* any less of a People's War novel. The sailors are mostly civilians, either conscripts or volunteers, and where there is a lack of sympathy with civilians it reflects no more than a feeling common among wartime servicemen. Monsarrat was a volunteer sailor and reported accurately what he saw. It is the Navy's myth of the Second World War, but it is not a fabrication. Rather, it is the experience witnessed from a particular angle. *The Cruel Sea* provides a brilliant insight into the psyche of corvette crews; it reflects their heroism and prejudices in equal turn. Monsarrat himself was too close to his subject to bother with explanations for sailors' prejudices or moderate them in anyway. In doing so he may well have done the civilians of wartime Britain a gross disservice, but it does not detract from the authenticity or value of his account.

Echoes of the war at sea linger still in strange and indirect ways. In the 1970s the BBC produced two fly-on-the-wall documentaries recording life on the modern (though soon to be scrapped) *Ark Royal. Sailor* gained large audiences. Although it was a piece about the modern Navy, *Sailor*'s attraction lay in the enduring fascination of examining closed communities and in its reminder of world power and world influence. HMS *Ark Royal* represented the best of the nation, just as the Navy had during the war itself. A stronger echo came in 1982 with the Falklands War. Britain's Navy became its shield once again and the Second World War was re-enacted in the media, as will be shown in the next chapter.

The British have simplified their war into chapters they find acceptable. This has often entailed elements of adaptation in order to ensure that the original story can be fitted into contemporary circumstances. However, certain aspects of the war have been left behind and are the preserve of those interested enough to investigate the history more deeply. Fascinatingly, the missing parts of the story are by no means entirely concerned with defeat, disgrace and ignominy. Rather, it is the result of a combination of circumstances, as elements ignored during the war have been joined by those deemed irrelevant or dubious since 1945. It reveals that the British myth of the Second World War may look static but has shifted and realigned over time while carrying the 'big facts' with it.

Notes

1 Henry Maule, *Great Battles of World War II* (London 1972), p. 408.

2 Martin Middlebrook and Patrick Mahoney, *Battleship: The Loss of the* Prince of Wales *and the* Repulse (London 1972), p. 32.

3 Ibid., p. 68.

4 *The Singapore Free Press* 3 December 1941. Also cited in Middlebrook and Mahoney, *Battleship*, p. 75.

5 Middlebrook and Mahoney, *Battleship*, p. 75.

6 Ibid.

7 Quoted in S.P. MacKenzie, *British War Firms 1939–1945* (London 2001), p. 82.

8 *Daily Telegraph* 16 February 1942.

9 Ibid.

10 James Chapman, *The British at War: Cinema, State and Propaganda, 1939–1945* (London 1998), p. 153.

11 Ivan Butler, *The War Film* (London 1974), p. 91. See also John Ramsden, 'Refocusing "The People's War": British War Films of the 1950s', *Journal of Contemporary History* 33, 1 (1998), p. 55.

12 *Daily Mail* 19 May 1944.

13 Quoted in Martin Gilbert, *Churchill: A Life* (London 1991), p. 767. For good examples of press reactions to the Italian campaign, see *Sunday Express* 20 February 1944 and *Daily Telegraph* 31 January 1944.

14 Interestingly, over the last five or six years there has been some interest shown in 1945 and the last episodes of the war, but much of it is dedicated to the fall of Berlin and the advance of the Soviet armies. This is shown most clearly in the success of Antony Beevor's sequel to his remarkably popular *Stalingrad* (London 1998), *Berlin: The Downfall, 1945* (London 2002).

15 For details of how the media interpreted the British bomber war, see Mark Connelly, *Reaching for the Stars: A New History of RAF Bomber Command in World War II* (London 2000).

16 K.R.M. Short, 'RAF Bomber Command's *Target for Tonight*', *Historical Journal of Film, Radio and Television* 17, 2 (1987), pp. 181–218.

17 Ibid., pp. 137–40.

18 Clive Coultass, *Images for Battle: British Film and the Second World War 1939–1945* (London and Toronto 1989), p. 100.

19 *News Chronicle* 28 May 1941.

20 *Daily Express* 15 November 1941.

21 Ibid.

22 *Ark Royal: The Admiralty Account of Her Achievement* (London 1942), p. 63.

23 Jeffrey Richards, 'Wartime Cinema Audiences and the Class System: The Case of *Ships with Wings* (1941)', *Historical Journal of Film, Radio and Television* 7, 2 (1987), pp. 129–41.

24 Anthony Aldgate and Jeffrey Richards, *Britain Can Take It: The British Cinema in the Second World War* (Oxford 1986), p. 206.

25 Ramsden, 'Refocusing "The People's War"', p. 38.

26 Angus Calder, *The Myth of the Blitz* (London 1991), pp. 164–5.

CHAPTER 9

Gotcha!: recasting the Second World War, 1945–2002

ince 1945 Britain has entered into a process of decline and readjust-
ment. This process is, in part, a direct result of the Second World War.
Britain has been forced to accept the loss of its empire, the loss of
economic superpower status, the loss of naval supremacy, and the need
to see European nations as partners. Throughout the 1950s, 1960s and
1970s Britain's manufacturing base declined, and then suffered a cata-
strophic blow from the policies of the Conservative governments of the
1980s. Realigning itself as a service sector economy has provided some
stability for Britain, but the need to produce and export remains a problem. Alongside this, the nation has witnessed great demographic and
racial changes, which include a questioning of the union itself. The
United Kingdom today is a much looser institution than it was in 1939 or
1945; separate parliaments represent Scotland and Wales, and Northern
Ireland has regained its own assembly (albeit currently suspended).

Nevertheless, Britain still plays an influential role in world affairs. Its
armed forces are respected for their professionalism and have been
deployed in many of the world's 'hotspots'. The shadow of the Second
World War is a vital prop to this image. As a victor nation in 1945, Britain
held a reputation as a military power and gained a permanent place on
the United Nations' Security Council, a position the nation has striven to
maintain. It reflects a continuing appetite for major player status, but the

maintenance of that position depends largely on US approval and sustenance. At the same time, Britain's closer ties with its European partners have resulted in some realignments of foreign and defence policies. Surprisingly, this process has served to confirm the nation's military credentials. Despite the much larger army and navy of France, Britain is the soldier of the European Union; and Tony Blair has been just as forceful in this role as his Conservative predecessors.

Culturally, the Second World War underpins this position. The British people take pride in the country's international status, especially since its peers have overtaken it in so many other fields. Endless re-running of the Second World War through the media in every way possible has provided Britain with a security blanket in a changing world. The moment this truly hit the British people was 1956 and the Suez Crisis. Posing as a world power with the ability to force others to bend to its will, Britain's position was exposed as a sham. Open US opposition to Britain's policy confirmed both the dubious morality of the action to regain the Canal as well as Britain's utter lack of truly independent financial and military status. Humiliated and revealed as a paper tiger, Britain had to look to the past for reassurance. As will be argued, this search for national comfort is felt most distinctly in England and is the cause of concern and pride in equal measures.

Since 1945 nearly every international crisis involving Britain has been compared to, or seen through the lens of, the Second World War. Martin Shaw has noted in his work on the popular understanding of the Gulf War that 'memory and propaganda to do with past wars [are] . . . extremely important in our relationships to current conflicts'.[1] No longer subject to conscription, and with the vast majority of British people ignorant of life in the modern armed forces, wars are understood by drawing on a collective pool of knowledge, and that knowledge is based on images of the Second World War. Newspapers, radio, television and the British population as a whole have found it convenient, heartening and sensible to understand British involvement in conflict in this manner. Maintaining this standard of interpretation has two distinct benefits: first, it allows the British to ignore the decline of their nation by focusing on an earlier time; secondly, it proves reassuring, especially when there are setbacks, to remember that in the Second World War, despite the initial odds, Britain pulled through to victory. Events are therefore made to conform to a preconceived blueprint and unfold according to a simple set of rules. But this is not a simple case of the media dictating the terms of public understanding. Rather it is a complex two-way process. The media does not lead the public with a ring through its nose; it takes on board the dominant cultural atmosphere and, at the same time, reflexively ingests the feelings of its audience. Crucial to the creation of these broad interpretative laws of current events is the continual presence of the Second World War in our wider culture, in television dramas, documentaries and sitcoms, in film, popular literature and the heritage industry. Thus, the survival of the 'deep memory' of the Second World War is ensured by both the media and the British public, and plays an ongoing role in our understanding of events and the world around us.

Hitler ubiquitous

Almost as soon as the Second World War ended, Britain found itself caught up in various conflicts stretching from low-level 'imperial policing' actions through to large-scale, long-running commitments. On each occasion the scenario was almost inevitably perceived by reference to the Second World War. When the Suez Crisis irrupted in 1956, President Nasser's actions were often compared to those of Hitler. Prime Minister Anthony Eden, who remembered his dealings with Hitler while Foreign Secretary in the 1930s, became convinced that any form of dialogue with Nasser was akin to appeasement. Similar analogies had been drawn a few years earlier during the Korean War.[2] A template had been constructed and accepted, Britain was to reprise the Second World War during each future crisis.

Appeasement has proved to be a particularly fertile parallel. Britons born long after Chamberlain returned from Munich with his piece of paper still react to that word, determined that never again should a British leader be caught talking peace with a deceitful opponent. In the wake of the Iraqi occupation of Kuwait in August 1990, Saddam Hussein was easily vilified as a new Hitler, not to be negotiated with. Negotiating with such a man was, according to the British press, merely whetting his appetite for more easy conquests and fuelling his contempt for supine nations committed to open talks. A *Daily Mirror* editorial stated: 'The lesson of history is that appeasement never brings peace or security, it means only a harder, and bloodier, fight later on.'[3] Continuing in the same vein, the editorial claimed that Hussein's far-right Baathist party was based on National Socialist principles. It was not only the tabloids, however. Similar pools of imagery were fished by *The Guardian*; one article drew the parallel with the Austro-German *Anschluss* of 1938.[4] This was a rather curious example to pick on, for the *Anschluss* was achieved with at least some form of popular support from within Austria. The occupation of Czechoslovakia in March 1939 would have proved a far more effective comparison. Hitler's standards of behaviour are the touchstone for any journalist covering the aggressive ambitions of foreign nations and statesmen. 'Why is it any of our business what happens in Kosovo?', asked a *Sun* editorial in March 1999. 'For the same reason it mattered when the Nazis invaded Poland in 1939' it answered.[5] Seeing complex international issues in this way makes for clear and easily understood reportage, but whether it explains and explores them in a sensible and relevant manner is another matter.

During the Gulf Crisis and War the British press found many other echoes of the Second World War. The despatch of the Seventh Armoured Brigade was much commented upon because of its impressive pedigree. *The Times*, like most British newspapers, pointed out that in 1942 the original unit had taken on Rommel in North Africa and so the 'armoured brigade follows a proud desert tradition'.[6] In October, the anniversary of El Alamein was marked by a veterans' pilgrimage to the old battlefields. They were asked to provide advice for British troops dug-in on the Saudi Arabian border, while the tour leader said that the lessons of the 1942 desert war were equally applicable to the Gulf.[7] Similarly, former Battle of Britain pilots sent a message of support to their counterparts in the Saudi desert, and in September 1990 the sixtieth anniversary of the Battle of Britain saw an impressive RAF fly-past, which prompted the *Daily Mail* to compare the Few with their modern successors in the Gulf.[8] Other Second World War comparisons were deployed: *The Times* referred to the 'allied battle plan for breaching Iraq's Maginot Line' and claimed the 'Shadow of Kursk hangs over [the] desert battlefield'.[9] Journalists, it would seem, found it impossible to believe that their audience was capable of understanding the crisis in any other terms. No matter how true this was or not, the relationship between the Gulf (and all other recent conflicts) and the Second World War was important. For some Britons the comparisons provide the opportunity to emulate the qualities of their forebears. During the Gulf War, an 11-year-old girl told her nurse: 'I'm glad we're at war. I missed the other two.'[10] Like Jimmy Porter, many young Britons are caught in a world seemingly denuded of good causes commanding the moral high ground, demanding every drop of energy. In the absence of such causes there grows a bitter-sweet nostalgia for the Second World War, which becomes a symbiotic vicious circle by making our own world look all the more tawdry by comparison.

The new Few

The event most closely interpreted according to the script of the Second World War was the Falklands Conflict of 1982. Almost every aspect of the conflict over the islands was compared with the earlier struggle. At times the level of comparison was so heavy that events stopped unfolding unpredictably and became instead things that could be second-guessed thanks to Britain's history and experiences. Reassurance and comfort were therefore lent to an operation otherwise fraught with risk and danger. Eventually, the war also led to a revised popular history of the Second World War, a reframing according to Thatcherite tenets.

Initially, the crisis was seen as a humiliation comparable with Chamberlain's supposedly supine appeasement of Hitler. For much of the press the British government had acted like the guilty men of 1939–40, leaving Britain ill prepared to defend its citizens. Margaret Thatcher's government was subjected to a torrent of abuse for its lack of foresight, its lack of nerve and its lack of a defiant, Churchillian spirit. A cartoon in *The Sun* showed Churchill as a lion sitting on the white cliffs of Dover with the banner '1940 We Shall Defend Our Islands' and the Foreign Secretary, Lord Carrington, as a mouse on a tiny island with a banner saying '1982 We Shall Defend What's Left of Our Islands'.[11] Coming just a few days after the Argentine invasion, this was an amazing use of images. The *Sun*'s readership was clearly expected to understand references to Churchill, Dover and the iconic year of 1940. 1940 is the shorthand for fortitude and 'backs-against-the-wall' spirit, qualities, it was implied, that were sorely lacking in the government of the time. Images of Chamberlain's 1939 old gang were invoked by the *Daily Mail* in a tirade against Lord Carrington: 'Sack him and his whole rotten gang', urged

Andrew Alexander the political correspondent, 'The plain fact is that the Foreign Office is rotten to the core, rotten with appeasement, rotten with real scorn for British interests . . .'[12] Many wondered why Britain appeared so rudderless; a model of leadership was required and one historical parallel appealed beyond all others: 'If Churchill still controlled Britain's destiny would the Argentines have even contemplated tweaking the lion's tail, let alone done it with impunity?', asked a *Daily Mail* reader.[13] Most seemed to believe a clear historical comparison could be drawn: as in 1939, a Conservative government had been humiliated, largely due to its own spineless character; there could be only one solution, to adopt the mantle of Churchill. But the shock of the Argentine invasion to an unwitting government and public did allow one further element to manifest itself, and this was crucial to a British view of history: the nation had been placed very firmly on the back foot. If Britain was going to win, it would have to come from behind and start the race with the odds stacked against it. In 1940, people had been inspired by their history of bad starts. By 1982, 1940 was both a part of history and its most brilliant example of a bad start turned to triumph. According to this comforting reading of history, the thoroughly disastrous circumstances were guaranteed to result ultimately in a British victory.

Having established how alike and well-known everything was, the press pursued the Second World War parallels at every opportunity. When the RAF bombed Stanley airfield it was called a 'blitz'. Sir Arthur 'Bomber' Harris, Commander-in-Chief of Bomber Command for much of the Second World War, was asked for his reaction to the raid and gave his whole-hearted endorsement. Rather bizarrely Jon Akass stated: 'Forty Years after the River Plate we deliver another wallop.'[14] A 1939 naval victory against a German battleship, fought on the Uruguayan side of the River Plate, 300 or so miles from Stanley, was thought a valid comparison! On 25 April, the British scored their first major victory of the war retaking the island of South Georgia. Brian Young, commander of HMS *Antrim*, announced the feat in a wonderfully quaint message: 'Be pleased to inform Her Majesty that the White Ensign flies alongside the Union Jack at Grytviken, South Georgia. God save the Queen.' Here was the stirring stuff of the salt-water race; changing times clearly had no effect on the rhetoric of the Royal Navy. For the *Daily Mail* it was the most brilliant action since the gallant Commando raid on St Nazaire in

1942.[15] Showing the nation's continuing obsession with the idea of a fight against overwhelming numbers, *The Sun* urged that the Falkland Islands be awarded with the George Cross, just as Malta had been after its heroic resistance to the Italian and German air forces.[16] (By now, few remembered that the British government had been planning to strip the Falkland Islanders of their full passports in the immediate run-up to the crisis.) Inevitably, the landings at San Carlos water were framed by references to 6 June 1944.[17] Robert Fox of the BBC watched the landing craft go in 'exactly according to the D-Day model'. For those watching the television footage, the comparison must have been irresistible. Shots of landing craft bouncing and bumping on choppy waters, and the steely look on soldiers' faces bore an uncanny resemblance to the famous images of D-Day 1944. Eliding the two sets of images also maintains the justice of the British cause. Undoubtedly on the side of right and morality in the Second World War, the closer the resemblance between the two wars the easier it was to avoid deep debate over the legality of Britain's position. Writing in Geoff Hurd's edited collection of essays, *National Fictions: World War Two in British Film and Television* (1984), Julie Harper has noted:

> Film images from the South Atlantic war regenerate images from decades of war feature films and documentary programmes. What is finally celebrated in these representations are the traditional story-book values of male heroism, British unflappability, bravery ending in victory and what is, or is not, a 'good fight'.[18]

Most often couched in Second World War mythology was the air war. Outnumbered by their opponents, fighting a battle crucial to the outcome of the entire campaign, the RAF Harrier pilots quickly became the new Few. Aerial combat regained the good old boys' own appellation of 'dog-fight' and another version of the Battle of Britain was played out in the skies over the Falklands. *The Sun* announced:

> The few Harrier pilots defending the Falklands task force must now rank in glory alongside the men who fought off the Germans in 1940.
>
> They are living on their skill and their nerves, just like the Battle of Britain pilots – who were given the immortal title of The Few by Winston Churchill. . . . And like the Battle of Britain aces, they are intensely

proud of their aircraft. To them the Harrier is a Hurricane and Spitfire rolled into one.[19]

The *Daily Mail* agreed: 'Our Harrier pilots . . . are acquitting themselves in the finest tradition of The Few.'[20] Authority was given to such statements by a serving officer on HMS *Invincible* who said, 'Hitler tried to beat us and he had to win the air battle first. He failed. The Argies will too.'[21] In true 1940 style, the *News of the World* even drew on the sporting analogy, one front page carried a scorecard marked:

Britain 6
(South Georgia, two airstrips, three warplanes)
Argentina 0[22]

One of the reasons behind this framing of the war was the lack of visual images and words despatched from the Falklands. During the course of the war the media were very closely controlled, creating great problems for journalists hoping to supply exciting and dramatic coverage. The result was often patchy coverage and reportage.[23] Confronted with a news-hungry public, the press had little option but to speculate and piece snippets of information together. To fill in the void, journalists found themselves relating the unknown to a known experience of war, and in this particular case the known experience was the Second World War. The dearth of good pictures undoubtedly exacerbated the problem. The solution was the renaissance of the journal illustrator, a trade that had died out decades earlier. Thus British newspapers suddenly found themselves full of line drawings in the style of Caton Woodville and boys' comics. Air combat scenes were interchangeable with *Victor Book for Boys* stories about the Battle of Britain. Ironically, some events actually seemed more suited to this format than hard-nosed journalism, particularly the SAS raid on Pebble Island. Visualised in exactly the same way as a Commando book, this was war in the way millions of young Britons, in particular, expected it.

Victory against the Argentine forces was secured thanks to the professionalism of the British armed forces, but as General Sir Jeremy Moore said, recounting Wellington, there could be little doubt that it was a 'damn close run thing'. Far from taking the shine off the victory, damn close run things merely confirmed the Britishness of it all. Running things to the wire, improvising, pulling it off, were all great British characteristics and they had been proved once again. An editorial in the *Daily Mail* turned the Falklands War into Dunkirk, the other disaster transformed into triumph. Moreover, like Dunkirk, it was a triumph of the absurd, the sort of triumph only a sporting nation could engineer:

> This improbable, this gallant expedition to prise a lump of British territory from the maw of the aggressor, did not have proper air cover . . . did not have adequate early warning . . . was tragically vulnerable. But our men won through.[24]

Alan Miller, a Falkland Islander from San Carlos settlement, saw the war in a similar manner. For Miller, the whole affair was an example of British history in microcosm, which ensured the outcome was never in doubt:

> All of us here feel extremely humble at the incredible cost of sending the Task Force, so much being accomplished by so many for just so few. All through history, Britain has waited until she has been kicked, made a fool of, and almost too late before doing something about it. But once the British bulldog gets his teeth into something, look out! Three-to-one against at Goose Green and similar odds in the Battle for Stanley. Obviously British is Still Best.[25]

Using Miller's responses, it is possible to tick off the individual entries on the British popular history checklist one by one. First, Churchill and 'The Few' speech are here, but subtly recast this time with the Falkland Islanders becoming the Few. However, as has been noted in earlier chapters, this is actually an example of the distinction between the few, the fewer and the fewest. In effect, the British are always the few. Secondly, the slow start and national humiliation are absolutely vital prerequisites to a proper British victory. Lastly, there is the determination of the British to sort themselves out, make the best of it and reveal qualities of defiance and fortitude completely unexpected by the vast ranks of their foes. (And, by implication, Galtieri was, of course, another Hitler.)

As Miller stated, the crucial incident in terms of national character was the Battle for Goose Green. 2 Para's capture of the settlement immediately developed its own mythology. When the British took Goose

Green on 29 May, the British press, backed by official sources, expressed their astonishment that so few soldiers could have overwhelmed so many. Seemingly, 450 paratroopers had overwhelmed somewhere in the region of 1,200 Argentine soldiers. Despite much scholarly examination of the battle, picking away at these details, the image of Goose Green will never change because it fits so clearly the British outline of history.[26] Having such a strong sense of overarching principles for explaining the past, the British and their myth remain impervious to debunking. From Agincourt and the Spanish Armada through Rorke's Drift to Dunkirk and the Battle of Britain, the Brits are, and remain, the few. Secondly, the battle started with a blunder, another vital rule of the British time laws. On 27 May the BBC's World Service announced the movement of British troops towards Goose Green. Any lingering chance of surprising the Argentine garrison was ruined. But, once again, this was merely the British way. Why catch an enemy unawares when you can tie one hand behind your back and make a real contest of it? Victory would therefore have to be achieved from a less than ideal position. Simply perfect. Finally, at the moment of crisis the grit of the island race had shown itself as Colonel H. Jones took matters into his own hands by charging an enemy position. The Charge of the Light Brigade, the last stand at Kandahar, Captain Fegen steaming straight for the mighty *Admiral Scheer* in an old liner, all placed a man with as good a grip on British history as Colonel Jones in no doubt as to his duty. It wasn't so much a case of death *or* glory as death *and* glory. Goose Green was the new Dunkirk and Battle of Britain rolled into one.

Thatcher and the Second World War

Unlike the Second World War, however, the Falklands War has never been seen as a people's victory. Equally, and perhaps slightly more surprisingly, it has never come to be seen as a Conservative party victory either. Rather, the laurels have been placed on Margaret Thatcher's head, and many see it as her greatest personal achievement. The Prime Minister emerged from the Falklands War brimming with confidence. In a matter of months her government had been transformed from the reincarnation of Chamberlain's farcical administration to the embodiment of Churchillian values. However, the potential to turn the initial attack on the government into one that need not devour the entire Conservative party was present from the start of the conflict. The press sympathetic to the Prime Minister rapidly shifted the weight of its attack on to the section of the party it dubbed the wets thanks to its lack of commitment to Thatcherite tenets. For the Thatcherite press, the wets were the new Chamberlainites. A closer reading of the popular right-wing press in April 1982 reveals not so much an attack on Margaret Thatcher herself as a vilification of Lord Carrington, a leading wet, who became the new guilty man, the new Chamberlain. As in 1940, the Conservatives hoped for a change of image by dumping those perceived to be hopelessly old-fashioned and out of touch. But by seeing this triumph of Thatcherism in terms of Second World War parallels, a dangerous precedent had been set which created the conditions for a wholesale recasting of 1939–45 according to Thatcherite tenets. As Martin Shaw has put it:

> During the Falklands War Margaret Thatcher clearly tried, in a way in which no other British leader has done since 1945, to revive a wartime nationalism and beliefs about British heroism, to put as she phrased it 'the Great back into Great Britain'. . . . In Thatcher's appropriation of the Second World War memories there was, however, a particularly limited vision of wartime experience, since she wished to claim the patriotism while jettisoning the sharing of equality under threat.[27]

As the Second World War was reworked to fit a Thatcherite understanding of the experience, so too was the history of the 1970s and 1980s. The Second World War was transposed to Britain during these years, providing the Thatcherites with an alternative explanation of the nation's development. Almost every element of the Thatcherite struggle to build its version of the New Jerusalem was capable of interpretation according to the Second World War plot. The miner's strike became the new anti-democratic assault, led by a megalomaniac, dictatorial Arthur Scargill, a suspiciously close parallel with Hitler (or indeed Stalin – a representative of a nation wiped from most of the western world's heroic chapters on the Second World War). The drive towards European Union became a German plot aided by new Vichy regimes and Quislings. The plots of two separate myths can therefore be identified – that of the People's War and that of the Thatcherite/right-wing interpretation of the war:

The People's War myth

1930s

Years of Conservative neglect: locust years.

1940

Year of People's Glory and National Regeneration: the sweeping away of the old gang, replacement with a new, dynamic leader.

Dunkirk, the Battle of Britain and the blitz see all ranks, all classes pulling together.

1945

Year of People's Triumph: putting Britain on the road to the New Jerusalem.

The Thatcherite parallel to the Second World War

1970s

Years of Labour neglect: locust years.

1982

Year of National Regeneration: the sweeping away of the old gang, the flowering of a new, dynamic leader.

1983

Year of Thatcherite Triumph: putting Britain on the road to the New Thatcherite Jerusalem.

Seemingly trapped by the same inability to read the national story without reference to the Second World War, even Mrs Thatcher's critics succumbed to the same imagery. Leslie Gibbard, cartoonist of *The Guardian*, reworked the notorious *Daily Mirror* cartoon of March 1942. The original had sent Churchill's growing irritation with the combative stance of the *Mirror* soaring. Zec's cartoon of a merchant seamen clinging to a raft above the caption 'The price of petrol has been increased by one penny – Official' was read as a bitterly satirical comment on wartime profiteering and therefore extremely dangerous to morale. Churchill briefly considered closing down the *Mirror* altogether. In the wake of the loss of HMS *Sheffield* during the Falklands War, Gibbard reproduced this image, changing the caption to 'The price of sovereignty has been increased – Official'.[28] Clearly, the prism of the Second World War provided the vital lens for viewing, contextualising and understanding the Falklands conflict.

It is equally clear that Mrs Thatcher saw the triumph as a personal victory, in the process putting her on a par with Churchill. Few of her supporters failed to make this point again and again. Unsurprisingly, the voice of middle-class Thatcherite opinion, the *Daily Mail*, stressed the comparison with great gusto. Given the extreme criticism of the party in the early days of the crisis, it did not take long for Thatcher to be separated from the débâcle and absolved from blame. As early as 5 April the *Mail* had decided that she was Churchillian, while other members of the cabinet were Chamberlainites.[29] After the loss of the vital supply ship, *Atlantic Conveyor*, the editorial compared the trials and worries of Churchill with those of Margaret Thatcher. But, 'He was a fighter. And is there anyone who can doubt that we are being led by a fighter today?'[30] In the immediate wake of victory, Robin Oakley, the *Mail's* political correspondent, painted Mrs Thatcher in a very Churchillian hue: 'But the victory belongs also to one woman whose courage has carried Britain through the moments of doubt – Prime Minister Margaret Thatcher'. He concluded: 'This is more than a military victory. It is one of those moments which can lift a nation's mood and alter its history. It is the restoration of Britain's pride and self-confidence.'[31]

According to this hagiography, Margaret Thatcher had restored Britain's reputation as a world player and was the powerhouse behind the rebirth. It differed from Churchill's wartime reputation in a crucial way: no matter what Churchill might have thought about his own performance, he stressed the role of the people. He claimed the people were the lion and he was merely its roar, and on VE Day he told the British, 'this is *your* victory' (emphasis added).[32] However, the Thatcherite understanding of the Falklands was to stress her personal victory. In 1945, Churchill had been denied the opportunity to make a Conservative peace. In 1982, Mrs Thatcher was determined to rectify this perceived injustice. The Falklands War was the precursor and catalyst of the Thatcherite society; the 1945 general election was to be put right in that of 1983. *Spitting Image* leapt on this hijacking of Churchill, portraying Thatcher in his boiler suit smoking a large Havana cigar. But the success of such a caricature rests on the strength of its signs, in this case the boiler suit and cigar. The fact that people understood the comparison through these relatively oblique symbols is a tribute to the enduring quality of Churchill's image. In the 1990s a reaction against 'pure' Thatcherism set in, but the

Conservative party continued to link its contemporary position with Churchill and the Second World War. William Hague attempted an extremely neat trick, trying to bring together the People's War history with that of the new right. For Hague, the Conservatives were the true spirit and guardian of ordinary people's freedoms and aspirations; he saw the Conservative party and the British people walking hand in hand from 1940, sharing similar values and a similar spirit. Continuing his vision, he saw Conservative leaders as sharing similar aims and objectives since 1940, thus linking Thatcher, Major and himself with Churchill, Butler, Eden and Macmillan. It was a peculiar and particular vision of the past and present, perceiving it as a sacred union hostile to alien concepts of centralisation and over-regulation. This interpretation was therefore aimed not only at his domestic political opponents but also at the European Union:

> Winston Churchill and the British people, hand in hand, as we stood alone and saved Europe from tyranny. Rab Butler and the British people, hand in hand, as we extended free education and brought opportunity to millions of children. Harold Macmillan and the British people, hand in hand, as we brought prosperity to the cold, grey post-war era. Margaret Thatcher and John Major and the British people, hand in hand, as we freed the nation from state intervention.[33]

Taking on the right to summarise the People's War, Hague transformed it from a struggle to defeat totalitarian powers and establish a welfare state into the blueprint for a Conservative party manifesto.

Continuing to stand alone

Having a continual presence of highly coloured or reframed aspects of the Second World War in the national culture has created a situation that breeds mistrust of all foreigners. 1940 was crucial to this perception, reinforcing the idea that foreigners look with envy upon the sceptred isle and will do all in their power to wreck the tranquil existence of this happy breed. Since the early 1980s much Conservative party rhetoric has relied on this simplistic understanding of European union and integration. For Britain, 1940 was (and is) about us saving the world. But, as Malcolm Smith has argued, at the time (and for many since) the most significant fact about 1940 was the collapse of France and its political and military implications. As Britons we tend not to think about this, or it is taken as proof of the supine nature of foreigners when the going gets tough. As a nation we have no concept of the vital importance of France in 1940 as a great bastion against fascism, as a great nation, as a great military power, as a great empire. But, as Smith has also pointed out, this different point of view and emphasis of perception does not make Britain's survival in 1940 any less significant, it merely places it in a different context.[34] Britons should not feel ashamed of their wartime legends but they should understand the wider picture.

By not accepting a broader interpretation of the Second World War, the British have often misunderstood its implications, and this has led to confusion and malaise particularly with regard to Europe. In March 1947, David Low saw the new Anglo-French alliance in typically British terms. His *Evening Standard* cartoon revealed a jolly Ernest Bevin (then Foreign Secretary) trudging on to a beach dressed in soldier's uniform complete with rifle and pack. Anxiously looking out to sea is his French counterpart, Georges Bidault, dressed as a *poilu*. The caption reads: 'Return to Dunkirk.' The implications are unmistakable: Britain has returned not as an equal partner but as the protector of poor little France. France needs Britain but Britain does not need France; Britain has the sea as its guardian.[35]

Britain's ambiguity about Europe is, of course, no sudden development. The Second World War merely accentuated a distrust of, and distaste for, foreigners. A crucial binding element of the Union between the nations of the United Kingdom has been its suspicion of the outside Other.[36] However, since the Thatcherite–New Right's attempts to wrestle the memory and history of the Second World War away from the People's War camp (as defined in Chapter 5) began in the late 1970s, it can be argued that the British, and more obviously the English, have come to focus on the xenophobic elements of our national war myth to the exclusion of almost everything else. Whenever crisis threatens the nation the popular right-wing press asks a simple, but powerful, question: can we trust any nation to help us? The answer is intimately connected to a distinct reading of the Second World War, for the usual claim is only the USA will stand shoulder to shoulder with its fellow English-speaking democracy. European nations are often dismissed as spineless at best, outright anti-British conspirators at worst. This aspect of Anglo-Saxon glorious isolation was most clearly seen in the Falklands Conflict. A *Sun* editorial declared that any wavering from the United Nations or the Common Market over Britain's claim to the islands should be treated with the contempt it deserved. Britain knew where right and justice lay, which meant that 'We shall, if necessary, stand alone'.[37] Andrew Alexander, writing in the *Mail*, said 'Now we'll really know who our friends are . . .'. He clearly doubted whether Britain would find any loyal chums on the continent for he responded to the Common Market's deliberations with the comment: 'The Falklands Crisis throws a new light on our Common Market "allies". . . . We can go it alone!'[38] For Alexander this meant not only the mission to liberate the Falklands, but the world generally; the Common Market was a useless encumbrance. If ever we needed reminding, here was the proof, all foreigners are untrustworthy and European plots to inveigle us in their appalling chains of anti-British, anti-common sense regulations need to be resisted. During the recent Second Gulf War sections of the media echoed these opinions in the light of the European Union's reluctance to accept military action against Iraq.

Part of the problem lies in Britain's understanding of European union. Britain has never regarded membership of the European Community as an ideal in itself, viewing it instead as an economic necessity. A flawed lens through which to see European integration was created by this imperative: British politicians have played the utterly fallacious game of convincing themselves and the electorate that the concept of European co-operation was for economic purposes only. This ignored the definite cultural, social and political implications of integration, which were clear and obvious from the earliest days of its gestations. Clouded by self-delusion, the British have resisted all movement towards a deeper and more fundamental union, claiming it to be a corruption of the original intentions.

However, membership of the European Union threatens Britain's concept of itself in a deeper way. Both the concepts of subsidiarity and of pooling sovereignty have implications for the sanctity and usefulness of the United Kingdom. Scottish ambitions may be much better served by the European Union than those of the United Kingdom. In turn, this has important implications for England. A convincing case can be made to support the thesis that England has felt its decline in the post-war world most sharply. England, as the traditionally dominant nation of the United Kingdom, has never had to define itself as clearly as Ireland, Wales and Scotland. England could afford to luxuriate in the term 'Britain' because these labels seemed interchangeable for so long. Britain's decline was therefore more often England's decline. As a declining nation, unsure of what made it distinctive from its Celtic neighbours – other than not being Celtic – England has had to grab on tight to certain touchstones. The most important of those touchstones is the Second World War. The Second World War proved England's importance to the world and no one must be allowed to forget it. England lives in the past because the past is comforting, a reminder of when it was unproblematic to be English and British. Amity with former foes is then read not as a positive sign of evolving international relations but as the resurgence of evil foreign ambitions. If England is still the England under siege, then the French are still filthy collaborators and the Germans are still dastardly Nazis.

Exactly this spirit seems to infuse the wonderfully eccentric journal, *This England*. Founded in 1967 and each quarterly edition regularly selling a quarter of a million copies, *This England* is a publishing phenomenon. Lampooned for its sub-Betjmanesque quaintness, it nevertheless has a circulation envied by many, supposedly more fashionable, rivals.[39] Revelling in the idea of England under threat – countryside to be invaded by bulldozers, the BBC's lack of patriotism and obsession with politically correct attitudes – *This England* is most concerned about the threat of Europe and its desire to enslave us all to an undemocratic, centralised authority. Its summer 2000 issue marked the anniversaries of Dunkirk and the Battle of Britain less as celebrations than as a warning against the contention that proven leopards can change their spots:

Sixty years ago, as the springtime of 1940 began turning into what should have been the blissful days of another glorious English summer, our country, and indeed the whole world, held its breath. For civilisation was standing on the brink of disaster, threatened with the total destruction of democracy by the aggressive might of fascist Germany.

Without doubt, what came to be called 'The Battle of Britain' proved to be the most critical moment in our island's long history, for in a few short weeks it laid the foundation of our ultimate victory almost five years later. No other battle during that bitter conflict was so crucial to

our future as an independent nation and the cause of freedom
everywhere. Yet sadly, as we approach the 60th anniversary, many
members of the general public are still strangely unaware of its
tremendous significance in the outcome of the war, for to recount the
details of such a triumph over tyranny has long been deemed too
embarrassing for our 'European partners'. That is perhaps why there is
still no national monument in London to those who played a vital part in
what Churchill aptly described as our 'Finest Hour'.[40]

It is a perfect example of gentle, rather pathetic, chauvinism: no allies
are credited for having helped out and no one is deemed grateful for the
freedoms Englishmen won for them.

The flip side to this (perhaps) harmless nostalgia and one-sided interpretation of history is seen in English football hooligans. Hooliganism,
especially when connected with England's international matches, and
even more especially when connected with England's international
matches against Germany, reveals England's appallingly low self-esteem,
a low self-esteem that can be assuaged only by reminding all and sundry
of the final score in the Second World War.

British/English germanophobia is the result of a combination of factors. History is clearly important; twice in the twentieth century Britain
found itself involved in total war against Germany. During this same
period other nations experienced an equally traumatic relationship with
Germany, but have not allowed the memory of that experience to affect
continually their dealings with modern Germany. For Britain the real
difficulty has been the reversal of fortunes. German economic success
has often put Britain in the shade, German sporting success has been a
constant source of irritation to a nation that has so often under-performed
in major competitions, and Germany's wholehearted embrace, and economic dominance, of Europe has triggered both a sense of resentment
and fear: resentment at Germany's seemingly easy transformation from
tyrant to an open, friendly and co-operative nation, accepted as such
by so many of its former foes; fear at the thought that the easy-going
Germany might be an elaborate bluff concealing an unreconstructed
aggressively acquisitive state. In July 1990, Nicholas Ridley, then Trade
and Industry Minister, expressed the best – and most notorious – example
of this attitude. Interviewed by the *Spectator*, he claimed the Germans

were out to dominate Europe in much the same way as they had in 1939.[41] The subsequent fallout of this massive diplomatic gaffe was to force his resignation. Whether Germany actually equates fully to any of these images is irrelevant here. The perception is the important thing, and in the case of Ridley it is important to note that his resignation was more a consequence of international, rather than domestic, embarrassment.[42]

By contrast, Britain, and more particularly England, has seen its economic dominance dwindle. Particular national humiliation was felt when the Rover car manufacturing company was bought out and then rapidly sold on by BMW. The press both reflected and encouraged a wave of indignity against these supposedly haughty and contemptuous German impositions on the British people. In a world of multinationals that are expanding or contracting operations in Britain every day of the week, the reaction was extraordinary.[43]

In addition, on the sports field the nation that developed and codified virtually every modern game has had to remind itself constantly that competing is more important than winning. And, on so many occasions, even that cannot be considered true: a legion of abject performances require the more subtle term 'Britain took part', because competing implies actually making a game of it and therefore something a little more professional and polished. Finally, Germany's apparent ability to achieve consensus and agreement in Europe is even more galling to a nation convinced that no one remembers its wartime role in saving foreigners' bacon.

Jürgen Kroenig, London editor of the German daily *Die Zeit*, has a keen interest in British germanophobia. Significantly, he sees a marked decline in Anglo-German relations after German reunification in the wake of the Soviet bloc's collapse in 1989. An opinion poll conducted in 1986 revealed that 26 per cent of Britons called Germany their best friend (a long way ahead of the French) and 28 per cent believed Germany could be trusted as a faithful ally in wartime. Against this Anglo-German *rapprochement* in the 1980s, Kroenig cites post-reunification mood swings: in 1992 53 per cent of people approached by Gallup believed Nazism was capable of renaissance in Germany. When a poll of 10–16 year-olds was conducted, asking for their thoughts on Germany, 78 per cent mentioned the war and half mentioned Hitler. 'For these youngsters Germany is the most unpopular, boring and poorest country in Europe.'[44]

Basing his argument on a dumbing down of the media, leading to greater reliance on clichés and stereotypes, Kroenig's argument is extremely interesting. However, it appears to overestimate greatly the speed and nature of the decline. Britain in the 1980s was not the 'German-happy' state Kroenig claims it to be. Thatcher's term in office witnessed the rise of innate British suspicions of the other, particularly the others we had fought wars against. Perhaps the chink in Kroenig's argument is his search for germanophobia. Prior to reunification, Kroenig is unlikely to find examples of germanophobia, but it is all too easy to find examples of *west germanophobia*. Despite the Cold War, most Britons had precious little knowledge of East Germany and rarely perceived it as a threat. West Germany, on the other hand, was a different matter. All the problems listed above, revolving around economics, European integration and sporting success, were points of contention with West Germany. When reunification occurred, Britain simply transferred its west germano-phobia to the whole, new country. But it was a west germanophobia based on historical and cultural tenets, those which had found most potent expression in the two world wars, and summarised in Angus Calder's table in the Introduction (see page 22).

Until the late 1970s, British germanophobia was fairly humdrum and innocent, if any form of racism can ever be labelled as such. However, with national decline came a more violent chauvinism, greatly aided by the Thatcher governments' obsessive desire to identify enemies of Britain, whether they were domestic trade unions or foreign countries. At the same time, more assertive Scottish and Welsh national movements restored some pride to sections of the United Kingdom which were under-represented and undervalued by Thatcher's Conservative gov-ernments. Ironically, this converse concentration on England did very little to divert or arrest its people's popular sense of decline. England's national prowess so obviously lost, and its achievements seemingly either forgotten or thought to be dubious, engineered a nasty backlash. For the English, lost in a world in which former certainties had been undermined, the past alone seems solid, and the most prominent, most solid fact of the nation's past was its righteous crusade in the Second World War. Armed with a perverted reading of this fact, English football hooligans have made international fixtures the new Second World War. The perversion lies in the simplistic misunderstanding of the national position in the Second World War. In 1945 Britain was in a position of (relatively) great military strength and power. It also had a great deal of moral power, won largely by its brave stand in 1940. Britain thus had a high profile and exerted authority. Since 1945 the former has declined (but, thanks to a set of historical accidents, not as sharply as Britain's economic position, as noted earlier) and the latter became more important. But this moral standing is of no interest to the football hooligan. Physically dominating power is the only thing that matters, is the only thing that can make ill-informed, aimless young men feel better. Understanding 'respect' to mean 'fear' and 'reputation' as 'presence', the English football hooligan has drawn a set of dysfunctional lessons from the nation's Second World War experiences, often encouraged and abetted by the popular press with its use of crude parallels alternated with crocodile tears of disgust. Mindlessly misunderstanding that British soldiers arrived in cities such as Brussels, Antwerp and Eindhoven as honoured liberators in 1944 and 1945, English hooligans have taken the historical masculine prowess of their race to mean treating all foreign cities as places of legitimate despoliation in order to let these people know who and what we are.

But before this begins to read like a *Guardian* editorial on the problems of Thatcherism and contemporary British/English history, it should be noted that the potential for this type of behaviour has always been present. In broader, structural terms, commentators on English national character such as Jeffrey Richards and Jeremy Paxman have noted the transformation of the English from a singularly violent people to a singularly civilised one.[45] Perhaps we are witnessing the turn of the wheel back to pre-modern national characteristics? Glimpses of England's older national stereotype can be detected in the war itself; ironically, the most potent symbol of this, and precursor of later violence, can be found in *British Movietone News'* newsreel special to mark Victory in Europe. Coverage of street parties includes interviews with the residents of south London's famous Lambeth Walk. One man – obviously slightly the worse for drink – faces the camera and says: 'You can always bet that when Lambeth people are about there'll only be one winner. That's the Lambeth people will fight anyone in the United Kingdom or outside the United Kingdom.'[46] The terrifying element of power and status achieved through indiscriminate violence combined with the English disease of parochial

ignorance is obvious. Viewed now, this section of the newsreel is discon-
certingly jarring, appearing utterly ignoble and sits uneasily with our
vision of a glorious people come to their righteous reward. This disturbing footnote became the main text in the 1970s, 1980s and 1990s.

Neil Blain, Raymond Boyle and Hugh O'Donnell have studied the
relationship between the British media, sport and hooliganism. Their
fascinating work confirms the British media's obsessive desire to cast
England–Germany football matches as re-runs of the Second World War.
The Second World War is used as the entrance to a wider collection of
images: 'Everything is referred to periods of history where England/
Britain was not only on the winning side, but was also on the side of
rectitude and was seen by all to occupy the high moral ground.'[47]

In turn, the qualities demanded by the war are those shown by the
international sides of the home nations, significantly not England alone.
These qualities, lionised in the press, are actually very close to the
People's War version of the blitz: endeavour and endurance, teamwork,
humour, fair play, honesty.[48] Often the sense of battling overwhelming
odds is also part of the equation, seen most potently in the eulogies
surrounding England's 'backs-against-the-wall' performance against
Argentina following Beckham's sending off in the 1998 World Cup
Finals. Twisted, misapplied and misunderstood, these same characteristics, supposedly inherited from the chirpy types who clambered from
the air-raid shelters, inform the attitude and behaviour of the football
hooligans. The havoc wrought in quiet bars situated on charming squares
by English hooligans is often justified by the claim that vast hordes of
local troublemakers came to taunt them, backed up by incompetent and
partial policemen. Thus the hooligans automatically qualify as the new
few, bravely fighting against the odds. As Billy Bragg's ironic and satirical
indictment of such attitudes, 'The Few', states:

> Our neighbours shake their heads
> And take their valuables inside
> While my countrymen piss in the fountains
> To express our national pride[49]

When England, far from showing their renowned mettle, melt into an
incoherent mess on the football field, the fans on the terraces salvage
national pride by tapping all the endeavour and endurance of their

forebears, allowing them to tear down fences and show Johnny Foreigner that Britons never, never, never will be slaves. Humorously providing advice on *How to be a Wally*, Paul Manning told his audience that showing good old-fashioned British guts in a foreign football stadium would prove '[t]here's nothing that Hitler could do with a couple of Panzer divisions that you and the lads can't tackle comfortably with your bare hands'.[50] Inadvertently, Manning has hit upon the point made earlier – the English have become the new Hun. To draw on Bragg's song, *The Few*, again: 'And they salute the foes their fathers fought / By raising their right arms in the air.' But this transformation has been made unwittingly. Far from being the preserve of evil foreigners, many English fans seem to believe that such excesses represent the behaviour demanded of them by their history; they are merely conforming to the standard set by our lads and lasses in 1940. They are regaining respect for all things English. This is the defiance of the utterly defeated. During 1940, with defeat staring the nation in the face, such an attitude was a virtue, as identified by Churchill in his history of the Second World War. With that wonderful command of rhetoric he was so famous for, Churchill proclaimed the moral of his history to be:

In War: *Resolution*
In Defeat: *Defiance*
In Victory: *Magnanimity*
In Peace: *Goodwill*[51]

Armed with the second moral, the English football hooligan is utterly bereft of the third and fourth, ignorant of the fact that to maintain the spirit of one alone is to maintain the spirit of none. Occasionally this lack of Churchill's four great morals has been seen to affect the highest of the country as well as the lowest. Following the Falklands Thanksgiving Service at St Paul's Cathedral in July 1982, Mrs Thatcher let it be known that she was singularly displeased with Archbishop Robert Runcie's sermon. Acting with Christian humility and truly British reservation, he failed to inject a suitably triumphant note, relying instead on true Churchillianism: in victory magnanimity, in peace goodwill.

Regardless of the protestations of the media, hooliganism is some-thing encouraged by its continued misreading of the national character, the Second World War and constant, facile xenophobia. In July 1990,

England reached the semi-finals of the World Cup where its opponent was Germany. *The Sun* carried a photograph of the father of England star striker Gary Lineker on his fruit and vegetable stall bearing a sign saying 'No Germans, Italians or Argies'. A range of minor celebrities were asked their opinion on the match. Bernard Manning based his on the axiom 'two world wars and one world cup', while Clive Dunn drew on his best-loved role, Private Jones of *Dad's Army*, declaring 'they don't like it up 'em'. The next day an unfunny cartoon added to the anti-German atmosphere: running out on to the pitch, the German team are being berated by Hitler and a gang of Nazis sitting in the crowd, 'who's the nut shouting "victory or the firing squad"?', asks the bemused German captain.[52]

Matters reached a head in 1996 when England hosted the European Championship and were once again fated to play Germany in the semi-final of a major competition. The *Mirror* rose to the occasion by providing a bizarre reworking of Chamberlain's declaration of war:

> *I am writing to you from the Editor's office at Canary Wharf, London.*
>
> *Last night the* Daily Mirror*'s ambassador in Berlin handed the German government a final note stating that, unless we heard from them by 11 o'clock that they were prepared at once to withdraw their football team from Wembley, a state of soccer war would exist between us.*
>
> *I have to tell you now that no such undertaking has been received, and that consequently we are at soccer war with Germany . . .*[53]

Pushing the puerile joke to its limits, the front page punned on the name of England's left back, promising 'Pearce in our time' alongside photographs of Stuart Pearce and Paul Gascoigne with superimposed tin hats. Parodying the clichéd lines of the war film genre, another headline ran: 'Achtung! Surrender / For You Fritz, ze Euro 96 Championship is over.' The back page carried a photograph of the German striker Jürgen Klinsmann along with another parody, this time of *Dad's Army* lyrics, 'Who do you think you are kidding Mister Hitman?' The impact of the Second World War appears to have achieved a double consciousness: on the first level there is the war itself and on the second that of its post-war cultural artefacts and reinterpretations. Although amusing on the surface, it is deeply problematic for it implies an inability to discriminate between the myth of the war and the present reality.

Continuing the Second World War theme, the *Daily Mirror* gained intelligence on the mood of the Germans by sending a correspondent to Berlin. In a stunningly pointless piece of journalism, two whole pages were taken up with an article written in cod spy language. On another page, readers were urged to cover up street signs so as to confuse the Germans, following the example of the Home Guard in 1940. The editorial drew upon an older parallel, stressing English resilience in the face of ominous odds by demanding: 'We must pull together, just as we pulled together to repulse the Spanish Armada.'[54] What the readers of the *Mirror* made of this is hard to tell, but there can be no doubt that the editor, involved in a capitalist war of ratings and reader loyalty, must have assumed his readership would understand, sympathise with, and accept these images.

But confusion lies at the heart of so much of this posturing and posing, most significantly on this vexed question of the difference between Englishness and Britishness. Richard Littlejohn, columnist of *The Sun*, tried to inflame anti-German passions in the run-up to the 1999 European Champions' League final contested by Manchester United and Bayern Munich. His examples barely make sense, citing an English football team consisting of an array of foreign-born talent as an example of British historical virtues against a German side that was the supposed reincarnation of Nazi ideals:

> It is fitting that in the final of the European Champions' League
> Manchester United will face Bayern Munich. Britain versus Germany –
> two world wars and one world cup. You couldn't ask for a more perfect
> clash of cultures. Cool Britannia versus the master race. Bayern might
> field a Ghanaian and the Brazilian Elber, but they are probably the only
> black men in Munich, the crucible of Nazism.[55]

Such journalism is so confusing, so muddled in its imagery and understanding of the situation that it is almost impossible to deduct any sense from it. All that can be understood for certain is a dislike of the Germans who, according to Littlejohn, have changed little since 1939.

To those concerned by the rise in anti-European sentiment and the popularity of isolationist views in Britain, the constant presence of the war in our national imagery is something to be resisted and frowned upon. At times, and in certain circumstances, just as with germanophobia, this can be taken too far. Humorous parodies of German wartime values can often be just as much of a send-up of British attitudes. However, such approaches can appear to sit on the cusp of the two interpretations of the war, that of the People's War myth and that of the New Right myth. The People's War myth is intimately connected with a sense of humour which is about taking a joke as well as handing them out, whereas the New Right myth is far more aggressive and confrontational. Perhaps the best illustration of this duality is Shepherd Neame's famous (bordering on notorious) advertisements for their Spitfire bitter. On the one hand, these very corny jokes about the war have a self-deprecating edge, mocking our inability to move on and form a new relationship with our past and our present. However, on the other hand, this material can also be read as lending tacit support to a continued anti-German and anti-foreign culture in Britain. Under the slogans 'The Bottle of Battle', 'Downed all over Kent, Just like the Luftwaffe', 'No Fokker Comes Close' and one showing beer glasses – a British mug and a German stein – in silhouette form, in imitation of a wartime aircraft recognition poster, with the inscription 'Ours' and 'Theirs', Shepherd Neame's adverts caused amusement and controversy in equal measure. Reacting to complaints from German tourists, the London Underground removed the adverts from their trains. Shepherd Neame disputed these claims of racism (and homophobia after a joke about rear-gunners, showing that even jibes about gays can be connected with wartime imagery) and had their case upheld by the Advertising Standards Authority.[56] Whether the campaign is thought to be in bad taste or not, its impact cannot be disputed. Mining the deep 'big facts' of the Second World War, Shepherd Neame touched upon the vital images of the Spitfire and the countryside of south-east England in the Battle of Britain.

The advertisements also follow a familiar line in British humour about the war, the best examples of which have an ambivalence seemingly mocking the Germans combined with an attack on British prejudice and our inability to cope with the modern world. John Cleese took exactly this line in *Fawlty Towers* in the famous Germans episode, though it is hard to know whether people laughed with Basil Fawlty or at him. A similarly problematic example is Johnny Speight's character, Alf Garnett. In Norman Cohen's film version of *Till Death Do Us Part* (1969), Alf attends the 1966 World Cup Final at Wembley. Finding himself

What makes Britain great: the Second World War and beer (Shepherd Neame Brewery).

standing behind a patriotic young German who cheers wildly when West Germany scores first, he taps him on the shoulder and says 'Same as in the war mate, same as in the war. Started it off well, started off well but got well clobbered in the end didn't ya?' Later, when Geoff Hurst scores his second goal he cannot resist saying, 'He's done it again hasn't he, mate? Bleedin' Blitzkrieg eh?!' We laugh at Alf's ridiculous comparisons but we also laugh with him: most Britons cannot help siding with him against the Germans.

Becoming nephews of our Uncle Sam

Ironically, however, it is not just our former enemies who continue to attract our scorn and sarcasm. The nation often thought to be our greatest ally is now in danger of losing its sacred aura. Having been linked so firmly with the USA, Britain has allowed itself to believe in an Anglo-Saxon understanding of the planet based on a shared heritage, proven by the bonds of blood shed in a common cause on the sands of North Africa, in the hills and valleys of Italy, the jungles of South-East Asia and the bocage of Normandy. The Second World War is a vital element in every aspect of Anglo-American relations. During the Cold War Britain and America could claim to be continuing their common struggle for freedom initiated in the Second World War. Most recently, the terrorist attacks on New York, Washington D.C. and Pennsylvania in September 2001 have allowed Tony Blair, Rudolph Guiliani and George Bush to play on images of the blitz, Lend-Lease (Roosevelt's decision to supply Britain with vital war materials on a pay later basis), D-Day and the full panoply of Anglo-American Second World War memories to justify their approaches to international relations and to sell the idea of a continuing common destiny of their peoples.

Although support for this stance is generally steady and accepted, the British have been adjusting their view of the USA and its role in their history. While the Cold War was ongoing the Americans needed a firm, resolute Britain and so had to pander to certain British sensitivities, most obviously over Britain's role in the Second World War. America's vast contribution to the victory of the allies was a clear and obvious fact to all in the West, but the British were eager to be seen as equal partners who had played a consistently significant role in the struggle. Given Hollywood's desire to cash in on the popularity of war movies in the wake of the conflict, this was a tricky proposition as films tended to support an American-centric vision of the war. British feathers were severely ruffled by Warner Brothers' 1945 Errol Flynn adventure, *Objective Burma*, which implied that American, rather than Commonwealth, forces had liberated Burma. A howl of indignation arose in Britain and America was accused of arrogantly appropriating the entire catalogue of allied Second World War successes into its own history.[57] However, with the British film industry capable of turning out more than enough reminders of the old country's days of glory, the score was just about evened out. Everything changed with the end of the Cold War, followed by easy victory in the Gulf War. America suddenly found it had exorcised Vietnam and was, in Fukuyama's phrase, the last man standing.[58]

Politically, economically and culturally dominant, America now had no need to pander to any allies, and with a new generation growing up completely disconnected from the Second World War there was an opportunity to revisit the old battlefields and re-imagine them. Buoyed by the interest of young Americans in a war they had no knowledge of and aware of the looming fiftieth anniversary celebrations, the Hollywood companies returned to the Second World War epic in the 1990s. But this time there were no allies; this was America's war. America had fought it alone, America had won it alone and America alone deserved the laurels of victory. Films such as *Saving Private Ryan* (1998), *U571* (2000) and *Pearl Harbor* (2001) have rewritten history and caused offence as they have done so, particularly in Britain. Despite the commercial success of these films in this country, Britain has shown extreme sensitivity to its sudden demotion. There were outcries over the lack of British representation in *Saving Private Ryan* and *U571*. When the BBC bought the hugely expensive series spawned by the success of *Saving Private Ryan*, *Band of Brothers*, great efforts were made to explain its British credentials, stressing that it starred British actors, was made in Britain by British production teams and was in fact a major coup for the British entertainment industry. However, it did not wash, for only a positive acknowledgement of Britain's role in the war could convince people it was not in fact another example of the Second World War according to America, and that was not on the agenda. Having spent so much money in securing the series, the BBC was remarkably downbeat in its publicity and eventually screened it on BBC2 rather than on the flagship channel BBC1.

Although media pundits have speculated over whether this reflected difficulties in identifying a core audience for the drama, part of the reason must surely lie in BBC sensitivity to the charge that it was supporting an American propaganda campaign.[59] Why should interpretations of events so long ago prove capable of arousing such high passions? The answer must return us to the decline of the nation argument. Having so little sense of who and what we are in the here and now, the solidity of the past becomes much more important, and any attempt to smudge it or recast it is viewed as a slur and an attack on the nation's honour and glory. By dominating popular culture, American media companies have the ability to revise the popular understanding of the Second World War, and in doing so they have chipped away at the most important British fact of the war – that we did it alone. America is the most potent reminder that Britain was not alone for six years. But, ironically, America now wants to take Britain's Second World War mantle for itself – the USA as a fortress of decency in a world corrupted by evil dictators, the USA alone and majestic against all comers, the USA fighting for the survival of democratic rule, whether that be on the imagined shores of Utah beach or in the hills of Afghanistan.

The British have not managed to escape the Second World War yet. International decline and internal realignments have not been easy processes for the British people. Standing up like a rock in a sea of mediocrity is the nation's performance in the Second World War, and the British keep their eyes fixed on this reassuring vision. Some find added comfort in Britain's continued high profile in military affairs, and some have taken matters into their own hands by causing mayhem in European cities, thus proving national solidarity and virility to all. The left has become faintly embarrassed by British and English patriotism, uncomfortable with the nation's pride in its achievements, ironically abandoning the people of the People's War. By implication, the left seems to find Britain's victory rather distasteful, as if submission to fascism would have been slightly better than this gauche nationalism. However, in abandoning the field, the left opened the way to a right-wing domination of the myth-history of the Second World War. The left did not completely reject the history and memory of the Second World War. Rather it took a different strand, being more interested in the everyday experiences of 'ordinary people' as opposed to the Churchillian 'grand narrative'. However, by failing to find adequate ways to deal with the *stereotypes* of chirpy cockneys, resolute Plymtonians and the gentle humour of *Dad's Army*, the left committed a tactical mistake and helped to undermine the healthy myth of the war. It appeared as if the left was deserting the British people, their patriotic pride and their desire to feel proud of Britain's Second World War achievements – the achievements of ordinary people in a People's War. For some people infused with this sense of pride, it seemed to leave only one option – acceptance of the right-wing version of the war. When combined with the disastrous social policies of Thatcher's governments, and economic dislocation and decline, a situation was created in which the nation's comforting, but rather placid, myth became one of ugly violence. The British people need to be reassured that the nation's role in the Second World War is something to be proud of and the sacrifices of its people something to remember with gratitude and honour. But, at the same time, they also need to be told that it is over, over for good, over once and for all. Now more than ever Britain, and England in particular, needs the patriotism of Cecil Spring-Rice: all our ways are ways of gentleness and all our paths are peace. In this manner alone can Britain honour its past and recover a sense of national magnanimity and goodwill.

Notes

1 Martin Shaw, 'Past Wars in Present Conflicts: From the Second World War to the Gulf', in Martin Evans and Ken Lunn (eds), *War and Memory in the Twentieth Century* (Oxford 1997), pp. 191–204.

2 Tony Shaw, *Eden, Suez and the Mass Media: Propaganda and Persuasion during the Suez Crisis* (London 1996), p. 113.

3 *Daily Mirror* 3 August 1990.

4 *The Guardian* 3 August 1990.

5 *The Sun* 24 March 1999.

6 *The Times* 15 September 1990.

7 *The Times* 22 October 1990.

8 *Daily Mail* 17 September 1990. See also *The Times* 19 January 1991.

9 *The Times* 23 and 30 January 1991.

10 Quoted in Martin Shaw, 'Past Wars in Present Conflicts', p. 198.

11 *The Sun* 5 April 1982.

12 *Daily Mail* 5 April 1982.

13 *Daily Mail* 17 April 1982.

14 All taken from *The Sun* 3 May 1982.

15 *Daily Mail* 26 April 1982.

16 *The Sun* 24 May 1982.

17 See, for example, *The Sun* 23 May 1982.

18 Julie Harper 'Join the Professionals! Militarism, Masculinity and the South Atlantic', in Geoff Hurd (ed.), *National Fictions: World War Two in British Film and Television* (London 1984) pp. 51–3.

19 *The Sun* 3 May and 10 June 1982.

20 *Daily Mail* 31 May 1982.

21 *The Sun* 20 May 1982.

22 Quoted in Robert Harris, *Gotcha! The Media, the Government and the Falklands Crisis* (London 1983), p. 48.

23 See Harris, *Gotcha!* and Valerie Adams, *The Media and the Falklands Campaign* (Basingstoke 1986).

24 *Daily Mail* 15 June 1982.

25 Martin Middlebrook, *Operation Corporate: The Story of the Falklands War 1982* (London 1985) p. 388.

26 For a detailed discussion of the numbers involved, see Spencer Fitz-Gibbon, *Not Mentioned in Despatches . . . The History and Mythology of the Battle of Goose Green* (Cambridge 1995), pp. 1–10.

27 Martin Shaw, 'Past Wars in Present Conflicts', p 193.

28 Harris, *Gotcha!*, p. 49.

29 *Daily Mail* 5 April 1982.

30 *Daily Mail* 27 May 1982.

31 *Daily Mail* 15 June 1982.

32 Charles Eade (ed.), *War Speeches of Winston Churchill*, 3 vols (London 1951), vol. III, pp. 438–9.

33 Quoted in Malcolm Smith, *Britain and 1940* (London 2000), p. 128.

34 Ibid., p. 8.

35 *Evening Standard* 4 March 1947.

36 See Linda Colley, *Britons: Forging the Nation 1707–1837* (London 1992), pp. 19–46.

37 *The Sun* 7 May 1982.

38 *Daily Mail* 26 April and 7 June 1982.

39 See Jeremy Paxman, *The English: A Portrait of a People* (London 1998), pp. 77–81.

40 *This England* 33, 2 (Summer 2000), p. 10.

41 *Spectator* 14 July 1990.

42 Alan Watkins, *A Conservative Coup: The Fall of Margaret Thatcher* (London 1992), pp. 133–5.

43 See, for example, *The Guardian* 2 April 2002.

44 Jürgen Kroenig, 'The Mass Media in the Age of Globalisation: Implications for Anglo-German Relations', 1999 Reuters Lecture, University of Kent at Canterbury.

45 See Paxman, *The English*; Jeffrey Richards, *Film and British National Identity, from Dickens to* Dad's Army (Manchester 1997).

46 *British Movietone News* 14 May 1945.

47 Neil Blain, Raymond Boyle and Hugh O'Donnell, *Sport and National Identity in the European Media* (Leicester 1993), p. 148.

48 Ibid., pp. 65–7. Fascinatingly, the continental media use exactly the same set of stereotypes to describe the British sides.

49 Billy Bragg, 'The Few', on *Don't Try This at Home* album, Catalogue No.: COOKCD062.

50 Paul Manning, *How to be a Wally* (London 1983), p. 100.

51 Winston Churchill, Frontispiece in *The Second World War*, 6 vols (London 1948–54).

52 *The Sun* 3 and 4 July 1990.

53 *Daily Mirror* 24 June 1996.

54 Ibid.

55 *The Sun* 25 April 1999. Also cited in Kroenig, 'Mass Media'.

56 See *The Times* and *The Guardian* 14 March 2001.

57 Ian Jarvie, 'Fanning the Flames: Anti-American Reaction to Operation Burma', *Historical Journal of Film, Radio and Television* 1, 2 (1981), pp. 117–37.

58 See Francis Fukuyama, *The End of History and the Last Man* (London 1992).

59 For examples of press reactions to these scheduling decisions, see *The Guardian* 14 May 2001 and 15 August 2001; and *Evening Standard* 4 October 2001.

Epilogue

The British myth of the Second World War was being made as the war itself unfolded. The myth was the result of collusion between the people and the government. Both accepted that in order to understand, endure and survive the experience of war an agreed explanation of events was required. Experience was therefore packaged and interpreted in particular ways. Those who see it as the imposition of a falsehood on reality are missing out on the subtlety of the process and certainly fail to understand that the myth could only survive and remain acceptable if it was based on reality. For this reason the broad outlines of the myth will stand up to close examination.

However, this book has not been an exercise in proving that there is no difference between all history and all myth. The popular version of the Second World War is the product and aggregate of a number of sources and a vast collection of individual experiences which have created a remarkably robust history. By contrast, the British myth of the Great War is very different and will not bear close scrutiny. The British memory of this conflict is one dominated almost entirely by an over-reliance on a very small pool of sources – the poetry and literature of educated, literary, young, unmarried junior officers.

Having defended the British myth of the Second World War, it is not the case that it has been entirely beneficial to Britain. In the post-war years it has certainly complicated Britain's relationship with its composite parts and the rest of the world, and it has clouded an objective reassessment of its international economic and military status.

Given the thrust of this book, it is perhaps somewhat ironic that it should also be noted that perhaps Britain might now be experiencing the final throes of the myth thanks to a whole range of social and economic factors. The cohesive, all-pervasive national culture that held on to the totems of the Second World War is now rapidly falling to pieces. White,

Anglo-Saxon racial homogeneity has been replaced with a far more complex tapestry, particularly in Britain's cities. Different communities with different interpretations and visions of the past have sprung up. The atomisation of family life, combined with the effect of intense diversity in television, broadcasting and leisure activities, means that British children will rarely now sit down to watch black-and-white war films on Sunday afternoons. New generations of toys and computer games have made Airfix Arnhem paratrooper figures look dated and boring. Unless museums can transfix their audiences with excitement and dynamism, they fail to make an impact. Words like 'Dunkirk' are still in the language but fewer and fewer young people, including history students, seem clear as to precisely what happened around that French port, why and when. Most of them won't have heard of Kenneth More let alone Douglas Bader.

It is significant that the recent Second Gulf War saw far fewer comparisons with the Second World War than the original Gulf Crisis of 1991. The media were far more interested in showing off their embedded reporters and exploring the technological specifications of weaponry that make Spitfires seem as ancient as knights in armour.

Unfortunately, the culture that is replacing it seems to have just as much to do with violence, but without any of the mitigating qualities demanded by the wartime struggle of good against evil. For, fascinatingly, interest in the Second World War still seems to be high among Britons, but the British element now often plays second fiddle to an obsession with Nazism, and the genocide in particular. A prurient interest in everything to do with the death camps is evident.

It is therefore hard to know whether the British myth of the Second World War will now take a new direction or whether the nation is witnessing the final manifestations of a national obsession that is about to pass into history. Britain has lived with its finest hour for a long time, but few would doubt that that hour has long since passed.

Bibliography

Sources

Mass-Observation Archive, University of Sussex

File Reports 1937–40: Report 167, 3 June 1940; Report 182, 10 June 1940

Public Records Office

INF1/264 Home Intelligence Daily Report, 15 July 1940

Ministry of Information pamphlets

Ark Royal: The Admiralty Account of Her Achievement (London 1942)

The Battle of Britain, August–October 1940: An Air Ministry Record of the Great Days from 8th August–31st October 1940 (London 1941)

The Battle of Egypt (London 1943)

Hay, Ian, *The Battle of Flanders, 1940* (London 1941)

Combined Operations, 1940–1942 (London 1943)

The Eighth Army, September 1941 to January 1943 (London 1943)

Newspapers and journals

Country Life; Daily Express; Daily Herald; Daily Mail; Daily Mirror; Daily Star; Daily Telegraph; Die Zeit; Evening Standard; The Gleaner; The Guardian; Illustrated London News; Kent Messenger; New Society; The Listener; Malaya Tribune; Manchester Guardian; Melody Maker; Monthly Film Bulletin; New Yorker; News Chronicle; News of the World; Observer; Picture Post; Radio Times; The Singapore Free Press; Spectator; The Sun; Sunday Express; The Sunday Times; The Times; The Times Literary Supplement; This England; TV Times; War Illustrated; Woman's Own.

Newsreels

British Gaumont News

British Movietone News and Gazette

British Paramount News

Pathé Gazette

Books

Adams, Valerie, *The Media and the Falklands Campaign* (Basingstoke 1986)

Addison, Paul, *Churchill on the Home Front* (London 1992)

Addison, Paul, *The Road to 1945* (London 1994; orig. 1975)

Addison, Paul and Crang, Jeremy (eds), *The Burning Blue: A New History of the Battle of Britain* (London 2000)

Aldgate, Anthony and Richards, Jeffrey, *Britain Can Take It: The British Cinema in the Second World War* (Oxford 1986)

Anderson, Benedict, *Imagined Communities: Reflections on the Origins and Spread of Nationalism* (London 1983)

Ashplant, T.G., Dawson, Graham and Roper, Michael (eds), *The Politics of War Memory and Commemoration* (London 2000)

Barnett, Correlli, *The Desert Generals* (London 1960)

Barnett, Correlli, *The Audit of War: The Illusion and Reality of Britain as a Great Nation* (London 1986)

Barnett, Correlli, *Engage the Enemy More Closely: The Royal Navy in the Second World War* (Harmondsworth 2000; orig. 1991)

Beevor, Antony, *Stalingrad* (London 1998)

Beevor, Antony, *Berlin: The Downfall, 1945* (London 2002)

Bierman, John and Smith, Colin, *Alamein: War Without Hate* (London 2002)

Billière, Peter de la, *Storm Command* (London 1992)

Blain, Neil, Boyle, Raymond and O'Donnell, Hugh, *Sport and National Identity in the European Media* (Leicester 1993)

Boulle, Pierre, *The Bridge on the River Kwai* (London 1954)

Brann, Christian, *The Little Ships of Dunkirk* (Cirencester 1989)

Brearley, Mike, *Phoenix from the Ashes* (London 1983)

Brickhill, Paul, *The Great Escape* (London 1951)

Brickhill, Paul, *Reach for the Sky* (London 2000; orig. 1954)

Briggs, Asa, *History of Broadcasting in the United Kingdom*, 3 vols (Oxford 1974)

Brogan, D.W., *The English People: Impressions and Observations* (London 1943)

Brooke-Taylor, Tim, *Rule Britannia: The Ways of the World and the True British Gentleman Patriot* (London 1983)

Brophy, John, *Britain's Home Guard: A Character Study* (London 1945)

Brown, Malcolm, *Spitfire Summer* (London 2000)

Butler, Ivan, *The War Film* (London 1974)

Calder, Angus, *The Myth of the Blitz* (London 1991)

Calder, Angus, *The People's War* (London 1997; orig. 1969)

Calder, Angus and Sheridan, Dorothy, *Speak for Yourself: A Mass-Observation Anthology, 1937–1949* (London 1984)

Carter, Dorothy, *Comrades of the Air* (London 1942)

'Cato', *The Guilty Men* (London 1940)

Chapman, James, *The British at War: Cinema, State and Propaganda, 1939–1945* (London 1998)

Charmley, John, *Churchill, the End of Glory: A Political Biography* (London 1993)

Childers, Erskine, *The Riddle of the Sands* (London 1903)

Churchill, Winston, *The Second World War*, 6 vols (London 1948–54)

Colley, Linda, *Britons: Forging the Nation 1707–1837* (London 1992)

Connelly, Mark, *Reaching for the Stars: A New History of RAF Bomber Command in World War II* (London 2000)

Connelly, Mark, *The Great War: Memory and Ritual* (London 2001)

Costello, John, *Love, Sex and War: Changing Values 1939–1945* (London 1985)

Coultass, Clive, *Images for Battle: British Film and the Second World War 1939–1945* (London and Toronto 1989)

Crompton, Richmal, *William at War* (Basingstoke 1995)

Crosby, T.L., *The Impact of Civilian Evacuation in the Second World War* (London 1986)

Dawson, Graham, *Soldier Heroes: British Adventure, Empire and the Imagining of Masculinities* (London 1994)

Deighton, Len, *Bomber* (London 1970)

Divine, A.D., *Dunkirk* (London 1945)

Doughty, C.M., *Travels in Arabia Deserta* (London 1888)

Dyer, Richard, *Brief Encounter* (London 1993)

Eade, Charles (ed.), *War Speeches of Winston Churchill*, 3 vols (London 1951)

Evans, Martin and Lunn, Ken (eds), *War and Memory in the Twentieth Century* (Oxford 1997)

Faulks, Sebastian, *Charlotte Gray* (London 1998)

Fielding, Steven, Thompson, Peter and Tiratsoo, Nick (eds), *England Arise! The Labour Party and Popular Politics in 1940s Britain* (Manchester 1995)

Fitchett, W.H., *Deeds That Won the Empire* (London 1897)

Fitz-Gibbon, Spencer, *Not Mentioned in Despatches . . . The History and Mythology of the Battle of Goose Green* (Cambridge 1995)

Fox, Caroline, *Dame Laura Knight* (Oxford 1988)

French, David, *Raising Churchill's Army: The British and the War against Nazi Germany 1919–1945* (Oxford 2000)

Fukuyama, Francis, *The End of History and the Last Man* (London 1992)

Gardiner, Juliet, *The 1940s House* (London 2000)

Gilbert, Martin, *The Second World War* (London 1989)

Gilbert, Martin, *Churchill: A Life* (London 1991)

Glancy, H. Mark, *When Hollywood Loved Britain: The Hollywood 'British' Film 1939–1945* (Manchester 1999)

Grahame, Kenneth, *The Wind in the Willows* (London 1908)

Grant, Neil, *Hamlyn Children's History of Britain* (London 1981)

Green, Oliver, *Underground Art: London Transport Posters 1908 to the Present* (London 1990)

Hadley, Patrick, *Third Class to Dunkirk* (London 1944)

Haining, Peter, *Spitfire Summer: The People's Eye View of the Battle of Britain* (London 1990)

Hamilton, Nigel, *Monty: The Man behind the Legend* (Wheathampstead 1987)

Hamilton, Nigel, *The Full Monty: Montgomery of Alamein 1887–1942* (London 2001)

Harman, Nicholas, *Dunkirk: The Necessary Myth* (London 1981)

Harper, Sue, *Picturing the Past: The Rise and Fall of the British Costume Film* (London 1994)

Harris, Robert, *Gotcha! The Media, the Government and the Falklands Crisis* (London 1983)

Harris, Robert, *Enigma* (London 1995)

Harrisson, Tom, *Living Through the Blitz* (Harmondsworth 1990; orig. 1976)

Hennessy, Peter, *Never Again, Britain 1945–1951* (London 1992)

Hillary, Richard, *The Last Enemy* (London 1997; orig. 1942)

Hughes, Thomas, *Tom Brown's Schooldays* (London 1857)

Hughes, Thomas, *The Manliness of Christ* (London 1880)

Hurd, Geoff (ed.), *National Fictions: World War Two in British Film and Television* (London 1984)

Hylton, Stuart, *Their Darkest Hour: The Hidden History of the Home Front 1939–1945* (Stroud 2001)

Irving, David, *The Trail of the Fox: The Life of Field Marshal Erwin Rommel* (London 1977)

Jerome, Jerome K., *Three Men in a Boat* (London 1889)

Johns, W.E., *Worrals of the WAAF* (London 1941)

Johns, W.E., *King of the Commandos* (London 1943)

Keegan, John, *Six Armies in Normandy* (London 1982)

Keegan, John, *The Second World War* (London 1989)

Kennington, Eric, *Drawing the RAF* (London 1942)

Kipling, Rudyard, *Stalky and Co* (London 1899)

Lant, Antonia, *Blackout: Reinventing Women for Wartime British Cinema* (Princeton, NJ 1991)

Lawrence, T.E., *Seven Pillars of Wisdom* (London 1935)

Lewis, Peter, *A People's War* (London 1986)

Lumley, Joanna, *Forces Sweethearts* (London 1993)

MacKenzie, J.M., *Propaganda and Empire* (Manchester 1984)

MacKenzie, J.M., *Imperialism and Popular Culture* (Manchester 1986)

MacKenzie, S.P., *The Home Guard* (Oxford 1995)

MacKenzie, S.P., *British War Films 1939–1945* (London 2001)

McKibbin, Ross, *Classes and Cultures in England 1918–1951* (Oxford 1998)

McLaine, Ian, *Ministry of Morale: Home Front Morale and the Ministry of Information in World War II* (London 1979)

Maclean, Alastair, *The Guns of Navarone* (London 1957)

McNab, Andy, *Bravo Two Zero* (London 1993)

Magorian, Michelle, *Goodnight Mister Tom* (London 1983)

Manning, Paul, *How to be a Wally* (London 1983)

Marwick, Arthur, *British Society since 1945* (London 1982)

Maule, Henry, *Great Battles of World War II* (London 1972)

Middlebrook, Martin, *Operation Corporate: The Story of the Falklands War 1982* (London 1985)

Middlebrook, Martin and Mahoney, Patrick, *Battleship: The Loss of the* Prince of Wales *and the* Repulse (London 1972)

Milligan, Spike, *Rommel? Gunner Who?* (Harmondsworth 1974)

Milligan, Spike, *Adolf Hitler: My Part in His Downfall* (Harmondsworth 1987; orig. 1971)

Milligan, Spike (ed.), *The Lost Goon Shows* (London 1987)

Monsarrat, Nicholas, *The Cruel Sea* (London 1951)

Mosley, Leonard, *The Battle of Britain: The Making of a Film* (London 1969)

Murphy, Robert, *British Cinema in the Second World War* (London 2000)

Nash, Paul, *Paul Nash: Paintings and Watercolours* (London 1975)

Nicholas, Sian, *The Echo of War: Home Front Propaganda and the Wartime BBC, 1939–45* (Manchester 1996)

Noakes, Lucy, *War and the British* (London 1998)

Noble, Ronnie, *Shoot First! Assignments of a Newsreel Cameraman* (London 1955)

Ogley, Bob, *Kent at War* (Westerham 2002; orig. 1994)

Paris, Michael, *From the Wright Brothers to* Top Gun: *Aviation, Nationalism and Popular Cinema* (Manchester 1995)

Paris, Michael, *Warrior Nation: Images of War in British Popular Culture 1850–2000* (London 2000)

Paxman, Jeremy, *The English: A Portrait of a People* (London 1998)

Ponting, Clive, *1940: Myth and Reality* (London 1990)

Pratt Boorman, H.R., *Hell's Corner: Kent Becomes the Battlefield of Britain* (Maidstone 1942)

Priestley, J.B., *Postscripts* (London 1940)

Reid, Pat, *The Colditz Story* (London 1952)

Richards, Jeffrey, *The Age of the Dream Palace: Cinema and Society in Britain 1930–1939* (London 1984)

Richards, Jeffrey, *Film and British National Identity, from Dickens to Dad's Army* (Manchester 1997)

Robinson, Derek, *Piece of Cake* (London 1983)

Ryan, Cornelius, *The Longest Day* (London 1960)

Samuel, Raphael (ed.), *Patriotism: The Making and Unmaking of British National Identity*, 3 vols (London 1989)

Saunders, H. St George, *Green Beret* (London 1959)

Savours, Ann (ed.), *Scott's Last Voyage Through the Antarctic Camera of Herbert Ponting* (London 1974)

Schama, Simon, *Landscape and Memory* (London 1995)

Shaw, Tony, *Eden, Suez and the Mass Media: Propaganda and Persuasion during the Suez Crisis* (London 1996)

Sheffield, Gary, *Forgotten Victory: The First World War, Myths and Realities* (London 2001)

Shute, Nevil, *A Town Like Alice* (London 1950)

Smith, Harold L. (ed.), *Britain and the Second World War: A Social History* (Manchester 1996)

Smith, Malcolm, *Britain and 1940* (London 2000)

Somerville, Christopher, *Our War: How the British Commonwealth Fought the Second World War* (London 1998)

Summerfield, Penny, *Women Workers in the Second World War* (London 1984)

Summerfield, Penelope, *Reconstructing Women's Wartime Lives: Discourse and Subjectivity in Oral Histories of the Second World War* (Manchester 1998)

Taylor, A.J.P., *English History 1914–1945* (Oxford 1965)

Taylor, Philip M. (ed.), *Britain and the Cinema in the Second World War* (Manchester 1988)

Thompson, Laurence, *1940: Year of Legend, Year of History* (London 1966)

Thomson, Alistair, *Anzac Memories: Living with the Legend* (Oxford 1994)

Titmuss, R.M., *Problems of Social Policy* (London 1950)

Turner, E.S., *Dear Old Blighty* (London 1980)

Twyford, H.P., *It Came to Our Door: Plymouth in the World War* (Plymouth 1975; orig. 1946)

Ward, Arthur, *Airfix: Celebrating Fifty Years of the World's Greatest Plastic Kits* (London 1999)

Watkins, Alan, *A Conservative Coup: The Fall of Margaret Thatcher* (London 1992)

Waugh, Alec, *Loom of Youth* (London 1917)

Wells, H.G., *The New World Order* (London 1940)

Wesley, Mary, *The Camomile Lawn* (London 1984)

Westall, Robert, *Children of the Blitz: Memories of Wartime Childhood* (London 1985)

Wicks, Ben, *No Time to Wave Goodbye* (London 1988)

Williams, Eric, *The Wooden Horse* (London 1949)

Wilmut, Roger (ed.), *The Complete Beyond the Fringe* (London 1987)

Winston, Brian, *Fires Were Started* (London 1999)

Wyndham, Joan, *Love Lessons: A Wartime Diary* (London 1986)

Wyndham, Joan, *Love is Blue: A Wartime Diary* (London 1986)

Young, Desmond, *Rommel* (London 1950)

Articles, chapters and lectures

Badsey, Stephen, 'British High Command and the Reporting of the Campaign', in Brian Bond and Michael D. Taylor (eds), *The Battle of France and Flanders Sixty Years On* (Barnsley 2001), pp. 137–56

Calder, Angus, 'The Battle of Britain and Pilots' Memoirs', in Paul Addison and Jeremy Crang (eds), *The Burning Blue: A New History of the Battle of Britain* (London 2000), pp. 191–206

Carmichael, Jane, 'Army Photographers in North-West Europe', *Imperial War Museum Review* 7 (no date), pp. 15–22

Dawson, Graham, 'History-writing on World War II', in Geoff Hurd (ed.), *National Fictions: World War Two in British Film and Television* (London 1984), pp. 1–7

Dawson, Graham and West, Bob, 'The Popular Memory of World War II and the Struggle over National Identity', in Geoff Hurd (ed.), *National Fictions: World War Two in British Film and Television* (London 1984), pp. 8–13

Harper, Julie, 'Join the Professionals! Militarism, Masculinity and the South Atlantic', in Geoff Hurd (ed.), *National Fictions: World War Two in British Film and Television* (London 1984), pp. 51–3

Harper, Sue, 'The Representation of Women in British Feature Films, 1939–1945', in Philip M. Taylor (ed.), *Britain and the Cinema in the Second World War* (Manchester 1988), pp. 168–202

Hurd, Geoff, 'Notes on Hegemony: The War and Cinema', in Geoff Hurd (ed.), *National Fictions: World War Two in British Film and Television* (London 1984), pp. 18–19

Jarvie, Ian, 'Fanning the Flames: Anti-American Reaction to Operation Burma', *Historical Journal of Film, Radio and Television* 1, 2 (1981), pp. 117–37

Jolly, Margaretta, 'Love Letters versus Letters Carved in Stone: Gender, Memory and the "Forces Sweethearts" Exhibition', in Martin Evans and Ken Lunn (eds), *War and Memory in the Twentieth Century* (Oxford 1997), pp. 105–24

Kroenig, Jürgen, 'The Mass Media in the Age of Globalisation: Implications for Anglo-German Relations', 1999 Reuters Lecture, University of Kent at Canterbury

Noakes, Lucy, 'Making Histories: Experiencing the Blitz in London's Museums in the 1990s', in Martin Evans and Ken Lunn (eds), *War and Memory in the Twentieth Century* (Oxford 1997), pp. 89–104

Orwell, George, 'The Art of Donald McGill', in *The Penguin Essays of George Orwell* (Harmondsworth 1984; orig. 1942), pp. 19–46

Orwell, George, 'The Lion and the Unicorn', in *The Penguin Essays of George Orwell* (Harmondsworth 1984; orig. 1941), pp. 149, 161–2

Ramsden, John, 'Churchill: "The Greatest Living Englishman"', *Contemporary British History* 12, 3 (Autumn 1998), pp. 1–40

Ramsden, John, 'Refocusing "The People's War": British War Films of the 1950s', *Journal of Contemporary History* 33, 1 (1998), pp. 35–64

Richards, Jeffrey, 'Wartime Cinema Audiences and the Class System: The Case of *Ships with Wings* (1941)', *Historical Journal of Film, Radio and Television* 7, 2 (1987), pp. 129–41

Sansom, William, 'The Wall', in Dan Davin (ed.), *The Oxford Book of Short Stories from the Second World War* (Oxford 1984), pp. 20–3

Shaw, Martin, 'Past Wars in Present Conflicts: From the Second World War to the Gulf', in Martin Evans and Ken Lunn (eds), *War and Memory in the Twentieth Century* (Oxford 1997), pp. 191–204

Short, K.R.M., 'RAF Bomber Command's *Target for Tonight*', *Historical Journal of Film, Radio and Television* 17, 2 (1987), pp. 181–218

Summerfield, Penelope, 'Education and Politics in the British Armed Forces in the Second World War', *International Review of Social History* 26 (1981), pp. 138–58

Theses

Semple, Rory, 'Dover's Bunker Mentality: Dover, Its People and Its Tunnels in Two World Wars', PhD University of Kent (forthcoming)

Sinclair, Gillian, 'Winston Churchill: Projection and Publicity 1939–1945', PhD University of Kent (forthcoming)

Comics, comic books and annuals

Battle

Battle Annual

Boys' Own Paper

Comic for Boys

Commando

Eagle

Hotspur

Lion

Rover

Swift

Victor

Victor Book for Boys 1980

The War Picture Library

Warlord

Warlord Annual 1985

Wizard

Films

Above Us the Waves (GB 1955)

All at Sea (GB 1939)

Angels One Five (GB 1952)

Appointment in London (GB 1953)

Ask a Policeman (GB 1938)

The Battle of Britain (GB/US 1969)

The Battle of the Bulge (US 1965)

The Battle of the River Plate (GB 1957)

The Belles of St Trinian's (GB 1954)

The Bridge on the River Kwai (US 1958)

A Bridge Too Far (GB/US 1977)

Brief Encounter (GB 1945)

Burma Victory (GB 1945)

Carve Her Name With Pride (GB 1958)

Charlotte Gray (GB 2001)

Christmas Under Fire (GB 1940)

The Cockleshell Heroes (GB 1955)

The Colditz Story (GB 1954)

The Cruel Sea (GB 1953)

Dad's Army (GB/US 1971)

The Dam Busters (GB 1955)

Dark Blue World (Czech 2001)

Dawn Guard (GB 1941)

Dawn Patrol (US 1938)

Demi-Paradise (GB 1943)

Desert Fox (US 1951)

Desert Rats (US 1953)

Desert Victory (GB 1943)

A Diary for Timothy (GB 1945)

Dover: Front Line City (GB 1940)

Dunkirk (GB 1958)

Eagle Squadron (US 1942)

The Early Bird (GB 1965)

The English Patient (GB/US 1996)

Enigma (GB 2001)

Fires Were Started (GB 1943)

The First Days (GB 1939)

The First of the Few (GB 1942)

For Freedom (GB 1940)

Gasbags (GB 1940)

The Gentle Sex (GB 1943)

The Great Escape (US 1963)

The Guns of Navarone (GB 1961)

Hanover Street (GB 1979)

Heart of Britain (GB 1941)

Hell's Angels (US 1930)

Hope and Glory (GB 1987)

How I Won the War (GB 1967)

Ice Cold in Alex (GB 1958)

In Which We Serve (GB 1942)

International Squadron (US 1942)

It's in the Air (GB 1938)

Lady Hamilton (US 1941)

Land Girls (GB 1998)

Laugh It Off (GB 1940)

Lawrence of Arabia (US 1962)

Let George Do It (GB 1940)

Listen to Britain (GB 1942)

London Can Take It! (British release title *Britain Can Take It!*) (GB 1940)

The Long and the Short and the Tall (GB 1961)

The Long Day's Dying (GB 1968)

The Longest Day (US 1962)

The Malta Story (GB 1953)

Millions Like Us (GB 1943)

Mrs Miniver (US 1942)

Next of Kin (GB 1942)

Objective Burma (US 1945)

Odette (GB 1950)

Old Mother Riley Joins Up (GB 1939)

Patton (US 1960)

Pearl Harbor (US 2001)

Play Dirty (GB 1968)

Porridge (GB 1979)

The Prime Minister (US 1941)

Privates on Parade (GB 1981)

Private's Progress (GB 1956)

Random Harvest (US 1942)

Reach for the Sky (GB 1956)

Rising Damp (GB 1980)

Saving Private Ryan (US 1998)

Sea of Sand (GB 1958)

Ships With Wings (GB 1941)

Sink the Bismarck (GB 1960)

633 Squadron (GB/US 1964)

Target for Tonight (GB 1941)

Theirs is the Glory (GB 1946)

They Made Me a Fugitive (GB 1947)

They Were Not Divided (GB 1950)

Thunder Rock (GB 1942)

Till Death Do Us Part (GB 1969)

A Town Like Alice (GB 1956)

True Glory (GB/US 1945)

Tunisian Victory (GB/US 1943)

U571 (US 2000)

Waterloo Bridge (GB 1940)

Waterloo Road (GB 1945)

Wavell's 30,000 (GB 1942)

The Way Ahead (GB 1944)

The Way to the Stars (GB 1945)

Where Eagles Dare (GB/US 1968)

The White Cliffs of Dover (US 1944)

The Wicked Lady (GB 1945)

Wild Geese (GB 1978)

Wings (US 1927)

The Wooden Horse (GB 1950)

A Yank in the RAF (US 1941)

Yanks (GB/US 1979)

Radio and sound recordings

Ack Ack – Beer Beer

Barnett, Correlli, BBC radio talk 'Myth Versus Reality', broadcast 6 December 1977

BBC 1922–72, fiftieth anniversary discs, BBC50

Bomber, ZBBC 1772

Brains Trust

Falklands War March–June 1982, original recordings from the BBC sound archives, ZBBC 1296

Garrison Theatre

The Goons

The Guns of Navarone, ZBBC 2061

ITMA [*It's That Man Again*]

Kitchen Front

Kuehl, Jerome, cassette liner notes, *The World at War*, Decca KDVC 6 820 013-4

Lenin of the Rovers, ZBBC 1257

Music While You Work

Round the Horne, BBC Enterprises 1988, ZBBC 1010

Russian Commentary

Shipmates Ahoy

Sincerely Yours – Vera Lynn

Spitfires over Britain

Victory in Europe 1945, original recordings from the BBC sound archives, ZCM 562

Workers' Playtime

Theatre

Beyond the Fringe

Paintings, photographs and posters

Alamein (Sergeant Chetwyn. This photograph was actually taken in a training exercise prior to the battle)

Squadron Leader Douglas Bader (Eric Kennington)

A Balloon Site, Coventry (Dame Laura Knight)

Battle of Britain (Paul Nash)

Wing Commander Francis Beamish (Eric Kennington)

British Troops on Queen Sector, Sword Beach (Sergeant Jimmy Mapham)

Falling Wall (Leonard Rosoman)

Richard Hillary (Eric Kennington)

Squadron Leader Joseph Kyall (Eric Kennington)

Ruby Loftus Screwing a Breech Ring (Dame Laura Knight)

'Sailor' Malan (Eric Kennington)

Sergeant B. Montague (H.M. Carr)

'Never was so much owed by so many to so few' (Poster. Artist anonymous)

Corporal Daphne Pearson GC (Dame Laura Knight)

'". . . the principal Ornament of our royal City, to the Honour of our Government, and of this our realm" from the "Letters Patent under the Great Seal of England the 12th day November 1675"' (Walter Spradberry)

Corporal Robbins with Assistant Section Leaders E. Henderson MN and Sergeant D. Turner (Dame Laura Knight)

St Bride's to St Paul's (Muirhead Bone)

Flight Lieutenant Alastair Taylor (Eric Kennington)

Tea Break (Edward Ardizzone)

23 Queen Victoria Street (PCs Arthur Cross and Fred Tibbs)

Your Britain Fight for It Now (Set of four by Frank Newbould)

Documentaries and television dramas

'Allo 'Allo (BBC)

The American Civil War (Ken Burns/ WGBH)

Band of Brothers (HBO/ BBC)

Britain at War in Colour (Carlton and Trans-World Sport)

The Camomile Lawn (Channel 4)

The Chancer (Granada)

Colditz (BBC)

Commando (Channel 4)

Dad's Army (BBC)

Das Boot (ZDF/BBC)

D-Day to Berlin (BBC)

The Evacuees (BBC)

Family at War (Granada)

The Fast Show (Talkback)

Fawlty Towers (BBC)

Finest Hour (BBC)

Fourth Arm (BBC)

Goodnight Mister Tom (Carlton)

Goodnight Sweetheart (Alamo)

Grange Hill (BBC)

Harry Enfield (BBC)

Hi-de-Hi (BBC)

How We Used to Live (Yorkshire)

Imitation Game (BBC)

It Ain't Half Hot Mum (BBC)

Licking Hitler (BBC)

Minder (Euston Films)

The Nazis: A Warning from History (BBC/WGBH)

1940 (BBC 1963)

The 1940s House (Channel 4)

Only Fools and Horses (BBC)

Paul Calf's Video Diary (BBC)

A People's War (Channel 4)

Piece of Cake (Witzend)

Porridge (BBC)

Q9 (BBC)

Rising Damp (Yorkshire)

Sailor (BBC)

The Second World War in Colour (Carlton – Trans-World Sport)

Secret Army (BBC)

Sir Norbert Smith – A Life (Hat Trick)

Spitting Image (Central)

Tenko (BBC)

Till Death Do Us Part (BBC)

Victoria Wood Christmas Special 2001 (BBC)

We'll Meet Again (Witzend)

Why We Fight (US Office of War Information)

Wish Me Luck (Central)

The World at War (Thames)

Websites consulted

Goodnight Mr Tom, see www.carltontv.co.uk/data/mistertom (23 February 2003)

Goodnight Sweetheart, see www.goodnightsweetheart.co.uk/fiction.html (23 February 2003)

Spitfires, see www.spitfires.flyer.co.uk (10 July 2001)

Tenko, see www.offthetelly.users.btopenworld.com/pdf/drama/tenko.pdf (23 February 2003)

Index